Quantum Fields and
Off-Shell Sciences

Quantum Fields and Off-Shell Sciences

Editor

Motoichi Ohtsu

MDPI • Basel • Beijing • Wuhan • Barcelona • Belgrade • Manchester • Tokyo • Cluj • Tianjin

Editor
Motoichi Ohtsu
Research Origin for Dressed
Photon, 3-13-19 Moriya-cho,
Kanagawa-ku, Yokohama,
Kanagawa 221-0022, Japan

Editorial Office
MDPI
St. Alban-Anlage 66
4052 Basel, Switzerland

This is a reprint of articles from the Special Issue published online in the open access journal *Symmetry* (ISSN 2073-8994) (available at: https://www.mdpi.com/journal/symmetry/special_issues/Quantum_Fields_Off-Shell_Sciences).

For citation purposes, cite each article independently as indicated on the article page online and as indicated below:

LastName, A.A.; LastName, B.B.; LastName, C.C. Article Title. *Journal Name* **Year**, *Volume Number*, Page Range.

ISBN 978-3-0365-5197-5 (Hbk)
ISBN 978-3-0365-5198-2 (PDF)

© 2022 by the authors. Articles in this book are Open Access and distributed under the Creative Commons Attribution (CC BY) license, which allows users to download, copy and build upon published articles, as long as the author and publisher are properly credited, which ensures maximum dissemination and a wider impact of our publications.

The book as a whole is distributed by MDPI under the terms and conditions of the Creative Commons license CC BY-NC-ND.

Contents

About the Editor vii

Preface to "Quantum Fields and Off-Shell Sciences" ix

Hirofumi Sakuma, Izumi Ojima
On the Dressed Photon Constant and Its Implication for a Novel Perspective on Cosmology
Reprinted from: *Symmetry* **2021**, *13*, 593, doi:10.3390/sym13040593 1

Hiroyuki Ochiai
Symmetry of Dressed Photon
Reprinted from: *Symmetry* **2021**, *13*, 1283, doi:10.3390/sym13071283 21

Kazuya Okamura
Towards a Measurement Theory for Off-Shell Quantum Fields
Reprinted from: *Symmetry* **2021**, *13*, 1183, doi:10.3390/sym13071183 29

Hayato Saigo
Category Algebras and States on Categories
Reprinted from: *Symmetry* **2021**, *13*, 1172, doi:10.3390/sym13071172 49

Hayato Saigo, Juzo Nohmi
Categorical Nonstandard Analysis
Reprinted from: *Symmetry* **2021**, *13*, 1573, doi:10.3390/sym13091573 61

Hayato Saigo
Quantum Fields as Category Algebras
Reprinted from: *Symmetry* **2021**, *13*, 1727, doi:10.3390/sym13091727 71

Suguru Sangu and Hayato Saigo
Description of Dressed-Photon Dynamics and Extraction Process
Reprinted from: *Symmetry* **2021**, *13*, 1768, doi:10.3390/sym13101768 89

Norio Konno, Etsuo Segawa and Martin Štefaňák
Relation between Quantum Walks with Tails and Quantum Walks with Sinks on Finite Graphs
Reprinted from: *Symmetry* **2021**, *13*, 1169, doi:10.3390/sym13071169 103

Kenta Higuchi, Takashi Komatsu, Norio Konno, Hisashi Morioka and Etsuo Segawa
A Discontinuity of the Energy of Quantum Walk in Impurities
Reprinted from: *Symmetry* **2021**, *13*, 1134, doi:10.3390/sym13071134 125

Leo Matsuoka, Kenta Yuki, Hynek Lavička and Etsuo Segawa
Maze Solving by a Quantum Walk with Sinks and Self-Loops: Numerical Analysis
Reprinted from: *Symmetry* **2021**, *13*, 2263, doi:10.3390/sym13122263 141

Shintaro Murakami, Okuto Ikeda, Yusuke Hirukawa and Toshiharu Saiki
Investigation of Eigenmode-Based Coupled Oscillator Solver Applied to Ising Spin Problems
Reprinted from: *Symmetry* **2021**, *13*, 1745, doi:10.3390/sym13091745 159

About the Editor

Motoichi Ohtsu

Motoichi Ohtsu (Director-in-chief of the Research Origin for Dressed Photon; Professor Emeritus, University of Tokyo and Tokyo Institute of Technology) received his Dr. Eng. Degree from the Tokyo Institute of Technology, Tokyo, in 1978. He was first appointed as a research associate, then an associate professor in 1982. From 1986 to 1987, while on leave from the Tokyo Institute of Technology, he joined the Crawford Hill Laboratory, AT&T Bell Laboratories, Holmdel, New Jersey, USA. In 1991, he became a professor at the Tokyo Institute of Technology. In 2004, he moved to the University of Tokyo as a professor. He has been the leader of the "Photon Control" project (1993–1998: the Kanawaga Academy of Science and Technology, Kanagawa, Japan), the "Localized Photon" project (1998–2003: ERATO, JST, Japan), the "Terabyte Optical Storage Technology" project (2002–2006: NEDO, Japan), the Near Field Optical Lithography System" project (2004–2006: Ministry of Education, Japan), the "Nanophotonics" team (2003–2009: SORST, JST, Japan), the "Innovative Nanophotonics Components Development" project (2006–2011: NEDO, Japan), the "Nanophotonics Total Expansion: Industry-University Cooperation and Human Resource Development" project (2006–2011: NEDO, Japan), and the "Development of a solar cell technology using dressed photons" project (2012–2014, NEDO, Japan).

Dr. Ohtsu has written over 588 papers and received 83 patents. He is the author, co-author, and editor of 85 books, including 46 in English. In 2000, He was appointed as President of the IEEE LEOS Japan Chapter. From 2000, he has been an executive director of the Japan Society of Applied Physics. His main fields of interests are off-shell science and dressed photon technology. He is a fellow of the Optical Society of America. He is also a fellow and life member of the Japanese society of Applied Physics. He is a member of the American Physical Society and the Laser Society of Japan. He has been awarded 21 prizes from academic institutions, including the Issac Koga Gold Medal of URSI in 1984; the Japan IBM Science Award in 1988; two awards from the Japan Society of Applied Physics in 1982 and 1990; the Inoue Science Foundation Award in 1999; the Japan Royal Medal with Purple Ribbon from the Japanese Government in 2004; the H. Inoue Award From JST in 2005; the Distinguished Achievement Award from the Institute of Electronics, Information and Communication, Engineering of Japan in 2007; the Julius Springer Prize for Applied Physics in 2009; the Okawa Publications Prize in 2016; and the IAAM Medal from the International Association of Advanced Materials in 2018.

He served as the committee member of 18 international conferences, including the Chair of the Executive Committee, the German–Japanese Symposium on Nanophotonics; the Chair of the Executive Committee, The US–Japan Symposium on Nanophotonics; the Chair of the Program Committee, the International Near-Field Optics Conference; the Chair of the Organizing Committee, the Asia-Pacific Near Field Optics Workshop; and the Chair of the Program Committee, the Pacific Rim Conference on Lasers and Electro-Optics.

Preface to "Quantum Fields and Off-Shell Sciences"

Intensive experimental studies on light–matter interactions and their associated technological breakthroughs, especially conducted in the field of dressed photon research, have led to a growing concern regarding unsettled off-shell quantum field interactions. In order to respond to the demand of this new tide of scientific progress, a new initiative has been recently launched. The Special Issue, entitled "Quantum Fields and Off-Shell Sciences", was organized in the academic journal *Symmetry* to promote the progress of such research activities from a wider perspective, not necessarily limited to dressed photon studies. The scope of the Special Issue covered quantum probability theory, quantum walk modeling, quantum measurement theory, micro–macro duality, category theory, the vortex structure of spacetime, off-the-mass-shell property of quantum field and symmetry, and symmetry breaking in quantum fields.

Eleven excellent original papers were successfully accepted for publication via an impartial peer-review process. This book contains these published papers. It will provide scientific and technical information on the quantum fields and off-shell sciences to scientists, engineers, and students who are and will be engaged in this field.

Motoichi Ohtsu
Editor

Article

On the Dressed Photon Constant and Its Implication for a Novel Perspective on Cosmology

Hirofumi Sakuma * and Izumi Ojima

Research Origin for Dressed Photon, 3-13-19 Moriya-cho, Kanagawa-ku, Yokohama 221-0022, Japan; ojima@gaia.eonet.ne.jp
* Correspondence: sakuma@rodrep.or.jp

Abstract: As an important follow-up report on the latest study of the first author (H.S.) on an off-shell quantum field causing a dressed photon and dark energy, we further discuss a couple of intriguing subjects based on the new notion of simultaneous conformal symmetry breaking. One is the dressed photon constant. If we use it, in addition to $\bar{h}$ and c, as the third component of natural units, it is defined as the geometric mean of the smallest and the largest lengths: Planck length and that relating to the cosmological constant. Interestingly, this length ($\approx$50 nanometers) seems to give a rough measure of the Heisenberg cut for electromagnetic phenomena. The other is a new perspective on cosmology that combines two original notions, i.e., twin universes and conformal cyclic cosmology, proposed, respectively, by Petit and Penrose, into one novel picture where universes expand self-similarly. We show the possibility that twin universes having a dual structure of (matter with (dark energy and matter)) vs. corresponding anti-entities, separated by an event horizon embedded in the geometric structure of de Sitter space, undergo endless cyclic processes of birth and death, as in the case of the pair creation and annihilation of elementary particles through the intervention of a conformal light field.

Keywords: dressed photon; dressed photon constant; natural units; Heisenberg cut; de Sitter space; dark energy; dark matter; cosmological constant; twin universes; conformal cyclic cosmology

Citation: Sakuma, H.; Ojima, I. On the Dressed Photon Constant and Its Implication for a Novel Perspective on Cosmology. *Symmetry* **2021**, *13*, 593. https://doi.org/10.3390/sym13040593

Academic Editor: Ignatios Antoniadis

Received: 2 March 2021
Accepted: 1 April 2021
Published: 2 April 2021

Publisher's Note: MDPI stays neutral with regard to jurisdictional claims in published maps and institutional affiliations.

Copyright: © 2021 by the authors. Licensee MDPI, Basel, Switzerland. This article is an open access article distributed under the terms and conditions of the Creative Commons Attribution (CC BY) license (https://creativecommons.org/licenses/by/4.0/).

1. Introduction

Application studies of quantum theory in nanosciences have continued to accomplish a variety of spectacular modern technological achievements. The technology involving the dressed photon (DP) phenomena is one such achievement that makes the impossible possible. While a reliable theory has not yet been established to explain the characteristic behaviors of DPs, a comprehensive review of DP studies, including the impossibility of understanding DP phenomena within the conventional framework of Maxwell's equation, was given by Ohtsu [1], together with a series of associated intriguing technologies and the status of theoretical attempts to understand DPs up to 2017. The research on the DP phenomena is now being pursued more actively than ever before both experimentally and theoretically. The most important point on the DP, clarified through decades-long investigations, is that the DP field is not a simple variant of the light field such as evanescent light, which is essentially a free mode, but involves largely transmuted and locally condensed (within an area smaller than several tens of nanometers) electromagnetic field energy achieved through light–matter field interactions involving point-like singularities, which seem to be a key factor for DP generation. The peculiarity of the DP field compared with the free light field is concisely summarized in Section 1 of the latest paper on DPs by Sakuma et al. [2] (S3O hereafter), where a new theory is proposed, focusing on the aspects of quantum field interactions thus far neglected.

The real reason for the unsuccessful attempts at a full-fledged theory of DPs seems to be related to the fact that a DP is not a free mode, but is the outcome of light–matter field interactions, the complexity of which makes constructing a simple mathematical model difficult. In fact, contrary to the above-mentioned remarkable technological successes of quantum theory, the current stage of development of quantum field theory (QFT) is far from a firmly established one, such as the theory of Newtonian mechanics. From this viewpoint, a major stumbling block might be the lack of mathematical support for interacting quantum field models satisfying the covariance under the Poincaré group $\mathcal{P}$ in 4-dimensional Minkowski spacetime (defined as the crossed product $\mathcal{P} := \mathbb{R}^4 \rtimes \mathcal{L}$ of the Lorentz group $\mathcal{L}$ acting on the 4-dimensional Minkowski spacetime $\mathbb{R}^4$). While the main subject here is the DP system, to be described as a subsystem of relativistic 4-dimensional QFT, a survey of the basic structure of the 4-dimensional QFT itself would be useful for our purpose of discussing the various aspects of the DP system.

First, the physical interpretations of QFT described by the interacting Heisenberg fields φ_H are realized by the notion of on-shell particles contained in φ_H with the 4-mometum p_μ given by Equation (1):

$$p^2 := \eta_{\mu\nu} p^\mu p^\nu := p_\nu p^\nu = (m_0 c)^2 \geq 0, \quad \mu, \nu = 0, 1, 2, 3, \tag{1}$$

where we adopt the sign convention $(+1, -1, -1, -1)$ for the Minkowski metric η given by

$$\eta_{\mu\nu} = \begin{pmatrix} +1 & 0 & 0 & 0 \\ 0 & -1 & 0 & 0 \\ 0 & 0 & -1 & 0 \\ 0 & 0 & 0 & -1 \end{pmatrix}.$$

The physical meaning of the asymptotic fields ϕ^{as} ($as = in$ or out) can be seen in their role in a scattering process formed by the in-fields $\phi_1^{in}(p_1), \cdots, \phi_m^{in}(p_m)$ with momenta $p_1, \cdots, p_m$ converging from the remote past to the scattering center and by the out-fields $\phi_1^{out}(q_1), \cdots, \phi_m^{out}(q_n)$ with momenta $q_1, \cdots, q_n$ diverging from the scattering center to the remote future. In contrast with the interacting Heisenberg field φ_H, which causes and controls the above scattering process behind the scenes, the asymptotic field ϕ^{as} carrying the above momentum spectrum as an observable quantity can be easily realized as a free field obtained by the so-called second quantization, as shown below. Owing to its linearity, the asymptotic field ϕ^{as} is governed by the well-known Klein–Gordon (KG) Equation (2).

In the simplest case of a scalar field ϕ^{as}, the first quantization $p_\mu \to i\hbar \partial_\mu$ applied to (1) realizes the KG equation:

$$[\hbar^2 \partial^\nu \partial_\nu + (m_0 c)^2]\phi^{as} = 0, \tag{2}$$

where the operand ϕ^{as} determined by the second quantization becomes a quantum field ϕ^{as} describing a multi-particle system given by

$$\phi^{as}(x^0, \tilde{x}) = \int \frac{d^3 \tilde{k}}{\sqrt{(2\pi)^3 2E_k}} [a(\tilde{k}) \exp(-i k_\nu x^\nu) + a^\dagger(\tilde{k}) \exp(i k_\nu x^\nu)]. \tag{3}$$

Here, $(a^\dagger(\tilde{k}), a(\tilde{l}))$ and $(\tilde{x}$ and $\tilde{k})$, respectively, denote a pair of creation-annihilation operators and of 3-vectors consisting of spatial components of x^μ and k_ν, with E_k defined by $E_k := \sqrt{(\tilde{k})^2 + (m_0)^2}$. A familiar Fock space is constructed on the basis of (3) and of the vacuum state vector $|0\rangle$ satisfying $a|0\rangle = 0$, according to which a positive energy spectrum is selected in the state vector space. While the field ϕ^{as} thus constructed embodies the *wave–particle duality* of a quantum system, it still lives in the realm of linearity due to the linear KG Equation (2). With the restriction due to this linearity (or the on-shell property (1)) overlooked, however, essential features of Fock spaces such as the positive energy spectra in the state vector space generated by repeated applications of the creation operators on the Fock vacuum $|0\rangle$ (under the cyclicity assumption) are misinterpreted as the universal structure to be found in interacting multiparticle systems. Accordingly, $|0\rangle$ becomes as mysterious as the creation of everything from emptiness. We return to this point in Section 4 on cosmology.

The mutual relations among the Poincaré group $\mathcal{P}$, Heisenberg field φ_H, asymptotic field ϕ^{as}, and momentum spectrum (p_μ) can be clearly visualized by means of the quadrality scheme to describe the duality relation between Micro and Macro (Micro-Macro duality based on the quadrality scheme [3]):

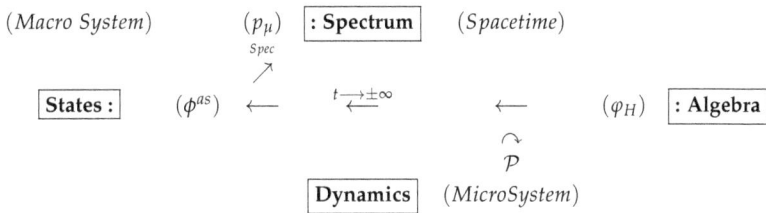

Remark 1. *In the specific example of scattering process with asymptotic completeness, the original quadrality scheme of micro–macro duality can be seen in the above relations among the dynamics $\mathcal{P}$ acting on the algebras of interacting Heisenberg fields φ_H and of their asymptotic fields ϕ^{as} and the spectrum of energy-momentum p_μ. It gives a unified categorical description of the system of interacting quantum fields in terms of quantum and classical systems, both of which are characterized dynamically by their non-commutative and commutative algebras. As our new ideas on quantum field theory of the dressed photons depends heavily on this quadrality scheme, it will be convenient to explain here its minimal essential points to those who are familiar only with quantum mechanics with finite degrees of freedom.*

The scheme is a theoretical framework consisting of a couple of different dualities that are interweaved to describe the theoretically phenomena under consideration: among the four basic ingredients in the scheme, Dynamics and the Algebra $\mathcal{X}$ of physical quantities belong to the micro side of the quantum system, while the remaining two elements—States (and their representations) and Spectrum— belong to the macro side. To visualize the invisible quantum micro system, we need to exert certain action $E : \mathcal{A} \to \mathcal{X}$ on the microscopic quantum system $\mathcal{X}$ from the macro side $\mathcal{A}$. The response of the acted micro side to the acting macro side is to be given by $F : \mathcal{A} \leftarrow \mathcal{X}$, according to which we have an adjoint pair of functors $\mathcal{A} \underset{E(a)}{\overset{F(x)}{\leftrightarrows}} \mathcal{X}$; ($x \in \mathcal{X}$ and $a \in \mathcal{A}$). In this way, we see that the basic structure of the quantum theory is mathematically formulated by the so-called "adjunction" in category theory, which can be understood as the precise mathematical form of "duality" $\mathcal{A} \simeq \mathcal{X}$ (one of the weaker forms of equivalence), where $\mathcal{X}$ and $\mathcal{A}$, respectively, denote unknown mathematical object belonging to micro system and known object (as the familiar vocabulary) in the classical macro system and symbol $\simeq$ denotes natural equivalence.

As we see in the above diagram, the abscissa axis represents the duality between the algebra $\mathcal{X}$ of quantum variables and its states with Gel'fand–Naimark–Segal (GNS) representations realized in a Hilbert space. Central problematic issues we have in considering quantum systems with infinite degrees of freedom would be those on unitary nonequivalence and the uniqueness of irreducible decomposition, which are usually regarded as a pathological aspect of systems with infinite degrees of freedom. However, omitting the details of extensive researches so far done on the generalized sector problem, we can briefly summarize the main conclusions of them as follows. A system with infinite degrees of freedom can be represented with multiple sectors where a sector is defined by a factor representation with trivial center containing only scalar multiples of the identity, which generalizes the notion of irreducible representations with trivial commutants. Here, disjointness means the absence of intertwiners, as the refined notion of unitary nonequivalence adapted to the situations with infinite degrees of freedom. By this kind of generalization, we also have the change in the classification of representation, that is to say, an irreducible representation is to be replaced by a factorial representation which has a self-evident center playing the role of a commutative (classical) order parameter. **Thus, we show that macroscopic order parameters emerge naturally from the disjoint representations appearing in the micro systems and the spectrum of those order parameters gives the classification space for describing a variety of configurations the micro system would take.** The duality relation illustrated in the ordinate axis, that is,

$[Dyn \leftrightarrows Spec]$ expresses the duality between invariability and variability of coupled micro and macro systems.

The asymptotic fields ϕ^{as} given by (3) are placed in this scheme in duality relation with the interacting Heisenberg fields φ_H, where ϕ^{as} itself consist only of linear free modes without anything to do with nonlinear field interactions having the off-shell property. Because the clear-cut mathematical criterion to distinguish nonlinear field interactions from the free time evolution of noninteracting modes, known as the Greenberg–Robinson theorem [4,5], states that *if the Fourier transform $\varphi(p)$ of a given quantum field $\phi^{as}(x)$ does not contain an off-shell spacelike momentum p_μ with $p_\nu p^\nu < 0$ (cf. Equation (1)), then $\phi^{as}(x)$ is a generalized free field.* A caveat to be made here is that a spacelike momentum field does not necessarily mean the presence of a tachyonic field representing particle-like *localized energy field* moving with superluminous velocity, which violates the Einstein causality. This localized field is known to be unstable such that the existing spacelike momentum fields take naturally simple wavy forms. Another crucial piece of knowledge necessary to understand the enigmatic DP phenomena is the important property of quantum fields with *infinite degrees of freedom*, referred to in the above remark. As is well known, we have only one sector in the familiar case of quantum mechanical systems with *finite degrees of freedom* which are governed by unitary time evolution (the Stone–von Neumann theorem [6]). In sharp contrast to this situation, quantum fields with infinite degrees of freedom have multiple sectors [3,7], which are mutually disjoint (i.e., separated by the absence of intertwiners), stronger than unitary inequivalence. Regarding the unitary equivalence, Haag's theorem [8] states that *any quantum field satisfying Poincaré covariance is a free field if it is connected to a free field by a unitary transformation*. According to this no-go theorem, it is meaningless to consider that an interacting Heisenberg field can be realized through a unitary transformation of a free field by means of the well-known Dyson S-matrix involving the interaction term. In this way, the essential part of our common knowledge cultivated in quantum mechanical systems with finite degrees of freedom is invalidated in relativistic QFT.

The notions of spacelike momentum field and the existence of multiple sectors must be quite foreign for many who are unfamiliar with quantum systems with infinite degrees of freedom, so that it is worthwhile to give a simple heuristic example. Let us consider a simple wave propagation, $\psi = \exp i(k_0 x^0 - k_1 x^1)$, in a certain background field. One may regard it as a wave, say, in the atmosphere. When the wave exists in a uniform background, it propagates such that it satisfies $(\partial^\nu \partial_\nu + k^2)\psi = 0$, with $k^2 := (k_0)^2 - (k_1)^2$, which may be compared to a "unitary" time evolution of a free mode in the timelike sector. If the background field becomes nonuniform but its degree of nonuniformity is rather smooth, then though its way of propagation is deformed to some extent, we can describe the deformed propagation pattern by employing perturbative methods, and the solution still remains in the timelike sector mentioned above. As an extreme case of severe interactions with the environmental field for which the perturbative method is break down, we can consider a frontal instability of the atmosphere in which the front is defined as a line of discontinuity of the temperature and velocity fields. A wavelike perturbation with small amplitude put into this frontal zone, due to hydrodynamic shear instability, can no longer keep its wavy form, and its amplitude starts to either (i) grow or to (ii) damp exponentially in a region that is narrow in the traverse direction. In view of such situations that QFT is basically a theory involving complex numbers and that the frequency and wave number of a given wavelike field represent the energy and momentum, the abrupt change in the energy and momentum brought about by a certain kind of discontinuity of the field can be represented in the simplest crude model by a discrete jump of (k_0, k_1) into $(\pm i l_0, -i l_1)$ with $l^2 := (l_0)^2 - (l_1)^2 > 0$. Note that with this abrupt change, $(\partial^\nu \partial_\nu + k^2)\psi = 0$ becomes $(\partial^\nu \partial_\nu - l^2)\psi = 0$, namely, the wave dynamics shifts abruptly from a timelike sector to a spacelike one with the properties $\exp(\mp l_0 x^0)$ and $\exp(-l_1 x^1)$ (valid in the domain $x^1 \geq 0$), respectively, corresponding to the above-mentioned properties of (i) and (ii). Needless to say, this example, due to the atmospheric dynamics, could be transferred to situations involving interactions among elementary particles, where a "severe interaction" would evoke these changes on the interacting Heisenberg fields to which on-shell field theory cannot be applied. We believe that this simple toy model gives an intuitive explanation of the essential features of severe field interactions involving a certain kind of discontinuity and why spacelike momentum modes are necessary to describe these field interactions. We will further discuss this problem in Section 2.2 on DP model.

Now, going back to the general argument on QFT, notice that the above two theorems in axiomatic QFT for relativistic quantum fields, especially the first one, justify our investigation into the existence of a spacelike momentum domain, *in the sense of a different sector*, with which the conventional Maxwell's equation is to be augmented for a complete description of electromagnetic field interactions. A helpful hint regarding an appropriate form of the spacelike momentum can be found in the longitudinal Coulomb mode or the virtual photon, which behaves as a carrier of electromagnetic force. In their series of papers, Sakuma et al. (and the latest S3O [9–12]) derived an extended field covering the spacelike momentum domain by applying a mathematical technique called *Clebsch parameterization* to electromagnetic 4-vector potential A_μ. The extension of the field was accomplished in two steps: (I) semi-spacelike and (II) spacelike extensions. To avoid confusion, here we replace the common notation A_μ for a 4-vector potential with U_μ. In step (I), U_μ satisfies

$$[\partial^\nu \partial_\nu - (\kappa_0)^2] U_\mu = 0, \quad U_\nu U^\nu = 0, \tag{4}$$

where κ_0 is an important constant, to be identified as the DP constant. At first glance, one may consider this to be the wrong equation, as a null (massless) condition $U_\nu U^\nu = 0$ seems to be incompatible with the first equation in (4). As shown in the next section, however, it is indeed correct. The reason why it looks bizarre is because it corresponds to a longitudinally propagating electromagnetic wave of which the quantum version is eliminated as unphysical in the conventional interpretation. We believe that this bizarre mode, massless in the sense of $U_\nu U^\nu = 0$, corresponds qualitatively to an *invisible virtual photon*, i.e., a $U(1)$ gauge boson, and in step (II), this field is extended further to the case of a genuine spacelike field satisfying $U_\nu U^\nu < 0$. As we will touch upon in Section 2.2, the formulation of steps (I) and (II) is generalized to cover the case of a curved spacetime. As the first equation in (4) can be considered a dual form of the timelike Proca equation, i.e., $[\partial^\nu \partial_\nu + (m_0)^2] A_\mu = 0$, we call it the Clebsch dual (CD) field and denote its skew-symmetric field strength by $S_{\mu\nu} := \partial_\mu U_\nu - \partial_\nu U_\mu$.

As the source-free Maxwell's equation is conformally invariant, the derivation of an augmented Maxwell field can be viewed mathematically as a conformal extension of the electromagnetic field $F_{\mu\nu}$. From this viewpoint, note that the derivation of the CD field is conceptually similar to the notion of a twistor introduced by Penrose [13], and in this sense, the essence of our new proposal on cosmology has a closer connection to the conformal cyclic cosmology (CCC) proposed by Penrose [14] than the antipodal twin universe model of Petit [15]. To see this, let us consider the rotation group $SO(3)$ acting on three-dimensional vectors. For $SO(3)$, the universal covering group $SU(2)$ exists, which is locally isomorphic to $SO(3)$ and in relation to which a spinor is defined as its irreducible representation. Extending this context to the Lorentz group $SO(1,3)$ in four-dimensional spacetime, $SL(2,C)$ arises as the universal covering group corresponding to $SU(2)$. If we further extend $SO(1,3)$ to a four-dimensional conformal group, then $SO(1,3)$ and $SL(2,C)$ are extended, respectively, to $SO(2,4)$ and $SU(2,2)$, and Penrose's twistor appears as an element of the complex four-dimensional space on which $SU(2,2)$ acts. As a parallel argument, we can consider the case of a conformal extension of the electromagnetic field $F_{\mu\nu}$ that acts on the spinor as a $U(1)$ gauge field. CD field $S_{\mu\nu}$, introduced as the spacelike extension of $F_{\mu\nu}$, is thus also regarded as a conformal extension of $F_{\mu\nu}$. As has been shown in S3O, we believe that this fact explains why the CD field plays an important role in the dark energy dynamics of the self-similarly (conformally) expanding universe described as a de Sitter space, in sharp contrast to the simple-minded intuition that the mutual relations between the DP and cosmological phenomena are irrelevant owing to their extremely large scale difference.

This paper is organized as follows. To discuss the theme addressed in the title, we first need prior knowledge on the CD field, which is a very new concept, and on several important conclusions on cosmology reported in S3O. We reserve Sections 2 and 3 for the purpose of recapitulating the minimal required knowledge in a simple way. Then, in Section 4, we discuss the main topics of this paper, namely, the dressed photon constant and a perspective on the possible relation between our novel cosmology and the CCC.

2. Augmented Maxwell's Theory
2.1. Clebsch Dual Field

As mentioned above, the CD field can be regarded as a field of longitudinal electromagnetic waves. To understand this, we first note that a serious misunderstanding regarding the longitudinally propagating wave modes has persisted. In the physical science communities, this misunderstanding has been prevailing and left untouched, but it cannot be overlooked in the present context. As a matter of fact, one frequently encounters this statement in standard textbooks on electromagnetism, which asserts that electromagnetic waves are not longitudinal but transversal. This concept seems, however, to be a superfluous reaction to the assertion in "advanced" quantum electrodynamics (QED), where longitudinal modes are eliminated as unphysical. In the classical theory of electromagnetism, however, the longitudinally propagating modes have been proved unmistakably to exist in *a light beam with finite width*, both theoretically in [16] and experimentally in [17]. In these papers, the existence of longitudinal modes is shown without using the electromagnetic 4-vector potential A_μ. Here, the significance of introducing the CD field can be seen in the following two aspects:

(i) in the above classical theory, the longitudinally propagating electric field can be reinterpreted as the null current vector $\partial_\mu \phi$ ($\phi := \partial_\nu A^\nu$), and

(ii) through a process similar to the analytic continuation in complex analysis, the electromagnetic field A_μ is extended to a CD field U_μ. Via the Clebsch parameterization of U_μ, A_μ is extended to the semi-spacelike momentum domain, which is regarded as the classical version of the $U(1)$ gauge boson as the mediator of the electromagnetic force. Thus, we can obtain a consistent picture of the classical electromagnetic longitudinal modes: the non-virtual one reported in [16,17] and the "virtual" one of the CD field.

To confirm what is stated above, let us consider Maxwell's Equation (5) and the associated energy-momentum tensor (7), together with its divergence (8):

$$\partial^\nu F_{\mu\nu} = \partial^\nu(\partial_\mu A_\nu - \partial_\nu A_\mu) = [-\partial^\nu \partial_\nu A_\mu + \partial_\mu(\partial^\nu A_\nu)] = j_\mu, \tag{5}$$

$$A_\mu = \alpha_\mu + \partial_\mu \chi, \quad (\partial_\nu \alpha^\nu = 0, \quad \phi := \partial_\nu A^\nu = \partial_\nu \partial^\nu \chi). \tag{6}$$

$$T_\mu^\nu = -F_{\mu\sigma} F^{\nu\sigma} + \frac{1}{4} \eta_\mu^\nu F_{\sigma\tau} F^{\sigma\tau}, \quad (F_{\sigma\tau} F^{\sigma\tau} = 0 \text{ for free wave modes}), \tag{7}$$

$$\partial_\nu T_\mu^\nu = \partial_\nu(-F_{\mu\sigma} F^{\nu\sigma}) = F_{\mu\nu} \partial_\sigma F^{\nu\sigma} = F_{\mu\nu} j^\nu. \tag{8}$$

If the Lorentz gauge condition $\partial^\nu A_\nu = 0$ is imposed, additionally or *formally*, to the above Maxwell's equation, then Equation (5) reduces to $\partial^\nu \partial_\nu A_\mu = 0$, according to which the free Maxwell's equation can be identified in the sense of $j_\mu = 0$. Apart from this conventional method, however, another possibility to find the free equation begins with

$$\partial^\nu \partial_\nu A_\mu = 0, \tag{9}$$

without assuming $\partial^\nu A_\nu = 0$. In this case, (5) tells us that we have a nontrivial ($\partial_\mu \phi \neq 0$) balance equation

$$\partial^\nu F_{\mu\nu} = \partial_\mu \phi, \quad \rightarrow \quad \partial^\mu \partial_\mu \phi = \partial^\mu \partial^\nu F_{\mu\nu} = 0. \tag{10}$$

The first equation in (10) can be justified in two steps: First, from (5) and (8), we see that the conservation law of $\partial_\nu T_\mu^\nu = 0$ is satisfied when $j^\nu = 0$ in the usual free case (8). In the case of (10), however, we use the expression $\partial_\nu T_\mu^\nu = F_{\mu\nu} \partial_\sigma F^{\nu\sigma}$ in (8) and $\partial^\nu F_{\mu\nu} = \partial_\mu \partial^\nu A_\nu$ in (5), which leads to

$$\partial_\nu T_\mu^\nu = F_{\mu\nu} \partial^\nu \phi = 0, \tag{11}$$

if $F_{\mu\nu} \perp \partial^\nu \phi$ with $\partial^\mu \partial_\mu \phi = 0$. This expression indicates that the longitudinally propagating vector $\partial^\nu \phi$ is physical in the sense that it satisfies the energy-momentum conservation.

In the second step of the physical justification of (10), we consider (9) in terms of α_μ and χ given in (6), which becomes

$$\partial^\nu \partial_\nu \alpha_\mu^{(h)} = 0, \quad \partial^\nu \partial_\nu \alpha_\mu^{(i)} + \partial^\nu \partial_\nu (\partial_\mu \chi) = 0, \tag{12}$$

with homogeneous and inhomogeneous solutions, i.e., $\alpha_\mu^{(h)}$ and $\alpha_\mu^{(i)}$, respectively, for a given χ satisfying the second equation in (10). $\alpha_\mu^{(h)}$ obviously represents a transverse mode, and the second equation gives a balance between the rotational and irrotational modes. The existence of this balance is well documented in the hydrodynamic literature explaining the mathematical description of the irrotational motion of a two-dimensional incompressible fluid. Due to the irrotationality of the motion, the velocity vector (v_1, v_2) is expressed in terms of the gradient of the vector potential $\hat{\phi}$, namely, $(v_1 = \partial_1 \hat{\phi}, v_2 = \partial_2 \hat{\phi})$; on the other hand, the incompressibility of the fluid makes its motion nondivergent such that (v_1, v_2) is alternatively expressed as $(v_1 = -\partial_2 \hat{\psi}, v_2 = \partial_1 \hat{\psi})$, where $\hat{\psi}$ denotes a stream function. Equating these two, we obtain $\partial_1 \hat{\phi} = -\partial_2 \hat{\psi}, \partial_2 \hat{\phi} = \partial_1 \hat{\psi}$, showing that $\hat{\phi}$ and $\hat{\psi}$ satisfy the Cauchy–Riemann relation in complex analysis. This heuristic example serves as a helpful reference in proving that *a null vector current $\partial_\mu \phi$ propagating along the x^1 axis perpendicular to $F_{\mu\nu}$ can be reinterpreted as the current of the longitudinal (x^1-directed) electric field, of which a detailed explanation is given in [10]*. As referred to at the beginning of this subsection, the existence of this longitudinally propagating electric field was actually reported in [16,17]. Thus, we can say that the vector field $\partial_\mu \phi$ is the physical mode that represents a longitudinally propagating electric field.

The orthogonality condition (11) is mathematically equivalent to the relativistic hydrodynamic equation of motion of a barotropic (isentropic) fluid [18]: $\omega_{\mu\nu}(w u^\nu) = 0$, where $\omega_{\mu\nu} := \partial_\mu(w u_\nu) - \partial_\nu(w u_\mu)$, u^ν, and w are the vorticity tensor, 4-velocity, and proper enthalpy density of the fluid, respectively. This observation suggests that the unknown form of the 4-vector potential U_μ can be clarified through the Clebsch parameterization [19] because the Clebsch parameterization is used to study the Hamiltonian structure of the above-mentioned barotropic fluid motion in terms of a couple of canonically conjugate scalar parameters (λ, ϕ) whose two degrees of freedom are equal to those of $(\vec{E}, \vec{M})$ in electromagnetic waves. Thus, in case (I) of the semi-spacelike CD field, the electromagnetic vector potential U_μ is parameterized as

$$U_\mu = \lambda \partial_\mu \phi, \quad (\phi = \partial_\nu A^\nu, \text{ which satisfies } \partial^\nu \partial_\nu \phi = 0), \tag{13}$$

$$\partial^\nu \partial_\nu \lambda - (\kappa_0)^2 \lambda = 0, \tag{14}$$

where κ_0 is a constant determined by DP experiments. If we introduce two gradient vectors—$L_\mu := \partial_\mu \lambda$ and $C_\mu := \partial_\mu \phi$, then the skew-symmetric field strength $S_{\mu\nu}$ can be represented by a simple bivector of the form

$$S_{\mu\nu} = L_\mu C_\nu - L_\nu C_\mu, \quad \to \quad Pf(S) := S_{01} S_{23} + S_{02} S_{31} + S_{03} S_{12} = 0, \tag{15}$$

which shows that, as in the case of $\vec{E}$ and $\vec{H}$ of an electromagnetic wave, the "electric" and "magnetic" fields of the CD field also satisfy the above orthogonality condition. $Pf(S)$ in (15) is the Pfaffian of the skew-symmetric matrix $S_{\mu\nu} : (Pf(S))^2 = Det(S_{\mu\nu})$ and the barotropic fluid motions governed by the equation of motion $\omega_{\mu\nu}(w u^\nu) = 0$ are characterized by the condition that the Pfaffian vanishes. Another important property of an electromagnetic wave is that $\vec{E}$ and $\vec{H}$ are advected along a null Poynting vector. In the CD model now under consideration, a null vector C^μ would naturally be expected to satisfy

$$C^\nu \partial_\nu L_\mu = 0, \tag{16}$$

from which we obtain

$$\begin{align} L^\mu(C^\nu \partial_\nu L_\mu) &= 0, \quad \rightarrow \quad C^\nu \partial_\nu(L^\mu L_\mu) = 0, \tag{17} \\ C^\mu(C^\nu \partial_\nu L_\mu) &= 0, \quad \rightarrow \quad C^\nu \partial_\nu(C^\mu L_\mu) = 0. \tag{18} \end{align}$$

In deriving (18), we utilized the fact that $C^\nu \partial_\nu C^\mu = 0$. For (18), the following orthogonality condition in the CD field

$$L_\nu C^\nu = 0 \tag{19}$$

can be imposed as an additional condition, which turns out later to be an important equation.

To see in what sense (19) is consistent with (15), we consider a null geodesic field ($U_\nu U^\nu = 0$):

$$U^\nu \partial_\nu U_\mu = U^\nu(\partial_\nu U_\mu - \partial_\mu U_\nu) = 0, \tag{20}$$

which is expected to satisfy an extended light field. Using (13) and (15), we readily obtain

$$U^\nu \partial_\nu U_\mu = -S_{\mu\nu}(\lambda C^\nu) = (C_\mu L_\nu - L_\mu C_\nu)(\lambda C^\nu) = (L_\nu C^\nu)\lambda C_\mu, \tag{21}$$

which vanishes by the orthogonality condition (19). The importance of (19) in the CD field formulation is that L_μ must be a spacelike vector, because L_μ satisfying (19) is either C_μ or a spacelike vector, which explains why the λ field introduced in the CD formulation satisfies the spacelike KG equation given in (14). Using the relations derived above between C_μ and L_μ, we can show the form of the extended Maxwell's equation:

$$\partial^\nu S_{\nu\mu} = (\kappa_0)^2 U_\mu \iff [\partial^\nu \partial_\nu - (\kappa_0)^2] U_\mu = 0, \quad (\text{with } \partial_\nu U^\nu = 0). \tag{22}$$

The energy-momentum tensor $\hat{T}_\mu^\nu$ of the lightlike CD field can be derived easily from the conventional one with the following form: $T_\mu^\nu = -F_{\mu\sigma} F^{\nu\sigma}$. Considering the sign change of the energy at the boundary between the timelike and spacelike domains, we define the tensor as

$$\begin{align} \hat{T}_{\mu\nu} : &= S_{\mu\sigma} S_\nu{}^\sigma = (L_\mu C_\sigma - C_\mu L_\sigma)(L_\nu C^\sigma - C_\nu L^\sigma) \\ &= (L_\sigma L^\sigma) C_\mu C_\nu = \rho C_\mu C_\nu, \quad \rho := L_\sigma L^\sigma < 0. \tag{23} \end{align}$$

The negative density ρ corresponds to the negative norm of the longitudinal modes in the QED, which makes this mode unphysical in the conventional interpretation. However, we believe that the usage of the term "unphysical" in this context is inappropriate, because if we regard the CD field as virtual photons, then the former is physical in the sense that the latter, as the mediator of the electromagnetic force, is physical though it is invisible. As the argument regarding the reference point of the gravitational potential energy shows, the decision regarding whether a given quantity under consideration is physical depends essentially on the physical setting of our problem; therefore, the Clebsch duality relation between $F_{\mu\nu}$ and $S_{\mu\nu}$ should not be viewed as the duality between physical and unphysical aspects but instead as the duality between the positive and negative sides of the light-cone $p^2 = 0$, the latter of which is, as we will see in Section 3 on cosmology, often closely related to the invisibility of a given quantity. Actually, the "state-dependent" physicality of the longitudinal photons was already pointed out by Ojima [20], who stated that while the longitudinal photons or unphysical Goldstone bosons in the Higgs mechanism are eliminated from the physical space of states in the usual formulation, this statement applies to the above modes only in their particle forms. In their non-particle forms, the former appear physically as infrared Coulomb tails, and the latter, as the so-called "macroscopic wave functions" arising from the Cooper pairs, both of which play essential physical roles. The CD formulation based on the Greenberg–Robinson theorem has revealed that the momenta of the non-particle forms in the above statement are invisible non-localized spacelike ones. Thus, regarding the negativity of ρ, we point out that it can be likened to the simple fact that the complexified time coordinate ict in Minkowski space is invisible, though it is an important element without which we cannot describe a given dynamical system in a satisfactory way.

In step (II) of the CD field formulation, we relax the condition $\partial^\nu \partial_\nu \phi = 0$ given by the second equation in (10) to allow the following extended vector potential U_μ, which is advected by itself along a geodesic:

$$U_\mu := \frac{1}{2}(\lambda C_\mu - \phi L_\mu), \implies U^\nu \partial_\nu U_\mu = -S_{\mu\nu}U^\nu + \frac{1}{2}\partial_\mu(U^\nu U_\nu) = 0,$$
$$U_\nu U^\nu < 0, \quad (24)$$
$$\partial^\nu \partial_\nu \lambda - (\kappa_0)^2 \lambda = 0, \quad \partial^\nu \partial_\nu \phi - (\kappa_0)^2 \phi = 0, \quad C^\nu L_\nu = 0. \quad (25)$$

The form of $S_{\mu\nu}$, given by the first equation in (15), remains unchanged in (24). Note that the condition $\partial^\nu \partial_\nu \phi = 0$ ($\phi = \partial_\nu A^\nu$) can certainly be considered a gauge fixing condition, but at the same time, the second equation in (10) can be interpreted as a special gauge condition where gauge invariance is represented by the charge conservation due to $\partial^\mu \partial^\nu F_{\mu\nu} = 0$, while $\partial_\mu \phi$ is not a usual timelike electric current.

In the extended Maxwell's equation given in (22), an electrically neutral current $(\kappa_0)^2 U_\mu = (\kappa_0)^2 (\lambda \partial_\mu \phi)$ behaves exactly like j_μ in the original Maxwell's equation, which shows that the constant κ_0 serves as a fundamental unit, such as the electric charge. Therefore, violation of condition (10) causes gauge symmetry breaking, according to which the CD field extended in step (II) suffers from breakdown of both the gauge symmetry and conformal symmetry in the sense of $U_\nu U^\nu = 0$.

Corresponding to the above extension, the energy-momentum tensor satisfying the conservation law of $\partial_\nu \hat{T}^\nu_\mu = 0$ is redefined as

$$\hat{T}_{\mu\nu} = \hat{S}_{\mu\sigma\nu}{}^\sigma - \frac{1}{2}\hat{S}_{\alpha\beta}{}^{\alpha\beta}\eta_{\mu\nu}, \quad \hat{S}_{\alpha\beta\gamma\delta} := S_{\alpha\beta}S_{\gamma\delta},$$
$$\iff G_{\mu\nu} := R_{\mu\nu} - Rg_{\mu\nu}/2. \quad (26)$$

Note that $\hat{S}_{\alpha\beta\gamma\delta}$ defined above has the same skew-symmetric properties as those of the Riemann tensor $R_{\alpha\beta\gamma\delta}$, including the first Bianchi identity, $S_{\alpha[\beta\gamma\delta]} = 0$ (equivalent to the second equation in (15)), which is valid as $S_{\mu\nu}$ is a bivector field given by the first equation in (15). Thus, $\hat{T}_{\mu\nu}$ given in (26) becomes isomorphic to the Einstein tensor $G_{\mu\nu} := R_{\mu\nu} - Rg_{\mu\nu}/2$, where the Ricci tensor $R_{\mu\nu} := R^\sigma_{\mu\nu\sigma}$.

2.2. Quantization of the CD Field and DP Model

Going back to (23), we note that it is isomorphic to the energy-momentum tensor of freely moving fluid particles. The ρ field for an actual fluid will be discretized if the kinetic theory of molecules is taken into account. When the light field is quantized, this form will obey Planck's quantization of light energy $E = h\nu$. As the CD field variable L^μ has the dimension of length, we introduce a certain quantized elemental length l_{dp} whose inverse is κ_0, namely, the discretization of ρ leads to

$$\kappa_0 := (l_{dp})^{-1}, \quad (27)$$

which can be considered an energy quantization of the CD field. Recall that the Dirac equation of the form

$$(i\gamma^\nu \partial_\nu + m)\Psi = 0 \quad (28)$$

can be regarded as the "square root" of the timelike KG equation $(\partial^\nu \partial_\nu + m^2)\Psi = 0$. Therefore, the Dirac equation for the spacelike KG equation $(\partial^\nu \partial_\nu - (\kappa_0)^2)\Psi = 0$ must be

$$i(\gamma^\nu \partial_\nu + \kappa_0)\Psi = 0. \tag{29}$$

On the other hand, an electrically neutral Majorana representation exists for (28), in which all the γ matrices become purely imaginary such that these matrices have the form $(\gamma^\nu_{(M)} \partial_\nu + m)\Psi = 0$, which is identical to (29). The Majorana field is fermionic with a half-integer spin 1/2; thus, the same (momentum) state cannot be occupied by two fields according to Pauli's exclusion principle. Note that by using the Pauli–Lubanski vector W_μ to describe the spin polarization of moving particles, we can find a specific orthogonal momentum configuration of a pair of Majorana fields whose resultant spin becomes 1, namely,

$$M_{\mu\nu} p^\nu = N_{\mu\nu} q^\nu = W_\mu, \tag{30}$$

where $M_{\mu\nu}$ and p^ν denote the angular and linear momenta of a given Majorana field, respectively, while $N_{\mu\nu}$ and q^ν are the corresponding momenta of the other, of which the linear momentum q^ν is perpendicular to p^ν. We believe that this configuration (30) gives a quantum mechanical justification for the orthogonality condition (19) and (25) of the CD field.

For a plane wave solution ($\lambda = \hat{\lambda}_c \exp[i(k_\nu x^\nu)]$) to the spacelike KG equation (14), $L_\nu = \partial_\nu \lambda$ satisfies

$$L^\nu L_\nu^* = -(\kappa_0)^2 (\hat{\lambda}_c \hat{\lambda}_c^*) = const. < 0, \tag{31}$$

which shows that the momentum vector L^μ lies in a submanifold of the Lorentzian manifold, called de Sitter space in cosmology, which is a pseudo-hypersphere with a certain constant radius embedded in R^5. Quite independent of the cosmological arguments on de Sitter space, Snyder [21] discussed the unique role of this space in spacetime quantization. He showed that with the introduction of the hypothetical momentum 5-vector $\eta^\mu (0 \leq \mu \leq 4)$ in R^5 constrained to lie on the de Sitter space, i.e., $\eta^\nu \eta_\nu^* = -(\eta_c)^2 = const.$, the following commutation relations are derived. For the definitions of p_μ, $\hat{p}_\mu$, and $\hat{x}^\mu$, we have

$$\begin{aligned} p_\mu &:= \frac{\hbar}{l_p} \frac{\eta_\mu}{\eta_4}, \quad \hat{p}_\mu := -\frac{i\hbar}{l_p \eta_4} \frac{\partial}{\partial \eta_\mu}, \quad \hat{x}^\mu := il_p \left(\eta_4 \frac{\partial}{\partial \eta_\mu} - \xi_\mu \eta_\mu \frac{\partial}{\partial \eta_4} \right); \\ (0 &\leq \mu \leq 3), \end{aligned} \tag{32}$$

where l_p denotes the Planck length, and ξ_μ takes a value of -1 when $\mu = 0$ and 1 when $\mu \neq 0$, from which we obtain

$$[\hat{x}^\mu, \hat{p}_\mu] = i\hbar \left[1 + \xi_\mu \left(\frac{l_p}{\hbar} \right)^2 (p_\mu)^2 \right],$$

$$[\hat{x}^\mu, \hat{p}_\nu] = [\hat{x}^\nu, \hat{p}_\mu] = i\hbar \left(\frac{l_p}{\hbar} \right)^2 p_\mu p_\nu \quad 0 \leq (\mu, \nu) \leq 3, \tag{33}$$

$$[\hat{x}^i, \hat{x}^j] = \frac{i(l_p)^2}{\hbar} \epsilon_{ijk} L_k, \quad [\hat{x}^0, \hat{x}^i] = \frac{i(l_p)^2}{\hbar} M_i; \quad 1 \leq (i, j, k) \leq 3, \tag{34}$$

where ϵ_{ijk} is Eddington's epsilon, and L_i and M_i are angular momentum vectors generated, respectively, by (spatial-spatial) and (spatial-temporal) rotations. *Snyder further showed that the "Lorentz transformation" in his spacelike momentum space* $\{\eta^\mu\}$, $(0 \leq \mu \leq 3)$ *naturally induces the Lorentz transformation in the usual spacetime* $\{x^\mu\}$. Thus, the energy-momentum tensor $\hat{T}_{\mu\nu}$ of the CD field given in (26) can be regarded as the one constructed on this Snyder's momentum "spacetime" η^μ with Lorentz invariance as in the case of $R_{\mu\nu}$, also constructed on the spacetime x^μ with Lorentz invariance, which becomes a very important property in the discussion of dark energy in the next section. In [12] and S3O, we showed that, by virtue of the bivector property of $S_{\mu\nu}$ given in (15), the form of $\hat{T}_{\mu\nu}$ can be extended to a curved spacetime. Thus, the intriguing isomorphism between $\hat{T}_{\mu\nu}$ and $G_{\mu\nu}$ in (26) seems to suggest an important consequence: the quantization of the CD field attained by the above commutation relations may also be applied to the quantization of the gravitational field. The research pursuing this goal can be found, for instance, Girelli [22] and Glikman [23].

Now, we move on to a new DP model. Although the constant κ_0 plays a crucial role in formulating the CD field, its value clearly cannot be determined solely by theoretical arguments. We already explained in S3O how the value of the DP constant κ_0 was estimated by the extensive DP experiments by Ohtsu, who utilized the photochemical vapor deposition and autonomous etching techniques [24]. Through those experiments, the maximum size of the DP that can be considered as l_{dp} introduced in (27) was estimated to be

$$50 \text{ nanometer } < l_{dp} = (\kappa_0)^{-1} < 70 \text{ nanometer}. \tag{35}$$

As emphasized in the introduction, we do not yet know a reliable QFT that can deal with the off-shell properties of the field playing an important role in the DP generating mechanism. Thus, we need to resort to a certain kind of simplified argument to bring in the experimental outcome to CD field theory. In the following, we give such a simplified argument. In the first paragraph of the introduction, we mentioned that the existence of point-like singularities, similar to the pointed end of a fiber probe or impurities with extremely tiny size scattered across a given background material, is the crucial element for generating DPs. We can safely say that field interactions in which these singularities come into play should be so serious that the involvement of the spacelike momenta predicted by the Greenberg–Robinson theorem will be crucial in these cases compared with those without singularities.

Remember that, in the introductory Section 1, we have touched upon a heuristic toy model with which we show the intervention of spacelike momentum in the field interactions. Aharonov et al. [25] conducted an advanced analysis of the response behavior of the spacelike KG equation perturbed by a point-like delta function $\delta(x^0)\delta(x^1)$, in which the above essential aspect was incorporated. They showed that the solutions excited by this point-like disturbance consist of two different types: the stable spacelike mode and the unstable timelike mode. The unstable timelike mode excited from the spacelike KG Equation (14) with spherical symmetry has the form $\lambda(x^0, r) = \exp(\pm k_0 x^0) R(r)$, where $R(r)$ satisfies

$$R'' + \frac{2}{r} R' - (\hat{\kappa}_r)^2 R = 0, \quad (\hat{\kappa}_r)^2 := (k_0)^2 - (\kappa_0)^2 > 0, \tag{36}$$

according to which $R(r)$ is the Yukawa potential of $R(r) = \exp(-\hat{\kappa}_r r)/r$. For a Majorana field, as with the quantum version of the λ field, the energy in terms of k_0 is discretized by κ_0, as shown in (27). Thus, the nonzero minimum $Min[\hat{\kappa}_r]$ in the Yukawa potential is κ_0, which gives the maximum size of the localized DP to be compared with the experimental result (35). Although the CD field consists of a pair of Majorana fields satisfying the orthogonality conditions (19) and (25), the orthogonal configuration must be broken down by the perturbation, and the timelike pair will turn, respectively, into $\lambda(x^0, r) = \exp(\pm k_0 x^0) R(r)$, namely, particle and antiparticle pairs, as an electrically neutral antiparticle can be considered a particle traveling backward in time. The excited field is non-propagating in nature; thus, a pair of particle and antiparticle fields will be combined into either an "electric" field with spin 0 or a "magnetic" field with spin 1 [26]. We believe that the DP is generated through this pair annihilation of the Majorana field. As the DP field is basically electromagnetic, once it is generated, its behavior in a uniform environment can be described by the Proca equation of the form $\partial^\nu \partial_\nu A_\mu + (\kappa_0)^2 A_\mu = 0$. From the viewpoint of nanophotonical engineering, however, what really matters is the control of the DP energy flows driven by the existence of point-like sources and sinks. In the above argument, we showed that the energy of incident photons working as the triggering cause of $\delta(x^0)$ at the singular point eventually turns into the energy of the DP. At the present stage, we do not have clear knowledge of the sink mechanisms, but the research on DP energy flow with source–sink-type driving forces is pursued actively by employing a certain class of quantum walk models [27–29]. Intuitively, however, we can expect that some kind of ζ-function enters here as the carrier to convey the above singularity waves, which explains the observation of ζ-function singularities in the quantum walks. Moreover, the parallelism between ζ-functions and partition functions (the latter appearing in statistical mechanics) explains the relevance of Tomita–Takesaki modular duality [30] to the basis of the conformal symmetry discussed below.

3. On Dark Energy and Dark Matter

In our discussion so far, we have developed a new concept of a CD field carrying spacelike momentum modes, which are required for electromagnetic field interactions. In comparison to the conventional QFT, the CD field can be compared with invisible virtual photons that can be excited from the vacuum ($|0\rangle = 0$), regarded as the ground state of a one-sided energy spectrum within the bound of the uncertainty principle. Apparently, simply employing this excitation scenario is problematic because the concept of the CD field contradicts the vacuum state mentioned above. We believe that the orthogonal relation between a pair of momentum vectors p^ν and q^ν given in (30) gives us a hint to solve this problem concerning the ground state. For spacetime with three spatial dimensions, as shown below, the maximum number of Majorana fermion fields as the limited capacity of spacetime is also three, of which the configuration is shown by

$$M_{\mu\nu}p^\nu = N_{\mu\nu}q^\nu = L_{\mu\nu}r^\nu = W_\mu. \tag{37}$$

This compound state with a resultant spin 3/2 is called a Rarita–Schwinger state, which we denote by $|M3\rangle_g$. The role of the vector $|M3\rangle_g$ is to give the GNS cyclic vector of a mixed state which is disjoint from the vacuum state whose cyclic vector is given by $|0\rangle$ [31]. The important characteristic of $|M3\rangle_g$ is that the CD vector boson field can be excited from any of the three different pairs, which propagates along one of the (x^1, x^2, x^3) directions. In view of the universality of electromagnetic interactions, the incessant occurrence of excitation–de-excitation cycles between $|M3\rangle_g$ and non-ground states makes $|M3\rangle_g$ a fully occupied state in the macroscopic time scale. Therefore, we can say that $|M3\rangle_g$ exists not as a momentary virtual state, but also as a stable invisible off-shell state. In the following, we show that $|M3\rangle_g$ exerts on the universe a cosmological effect identified as dark energy.

To investigate the property of $|M3\rangle_g$, let us consider plane wave solutions λ and ϕ for the spacelike case of $U_\nu U^\nu < 0$, in which $\lambda = N_\lambda \hat{\lambda}_c \exp(ik_\nu x^\nu)$ and $\phi = N_\phi \hat{\phi}_c \exp(ik_\nu x^\nu)$, with $k_\nu k^\nu = -(\kappa_0)^2$, where $\hat{\lambda}_c$ and $\hat{\phi}_c$ denote elemental amplitudes of the respective fields, and N_λ and N_ϕ are the numbers of the respective modes. As Equation (15) shows, λ and ϕ always appear in the form of a product; thus, we may rewrite these two expressions as

$$\lambda = N(\kappa_0)^{-2}\exp(ik_\nu x^\nu), \quad \phi = \hat{\phi}_c \exp(ik_\nu x^\nu), \tag{38}$$

where N is a combined number $N := N_\lambda N_\phi$, and we can identify $\hat{\lambda}_c$ as $\hat{\lambda}_c = (\kappa_0)^{-2}$, as $\hat{\lambda}_c$ has the dimension of $(length)^2$. By substituting these into the first equation in (26) and setting $N = 1$, we obtain the absolute value of $\hat{T}_\nu^\nu(1)$, denoted as $|\hat{T}_\nu^\nu(1)|$:

$$|\hat{T}_\nu^\nu(1)| = -2[\hat{\phi}_c(\hat{\phi}_c)^*] < 0, \tag{39}$$

where $(\bullet)^*$ denotes the complex conjugate of $(\bullet)$. The right-hand side of (39) can be evaluated by the light-like case of the CD field (23), in which we have $\hat{T}_{\mu\nu} = \rho C_\mu C_\nu$. For the light-like case, we have $\phi = \hat{\phi}_c \exp(ik_\nu x^\nu)$, $k_\nu k^\nu = 0$ and $\lambda = N(\kappa_0)^{-2}\exp(il_\nu x^\nu)$, $l_\nu l^\nu = -(\kappa_0)^2$, from which we have

$$(C_\mu)^* C^\nu = k_\mu k^\nu \hat{\phi}_c(\hat{\phi}_c)^*, \quad \rho = -N^2(\kappa_0)^{-2}. \tag{40}$$

Next, we consider a case in which the k^μ vector of ϕ is parallel to the x^1 direction and consider a rectangular parallelepiped V spanned by the vectors $(1/k_1, 1, 1)$. For $k_0 = v_0/c$, where c and v_0 denote the light velocity and the frequency of the ϕ field, the volume integral of $\hat{T}_0^{\ 0}/(-N^2)$ over V as the energy per quantum is

$$\frac{1}{(-N^2)} \int_V \hat{T}_0^{\ 0} dx^1 dx^2 dx^3 = (\kappa_0)^{-2} \epsilon [\hat{\phi}_c (\hat{\phi}_c)^*] \frac{v_0}{c}, \tag{41}$$

where ϵ denotes the unit length squared. Equating (41) with $E = hv_0$, we obtain

$$hc(\kappa_0)^2 = \epsilon [\hat{\phi}_c (\hat{\phi}_c)^*], \quad \epsilon = 1 (\text{meter})^2. \tag{42}$$

As stated after (37), we need three fields propagating along the x^1, x^2, and x^3 directions to achieve isotropic radiation of the CD field. These three fields are given by (S_{23}, S_{02}), (S_{31}, S_{03}), and (S_{12}, S_{01}). The energy-momentum tensor $\hat{T}_\mu^{\ \nu}(3)$ derived by the superposition of these fields becomes

$$\hat{T}_\mu^{\ \nu}(3) = \begin{pmatrix} -3\sigma^2 & -\tau\sigma & -\tau\sigma & -\tau\sigma \\ \tau\sigma & 2\tau^2 - \sigma^2 & 0 & 0 \\ \tau\sigma & 0 & 2\tau^2 - \sigma^2 & 0 \\ \tau\sigma & 0 & 0 & 2\tau^2 - \sigma^2 \end{pmatrix}. \tag{43}$$

In deriving (43), we set $S_{23} = S_{31} = S_{12} = \sigma$ and $S_{01} = S_{02} = S_{03} = \tau$. We note that $\hat{T}_\mu^{\ \nu}(3)$ can be regarded as the energy-momentum tensor of the anti-dark energy (dark energy with a negative energy density, that is, $\hat{T}_0^{\ 0}(3) = -3\sigma^2 < 0$). Dark energy (with positive energy density) $^*\hat{T}_\mu^{\ \nu}(3)$ having exactly the same trace as that of the anti-dark energy $\hat{T}_\mu^{\ \nu}(3)$ can be introduced by the Hodge dual exchange between (σ, τ) and $(i\tau, i\sigma)$ in (43), which becomes

$$^*\hat{T}_\mu^{\ \nu}(3) = \begin{pmatrix} 3\tau^2 & \tau\sigma & \tau\sigma & \tau\sigma \\ -\tau\sigma & -2\sigma^2 + \tau^2 & 0 & 0 \\ -\tau\sigma & 0 & -2\sigma^2 + \tau^2 & 0 \\ -\tau\sigma & 0 & 0 & -2\sigma^2 + \tau^2 \end{pmatrix}. \tag{44}$$

At this point, we recall the important remark on the validity of extending our discussion, which started from Minkowski space, to the case of a curved spacetime. As already pointed out in the explanation of Snyder space written in italics below in Equation (34), the isomorphism between $\hat{T}_{\mu\nu}$ and $G_{\mu\nu}$ given in (26) can be extended to a curved spacetime by virtue of the bivector property of (15). If the dark energy is modeled by a cosmological term of $\Lambda g_{\mu\nu}$, then the Einstein field equation with the sign convention of $R_{\mu\nu} = R^\sigma_{\mu\nu\sigma}$ together with the metric convention of $(+1, -1, -1, -1)$ becomes

$$R_\mu^{\ \nu} - \frac{R}{2} g_\mu^{\ \nu} + \Lambda g_\mu^{\ \nu} = -\frac{8\pi G}{c^4} T_\mu^{\ \nu}, \tag{45}$$

where Λ becomes negative for an expanding universe. Before proceeding further, we note that $^*\hat{T}_\mu^{\ \nu}(3)$ is not a quantity that directly fits into the conventional cosmological analysis utilizing the isotropic spacetime structure assumed by Weyl's hypothesis on the cosmological principle. First, as $^*\hat{T}_\mu^{\ \nu}(3)$ is spacelike in nature, it cannot be reduced to a diagonalized matrix form. Second, it is the energy-momentum tensor of fermionic $|M3\rangle_g$ with spin 3/2. The crucial problem in our analysis therefore is whether we can find observable quantities in $^*\hat{T}_\mu^{\ \nu}(3)$. Because the relevant criterion for singling out an observable quantity may depend on the situation, we have no choice but to make a good guess. The fact that seems to work as "the guiding principle" is that within the framework of relativistic QFT, any observable without exception associated with a given internal symmetry is invariant under the action of a transformation group materializing the symmetry under consideration. By extending this knowledge on the internal symmetry to the external (spacetime) one, we assume that the trace $\Lambda_{de} g_\nu^\nu$ defined by

$$\Lambda_{de} g_\nu^\nu := -\frac{8\pi G}{c^4} {}^*\hat{T}_\nu^\nu(3) > 0, \quad \rightarrow \quad \Lambda_{de} = \frac{12\pi G h}{c^3 \epsilon}(\kappa_0)^2 \qquad (46)$$

is observable as the invariant of the general coordinate transformation, which is consistent with the built-in Lorentz invariance of Snyder's momentum space on which the CD field is constructed. Thus, the validity of our new model on dark energy can be checked by comparing the following two models:

$$\begin{aligned} R_\mu^\nu - \frac{R}{2} g_\mu^\nu - \Lambda_{obs} g_\mu^\nu &= -\frac{8\pi G}{c^4} T_\mu^\nu, \\ R_\mu^\nu - \frac{R}{2} g_\mu^\nu &= -\frac{8\pi G}{c^4} T_\mu^\nu + \Lambda_{de} g_\mu^\nu, \end{aligned} \qquad (47)$$

where Λ_{obs} denotes the value obtained by Planck satellite observations. (In S3O, Λ_{obs} in the above Equation (47) appeared with the wrong sign in the corresponding Equation (25), which should be corrected.) Using (39), ${}^*\hat{T}_\nu^\nu(3) = 3\hat{T}_\nu^\nu(1)$, and (42), we obtain $\Lambda_{de} \approx 2.47 \times 10^{-53}$ m^{-2} and $\Lambda_{obs} \approx 3.7 \times 10^{-53}$ m^{-2} [32]. Thus, $|M3\rangle_g$ seems to be a promising candidate model for dark energy.

In the above arguments on the dark energy model, the physical meaning of the "real" cosmological term $\Lambda g_{\mu\nu}$ should be revised, because it does not correspond in our model to dark energy. We believe that one of the intriguing possibilities is that $\Lambda_{dm} g_{\mu\nu}$ with $\Lambda_{dm} > 0$ (valid in our sign convention) represents dark matter. The main reason for this is due to a simple fact that we can represent the metric tensor $g_{\mu\nu}$ in terms of the Weyl (conformal) curvature tensor $W_{\alpha\beta\gamma\delta}$ as long as its magnitude does not vanish, namely,

$$g_{\mu\nu} = \frac{4}{W^2} W_{\mu\alpha\beta\gamma} W_\nu^{\alpha\beta\gamma}, \quad W^2 := W_{\alpha\beta\gamma\delta} W^{\alpha\beta\gamma\delta} \neq 0, \qquad (48)$$

as shown by straightforward calculations [33]. Recall that Weyl curvature represents the deviation of spacetime from the conformally flat Friedmann–Robertson–Walker (FRW) metric for an isotropic universe. In addition, the monotonic decrease in W^2 along the radial direction in the field of $W_{\alpha\beta\gamma\delta}$ in the well-known spherically symmetric Schwarzschild outer solution of a given star suggests that the local maxima of W^2 would behave as "particles" or that its existence tends to correlate with the created matter field. Therefore, $\tilde{T}_{\mu\nu}$, defined as

$$\tilde{T}_{\mu\nu} := \Lambda_{dm} g_{\mu\nu}, \quad \Lambda_{dm} > 0, \quad g_{00} > 0, \qquad (49)$$

to be put on the left-hand side of (45), gives an energy-momentum tensor of this pseudo-matter field as a candidate for dark matter. The existence of $\tilde{T}_{\mu\nu}$ will further accelerate the deviation of spacetime from the FRW metric and thus serve as the fostering mechanism of galaxy formation. (In Equation (30) of S3O, the above $\tilde{T}_{\mu\nu}$ was defined with negative Λ_{dm}, which is a second error related to the first error of $+\Lambda_{obs}$ in (47)). In determining the magnitude of Λ_{dm}, we first refer to the observational fact that the estimated abundance ratio of dark energy to dark matter is 3 : 1. AS $\Lambda_{de} = -{}^*\hat{T}_\nu^\nu(3) = -3\hat{T}_\nu^\nu(1)$, we have

$$\Lambda_{dm} = -\hat{T}_\nu^\nu(1) = \frac{\Lambda_{de}}{3}, \qquad (50)$$

the theoretical justification of which is given in the next section. Notice that the constant $\hat{T}_\nu^\nu(1)$ appearing first in (39) is a quantity belonging to the off-shell electromagnetic field discussed in Section 2.1 in which spacelike CD field is introduced by the conformal symmetry breaking (CSB) of light-like CD field. Although we already alluded to the importance of CSB in our previous paper (S3O), our discussion on it in the context of cosmological dynamics remains quite vague. In the subsequent section covering the main theme of this paper, we will show that the new notion of CSB which applies simultaneously to electromagnetic as well as gravitational fields will play an important role in connecting our novel cosmological model to the preceding intriguing CCC proposed by Penrose [14,34].

4. Dressed Photon Constant and a New Version of CCC

4.1. Dressed Photon Constant

Using (39), (42), and (50), we have

$$\Lambda_{dm} = \frac{4\pi G h(\kappa_0)^2}{c^3 \epsilon},\quad(51)$$

which is rewritten as follows in terms of the Planck length l_p, length scales of the universe l_{dm}, and DP:

$$l_p := \sqrt{hG/c^3},\ l_{dm} := \sqrt{(\Lambda_{dm})^{-1}},\ l_{dp} = (\kappa_0)^{-1},\quad(52)$$

$$l_p l_{dm} = \frac{\sqrt{\epsilon}}{2\sqrt{\pi}} l_{dp} \quad \rightarrow \quad \left[l_p l_{dm} = (\hat{l}_{dp})^2\right].\quad(53)$$

Equation (53) reveals that if we choose $\hat{l}_{dp} := l_{dp}/2\sqrt{\pi}$ as the third component of a natural unit in which we set $\hat{l}_{dp} = 1$, then $\hat{l}_{dp}$ gives the geometric mean of the smallest scale l_p and the largest one of l_{dm} in that natural unit system. By rewriting the second equation in (46) as

$$l_{dp} = \sqrt{\frac{12\pi G h}{c^3 \epsilon}}(\Lambda_{de})^{-1/2},\quad \rightarrow \quad l_{dp}^\dagger = \sqrt{\frac{12\pi G h}{c^3 \epsilon}}(\Lambda_{obs})^{-1/2},\quad(54)$$

we can use this equation to estimate the DP constant $l_{dp}^\dagger$ solely by the fundamental physical constants G, h, and c together with the observed cosmological constant Λ_{obs} in place of the above Λ_{de}. Directly from the second equation in (54), we obtain

$$l_{dp}^\dagger \approx 40.0\ \text{nm},\quad \left[\text{Experiments}: 50\ \text{nm} < l_{dp} < 70\ \text{nm}\right].\quad(55)$$

4.2. New Version of CCC

The main aim of this subsection is to explain a new factor we would like to add to the CCC which has more than a decade of research history. At the present moment, we are not sure whether our new factor will fit consistently into the basic schemes of the CCC so far investigated. However, we hope that our proposal presented here could be a somewhat useful contribution to the CCC which is related, for instance, to a particular study by Lübbe [35] who discussed the inclusion problem of a cosmological constant. As our dark energy model introduced in (47) is related to de Sitter space, we start from the run-through of the well-known characteristics of it by looking into the Einstein field equation

$$R_\mu^\nu - \frac{R}{2} g_\mu^\nu - \Lambda_{de} g_\mu^\nu = 0,\quad(56)$$

which yields a familiar solution given by

$$ds^2 = (cdt)^2 - (R_0)^2 \exp[2\sqrt{\frac{\Lambda_{de}}{3}}ct][dr^2 + r^2(d\theta^2 + \sin^2\theta)d\varphi^2],\quad(57)$$

where the constant R_0 serves as the coefficient of the time-dependent scale factor. In the use of (50), this solution can be simplified by taking $R_0 = l_p$ into

$$ds^2 = (cdt)^2 - (l_p)^2 \exp[2\sqrt{\Lambda_{dm}}ct][dr^2 + r^2(d\theta^2 + \sin^2\theta)d\varphi^2].\quad(58)$$

At the end of Section 3, the simultaneous CSB in electromagnetic and gravitational fields was mentioned. We now explain what this exactly means. Recall that the energy-momentum tensor $\hat{T}_\mu^\nu$ of the spacelike ($l_\nu l^\nu < 0$) CD field is given in Section 2.1 by (26), which is isomorphic to the Einstein tensor G_μ^ν. The same quantity $\hat{T}_\mu^\nu$ also emerges from the light-like case of $U_\nu U^\nu = 0$ by replacing $\partial^\nu \partial_\nu \phi = 0$ with $[\partial^\nu \partial_\nu - (\kappa_0)^2]\phi = 0$, which can be regarded as the breaking of both symmetries, i.e., conformal and gauge (cf. (10)). Therefore, this CSB from the light-like to the spacelike CD field can be seen as responsible simultaneously for the breaking from $ds^2 = 0$ to nonzero ds^2 in (58) through (53), which corresponds to the CSB of gravitational field with the scale parameter Λ_{dm}.

A well-known remarkable characteristic of the solution (58) is that it is transformed into a stationary solution

$$ds^2 = \left(1 - \Lambda_{dm}(r')^2\right)(cdt')^2 - \frac{(dr')^2}{(1 - \Lambda_{dm}(r')^2)} - (r')^2(d\theta^2 + \sin^2\theta d\varphi^2) \tag{59}$$

by the following variable changes:

$$l_p r = \frac{r'}{\sqrt{D}} \exp[-\sqrt{\Lambda_{dm}} ct'], \quad t = t' + \frac{1}{2c}\sqrt{\frac{1}{\Lambda_{dm}}} \ln D, \tag{60}$$

where D is defined either by $1 > D := 1 - \Lambda_{dm}(r')^2 > 0$ (case I) or by $1 > D := \Lambda_{dm}(r')^2 - 1 > 0$ (case II). Note that the metric (59) is similar in form to the Schwarzschild metric given below, for which an event horizon exists at $r' = \alpha$, while that in (59) exists at $r' = \sqrt{1/\Lambda_{dm}}$. (See Figure 1)

$$ds^2 = \left(1 - \frac{\alpha}{r'}\right)(cdt')^2 - \frac{(dr')^2}{(1 - \frac{\alpha}{r'})} - (r')^2(d\theta^2 + \sin^2\theta d\varphi^2). \tag{61}$$

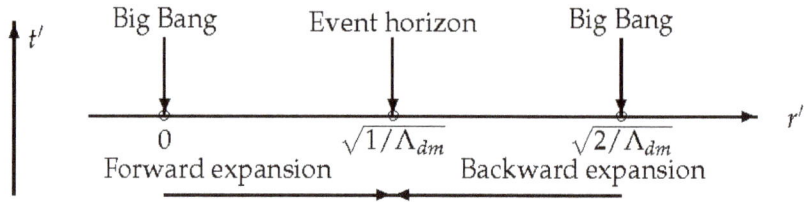

Figure 1. Dual configuration of twin universes.

In case I of the stationary metric (59), we have $r' = 0$ by the synchronization $t = t'$ of t and t' owing to (60). If t' is adjusted as $t' = \Theta t$, $(\Theta > 1)$, then we see that r' moves from 0 to $1/\sqrt{(\Lambda_{dm})}$ as t moves from 0 to $+\infty$. Similarly, in case II, we see that r' moves from $\sqrt{2/(\Lambda_{dm})}$ to $1/\sqrt{(\Lambda_{dm})}$ as t moves from 0 to $+\infty$. This dual structure, illustrated in Figure 1, clearly shows that by taking $t = 0$ as the origin of time from which twin Big Bang universes evolve, they will meet at the event horizon in (59) an eon later ($t = \infty$). To the best of our knowledge, the concept of twin universes with matter vs. antimatter duality was first discussed by Petit [15]. We believe that his cosmological model fits exactly into the configuration illustrated in Figure 1, which tells us that $\sqrt{(\Lambda_{dm})^{-1}}$ is a genuine characteristic length scale of our universe. This justifies the fact that Λ_{dm} defined in (50) is the cosmological constant that appears in the form of (49). The forward and backward time evolutions of twin universes correspond, respectively, to positive and negative field operators of the 4-momentum, while the existence of twin universes naturally explains the reason why one-sided energy spectra at the level of state vector space works for many practical situations in each universe. If the birth of these twin universes was brought about by conformal symmetry breaking of certain light fields in which the duality between "matter (with positive energy) and antimatter (with negative energy)" works as the separation rule of the twin structure, then the twin pair will return to the original light fields when they meet at the event horizon. The next Big Bangs of the twin pair will occur at certain locations on this event horizon distant from each other by $\sqrt{2/\Lambda_{dm}}$.

According to the arguments developed thus far, we can say that the original conformal light field is composed of light fields with the following duality structures:

$$\left[T_\mu^\nu = -F_{\mu\sigma}F^{\nu\sigma}, \ ^*\hat{T}_\mu^\nu =^* (S_{\mu\sigma}S^{\nu\sigma}), \ T_0^0 > 0, \ ^*\hat{T}_0^0 > 0\right], \tag{62}$$

$$\left[^*T_\mu^\nu = -^*(F_{\mu\sigma}F^{\nu\sigma}), \ \hat{T}_\mu^\nu = S_{\mu\sigma}S^{\nu\sigma}, \ ^*T_0^0 < 0, \ \hat{T}_0^0 < 0\right], \tag{63}$$

where the symbol * denotes the Hodge duality explained in the derivation of (44). Although (62) and (63) can be considered as light and anti-light (light with positive energy moving backward in time) fields, respectively, they can coexist as free modes without interacting with each other, unlike the case of matter and antimatter interactions. As all of these fields are trace free, the associated Ricci scalar curvature is zero. Equation (26) tells us that the Riemann curvature associated with these light fields takes the form $R_{\lambda\rho\mu\nu} = F_{\lambda\rho}F_{\mu\nu}(= S_{\lambda\rho}S_{\mu\nu})$. In addition to $R_\nu^\nu = 0$, we can readily show $R_{\mu\nu}R^{\mu\nu} = 0$ using (23). Under the former condition $R_\nu^\nu = 0$, the Weyl tensor $W_{\lambda\rho\mu\nu}$ assumes the form

$$W_{\lambda\rho\mu\nu} = R_{\lambda\rho\mu\nu} + \frac{1}{2}(R_{\lambda\mu}g_{\rho\nu} - R_{\lambda\nu}g_{\rho\mu} - R_{\rho\mu}g_{\lambda\nu} + R_{\rho\nu}g_{\lambda\mu}); \tag{64}$$

thus, by direct calculations using the latter condition of $R_{\mu\nu}R^{\mu\nu} = 0$, we obtain $W^2 = 0$. Therefore, for light fields (62) and (63), we have

$$R_\nu^\nu = 0, \quad W^2 = W_{\nu\alpha\beta\gamma}W^{\nu\alpha\beta\gamma} = 0. \tag{65}$$

The second equation in (65) is related to Penrose's Weyl curvature hypothesis [14].

In modern cosmology, cosmic inflation theory was introduced to explain the observed highly tuned initial condition of the Big Bang, in which the notion of "false vacua" plays a key role in explaining the tremendous exponential expansion of space. In the introduction, however, we pointed out that the notion of the vacuum state in conventional QFT is highly biased by the one in Fock space, which may be called "Fock vacuum prejudice" if adhering to the idea of creation from emptiness. One of the aims of our present paper is to overcome this prejudice in the spirit of Occam's razor as follows: in view of the present circumstances showing that inflation theory seems to be "lost in a maze" in achieving the above-mentioned original goal, the basic premise of our working hypothesis in cosmology can be shifted from the Fock vacuum to the phase transition of the extended light field arising from its CSB, according to which a simpler alternative view emerges such that the initial condition of the Big Bang and the dynamics of both dark energy and matter can be naturally explained.

For light fields, $ds^2 = 0$, the amplitude of the smallest perturbations of CSB in the length scale would be l_p in (58), but its magnitude in the converted energy scale is tremendously large because energy is inversely proportional to length. By virtue of the Weyl curvature hypothesis of (65), and especially of the peculiar form of (49) through which the Weyl tensor contributes to part of the energy-momentum field, we see that the Weyl contribution to the energy field is a very low value of Λ_{dm}. Therefore, the energy field with extremely high density thus created must have a distribution in spacetime very close to the FRW metric on which small amplitude perturbations of W^2 exist. The emergence of the FRW metric is the result of unfolding the "blueprint" (14) encoded in the lightlike CD field. Note that in the limit of $W^2 \to 0$, the energy-momentum field (49) approaches the anti-de Sitter (AdS) space; thus, the weak gravitational field and high energy conformal field share a common AdS spacetime, which is an essential part of the Maldacena duality [36]. In our new revised version of the CCC of twin universes, the beginning and end of the cycle are, respectively, compared to the pair creation and annihilation of elementary particles through the intervention of conformal light fields. Within the cycle in each universe, a couple of different classes of entities exist, i.e., both visible matter and invisible dark energy and dark matter exist. In S3O, we already discussed an extended thermodynamical viewpoint on the dynamics at cosmological scales.

When we take into account the remarkable abundance ratios of invisible dark energy and dark matter in comparison to the negligible one of ordinary visible matter, the time evolution of visible material subsystems in the universe, for instance, galaxy cluster formations, may be compared to the "heat engines" working between invisible "heat reservoirs" with higher and lower temperature, which, respectively, correspond to dark matter with positive energy and negative dark energy. If we denote the space averaged W^2 by $W^2|_{ave.}$, then due to the property of universal gravitation, it will increase with the passage of time and thus may be related to the gravitational entropy of the visible subsystem in the universe. From this viewpoint, the effect of the gravitational field, including that of dark matter, modeled as $\Lambda_{dm} g_{\mu\nu}$ in our theory, can be interpreted by a certain model of thermodynamics. Actually, attempts at this have already been made, for instance, in [37,38].

As the final remarks on CCC, first, we note that the conformal symmetry of source-free Maxwell's equation holds well only in four dimensions, which may explain why the dimensions of spacetime in which we live are four. Second, the first author would appreciate if his philosophical preference of helical evolution to cyclic motion is reflected in CCC. His speculative "Book of Genesis" on CCC is as follows:

In the beginning, God, as a mathematician, created the primordial light with conformal symmetry, and God said: "Let there be conformal symmetry breaking, and there were twin universes, beginning their long journey towards a brighter future of a light world one stage higher in eternal evolution."

Author Contributions: H.S. contributed to the basic structure of this article. I.O. provided the knowledge on fundamental quantum field theory and the new perspective on the involvement of the ζ-function singularity in the quantum walk models describing the behaviors of dressed photons. All authors have read and agreed to the published version of the manuscript.

Funding: This research received no external funding.

Institutional Review Board Statement: Not applicable.

Informed Consent Statement: Not applicable.

Data Availability Statement: Not applicable.

Acknowledgments: This research was partially supported in the form of a collaboration with the Institute of Mathematics for Industry, Kyushu University. We thank anonymous reviewers for their helpful comments and suggestions to improve the quality of this paper.

Conflicts of Interest: The authors declare no conflict of interest.

References

1. Ohtsu, M. *Dressed Photons*; Springer: Berlin, Germany, 2014; pp. 89–214.
2. Sakuma, H.; Ojima, I.; Ohtsu, M.; Ochiai, H. Off-Shell Quantum Fields to Connect Dressed Photons with Cosmology. *Symmetry* **2020**, *12*, 1244. [CrossRef]
3. Ojima, I. Micro-Macro duality and emergence of macroscopic levels. *Quantum Probab. White Noise Anal.* **2008**, *21*, 217–228.
4. Jost, R. *The General Theory of Quantized Fields*; American Mathematical Society: Providence, RI, USA, 1963.
5. Dell'Antonio, G.F. Support of a field in *p* space. *J. Math. Phys.* **1961**, *2*, 759–766. [CrossRef]
6. Mackey, G.W. A theorem of Stone and von Neumann. *Duke Math. J.* **1949**, *16*, 313–326. [CrossRef]
7. Ojima, I. A unified scheme for generalized sectors based on selection criteria–order parameters of symmetries and of thermal situations and physical meanings of classifying categorical adjunctions. *Open Syst. Inf. Dyn.* **2003**, *10*, 235–279. [CrossRef]
8. Streater, R.F.; Wightman, A.S. *PCT, Spin and Statistics and All That*; Benjamin, Inc.: Big Bear Lake, CA, USA, 1964.
9. Sakuma, H.; Ojima, I.; Ohtsu, M. Dressed photons in a new paradigm of off-shell quantum fields. *Progr. Quantum Electron.* **2017**, *55*, 74–87. [CrossRef]
10. Sakuma, H.; Ojima, I.; Ohtsu, M. Gauge symmetry breaking and emergence of Clebsch-dual electromagnetic field as a model of dressed photons. *Appl. Phys. A* **2017**, *123*, 750. [CrossRef]
11. Sakuma, H. Virtual Photon Model by Spatio-Temporal Vortex Dynamics. In *Progress in Nanophotonics*; Yatsui, T., Ed.; Springer Nature: Cham, Switzerland, 2018; Volume 5, pp. 53–77.

12. Ohtsu, M.; Ojima, I.; Sakuma, H. *Progress in Optics*; Chapter 1; Visser, T., Ed.; Elsevier: Amsterdam, The Netherlands, 2019; Volume 62, pp. 45–97.
13. Huggett, S.A.; Tod, K.P. *An Introduction to Twistor Theory*, 2nd ed.; Cambridge University Press: Cambridge, UK, 1994.
14. Penrose, R. Before the Big Bang: An outrageous new perspective and its implications for particle physics. *Proc. EPAC* **2006**. Available online: https://accelconf.web.cern.ch/e06/PAPERS/THESPA01.PDF (accessed on 1 January 2021).
15. Petit, J.P. Twin Universes Cosmology. *Astrophys. Space Sci.* **1995**, *226*, 273–307. [CrossRef]
16. Lax, M.; Louisell, W.H.; McKnight, W.B. From Maxwell to paraxial optics. *Phys. Rev. A* **1975**, *11*, 1365–1370. [CrossRef]
17. Cicchitelli, L.; Hora, H.; Postle, R. Longitudinal field components for laser beams in vacuum. *Phys. Rev. A* **1990**, *41*, 3727–3732. [CrossRef]
18. Landau, L.D.; Lifshitz, E.M. *Course of Theoretical Physics*, 2nd ed.; Volume 6 Fluid Mechanics; Elsevier: Oxford, UK, 1987.
19. Lamb, S.H. *Hydrodynamics*, 6th ed.; Cambridge University Press: Cambridge, UK, 1930.
20. Ojima, I. Nakanishi-Lautrup B-Field, Crossed Product & Duality. *RIMS Kokyuroku* **2006**, *1524*, 29–37.
21. Snyder, H.S. Quantized space-time. *Phys. Rev.* **1947**, *71*, 38. [CrossRef]
22. Girelli, F.; Livine, E.R.; Oriti, D. Deformed special relativity as an effective flat limit of quantum gravity. *Nucl. Phys. B* **2005**, *708*, 411–433. [CrossRef]
23. Kowalski-Glikman, J. Introduction to Doubly Special Relativity. *arXiv* **2004**, arXiv:hep-th/0405273v1
24. Ohtsu, M. History, current developments, and future directions of near-field optical science. *Opto-Electron. Adv.* **2020**, *3*, 190046. [CrossRef]
25. Aharonov, Y.; Komar, A.; Susskind, L. Superluminal behavior, causality, and instability. *Phys. Rev.* **1969**, *182*, 1400–1402. [CrossRef]
26. Kadowaki, T.; Kawazoe, T.; Ohtsu, M. SiC transmission-type polarization rotator using a large magneto-optical effect boosted and stabilized by dressed photons. *Sci. Rep.* **2020**, *10*, 12967. [CrossRef] [PubMed]
27. Hamano, M.; Saigo, H. Quantum walk and dressed photon. In Proceedings of the 9th International Conference on Quantum Simulation and Quantum Walks (QSQW 2020), Electronic Proceedings in Theoretical Computer Science 315, Marseille, France, 20–24 January 2020; pp. 93–99.
28. Higuchi, Y.; Segawa, E. A dynamical system induced by quantum walk. *J. Phys. A Math. Theor.* **2019**, *52*, 39. [CrossRef]
29. Higuchi, Y.; Sabri, M.; Segawa, E. Electric Circuit Induced by Quantum Walk. *J. Stat. Phys.* **2020**, *181*, 603–617. [CrossRef]
30. Takesaki, M. Duality for crossed products and the structure of von Neumann algebras of type III. *Acta Math.* **1973**, *131*, 249–310.
31. Ojima, I. Gauge fields at finite temperatures—"Thermo Field Dynamics"and the KMS condition and their extension to gauge theories. *Ann. Phys.* **1981**, *137*, 1–32. [CrossRef]
32. Liu, H. What-Is-the-Best-Estimate-of-the-Cosmological-Constant. Available online: https://www.quora.com (accessed on 1 January 2021).
33. Sakuma, H.; Ochiai, H. Note on the physical meaning of the cosmological term. OffShell: 1909O.001.v2. 2019. Available online: http://offshell.rodrep.org/?p=249 (accessed on 1 January 2021).
34. Tod, P. The equation of CCC. *arXiv* **2013**, arXiv:1309.7248.
35. Lübbe, C. Conformal scalar fields, isotropic singularities and conformal cyclic cosmology. *arXiv* **2013**, arXiv:1312.2059.
36. Maldacena, J. The large N limit of superconformal field theories and supergravity. *Adv. Theor. Math. Phys.* **1998**, *2*, 231–252. [CrossRef]
37. Verlinde, E. On the origin of gravity and the laws of Newton. *High Energy Phys.* **2011**, *4*, 29. [CrossRef]
38. Brouwer, M.M.; Visser, M.R.; Dvornik, A.; Hoekstra, H.; Kuijken, K.; Valentijn, E.A.; Bilicki, M.; Blake, C.; Brough, S.; Buddelmeijer, H.; et al. First test of Verlinde's theory of Emergent Gravity using Weak Gravitationsl Lensing measurements. *Mon. Not. R. Astron. Soc.* **2017**, *466*, 2547–2559. [CrossRef]

Article

Symmetry of Dressed Photon

Hiroyuki Ochiai

Institute of Mathematics for Industry, Kyushu University, Fukuoka 819-0395, Japan; ochiai@imi.kyushu-u.ac.jp

Abstract: Motivated by describing the symmetry of a theoretical model of dressed photons, we introduce several spaces with Lie group actions and the morphisms between them depending on three integer parameters $n \geq r \geq s$ on dimensions. We discuss the symmetry on these spaces using classical invariant theory, orbit decomposition of prehomogeneous vector spaces, and compact reductive homogeneous space such as Grassmann manifold and flag variety. Finally, we go back to the original dressed photon with $n = 4, r = 2, s = 1$.

Keywords: dressed photon; Grassmann manifold; flag manifold; pre-homogeneous vector space; invariants

Citation: Ochiai, H. Symmetry of Dressed Photon. *Symmetry* **2021**, *13*, 1283. https://doi.org/10.3390/sym13071283

Academic Editor: Ignatios Antoniadis

Received: 1 July 2021
Accepted: 14 July 2021
Published: 16 July 2021

Publisher's Note: MDPI stays neutral with regard to jurisdictional claims in published maps and institutional affiliations.

Copyright: © 2021 by the author. Licensee MDPI, Basel, Switzerland. This article is an open access article distributed under the terms and conditions of the Creative Commons Attribution (CC BY) license (https://creativecommons.org/licenses/by/4.0/).

1. Introduction

A formulation of dressed photons in quantum field theory is given by the Clebsch dual variable, motivated by fluid dynamics [1–3]. The Clebsch parametrization of the rotational model of the velocity field U_μ is formulated of the form $U_\mu = \lambda \nabla_\mu \phi$ with two scalar fields λ, ϕ. We define the covariant vectors $C_\mu = \nabla_\mu \phi$ and $L_\mu = \nabla_\mu \lambda$, and the bi-vector $S_{\mu\nu} = C_\mu L_\nu - L_\mu C_\nu$. The energy–momentum tensor is defined by $\hat{T}^\nu_\mu = -S_{\mu\sigma} S^{\nu\sigma}$. It is shown

$$\hat{T}^\nu_\mu = \rho C_\mu C^\nu \quad (1)$$

by a simple computation [1].

Our main concern is this last Equation (1). This looks like Veronese embedding in projective geometry. In this paper, we introduce the model in arbitrary dimension and describe the symmetry of this model. Most of the material comes from the modern treatment of classical invariant theory [4,5]. Especially, the quadratic map arising in reductive dual pair [6,7] is used as one of the key ingredients in this paper to construct geometric objects describing the symmetry. This enables us to give another explanation of the last Equation (1) on $\hat{T}$.

Physical study of dressed photons, including experiments and related applications, called dressed photon phenomenon, has already been summarized in our previous paper [8]. This paper serves as a complementary observation on symmetry of theoretical foundations of dressed photon Equation [1], which would be expected as is in classical electromagnetism. We conclude that the symmetry is well described in terms of compact homogeneous space, such as Grassmann manifolds and flag manifolds, as well as pre-homogeneous vector spaces, which is not a homogeneous space, but still has a large symmetry. It is also significant that a part of discussion is not restricted to a specific dimension, so that half of them are formulated in arbitrary dimension.

The construction of this paper is as follows: In Section 2, we work over the complex number field $\mathbb{C}$, and do si in arbitrary dimensions $n \geq r \geq s$. In Section 3, we consider the special case $n = 4, r = 2, s = 1$ with the real number field $\mathbb{R}$. The symmetry and invariants are mostly the same for $\mathbb{C}$ and for $\mathbb{R}$; however, there is a subtle and rather complicated problem on connected components over $\mathbb{R}$. In order to concentrate this complication for $\mathbb{R}$, the common features of the model are discussed over $\mathbb{C}$, and the different point is separately treated in Section 3.

2. The Model over the Complex Numbers

2.1. Symmetry in Arbitrary Dimension

Let $M(n,r,\mathbb{C})$, $\text{Sym}(n,\mathbb{C})$, $\text{Alt}(n,\mathbb{C})$ be the set of n by r matrices, symmetric matrices, and skew-symmetric matrices with complex entries. We denote by $M(n,r,\mathbb{C})_{\text{rk}\leq i}$ the subset consisting of matrices of rank at most i. The transpose of a matrix X is denoted by X^T. Classical invariant theory gives the following maps:

Let $J \in \text{Alt}(r,\mathbb{C})_{\text{rk}=r}$. We define the map

$$\mathbb{S} : M(n,r,\mathbb{C}) \longrightarrow \text{Alt}(n,\mathbb{C}) \quad \text{by} \quad X \mapsto XJX^T.$$

If $r \geq n$, then this map is surjective. If $r < n$, then the image of this map is $\text{Alt}(n,\mathbb{C})_{\text{rk}\leq r}$. This map is $GL(n,\mathbb{C}) \times Sp(r,\mathbb{C})$-equivariant, in the sense that $\mathbb{S}(lXh) = l\mathbb{S}(X)l^T$ for any $l \in GL(n,\mathbb{C})$ and $h \in Sp(r,\mathbb{C})$, where the symplectic group attached to J is defined by $Sp(r,\mathbb{C}) = Sp(J,\mathbb{C}) = \{h \in M(r,\mathbb{C}) \mid hJh^T = J\}$.

Let $g \in \text{Sym}(n,\mathbb{C})_{\text{rk}=n}$. We define the map

$$\mathbb{G} : M(n,r,\mathbb{C}) \longrightarrow \text{Sym}(r,\mathbb{C}) \quad \text{by} \quad X \mapsto X^T g X.$$

If $r \geq n$, then this map is surjective. If $r < n$, then the image of this map is $\text{Sym}(r,\mathbb{C})_{\text{rk}\leq n}$. This map is $O(n,\mathbb{C}) \times GL(r,\mathbb{C})$-equivariant, in the sense that $\mathbb{G}(lXh) = h^T\mathbb{G}(X)h$ for any $l \in O(n,\mathbb{C})$ and $h \in GL(r,\mathbb{C})$, where the orthogonal group attached to g is defined by $O(n,\mathbb{C}) = O(g,\mathbb{C}) = \{l \in M(n,\mathbb{C}) \mid l^T g l = g\}$. Especially, put $r = n$ and restrict the domain, we define

$$\mathbb{T} : \text{Alt}(n,\mathbb{C}) \longrightarrow \text{Sym}(n,\mathbb{C}) \quad \text{by} \quad X \mapsto XgX^T = -XgX = X^TgX.$$

This is $O(n,\mathbb{C})$-equivariant: $\mathbb{T}(lXl^T) = l\mathbb{T}(X)l^T$.

From now on, we assume that $n \geq r \geq s$. Each $GL(r,\mathbb{C})$-orbit on $\text{Sym}(r,\mathbb{C})$ is parametrized by the rank. The closure relation of orbits is linear, so that the closure of $\text{Sym}(r,\mathbb{C})_{\text{rk}=s}$ is $\text{Sym}(r,\mathbb{C})_{\text{rk}\leq s}$. We define

$$Y(\mathbb{C}) = M(n,r,\mathbb{C})_{\text{rk}=r} \cap \mathbb{G}^{-1}(\text{Sym}(r,\mathbb{C})_{\text{rk}\leq s})$$

Our main target is the description of the image of $Y(\mathbb{C})$ by the map $\mathbb{T} \circ \mathbb{S}$:

$$\text{Sym}(r,\mathbb{C})_{\text{rk}\leq s} \xleftarrow{\mathbb{G}} M(n,r,\mathbb{C})_{\text{rk}=r} \xrightarrow{\mathbb{S}} \text{Alt}(n,\mathbb{C}) \xrightarrow{\mathbb{T}} \text{Sym}(n,\mathbb{C}). \tag{2}$$

In order to state the main result, we introduce several auxiliary spaces and maps. We fix $g' \in \text{Sym}(s,\mathbb{C})_{\text{rk}=s}$. We define the maps

$$\mathbb{V} : M(n,s,\mathbb{C}) \longrightarrow \text{Sym}(n,\mathbb{C}) \quad \text{by} \quad \mathbb{V}(X) = Xg'X^T.$$

$$\mathbb{V}' : M(r,s,\mathbb{C}) \longrightarrow \text{Sym}(r,\mathbb{C}) \quad \text{by} \quad \mathbb{V}'(X') = X'g'X'^T,$$

Note that these maps are similar to $\mathbb{G}$, but transposed. Especially, the orthogonal group $O(g',\mathbb{C})$ acts transitively on each fiber of an element of $\text{Sym}(r,\mathbb{C})_{\text{rk}=s}$.

We define $Z(\mathbb{C})$ to be the fiber product of the map $\mathbb{G} : Y(\mathbb{C}) \to \text{Sym}(r,\mathbb{C})_{\text{rk}\leq s}$ and $\mathbb{V}' : M(r,s,\mathbb{C})_{\text{rk}=s} \to \text{Sym}(r,\mathbb{C})_{\text{rk}\leq s}$:

$$Z(\mathbb{C}) = Y(\mathbb{C}) \times_{\text{Sym}(r,\mathbb{C})_{\text{rk}\leq s}} M(r,s,\mathbb{C})_{\text{rk}=s}$$
$$= \{(X,X') \in M(n,r,\mathbb{C}) \times M(r,s,\mathbb{C}) \mid \text{rk}(X) = r, \text{rk}(X') = s, X^TgX = X'g'X'^T\}.$$

We have the commutative diagram

$$
\begin{array}{ccccc}
M(n,r,\mathbb{C}) & \longleftarrow & Y(\mathbb{C}) & \xleftarrow{\widetilde{\mathbb{V}}'} & Z(\mathbb{C}) \\
\mathbb{G} \downarrow & & \mathbb{G} \downarrow & \square & \widetilde{\mathbb{G}} \downarrow \\
\mathrm{Sym}(r,\mathbb{C}) & \longleftarrow & \mathrm{Sym}(r,\mathbb{C})_{\mathrm{rk}\leq s} & \xleftarrow{\mathbb{V}'} & M(r,s,\mathbb{C})_{\mathrm{rk}=s}
\end{array}
\qquad (3)
$$

where the right square is Cartesian.

The map $\mathbb{T}\circ\mathbb{S}$ does not factor through the map $\mathbb{V}$. However, when we lift the map from $Y(\mathbb{C})$ to $Z(\mathbb{C})$, the map factor through $\mathbb{V}$. To be more precise, we have the following:

Theorem 1. $(\mathbb{T}\circ\mathbb{S})(X) = (\mathbb{V}\circ\phi)(X,X')$ *for all* $(X,X')\in Z(\mathbb{C})$, *where we define*

$$\phi: M(n,r,\mathbb{C})_{\mathrm{rk}=r} \times M(r,s,\mathbb{C})_{\mathrm{rk}=s} \longrightarrow M(n,s,\mathbb{C})_{\mathrm{rk}=s} \quad \text{by} \quad (X,X') \mapsto XJX' \qquad (4)$$

Proof. $(\mathbb{T}\circ\mathbb{S})(X) = \mathbb{T}(XJX^T) = (XJX^T)g(XJX^T)^T = XJ\mathbb{G}(X)J^T X^T$
$= XJ\mathbb{V}'(X')J^T X^T = (XJX')g'(XJX')^T = \mathbb{V}(XJX') = (\mathbb{V}\circ\phi)(X,X')$. □

This theorem is illustrated as the following commutative diagram:

$$
\begin{array}{ccccc}
Z(\mathbb{C}) & \longrightarrow & M(n,r,\mathbb{C})_{\mathrm{rk}=r}\times M(r,s,\mathbb{C})_{\mathrm{rk}=s} & \xrightarrow{\phi} & M(n,s,\mathbb{C})_{\mathrm{rk}=s} \\
\widetilde{\mathbb{V}}' \downarrow & & \downarrow & & \downarrow \mathbb{V} \\
Y(\mathbb{C}) & \longrightarrow & M(n,r,\mathbb{C})_{\mathrm{rk}=r} & \xrightarrow{\mathbb{S}} \mathrm{Alt}(n,\mathbb{C}) \xrightarrow{\mathbb{T}} & \mathrm{Sym}(n,\mathbb{C})
\end{array}
\qquad (5)
$$

Note that the maps $\mathbb{S},\mathbb{G},\mathbb{T},\mathbb{V},\mathbb{V}'$ are common in classical invariant theory and theory of reductive dual pair, though the space $Y(\mathbb{C})$ and $Z(\mathbb{C})$ is unique in our setting.

2.2. Grassmann and Flag Manifold

We will show that the map ϕ introduced in Theorem 1 has an interpretation in the projective setting. We still assume $n \geq r \geq s$. The Grassmann manifold $\mathrm{Grass}(n,r,\mathbb{C})$ is the set of r-dimensional subspace of $\mathbb{C}^n$. This is identified with

$$M(n,r,\mathbb{C})_{\mathrm{rk}=r}/GL(r,\mathbb{C}) \cong \mathrm{Grass}(n,r,\mathbb{C}).$$

Every r-dimensional subspace of $\mathbb{C}^n$ is spanned by r linear independent column vectors in $\mathbb{C}^n$.

The flag manifold $\mathrm{Flag}(n;k_1,\ldots,k_m,\mathbb{C})$ is the set of flags of type $(k_1,k_2,\ldots,k_m)$, which is defined to be a sequence of subspaces $V_1\subset V_2 \subset \cdots \subset V_m$ of $\mathbb{C}^n$, where $1 \leq k_1 < k_2 < \cdots < k_m < n$, with $\dim V_i = k_i$ ($i=1,\ldots,m$). Grassmann manifold is a special case of flag manifolds with $m=1$. On the other hand, a flag variety is regarded as the incidence variety of the product of Grassmann manifolds. For example, $\mathrm{Flag}(n;k_1,k_2,\mathbb{C}) = \{(V_1,V_2) \in \mathrm{Grass}(N,k_1,\mathbb{C}) \times \mathrm{Grass}(N,k_2,\mathbb{C}) \mid V_1 \subset V_2\}$. We have an isomorphism

$$(M(n,r,\mathbb{C})_{\mathrm{rk}=r}\times M(r,s,\mathbb{C})_{\mathrm{rk}=s})/(GL(r,\mathbb{C})\times GL(s,\mathbb{C})) \cong \mathrm{Flag}(n;s,r,\mathbb{C}).$$

In the following commutative diagram, each space in the upper line, which arises in Theorem 1, is a locally closed subset of an affine space, while each space in the lower line is a projective variety.

$$
\begin{array}{ccccc}
M(n,r,\mathbb{C})_{\mathrm{rk}=r} & \longleftarrow & M(n,r,\mathbb{C})_{\mathrm{rk}=r}\times M(r,s,\mathbb{C})_{\mathrm{rk}=s} & \xrightarrow{\phi} & M(n,s,\mathbb{C})_{\mathrm{rk}=s} \\
\downarrow & & \downarrow & & \downarrow \\
\mathrm{Grass}(n,r,\mathbb{C}) & \longleftarrow & \mathrm{Flag}(n;s,r,\mathbb{C}) & \longrightarrow & \mathrm{Grass}(n,s,\mathbb{C}).
\end{array}
\qquad (6)
$$

The maps in the lower line are given by $V_2 \leftarrow (V_1, V_2) \mapsto V_1$. This double fibration is often used in Radon transform and Heck correspondence [9].

In the case $r = 2$, the map

$$\mathbb{S} : M(n, 2, \mathbb{C})_{\text{rk}=2} \longrightarrow \text{Alt}(n, \mathbb{C})_{\text{rk}=2}$$

induces the Plücker embedding

$$\text{Grass}(n, 2, \mathbb{C}) \longrightarrow \text{Alt}(n, \mathbb{C})_{\text{rk}=2}/\mathbb{C}^\times \subset \mathbb{P}^{n(n-1)/2-1}(\mathbb{C}).$$

3. The Model over Real Numbers

We now consider the special case $n = 4, r = 2, s = 1$, and replace $\mathbb{C}$ by $\mathbb{R}$. Let $J = \begin{pmatrix} 0 & 1 \\ -1 & 0 \end{pmatrix}$ be the standard non-degenerate skew-symmetric matrix. Note that $J^T = -J$ and $\det J = 1$. Let g be the diagonal matrix with diagonal entries $(1, -1, -1, -1)$. Finally, we put $g' = 1$.

Most of the story in the previous section does hold over the real number field $\mathbb{R}$ as well. However, the disconnectedness makes things complicated. For example, although the map $\mathbb{V}' : M(2, 1, \mathbb{C}) \longrightarrow \text{Sym}(2, \mathbb{C})_{\text{rk} \leq 1}$ given by $\mathbb{V}'(X') = X'X'^T$ is surjective, the map $\mathbb{V}' : M(2, 1, \mathbb{R}) \longrightarrow \text{Sym}(2, \mathbb{R})_{\text{rk} \leq 1}$ is not surjective, because $\begin{pmatrix} 0 & 0 \\ 0 & -1 \end{pmatrix}$ is not in the image. In order to improve this defect, we introduce a non-zero scalar multiplication so that we modify the map $\mathbb{V}'$ by $\mathbb{V}_2$ given below (7).

3.1. Quadratic Polynomial

Let us consider the matrix $X = (C, L) = \begin{pmatrix} C_0 & L_0 \\ C_1 & L_1 \\ C_2 & L_2 \\ C_3 & L_3 \end{pmatrix} \in M(4, 2, \mathbb{R})$ with the column vectors $C, L \in \mathbb{R}^4$. Here, $M(m, n, \mathbb{R})$ the set of m by n matrices with real coefficients. The entry of the map

$$\mathbb{S} : M(4, 2, \mathbb{R}) \ni X \mapsto XJX^T \in \text{Alt}(4, \mathbb{R})_{\text{rk} \leq 2}$$

is given by

$$\mathbb{S}_{\mu\nu}(X) = (XJX^T)_{\mu\nu} = C_\mu L_\nu - L_\mu C_\nu,$$

which realizes the definition of $S_{\mu\nu}$. The map $\mathbb{S}$ is $GL(4, \mathbb{R}) \times SL(2, \mathbb{R})$-equivariant, where we remark the accidental isomorphism of lower rank groups:

$$SL(2, \mathbb{R}) = \{h \in M(2, \mathbb{R}) \mid \det h = 1\} = Sp(2, \mathbb{R}) = \{h \in M(2, \mathbb{R}) \mid hJh^T = J\}$$

The action of $GL(4, \mathbb{R})$ on $\text{Alt}(4, \mathbb{R})$ is prehomogeneous [10]. The image $\text{Alt}(4, \mathbb{R})_{\text{rk} \leq 2}$ is the complement of the open $GL(4, \mathbb{R})$-orbit $\text{Alt}(4, \mathbb{R})_{\text{rk}=4}$, and its defining equation is given by the basic relative invariant, Pfaffian

$$\text{Pf}(S) = S_{01}S_{23} + S_{02}S_{31} + S_{03}S_{12}.$$

Then, the singular set $\text{Alt}(4, \mathbb{R})_{\text{rk} \leq 2} = \{S \in \text{Alt}(4, \mathbb{R}) \mid \text{Pf}(S) = 0\}$ is the zero locus of Pfaffian, and the open orbit $\text{Alt}(4, \mathbb{R})_{\text{rk}=4}$ has two connected components $\{S \in \text{Alt}(4, \mathbb{R}) \mid \pm\text{Pf}(S) > 0\}$. The relation $\text{Pf}(S) = 0$ is considered as a Plücker relation of Grassmann manifold $\text{Grass}(4, 2, \mathbb{R})$.

3.2. Symmetry Breaking

We restrict the general linear group $GL(4, \mathbb{R})$ to the subgrouop $O(1,3)$. Let $g = \begin{pmatrix} 1 & 0 & 0 & 0 \\ 0 & -1 & 0 & 0 \\ 0 & 0 & -1 & 0 \\ 0 & 0 & 0 & -1 \end{pmatrix}$ be the standard non-degenerate symmetric matrix with signature $(1,3)$. Define Lorentz group (indefinite orthogonal group of signature $(1,3)$) by

$$O(1,3) = \{l \in M(4, \mathbb{R}) \mid l^T g l = g\}.$$

Gram matrix with respect to this metric is given by the map

$$\mathbb{G} : M(4, 2, \mathbb{R}) \ni X \mapsto X^T g X \in \mathrm{Sym}(2, \mathbb{R})$$

where $\mathrm{Sym}(n, \mathbb{R})$ is the set of real symmetric matrices of size n. The map $\mathbb{G}$ is $O(1,3) \times GL(2, \mathbb{R})$-equivariant:

$$\mathbb{G}(lXh) = h^T \mathbb{G}(X) h, \quad \forall l \in O(1,3), h \in GL(2, \mathbb{R}).$$

We define

$$Y(\mathbb{R}) := M(4, 2, \mathbb{R})_{\mathrm{rk}=2} \cap \mathbb{G}^{-1}(\mathrm{Sym}(2, \mathbb{R})_{\mathrm{rk} \leq 1}),$$

an $O(1,3) \times SL(2, \mathbb{R})$-invariant subset of $M(4, 2, \mathbb{R})$. Moreover, let

$$S^1 := \{\mathbf{v} = \begin{pmatrix} v_1 \\ v_2 \end{pmatrix} \in \mathbb{R}^2 \mid v_1^2 + v_2^2 = 1\}$$

and an analogue of Veronese map is defined by

$$\mathbb{V}_2 : S^1 \times \mathbb{R}^\times \ni (\mathbf{v}, -\rho) \mapsto -\rho \mathbf{v} \mathbf{v}^T \in \mathrm{Sym}(2, \mathbb{R})_{\mathrm{rk} \leq 1}. \quad (7)$$

The fiber product of two maps

$$\mathbb{G} : Y(\mathbb{R}) \longrightarrow \mathrm{Sym}(2, \mathbb{R})_{\mathrm{rk} \leq 1}, \qquad \tilde{C} \mapsto \mathbb{G}(\tilde{C}),$$
$$\mathbb{V}_2 : S^1 \times \mathbb{R}^\times \to \mathrm{Sym}(2, \mathbb{R})_{\mathrm{rk} \leq 1}, \qquad (\mathbf{v}, -\rho) \mapsto -\rho \mathbf{v} \mathbf{v}^T$$

is defined by

$$Z(\mathbb{R}) := Y(\mathbb{R}) \times_{\mathrm{Sym}(2,\mathbb{R})_{\mathrm{rk} \leq 1}} (S^1 \times \mathbb{R}^\times)$$
$$= \{(X, \mathbf{v}, -\rho) \in M(4, 2, \mathbb{R})_{\mathrm{rk}=2} \times S^1 \times \mathbb{R}^\times \mid \mathbb{G}(X) = -\rho \mathbf{v} \mathbf{v}^T\},$$

then we obtain a real counterpart of (3):

$$\begin{array}{ccc} Z(\mathbb{R}) & \xrightarrow{\tilde{\mathbb{V}}_2} & Y(\mathbb{R}) \\ \tilde{\mathbb{G}} \downarrow & \square & \downarrow \mathbb{G} \\ S^1 \times \mathbb{R}^\times & \xrightarrow{\mathbb{V}_2} & \mathrm{Sym}(2, \mathbb{R})_{\mathrm{rk} \leq 1} \end{array}$$

3.3. Tensor $\hat{T}$

The map

$$\mathbb{T} : \mathrm{Alt}(4, \mathbb{R}) \ni S \mapsto -SgS \in \mathrm{Sym}(4, \mathbb{R})$$

has been defined to be compatible with $\hat{T}^\nu_\mu = -S_{\mu\sigma} S^{\nu\sigma}$. This map is $O(1,3)$-equivariant

$$\mathbb{T}(l S l^T) = l \mathbb{T}(S) l^T, \quad \forall l \in O(1,3)$$

We replace ϕ by Φ, and $\mathbb{V}$ by $\mathbb{V}_4$ given as follows:

$$\Phi: Z(\mathbb{R}) \ni (X, \mathbf{v}, -\rho) \mapsto (XJ\mathbf{v}, -\rho) \in M(4,1,\mathbb{R})_{rk=1} \times \mathbb{R}^\times,$$
$$\mathbb{V}_4: \mathbb{R}^4 \times \mathbb{R}^\times \ni (\mathbf{w}, -\rho) \mapsto \rho \mathbf{w}\mathbf{w}^T \in \text{Sym}(4,\mathbb{R})_{rk\leq 1}.$$

Theorem 2. $(\mathbb{T} \circ \mathbb{S})(X) = (\mathbb{V}_4 \circ \Phi)(X, \mathbf{v}, -\rho)$ for all $(X, \mathbf{v}, -\rho) \in Z(\mathbb{R})$.

Proof. $(\mathbb{T} \circ \mathbb{S})(X) = (XJX^T)g(XJX^T)^T = XJ\mathbb{G}(X)J^T X^T = -XJ\rho\mathbf{v}\mathbf{v}^T J^T X^T$
$= \mathbb{V}_4((XJ\mathbf{v}, -\rho)) = (\mathbb{V}_4 \circ \Phi)((X, \mathbf{v}, -\rho))$. □

This theorem is illustrated as

$$\begin{array}{ccccc}
Z(\mathbb{R}) & \longrightarrow & M(4,2,\mathbb{R})_{rk=2} \times S^1 \times \mathbb{R}^\times & \xrightarrow{\Phi} & M(4,1,\mathbb{R})_{rk=1} \times \mathbb{R}^\times \\
{\tilde{\mathbb{V}}_2}\downarrow & & \downarrow & & \downarrow \mathbb{V}_4 \\
Y(\mathbb{R}) & \longrightarrow & M(4,2,\mathbb{R})_{rk=2} \xrightarrow{\mathbb{S}} \text{Alt}(4,\mathbb{R})_{rk=2} & \xrightarrow{\mathbb{T}} & \text{Sym}(4,\mathbb{R})
\end{array}$$

3.4. Grassmann and Flag Manifold

$$\begin{array}{ccccc}
Y(\mathbb{R}) & \xleftarrow{\tilde{\mathbb{V}}_2} & Z(\mathbb{R}) & \xrightarrow{\Phi} & M(4,1,\mathbb{R})_{rk=1} \times \mathbb{R}^\times \\
\downarrow & & \downarrow & & \downarrow \\
M(4,2,\mathbb{R})_{rk=2} & \longleftarrow & M(4,2,\mathbb{R})_{rk=2} \times S^1 \times \mathbb{R}^\times & \xrightarrow{\Phi} & M(4,1,\mathbb{R})_{rk=1} \times \mathbb{R}^\times \\
\downarrow & & \downarrow & & \downarrow \\
\text{Grass}(4,2,\mathbb{R}) & \longleftarrow & \text{Flag}(4;1,2,\mathbb{R}) & \longrightarrow & \text{Grass}(4,1,\mathbb{R})
\end{array}$$

The flag manifold is realized as an incidence variety of the product of two Grassmann manifold:

$$\text{Flag}(4;1,2,\mathbb{R}) = \{(V_1, V_2) \mid \dim V_1 = 1, \dim V_2 = 2, V_1 \subset V_2 \subset \mathbb{R}^4\}$$
$$\text{Flag}(4;1,2,\mathbb{R}) = \{(V_1, V_2) \in \text{Grass}(4,1,\mathbb{R}) \times \text{Grass}(4,2,\mathbb{R}) \mid V_1 \subset V_2\}.$$

For $(X, \mathbf{v}) \in M(4,2,\mathbb{R})_{rk=2} \times S^1$, two column vectors of X spans a two-dimensional subspace V_2, and a column vector $XJ\mathbf{v}$ generate a one-dimensional subspace V_1 in V_2. The map

$$\begin{array}{ccccc}
\text{Grass}(4,2,\mathbb{R}) & \longleftarrow & \text{Flag}(4;1,1,2,\mathbb{R}) & \longrightarrow & \text{Grass}(4,1,\mathbb{R}) \\
V_2 & \leftarrow & (V_1, V_2) & \mapsto & V_1 \\
X & \leftarrow & (X, \mathbf{v}) & \mapsto & XJ\mathbf{v}
\end{array}$$

is the double fibration.

3.5. The Interpretation of the Off-Shell Condition

The vectors C and L in Clebsch parametrization should satisfy the following off-shell conditions [2]:

$$C_\nu C^\nu = 0, \quad L_\nu C^\mu = 0, \quad L_\nu L^\mu = -\rho. \tag{8}$$

We put $\bar{R} := \begin{pmatrix} 0 & 0 \\ 0 & -\rho \end{pmatrix}$. Then, the condition (8) is written as

$$\mathbb{G}(X) = \bar{R}.$$

In particular, in the case $\mathbf{v} = \begin{pmatrix} 0 \\ 1 \end{pmatrix} \in S^1$, we compute the maps $\mathbb{V}_2, \Phi$ and $\mathbb{V}_4$:

- $\mathbb{V}_2((\mathbf{v}, -\rho)) = -\rho \mathbf{v}\mathbf{v}^T = \bar{R}$,

- $(\mathbf{w}, -\rho) = \Phi((X, \mathbf{v}, -\rho)) = (XJ\mathbf{v}, -\rho) = (C, -\rho)$, this implies $\mathbf{w} = C$,
- $\mathbb{V}_4((\mathbf{w}, -\rho)) = \rho \mathbf{w}\mathbf{w}^T = \rho CC^T = \hat{T}$.

This coincides with the result in [2]. An unnatural J in the definition of Φ is for the sake of compatibility with the existing formula.

We now remark $R \in \mathrm{Sym}(2, \mathbb{R})_{\mathrm{rk} \leq 1}$.

$$\begin{array}{ccc}
 & & Z(\mathbb{R}) \\
 & & \downarrow \\
\mathbb{G}^{-1}(\bar{R}) & \longrightarrow & Y(\mathbb{R}) \\
\downarrow & & \downarrow \mathbb{G} \\
\bar{R} & \in & \mathrm{Sym}(2,\mathbb{R})_{\mathrm{rk}=1}
\end{array}$$

The group $GL(2, \mathbb{R})$ acts on $\mathrm{Sym}(2, \mathbb{R})_{\mathrm{rk}=1}$ and the stabilizer at $\bar{R}$ is a Borel subgroup

$$B = \left\{ \begin{pmatrix} a & 0 \\ c & d \end{pmatrix} \right\} \subset GL(2, \mathbb{R}).$$

Then, $\mathbb{G} : Y(\mathbb{R}) \longrightarrow \mathrm{Sym}(2,\mathbb{R})_{\mathrm{rk}=1}$ is a $GL(2,\mathbb{R})$-equivariant bundle. We regard the off-shell condition specifies a fiber of this bundle. A symmetry is hidden in the horizontal direction of this bundle, the group action of $GL(2, \mathbb{R})$. Of course, form the Clebsch parametrization point of view, the role of C and L is not the same; the off-shell condition specifies the special isotropic direction for C: the choice of this direction is controlled by the homogeneous space $GL(2, \mathbb{R})/B$.

4. Discussion

We describe the symmetry of equations of dressed photon in a general manner. The tensor S is understood as an affine version of Plücker coordinates of Grassmann manifold $\mathrm{Grass}(4, 2, \mathbb{R})$. The splitting expression of the tensor $\hat{T}$ is related with an affine version of flag manifold $\mathrm{Flag}(4; 1, 2, \mathbb{R})$. We find the off-shell condition (8) chooses the special fiber of the homogeneous bundle. This mathematical interpretation of the choice may have a physical interpretation, especially in the context of Clebsch variables, however, which must be a future work. We also remark that the existence of the symmetry in arbitrary dimension suggests a feedback from the theory of dressed photon to the theory of reductive dual pairs on the pullback of nilpotent orbits [6], which is also a topic of future study.

Funding: This research received no external funding.

Institutional Review Board Statement: Not applicable.

Informed Consent Statement: Not applicable.

Data Availability Statement: Not applicable.

Acknowledgments: This research was partially supported by 2019 IMI Joint Use Research Program Workshop "Basic mathematical studies on dressed photon phenomena". The author thanks the anonymous reviewer for their questions and comments, which helped them to improve the quality of this article.

Conflicts of Interest: The author declares no conflict of interest.

References

1. Sakuma, H.; Ojima, I.; Ohtsu, M. Dressed photons in a new paradigm of off-shell quantum fields. *Prog. Quantum Electron.* **2017**, *55*, 74–87. [CrossRef]
2. Sakuma, H.; Ojima, I.; Ohtsu, M. Gauge symmetry breaking and emergence of Clebsch-dual electromagnetic field as a model of dressed photons. *Appl. Phys. A* **2017**, *123*, 750. [CrossRef]
3. Saigo, H.; Ojima, I.; Ohtsu, M. Dressed photons from the viewpoint of photon localization: The entrance to the off-shell science. *Appl. Phys. A* **2017**, *123*, 724. [CrossRef]
4. Howe, R. Transcending classical invariant theory. *J. Am. Math. Soc.* **1989**, *2*, 535–552. [CrossRef]

5. Howe, R. Remarks on classical invariant theory. *Trans. Am. Math. Soc.* **1989**, *313*, 539–570. [CrossRef]
6. Nishiyama, K.; Ochiai, H.; Taniguchi, K. Bernstein degree and associated cycles of Harish-Chandra modules–Hermitian symmetric case. *Asterisque* **2001**, *273*, 13–80.
7. Nishiyama, K.; Zhu, C.-B. Theta lifting of unitary lowest weight modules and their associated cycles. *Duke Math. J.* **2004**, *125*, 415–465. [CrossRef]
8. Sakuma, H.; Ojima, I.; Ohtsu, M.; Ochiai, H. Off-Shell Quantum Fields to Connect Dressed Photons with Cosmology. *Symmetry* **2020**, *12*, 1244. [CrossRef]
9. Helgason, S. *The Radon Transform*; Progress in Mathematics; Birkhäuser: Basel, Switzerland, 1969.
10. Kimura, T. *Introduction to Prehomogeneous Vector Spaces*; American Mathematical Society: Providence, RI, USA, 2003.

Article

Towards a Measurement Theory for Off-Shell Quantum Fields

Kazuya Okamura [1,2]

[1] Research Origin for Dressed Photon, 3-13-19 Moriya-cho, Kanagawa-ku, Yokohama 221-0022, Japan; k.okamura.renormalizable@gmail.com or okamura@math.cm.is.nagoya-u.ac.jp

[2] Graduate School of Informatics, Nagoya University, Chikusa-ku, Nagoya 464-8601, Japan

Abstract: In this study, we develop quantum measurement theory for quantum systems described by C*-algebras. This is the first step to establish measurement theory for interacting quantum fields with off-shell momenta. Unlike quantum mechanics (i.e., quantum systems with finite degrees of freedom), measurement theory for quantum fields is still in development because of the difficulty of quantum fields that are typical quantum systems with infinite degrees of freedom. Furthermore, the mathematical theory of quantum measurement is formulated in the von Neumann algebraic setting in previous studies. In the paper, we aim to extend the applicable area of quantum measurement theory to quantum systems described by C*-algebras from a mathematical viewpoint, referring to the sector theory that is related to symmetry and based on the theory of integral decomposition of states. In particular, we define central subspaces of the dual space of a C*-algebra and use them to define instruments. This attempt makes the connection between measurement theory and sector theory explicit and enables us to understand the macroscopic nature and the physical meaning of measurement.

Keywords: quantum measurement; C*-algebra; algebraic quantum field theory; local net; extension of local net; completely positive instrument; macroscopic distinguishability

Citation: Okamura, K. Towards a Measurement Theory for Off-Shell Quantum Fields. *Symmetry* **2021**, *13*, 1183. https://doi.org/10.3390/sym13071183

Academic Editor: Motoichi Ohtsu

Received: 1 June 2021
Accepted: 28 June 2021
Published: 30 June 2021

Publisher's Note: MDPI stays neutral with regard to jurisdictional claims in published maps and institutional affiliations.

Copyright: © 2021 by the author. Licensee MDPI, Basel, Switzerland. This article is an open access article distributed under the terms and conditions of the Creative Commons Attribution (CC BY) license (https://creativecommons.org/licenses/by/4.0/).

1. Introduction

In this study, we develop a measurement theory for quantum systems described by C*-algebras. Interacting quantum fields assumed in this study are quantum systems with infinite degrees of freedom and with off-shell momenta, whose observables are given by self-adjoint elements of C*-algebras. The C*-algebraic approach to quantum fields is not unrelated to the usual approach by field operators. It is a powerful way to remove the difficulty of unbounded operators by making them bounded operators. For example, in a free real Bose field, the exponential $e^{i\phi(f)}$ (or resolvent) of the field operator $\phi(f)$, where f is a real function, is a bounded operator, and the collection of them generates a C*-algebra. This study is inspired by the measurement of the quantum field generated by the interaction between the electromagnetic field and electrons at the nanoscale, which is called the dressed photon (DP) phenomenon [1]. It is known to behave completely differently from electromagnetic waves propagating in free space or electromagnetic fields in a uniform medium, and has long been studied as near-field optics. The measurement theory for such systems is still unexplored, and we believe that a framework extending the current theory is necessary. For this reason, we adopt an approach based on both algebraic quantum field theory (AQFT) and quantum measurement theory and their mathematics. There are many examples of the contribution of mathematics to the progress of physical theories, and the introduction of new mathematics contributes greatly to the implementation of new physical concepts. In the study, we will actively use the mathematical framework for conceptual advancement.

In the algebraic formulation of quantum theory, the observable algebra of a quantum system is described by a *-algebra $\mathcal{X}$, and a state is described by an expectation functional ω on $\mathcal{X}$. From an algebraic point of view, Hilbert space is treated as a secondary one to be used in analysis as needed. For each state ω, a Hilbert space is given by the GNS representation $(\pi_\omega, \mathcal{H}_\omega, \Omega_\omega)$:

$$\omega(X) = \langle \Omega_\omega | \pi_\omega(X) \Omega_\omega \rangle \qquad (1)$$

for all $X \in \mathcal{X}$. C*-algebras, a special case of *-algebra, are used in AQFT [2–4]. Various Hilbert spaces can be given by the GNS representation, and the fact that the representation has a physical meaning as well as the Hilbert space itself primarily promotes the conceptual understanding of the algebraic formulation. The contribution of Haag and Kastler [2] to this progress has been significant. Although there are studies on the algebraic formulation prior to their study, Ref. [2] is probably the first to successfully confront the fact that there are many different representations (depending on the choice of state). In [2], the "physical equivalence" of representations (also called weak equivalence) was used to give a clear meaning to the replacement between equivalent representations. In [5–8], a physical meaning was given to the situation in (A)QFT where different representations chosen by the DHR selection criterion coexist. It is a criterion that selects representations equivalent (through unitary transformations) to the vacuum representation (obtained from the GNS representation from the vacuum state) of the observable algebra on the domain which is spatial to some bounded domain. A representation satisfying this criterion describes a situation in which localized excitations of the quantum field exist. It was shown in [9] that a class (collection) of representations satisfying certain conditions corresponds to a situation where topological charges exist, and that, by using these representations, field algebra $\mathcal{F}$ and global gauge group G are reconstructed from observable algebra $\mathcal{A}$. This result is known as an iconic result in AQFT. Representations with different charges form their own sectors (with unitary equivalence), which are not only unitarily inequivalent but also mutually "disjoint", giving rise to the so-called "superselection rule". This result is closely related to the representation theory of field operators including the algebra of canonical commutation relations, where unitarily inequivalent representations arise (see [10–13] and references therein). Global gauge group G here is an unbroken symmetry, and the results of [9] are not valid for broken symmetries [14]. The extension of Ref. [9]'s results to broken symmetry situations was done in [14,15], and Ojima [16] defined the generalized sector as a "quasi-equivalence class of factor states", allowing for a unified treatment of macroscopic aspects in quantum systems in various contexts, including measurement.

To date, the instrument introduced by Davies and Lewis [17] has contributed greatly to the development of quantum measurement theory. They introduced instruments from a statistical viewpoint, and specified probability distributions and states after the measurement obtained by measuring a system using the measurement apparatus. However, because the relationship between the instrument and the usual quantum mechanical description was not clear at first, the analysis using the instrument did not progress until the investigation by Ozawa [18]. He introduced a completely positive instrument and a measuring process, the latter being used for quantum mechanical modeling of measurement. Every measuring process defines a completely positive instrument. The main result of [18] is the converse in a quantum system with finite degrees of freedom, i.e., every completely positive instrument in such a system is defined by a measuring process. This is a standard fact in quantum measurement theory now. Furthermore, the theory of completely positive instruments in quantum systems with infinite degrees of freedom described by the general von Neumann algebra has recently been developed in [19,20]. C*-algebras and von Neumann algebras can be viewed as non-commutative versions of topological and measurable spaces, respectively. The latter is a special case of the former, but their analysis methods are very different. In the current measurement theory, focusing on probability distributions and states after the measurement has led to the selection of components to be macroscopic by the measurement and the successful investigation of the relationship with quantum mechanical modeling.

In order to formulate the measurement theory for quantum systems described by C*-algebras, the more general case compared to von Neumann algebras, we believe that it is necessary to integrate a completely positive instrument and the sector theoretical treatment of the macroscopic aspect of the quantum system. The reason for this is that, because the concept of state is statistically characterized, we consider that the difference of values output by the measurement should be macroscopically distinguished by the disjointness of states of the composite system of the system and the measuring apparatus. In other words, a measurement is a physical process that leads to the situation wherein different output values of the measuring apparatus correspond to mutually disjoint states of the composite system. From this viewpoint, a measuring process, a quantum mechanical modeling of the measurement, is of course important historically and theoretically, but it should not necessarily be the first consideration in establishing the physical meaning and description of the measurement. On the other hand, this study is advantageous in that the identification of sectors by the measurement is justified by the measurement-theoretic description. We are convinced that the establishment of the measurement theory in quantum systems described by C*-algebras will open up new perspectives for the understanding of macroscopic aspects of quantum systems. Herein, we reexamine the result of [21]. While [21] focused on the use of measuring processes, we make thorough use of the instrument in this study.

In Section 2, the local net and open system are discussed and the description of dynamics as an open system in AQFT is stated. In Section 3, we review the sector theory and its mathematics. In Section 4, the central subspaces of the dual of a C*-algebra are defined. In the C*-algebraic setting, we define instruments in terms of central subspaces. Furthermore, we define and characterize central instruments in order to examine the differences between the C*-algebraic setting and the von Neumann algebraic setting. In Section 5, we summarize the results of the study and present the perspective.

2. Systems of Interest: Local Nets and Open System

2.1. C*-Algebraic Quantum Theory

All the statistical aspects of a physical system **S** are registered in a C*-probablity space $(\mathcal{X}, \omega)$, a pair of a C*-algebra $\mathcal{X}$, and a state ω on $\mathcal{X}$ [21]. Observables of **S** are described by self-adjoint elements of $\mathcal{X}$. On the other hand, the state ω is an expectation functional on $\mathcal{X}$ and statistically describes a physical situation (or an experimental setting) of **S**. We keep claiming that every quantum system is described in the language of noncommutative (quantum) probability theory (see [22] for an introduction to quantum probability theory). In Appendix A, the basic facts on operator algebras are summarized.

2.2. Local Net

Let M be a manifold or a (locally finite) graph. We suppose that M describes the space-time or the space under consideration. $\mathcal{R}$ denotes the set of bounded regions of M, which satisfies $\cup \mathcal{R} = M$. $M \in \mathcal{R}$ is assumed when M is bounded.

Definition 1 (local net). *A family $\{\mathcal{A}(\mathcal{O})\}_{\mathcal{O} \in \mathcal{R}}$ of C*-algebras is called a local net on M if it satisfies the following conditions:*
(i) For every inclusion $\mathcal{O}_1 \subset \mathcal{O}_2$, we have $\mathcal{A}(\mathcal{O}_1) \subset \mathcal{A}(\mathcal{O}_2)$.
(ii) For any mutually causally separated (spatial) regions $\mathcal{O}_1$ and $\mathcal{O}_2$,

$$[\mathcal{A}(\mathcal{O}_1), \mathcal{A}(\mathcal{O}_2)] = \{AB - BA | A \in \mathcal{A}(\mathcal{O}_1), B \in \mathcal{A}(\mathcal{O}_2)\} = \{0\}. \tag{2}$$

For every local net $\{\mathcal{A}(\mathcal{O})\}_{\mathcal{O} \in \mathcal{R}}$ on M, there exists a C*-algebra

$$\mathcal{A} = \overline{\bigcup_{\mathcal{O} \in \mathcal{R}} \mathcal{A}(\mathcal{O})}^{\|\cdot\|}, \tag{3}$$

called the global algebra of $\{\mathcal{A}(\mathcal{O})\}_{\mathcal{O} \in \mathcal{R}}$. If M is bounded, then $\mathcal{A} = \mathcal{A}(M)$ since $M \in \mathcal{R}$ and $\mathcal{O} \subset M$ for all $\mathcal{O} \in \mathcal{R}$. When a group G acts on $\mathcal{R}$ as a symmetry, we assume the covariance condition for $\{\mathcal{A}(\mathcal{O})\}_{\mathcal{O} \in \mathcal{R}}$: there exists an automorphic action α of G on $\mathcal{A}$ such that

$$\alpha_g(\mathcal{A}(\mathcal{O})) = \mathcal{A}(g\mathcal{O}) \qquad (4)$$

for all $g \in G$ and $\mathcal{O} \in \mathcal{R}$, where $g\mathcal{O} = \{gx | x \in \mathcal{O}\}$.

To describe the statistical aspect of quantum fields by a local net $\{\mathcal{A}(\mathcal{O})\}_{\mathcal{O} \in \mathcal{R}}$, states on the global algebra $\mathcal{A}$ or "local states" [23] are used.

2.3. Open System

We shall discuss how to describe the dynamics of open systems. In the context of quantum statistical mechanics, open systems are a subject that has been discussed for a long time. Open systems are also fundamental in quantum field theory, and are closely related to scattering theory. In particular, it is a necessary description of the dynamics in the paper concerning the DP as a typical example of off-shell quantum fields. This is because the DP phenomena are known to involve the process of generation by incident light and annihilation that changes to scattered light. On the other hand, it is essential that the quantum field considered here is a quantum system with an infinite degree of freedom system, and we should pay attention to the description of its dynamics (see Section 4 for details). In the following, we introduce the mathematical concepts necessary to describe the dynamics of open systems.

The discussion below is based on the understanding that closed systems are a special case of open systems. We consider a quantum system **S** described by a C*-algebra $\mathcal{X}$. Every time evolution of **S** as a closed system is described by an automorphism of $\mathcal{X}$. Furthermore, when the time t is parametrized by $\mathbb{R}$, the time evolution of **S** as a closed system is described by a strongly continuous automorphism group $\alpha : \mathbb{R} \ni t \mapsto \alpha_t \in Aut(\mathcal{X})$ satisfying $\alpha_0 = \mathrm{id}_\mathcal{X}$, $\alpha_s \circ \alpha_t = \alpha_{s+t}$ and $\alpha_{-t} = \alpha_t^{-1}$ for all $s, t \in \mathbb{R}$. In contrast to a closed system, the time evolution of an open system is described by a completely positive map $T : \mathcal{X} \to \mathcal{X}$. The complete positivity of maps between C*-algebras is defined as follows:

Definition 2 (Complete positivity [24–27]). *Let $\mathcal{C}$ and $\mathcal{D}$ be C*-algebras. A linear map $T : \mathcal{C} \to \mathcal{D}$ is said to be completely positive (CP) if*

$$\sum_{i,j=1}^{n} D_i^* T(C_i^* C_j) D_j \geq 0 \qquad (5)$$

for all $n \in \mathbb{N}$, $C_1, \cdots, C_n \in \mathcal{C}$ and $D_1, \cdots, D_n \in \mathcal{D}$.

It is known that a CP map is positive, but the converse is not true. Every homomorphism of a C*-algebra $\mathcal{C}$ into a C*-algebra $\mathcal{D}$ is CP. In particular, all automorphisms of a C*-algebra $\mathcal{C}$ are CP. For every C*-algebra $\mathcal{C}$ and $n \in \mathbb{N}$, $M_n(\mathcal{C})$ denotes the C*-algebra of square matrices of order n whose entries are elements of $\mathcal{C}$. For every linear map $T : \mathcal{C} \to \mathcal{D}$ and $n \in \mathbb{N}$, a linear map $T^{(n)} : M_n(\mathcal{C}) \to M_n(\mathcal{D})$ is defined by $T^{(n)}(C) = (T(C_{ij}))$ for all $C = (C_{ij}) \in M_n(\mathcal{C})$. A linear map $T : \mathcal{C} \to \mathcal{D}$ is said to be n-positive if $T^{(n)} : M_n(\mathcal{C}) \to M_n(\mathcal{D})$ is positive. A linear map $T : \mathcal{C} \to \mathcal{D}$ is CP if and only if it is n-positive for all $n \in \mathbb{N}$. The dual map $T^* : \mathcal{D}^* \to \mathcal{C}^*$ of $T : \mathcal{C} \to \mathcal{D}$ is defined by

$$(T^*\varphi)(C) = \varphi(T(C)) \qquad (6)$$

for all $\varphi \in \mathcal{D}^*$ and $C \in \mathcal{C}$. T is CP if and only if the linear map $\mathcal{D}^* \ni \varphi \mapsto \sum_{i,j=1}^{n} C_i T^*(D_i \varphi D_j^*) C_j^* \in \mathcal{C}^*$ is positive for all $n \in \mathbb{N}$, $C_1, \cdots, C_n \in \mathcal{C}$ and $D_1, \cdots, D_n \in \mathcal{D}$. Here, for every $A, B \in \mathcal{D}$ and $\varphi \in \mathcal{D}^*$, $A\varphi, \varphi B, A\varphi B \in \mathcal{D}^*$ are defined by

$$(A\varphi)(D) = \varphi(DA), \qquad (7)$$
$$(\varphi B)(E) = \varphi(BE), \qquad (8)$$
$$(A\varphi B)(F) = \varphi(BFA), \qquad (9)$$

respectively, for all $D, E, F \in \mathcal{D}$.

The following structure theorem for normal CP maps defined on $B(\mathcal{H})$ is well-known.

Theorem 1. *Let $\mathcal{H}$ be a separable Hilbert space. Let T be a normal CP map on $B(\mathcal{H})$.*
(1) There exist a separable Hilbert space $\mathcal{K}$, an element ξ of $\mathcal{K}$, a positive operator R on $\mathcal{K}$, and a unitary operator U on $\mathcal{H} \otimes \mathcal{K}$ such that

$$T(X) = \text{Tr}_{\mathcal{K}}[U^*(X \otimes R)U(1 \otimes |\xi\rangle\langle\xi|)] \tag{10}$$

for all $X \in B(\mathcal{H})$.
(2) There exists a family $\{K_i\}_{i=1}^{\infty}$ of bounded operators on $\mathcal{H}$ such that

$$T(X) = \sum_{i=1}^{\infty} K_i^* X K_i \tag{11}$$

for all $X \in B(\mathcal{H})$.

The proof of this theorem is given in Appendix B. The dynamics of open systems in the Heisenberg picture are described by a quantum stochastic process in the sense of Accardi–Frigerio–Lewis [28,29]. Following their study, measurement theory in the Heisenberg picture is formulated in [20].

3. Sector Theory

The concept of sector is defined by Ojima [16] as follows:

Definition 3. *A sector of $\mathcal{X}$ is a quasi-equivalence class of a factor state.*

A state on $\mathcal{X}$ is called a factor if the center $\mathcal{Z}_\omega(\mathcal{X}) = \pi_\omega(\mathcal{X})'' \cap \pi_\omega(\mathcal{X})'$ of $\pi_\omega(\mathcal{X})''$ is trivial, i.e., $\mathcal{Z}_\omega(\mathcal{X}) = \mathbb{C}1$. Let π be a representation of $\mathcal{X}$ on a Hilbert space $\mathcal{H}$. We say that a linear functional ω on $\mathcal{X}$ is π-normal if there exists a trace-class operator σ on $\mathcal{H}$ such that

$$\omega(X) = \text{Tr}[\pi(X)\sigma] \tag{12}$$

for all $X \in \mathcal{X}$.

Definition 4. *Let π_1 and π_2 be a representation of $\mathcal{X}$ on Hilbert spaces $\mathcal{H}_1$ and $\mathcal{H}_2$, respectively.*
(1) π_1 and π_2 are quasi-equivalent, written as $\pi_1 \approx \pi_2$, if every π_1-normal state is π_2-normal and vice versa.
(2) π_1 and π_2 are mutually disjoint, written as $\pi_1 \,\delta\, \pi_2$, if no π_1-normal state is π_2-normal and vice versa.

Two states ω_1 and ω_2 on $\mathcal{X}$ are quasi-equivalent (mutually disjoint, resp.), written as $\omega_1 \approx \omega_2$ ($\omega_1 \,\delta\, \omega_2$, resp.), if π_{ω_1} and π_{ω_2} are quasi-equivalent (mutually disjoint, resp.).

The sector theory based on sector defined above has already been discussed in [16,21]. However, we believe that mathematics related to sector theory should be reexamined in order to develop measurement theory for quantum systems described by C*-algebras. The following theorem mathematically justifies the definition of sector, which is obvious from [30] (Corollary 5.3.6).

Theorem 2. *Two factor states ω_1 and ω_2 are either quasi-equivalent or disjoint.*

By the above theorem, two factor states ω_1 and ω_2 belong to different sectors if and only if $\omega_1 \,\delta\, \omega_2$. A sector corresponds to a macroscopic situation where order parameters of the system have definite values. Although the unitary equivalence of states is efficient for pure states, physically important states are not always pure. For example, KMS states in some quantum system with infinite degrees of freedom are of type III. We would like to stress that the unitary equivalence class of a pure state is not appropriate for a unit of the state space. The reason will be discussed later.

Next, we shall define the notion of orthogonality of states. The order relation $\omega_1 \leq \omega_2$ for two positive linear functionals ω_1 and ω_2 on $\mathcal{X}$ is defined by

$$\omega_1(X) \leq \omega_2(X) \tag{13}$$

for all $X \in \mathcal{X}_+$.

Definition 5. *Let ω_1, ω_2 be positive linear functionals on $\mathcal{X}$. We say that ω_1 and ω_2 are mutually orthogonal, written as $\omega_1 \perp \omega_2$, if there exists no non-zero positive linear functional ω' such that $\omega' \leq \omega_1$ and $\omega' \leq \omega_2$.*

The following theorem shows the gap between the disjointness and the orthogonality of states.

Theorem 3 ([31] (Lemma 4.1.19 and Lemma 4.2.8)). *Let ω_1, ω_2 be positive linear functionals on $\mathcal{X}$. Put $\omega = \omega_1 + \omega_2$.*
(1) If ω_1 and ω_2 are mutually orthogonal, then there exists an orthogonal projection $P \in \pi_\omega(\mathcal{X})'$ such that

$$\omega_1(X) = \langle \Omega_\omega | P \pi_\omega(X) \Omega_\omega \rangle, \quad \omega_2(X) = \langle \Omega_\omega | (1-P) \pi_\omega(X) \Omega_\omega \rangle \tag{14}$$

for all $X \in \mathcal{X}$.
(2) If ω_1 and ω_2 are mutually disjoint, then there exists an orthogonal projection $C \in \mathcal{Z}_\omega(\mathcal{X})$ such that

$$\omega_1(X) = \langle \Omega_\omega | C \pi_\omega(X) \Omega_\omega \rangle, \quad \omega_2(X) = \langle \Omega_\omega | (1-C) \pi_\omega(X) \Omega_\omega \rangle \tag{15}$$

for all $X \in \mathcal{X}$.

The topology of $\mathcal{S}(\mathcal{X})$ used here is the restriction of the weak*-topology of $\mathcal{X}^*$ to $\mathcal{S}(\mathcal{X})$. That is to say, it is generated by the basis $\mathcal{B} = \{O_\omega(\{X_i, \varepsilon_i\}_{i=1}^n) \mid \omega \in \mathcal{S}(\mathcal{X}), n \in \mathbb{N}, X_1, \cdots, X_n \in \mathcal{X}, \varepsilon_1, \cdots, \varepsilon_n > 0\}$, where $O_\omega(\{X_i, \varepsilon_i\}_{i=1}^n) = \{\omega' \in \mathcal{S}(X) \mid \forall i = 1, \cdots, n, |\omega(X_i) - \omega'(X_i)| < \varepsilon_i\}$. Then, $\mathcal{S}(\mathcal{X})$ is a compact convex set, and we use the Borel field $\mathcal{B}(\mathcal{S}(\mathcal{X}))$ of $\mathcal{S}(\mathcal{X})$ generated by this topology. A positive linear functional ω on $\mathcal{X}$ is called a barycenter of a regular Borel measure μ on $\mathcal{S}(\mathcal{X})$ if

$$\omega = \int_{\mathcal{S}(\mathcal{X})} \rho \, d\mu(\rho). \tag{16}$$

μ is then called a barycentric measure of ω.

Definition 6. *A regular Borel measure μ on $\mathcal{S}(\mathcal{X})$ is orthogonal if*

$$\int_\Delta \rho \, d\mu(\rho) \perp \int_{\Delta^c} \rho \, d\mu(\rho) \tag{17}$$

for all $\Delta \in \mathcal{B}(\mathcal{S}(\mathcal{X}))$. $\mathcal{O}_\omega(\mathcal{S}(\mathcal{X}))$ denotes the set of orthogonal measures on $\mathcal{S}(\mathcal{X})$ with barycenter ω.

The following theorem characterizes orthogonal measures of a state.

Theorem 4 ([31] (Theorem 4.1.25)). *Let $\mathcal{X}$ be a unital C*-algebra and ω a state on $\mathcal{X}$. There is a one-to-one correspondence between the following three sets:*
(i) the orthogonal measures $\mu \in \mathcal{O}_\omega(\mathcal{S}(\mathcal{X}))$;
(ii) the abelian von Neumann subalgebras $\mathcal{B}$ of $\pi_\omega(\mathcal{X})'$;
(iii) the orthogonal projections P on $\mathcal{H}_\omega$ such that $P\Omega_\omega = \Omega_\omega$ and $P\pi_\omega(\mathcal{X})P \subseteq \{P\pi_\omega(\mathcal{X})P\}'$.

If μ, $\mathcal{B}$ and P are in correspondence, one has the following conditions:
(1) $\mathcal{B} = (\pi_\omega(\mathcal{X}) \cup \{P\})'$;
(2) P is the orthogonal projection onto $\mathcal{B}\Omega_\omega$;
(3) $\mu(\hat{X}_1 \cdots \hat{X}_n) = \langle \Omega_\omega | \pi_\omega(X_1) P \pi_\omega(X_2) P \cdots P \pi_\omega(X_n) \Omega_\omega \rangle$;
(4) $\mathcal{B}$ is $*$-isomorphic to the range of the map $\kappa_\mu : L^\infty(\mathcal{S}(\mathcal{X}), \mu) \ni f \mapsto \kappa_\mu(f) \in \pi_\omega(\mathcal{X})'$ defined by

$$\langle \Omega_\omega | \kappa_\mu(f) \pi_\omega(X) \Omega_\omega \rangle = \int_{\mathcal{S}(\mathcal{X})} f(\rho) \, \hat{X}(\rho) \, d\mu_\omega(\rho) \tag{18}$$

for all $X \in \mathcal{X}$ and $f \in L^\infty(\mathcal{S}(\mathcal{X}), \mu)$, where $\hat{X} \in C(\mathcal{S}(\mathcal{X}))$ is defined by $\hat{X}(\rho) = \rho(X)$ for all $\rho \in \mathcal{S}(\mathcal{X})$. κ_μ satisfies

$$\kappa_\mu(\hat{X}) \pi_\omega(Y) \Omega_\omega = \pi_\omega(Y) P \pi_\omega(X) \Omega_\omega \tag{19}$$

for all $X, Y \in \mathcal{X}$.

By Theorems 3 and 4, we have the following theorem:

Theorem 5 ([31] (Proposition 4.2.9)). *Let ω be a state on $\mathcal{X}$ and μ a barycentric measure of ω. The following conditions are equivalent.*
(1) *For every $\Delta \in \mathcal{B}(\mathcal{S}(\mathcal{X}))$,*

$$\int_\Delta \rho \, d\mu(\rho) \, \between \, \int_{\Delta^c} \rho \, d\mu(\rho). \tag{20}$$

(2) *μ is orthogonal, and $\kappa_\mu(L^\infty(\mathcal{S}(\mathcal{X}), \mu))$ is a von Neumann subalgebra of the center $\mathcal{Z}_\omega(\mathcal{X})$ of $\pi_\omega(\mathcal{X})''$.*

For every $\omega \in \mathcal{S}(\mathcal{X})$, μ_ω denotes the orthogonal measure with barycenter ω corresponding to the center $\mathcal{Z}_\omega(\mathcal{X})$ of $\pi_\omega(\mathcal{X})''$. μ_ω is called the central measure of ω. The following theorem shows that the central measure gives the unique integral decomposition into mutually different sectors.

Theorem 6 ([31] (Theorem 4.2.11)). *The central measure μ_ω of a state ω on $\mathcal{X}$ is pseudosupported by the set $\mathcal{S}_f(\mathcal{X})$ of factor states on $\mathcal{X}$, i.e., $\mu_\omega(\Delta) = 0$ for all $\Delta \in \mathcal{B}(\mathcal{S}(\mathcal{X}))$ such that $\Delta \cap \mathcal{S}_f(\mathcal{X}) = \emptyset$. If $\mathcal{X}$ is separable, then μ_ω is supported by $\mathcal{S}_f(\mathcal{X})$.*

That is to say, the concept of sector is applicable to any states via their central measures. $L^\infty(\mathcal{S}(\mathcal{X}), \mu_\omega)$ then describes the observable algebra that distinguishes sectors in ω and is $*$-isomorphic to $\mathcal{Z}_\omega(\mathcal{X})$. The $*$-isomorphism $\kappa_\omega := \kappa_{\mu_\omega} : L^\infty(\mathcal{S}(\mathcal{X}), \mu_\omega) \to \mathcal{Z}_\omega(\mathcal{X})$, defined by

$$\langle \Omega_\omega | \kappa_\omega(f) \pi_\omega(X) \Omega_\omega \rangle = \int_{\mathcal{S}(\mathcal{X})} f(\rho) \, \hat{X}(\rho) \, d\mu_\omega(\rho) \tag{21}$$

for all $X \in \mathcal{X}$ and $f \in L^\infty(\mathcal{S}(\mathcal{X}), \mu_\omega)$, justifies this statement. By the definition, all elements of the center $\mathcal{Z}_\omega(\mathcal{X})$ of $\pi_\omega(\mathcal{X})''$ are compatible with those of $\pi_\omega(\mathcal{X})''$. The following theorem is also shown.

Theorem 7 ([31] (Theorem 4.2.5)). *Let ω be a state on $\mathcal{X}$ and μ an orthogonal measure with barycenter ω corresponding to a maximal abelian von Neumann subalgebra (MASA) of $\pi_\omega(\mathcal{X})'$. Then, μ is pseudosupported by the set $\mathcal{S}_e(\mathcal{X})$ of pure states on $\mathcal{X}$. If $\mathcal{X}$ is separable, then μ is supported by $\mathcal{S}_e(\mathcal{X})$.*

An orthogonal measure corresponding to a MASA of $\pi_\omega(\mathcal{X})'$ gives an irreducible decomposition of the state. In general, MASA of $\pi_\omega(\mathcal{X})'$ is not unique. The situation where MASA of $\pi_\omega(\mathcal{X})'$ is unique is special. This is the reason why the unitary equivalence class of a pure state is not appropriate for a unit of the state space. It is known that $\pi_\omega(\mathcal{X})''$ is a type I von Neumann algebra if $\pi_\omega(\mathcal{X})'$ is abelian. The following theorem characterizes such a situation in the context of orthogonal decompositions of states.

Theorem 8 ([31] (Theorem 4.2.3)). *Let ω be a state on $\mathcal{X}$, and P the projection operator on $\mathcal{H}_\omega$ whose range is $\pi_\omega(\mathcal{X})'\Omega_\omega$. The following conditions are equivalent:*
(1) $\pi_\omega(\mathcal{X})'$ *is abelian;*
(2) $P\pi_\omega(\mathcal{X})P$ *generates an abelian algebra.*

4. Completely Positive Instrument

In this section, we analyze the concept of CP instrument in the C*-algebraic setting. In previous investigations [17–20], it has been examined in the von Neumann algebraic formulation of quantum theory. The generalization to C*-algebra is realized in terms of central subspaces of the dual of a C*-algebra. Our approach enables us to unify the measurement theory with sector theory.

4.1. Definition

Since the investigation [17] by Davies and Lewis, instruments have been defined on the predual of a von Neumann algebra. In order to define its C*-algebraic generalization, the dual space of a C*-algebra is too big in general. When a von Neumann algebra $\mathcal{M}$ on a Hilbert space $\mathcal{K}$ is not finite-dimensional, the predual $\mathcal{M}_*$ of $\mathcal{M}$ does not coincide with $\mathcal{M}^*$, i.e., $\mathcal{M}_* \subsetneq \mathcal{M}^*$. In addition, in the case where all physically relevant states are contained in $\mathcal{M}_*$, the whole space $\mathcal{M}^*$ is not needed. This does not depend on whether $\mathcal{M}$ is treated as a C*-algebra or a von Neumann algebra. In the C*-algebraic formulation introduced here, we can naturally use $\mathcal{M}_*$ as a domain of instruments.

Let $\mathcal{X}$ be a C*-algebra and π a representation of $\mathcal{X}$ on a Hilbert space $\mathcal{H}$. Let $\mathcal{M}$ be a von Neumann algebra on a Hilbert space $\mathcal{K}$. $\mathcal{Z}(\mathcal{M})$ denotes the center of $\mathcal{M}$. We define the subset $V(\pi)$ of $\mathcal{X}^*$ by

$$V(\pi) = \{\varphi \in \mathcal{X}^* \mid \exists \rho \in (\pi(\mathcal{X})'')_*, \forall X \in \mathcal{X}, \varphi(X) = \rho(\pi(X))\}. \tag{22}$$

A subspace $\mathcal{L}$ of $\mathcal{X}^*$ is said to be central if there exists a central projection C of $\mathcal{X}^{**}$, i.e., $C \in \mathcal{Z}(\mathcal{X}^{**})$, such that $\mathcal{L} = C\mathcal{X}^*$. Central subspaces of $\mathcal{X}^*$ are characterized as closed invariant subspaces (see [26] (Chapter III, Theorem 2.7)). A central subspace $\mathcal{L}(=C\mathcal{X}^*)$ is said to be σ-finite if its dual $\mathcal{L}^*(\cong C\mathcal{X}^{**})$ is a σ-finite W^*-algebra. For every $M_1, M_2 \in \mathcal{V}^*$ and $\rho \in \mathcal{V}$, we define $M_1\rho, \rho M_2, M_1\rho M_2 \in \mathcal{V}$ by

$$\langle M, M_1\rho \rangle = \langle MM_1, \rho \rangle, \tag{23}$$

$$\langle M, \rho M_2 \rangle = \langle M_2 M, \rho \rangle, \tag{24}$$

$$\langle M, M_1\rho M_2 \rangle = \langle M_2 M M_1, \rho \rangle, \tag{25}$$

respectively, for all $M \in \mathcal{V}^*$. The usefulness of the central subspace can be seen in the following example:

Example 1 (See [26] (Chapter III) for example). *(1) Let $\mathcal{X}$ be a C*-algebra and π a representation of $\mathcal{X}$ on a Hilbert space $\mathcal{H}$. There exists a central projection $C(\pi)$ of $\mathcal{X}^{**}$ such that*

$$V(\pi) = C(\pi)\mathcal{X}^* = \{C(\pi)\varphi \mid \varphi \in \mathcal{X}^*\} = \{\varphi \in \mathcal{X}^* \mid C(\pi)\varphi = \varphi\}. \tag{26}$$

(2) Let $\mathcal{M}$ be a von Neumann algebra on a Hilbert space $\mathcal{H}$. There exists a central projection C of $\mathcal{M}^{**}$ such that $\mathcal{M}_* = C\mathcal{M}^*$.

The following theorem is known.

Theorem 9. *Let $\mathcal{X}$ be a C*-algebra and π_1 and π_2 representations of $\mathcal{X}$ on Hilbert spaces $\mathcal{H}_1$ and $\mathcal{H}_2$, respectively. The following conditions are equivalent:*
(1) $\pi_1 \approx \pi_2$. (2) $V(\pi_1) = V(\pi_2)$. (3) $C(\pi_1) = C(\pi_2)$.
Similarly, the following conditions are equivalent:
(4) $\pi_1 \mathrel{\text{\textbardbl}} \pi_2$ (5) $V(\pi_1) \cap V(\pi_2) = \{0\}$. (6) $C(\pi_1)C(\pi_2) = 0$.

The former part of this theorem is shown in [26] (Chapter III, Proposition 2.12). We can show the latter part in a similar way.

We shall define instruments in terms of central subspaces in the fully C^*-algebraic setting. Let $\mathcal{M}$ and $\mathcal{N}$ be W^*-algebras. $P(\mathcal{M}_*, \mathcal{N}_*)$ denotes the set of positive linear maps of $\mathcal{M}_*$ into $\mathcal{N}_*$. In addition, for any Banach space $\mathcal{L}$, $\langle \cdot, \cdot \rangle$ denotes the pairing of $\mathcal{L}^*$ and $\mathcal{L}$.

Definition 7 (instrument). *Let $\mathcal{V}_{\text{in}}$ and $\mathcal{V}_{\text{out}}$ be σ-finite central subspaces of C^*-algebras $\mathcal{X}$ and $\mathcal{Y}$, respectively, and $(S, \mathcal{F})$ a measurable space. $\mathcal{I}$ is called an instrument for $(\mathcal{X}, \mathcal{V}_{\text{in}}, \mathcal{Y}, \mathcal{V}_{\text{out}}, S)$ if it satisfies the following three conditions:*
(1) $\mathcal{I}$ is a map of $\mathcal{F}$ into $P(\mathcal{V}_{\text{in}}, \mathcal{V}_{\text{out}})$.
(2) $\langle 1, \mathcal{I}(S)\rho \rangle = \langle 1, \rho \rangle$ for all $\rho \in \mathcal{V}_{\text{in}}$.
(3) For every $\rho \in \mathcal{V}_{\text{in}}$, $M \in \mathcal{V}_{\text{out}}^*$ and mutually disjoint sequence $\{\Delta_j\}_{j \in \mathbb{N}}$ of $\mathcal{F}$,

$$\langle M, \mathcal{I}(\cup_j \Delta_j)\rho \rangle = \sum_{j=1}^{\infty} \langle M, \mathcal{I}(\Delta_j)\rho \rangle. \tag{27}$$

When $\mathcal{X} = \mathcal{Y}$, an instrument $\mathcal{I}$ for $(\mathcal{X}, \mathcal{V}_{\text{in}}, \mathcal{Y}, \mathcal{V}_{\text{out}}, S)$ is called that, for $(\mathcal{X}, \mathcal{V}_{\text{in}}, \mathcal{V}_{\text{out}}, S)$. Furthermore, when $\mathcal{V}_{\text{in}} = \mathcal{V}_{\text{out}} = \mathcal{V}$, an instrument $\mathcal{I}$ for $(\mathcal{X}, \mathcal{V}_{\text{in}}, \mathcal{V}_{\text{out}}, S)$ is called for $(\mathcal{X}, \mathcal{V}, S)$. In particular, an instrument for $(\mathcal{M}, \mathcal{M}_*, S)$ is called for $(\mathcal{M}, S)$. For every instrument $\mathcal{I}$ for $(\mathcal{V}_{\text{in}}, \mathcal{V}_{\text{out}}, S)$ and normal state φ on $\mathcal{V}_{\text{in}}^*$, we define the probability measure $\|\mathcal{I}\varphi\|$ on $(S, \mathcal{F})$ by $\|\mathcal{I}\varphi\|(\Delta) = \|\mathcal{I}(\Delta)\varphi\|$ for all $\Delta \in \mathcal{F}$. For every instrument $\mathcal{I}$ for $(\mathcal{X}, \mathcal{V}_{\text{in}}, \mathcal{Y}, \mathcal{V}_{\text{out}}, S)$, the dual map $\mathcal{I}^* : \mathcal{V}_{\text{out}}^* \times \mathcal{F} \to \mathcal{V}_{\text{in}}^*$ of $\mathcal{I}$ is defined by

$$\langle M, \mathcal{I}(\Delta)\rho \rangle = \langle \mathcal{I}^*(M, \Delta), \rho \rangle \tag{28}$$

for all $\rho \in \mathcal{V}_{\text{in}}$, $M \in \mathcal{V}_{\text{out}}^*$ and $\Delta \in \mathcal{F}$.

Definition 8. *An instrument $\mathcal{I}$ for $(\mathcal{X}, \mathcal{V}_{\text{in}}, \mathcal{Y}, \mathcal{V}_{\text{out}}, S)$ is said to be completely positive (CP) if the map $\mathcal{V}_{\text{out}}^* \ni M \mapsto \mathcal{I}^*(M, \Delta) \in \mathcal{V}_{\text{in}}^*$ is CP for all $\Delta \in \mathcal{F}$.*

For every map $\mathcal{J} : \mathcal{V}_{\text{out}}^* \times \mathcal{F} \to \mathcal{V}_{\text{in}}^*$ satisfying the following three conditions, there uniquely exists an instrument $\mathcal{I}$ for $(\mathcal{X}, \mathcal{V}_{\text{in}}, \mathcal{Y}, \mathcal{V}_{\text{out}}, S)$ such that $\mathcal{J} = \mathcal{I}^*$:
(1) For every $\Delta \in \mathcal{F}$, the map $\mathcal{V}_{\text{out}}^* \ni M \mapsto \mathcal{J}(M, \Delta) \in \mathcal{V}_{\text{in}}^*$ is normal, positive, and linear.
(2) $\mathcal{J}(1, S) = 1$.
(3) For every $\rho \in \mathcal{V}_{\text{in}}$, $M \in \mathcal{V}_{\text{out}}^*$ and mutually disjoint sequence $\{\Delta_j\}_{j \in \mathbb{N}}$ of $\mathcal{F}$,

$$\langle \mathcal{J}(M, \cup_j \Delta_j), \rho \rangle = \sum_{j=1}^{\infty} \langle \mathcal{J}(M, \Delta_j), \rho \rangle. \tag{29}$$

From now on, $\mathcal{I}$ denotes the dual map $\mathcal{I}^*$ of an instrument $\mathcal{I}$ for $(\mathcal{X}, \mathcal{V}_{\text{in}}, \mathcal{Y}, \mathcal{V}_{\text{out}}, S)$. The dual map of an instrument for $(\mathcal{X}, \mathcal{V}_{\text{in}}, \mathcal{Y}, \mathcal{V}_{\text{out}}, S)$ is also called an instrument for $(\mathcal{X}, \mathcal{V}_{\text{in}}, \mathcal{Y}, \mathcal{V}_{\text{out}}, S)$.

4.2. Central Decomposition of State via CP Instrument

Let $\mathcal{V}$ be a σ-finite central subspace of the dual space of a C^*-algebra $\mathcal{X}$ and $(S, \mathcal{F})$ a measurable space. Let $C : \mathcal{F} \to \mathcal{Z}(\mathcal{V}^*)$ be a projection valued measure (PVM). A CP instrument $\mathcal{I}_C$ for $(\mathcal{X}, \mathcal{V}, S)$ is defined by

$$\mathcal{I}_C(\Delta)\rho = C(\Delta)\rho \tag{30}$$

for all $\rho \in \mathcal{V}$ and $\Delta \in \mathcal{F}$.

Theorem 10. $\mathcal{I}_C$ satisfies the following conditions:
(1) $\mathcal{I}_C(S)\rho = \rho$ for all $\rho \in \mathcal{V}$.
(2) It is repeatable, i.e., it satisfies

$$\mathcal{I}_C(\Delta)\mathcal{I}_C(\Gamma) = \mathcal{I}_C(\Delta \cap \Gamma) \tag{31}$$

for all $\Delta, \Gamma \in \mathcal{F}$.
(3) For every $\rho \in \mathcal{V}_+ := \mathcal{V} \cap \mathcal{X}_+^*$ and $\Delta \in \mathcal{F}$, $\mathcal{I}_C(\Delta)\rho$ and $\mathcal{I}_C(\Delta^c)\rho$ are mutually disjoint.
(4) For every $\Delta \in \mathcal{F}$, $\mathcal{I}_C(\Delta)$ is $\mathcal{V}^*$-bimodule map, i.e., for every $\Delta \in \mathcal{F}$, $\rho \in \mathcal{V}$ and $M_1, M_2 \in \mathcal{V}^*$,

$$\mathcal{I}_C(\Delta)(M_1 \rho M_2) = M_1(\mathcal{I}_C(\Delta)\rho)M_2. \tag{32}$$

Conversely, if an instrument $\mathcal{I}$ for $(\mathcal{V}, S)$ satisfies the conditions (2) and (4), then there exists a spectral measure $C : \mathcal{F} \to \mathcal{Z}(\mathcal{V}^*)$ such that $\mathcal{I} = \mathcal{I}_C$.

Proof. We can easily check (1), (2), and (4). (3) is shown by using Theorem 9.
The converse is also obvious as follows. We define a map $C : \mathcal{F} \to \mathcal{V}^*$ by $C(\Delta) = \mathcal{I}(1, \Delta)$ for all $\Delta \in \mathcal{F}$. For every $\Delta \in \mathcal{F}$, $\rho \in \mathcal{V}$ and $M \in \mathcal{V}^*$, we have

$$\langle M, \mathcal{I}(\Delta)\rho \rangle = \langle 1, \mathcal{I}(\Delta)(\rho M) \rangle = \langle C(\Delta), \rho M \rangle = \langle MC(\Delta), \rho \rangle. \tag{33}$$

$\langle M, \mathcal{I}(\Delta)\rho \rangle = \langle C(\Delta)M, \rho \rangle$ is also shown in the same way. Therefore, we have $\langle [C(\Delta), M], \rho \rangle = 0$ for all $\Delta \in \mathcal{F}$, $\rho \in \mathcal{V}$ and $M \in \mathcal{V}^*$. When φ is normal faithful state on $\mathcal{V}^*$ and $\rho = \varphi([C(\Delta), M])^*$, $\langle ([C(\Delta), M])^*[C(\Delta), M], \varphi \rangle = 0$, so that $[C(\Delta), M] = 0$ for all $\Delta \in \mathcal{F}$ and $M \in \mathcal{V}^*$. We obtain $C(\Delta) \in \mathcal{Z}(\mathcal{V}^*)$ for all $\Delta \in \mathcal{F}$.
By the conditions (2) and (4),

$$\begin{aligned}\langle C(\Delta \cap \Gamma), \rho \rangle &= \langle 1, \mathcal{I}(\Delta \cap \Gamma)\rho \rangle = \langle 1, \mathcal{I}(\Delta)\mathcal{I}(\Gamma)\rho \rangle = \langle C(\Delta), \mathcal{I}(\Gamma)\rho \rangle \\ &= \langle 1, \mathcal{I}(\Gamma)(\rho C(\Delta)) \rangle = \langle C(\Gamma), \rho C(\Delta) \rangle = \langle C(\Delta)C(\Gamma), \rho \rangle.\end{aligned} \tag{34}$$

Thus, $C : \mathcal{F} \to \mathcal{Z}(\mathcal{V}^*)$ is a PVM, and we have $\mathcal{I} = \mathcal{I}_C$. □

An instrument $\mathcal{I}$ for $(\mathcal{X}, \mathcal{V}_{\text{in}}, \mathcal{Y}, \mathcal{V}_{\text{out}}, S)$ is said to be subcentral if, for every $\rho \in \mathcal{V}_{\text{in},+}$ and $\Delta \in \mathcal{F}$, $\mathcal{I}_C(\Delta)\rho$ and $\mathcal{I}_C(\Delta^c)\rho$ are mutually disjoint. The condition (3) in Theorem 10 is a special case of the subcentrality of instruments. $\mathcal{P}(\mathcal{X}, \mathcal{V})$ denotes the subset $\{\mathcal{I}_C | C : \mathcal{F} \to \mathcal{Z}(\mathcal{V}^*)$ is a PVM.$\}$ of the set of instruments defined on $\mathcal{V}$. An instrument $\mathcal{I}$ for $(\mathcal{X}, \mathcal{V}, S)$ is said to be central if it is an element of $\mathcal{P}(\mathcal{X}, \mathcal{V})$ and is the maximum in $\mathcal{P}(\mathcal{X}, \mathcal{V})$, where the maximum is due to the (pre)order $\prec$ on instruments defined as follows: For instruments $\mathcal{I}_1, \mathcal{I}_2$ for $(\mathcal{X}, \mathcal{V}_{\text{in}}, \mathcal{Y}, \mathcal{V}_{\text{out}}, S_1)$ and $(\mathcal{X}, \mathcal{V}_{\text{in}}, \mathcal{Y}, \mathcal{V}_{\text{out}}, S_2)$, respectively, $\mathcal{I}_1 \prec \mathcal{I}_2$ if $\mathcal{I}_1(\mathcal{F})\rho \subset \mathcal{I}_2(\mathcal{F})\rho$ for all $\rho \in \mathcal{S}(\mathcal{X}) \cap \mathcal{V}_{\text{in}}$, where $\mathcal{I}_i(\mathcal{F}_i)\rho$, $i = 1, 2$, is the subset of $(\mathcal{V}_{\text{in}})_+$ defined by $\mathcal{I}_i(\mathcal{F}_i)\rho = \{\mathcal{I}_i(\Delta_i)\rho \mid \Delta_i \in \mathcal{F}_i\}$. By Theorem 10, we have the following theorem.

Theorem 11. Let $(S, \mathcal{F})$ be a measurable space, $\mathcal{V}$ a σ-finite central subspace of the dual of a C^*-algebra $\mathcal{X}$, and $C : \mathcal{F} \to \mathcal{Z}(\mathcal{V}^*)$ a PVM. $\mathcal{I}_C$ is central if and only if the abelian W^*-algebra generated by $\{C(\Delta) | \Delta \in \mathcal{F}\}$ is isomorphic to $\mathcal{Z}(\mathcal{V}^*)$.

5. Operational Requirement and Macroscopic Distinguishability

In this section, we discuss the characterization of CP instruments. We deepen our conceptual understanding of measurement theory by referring to the mathematics of sector theory. In sector theory, we explained that a sector is a macroscopic unit. As an application of sector theory to measurement theory, we follow the macroscopic distinction made by the disjointness of states. That is, in contrast to the usual understanding of measurement, our understanding is that a measurement is a physical process that realizes macroscopically distinguishable situations when different values are output. In past investigations, the concept of CP instrument has been justified by clarifying the statistical properties that a measuring apparatus should satisfy from an operational point of view in the (extended)

Schrödinger picture. We first review this here. Next, we proceed to characterize CP instruments from the perspective of the macroscopic distinguishability of states, which is related to sector theory.

Here, we assume that the system **S** is described by a C^*-algebra $\mathcal{X}$ and that $\mathcal{V}_{in}$ a σ-finite central subspace of $\mathcal{X}^*$. We consider a measuring apparatus $\mathbf{A}(x)$ with output variable x to measure the system **S**, where x takes values in a measurable space $(S, \mathcal{F})$. In the following, we consider three assumptions from an operational point of view. They are modified from [19,32] in the C^*-algebraic setting.

Assumption 1. $\mathbf{A}(x)$ *statistically specifies the following two components:*
(1) *the probability measure* $\Pr\{x \in \Delta \| \omega\}$, $\Delta \in \mathcal{F}$, *on* $(S, \mathcal{F})$ *for every initial state* $\omega \in \mathcal{S}(\mathcal{X}) \cap \mathcal{V}_{in}$.
(2) *the state* $\omega_{\{x \in \Delta\}}$ *(on a C^*-algebra $\mathcal{Y}$) after the measurement under the condition that ω is an initial state and output values not contained in Δ are ignored. For every* $\omega \in \mathcal{S}(\mathcal{X}) \cap \mathcal{V}_{in}$ *and* $\Delta \in \mathcal{F}$, $\omega_{\{x \in \Delta\}}$ *is unique whenever* $\Pr\{x \in \Delta \| \omega\} \neq 0$, *or is indefinite otherwise.*

From now on, we consider only the case of $\mathcal{X} = \mathcal{Y}$ for simplicity. The joint probability distribution of the successive measurement of $\mathbf{A}(x)$ and $\mathbf{A}(y)$ in this order in a state $\omega \in \mathcal{V}_{in} \cap \mathcal{S}(\mathcal{X})$ is given by

$$\Pr\{x \in \Delta, y \in \Gamma \| \omega\} = \Pr\{x \in \Delta \| \omega\} \Pr\{y \in \Gamma \| \omega_{\{x \in \Delta\}}\} \tag{35}$$

for all $\Delta \in \mathcal{F}$ and $\Gamma \in \mathcal{F}'$.

Assumption 2. *For every* $\Delta \in \mathcal{F}$, *measuring apparatus* $\mathbf{A}(y)$ *whose output variable y takes values in a measurable space* $(S', \mathcal{F}')$, *and* $\Gamma \in \mathcal{F}'$, *the map* $\mathcal{S}(\mathcal{X}) \cap \mathcal{V}_{in} \ni \omega \mapsto \Pr\{x \in \Delta, y \in \Gamma \| \omega\}$ *is affine, that is,*

$$\Pr\{x \in \Delta, y \in \Gamma \| \alpha \omega_1 + (1-\alpha)\omega_2\} = \alpha \Pr\{x \in \Delta, y \in \Gamma \| \omega_1\} + (1-\alpha) \Pr\{x \in \Delta, y \in \Gamma \| \omega_2\} \tag{36}$$

for all $\alpha \in [0,1]$ *and* $\omega_1, \omega_2 \in \mathcal{S}(\mathcal{X}) \cap \mathcal{V}_{in}$.

The affine property of joint distributions of successive measurements characterizes the instrument as shown in the following theorem.

Theorem 12. *Let* $\mathbf{A}(x)$ *be a measuring apparatus satisfying Assumption 1. Suppose that there exists a σ-finite central subspace $\mathcal{V}_{out}$ of $\mathcal{X}$ such that* $\{\omega_{\{x \in \Delta\}} | \omega \in \mathcal{S}(\mathcal{X}) \cap \mathcal{V}_{in}, \Delta \in \mathcal{F}\} \subset \mathcal{V}_{out}$. *The following conditions are equivalent:*
(1) $\mathbf{A}(x)$ *satisfies Assumption 2.*
(2) *There exists an instrument $\mathcal{I}$ for* $(\mathcal{V}_{in}, \mathcal{V}_{out}, S)$ *such that*

$$\Pr\{x \in \Delta \| \omega\} = \|\mathcal{I}(\Delta)\omega\| \tag{37}$$

for all $\omega \in \mathcal{S}(\mathcal{X}) \cap \mathcal{V}_{in}$ *and* $\Delta \in \mathcal{F}$, *and that*

$$\omega_{\{x \in \Delta\}} = \frac{\mathcal{I}(\Delta)\omega}{\|\mathcal{I}(\Delta)\omega\|} \tag{38}$$

whenever $\Pr\{x \in \Delta \| \omega\} \neq 0$.

The complete positivity of instrument is based on the general description of the dynamics of open systems. In Section 2, we discussed the dynamics of open systems state/representation-independently. We consider the following assumption that is called the trivial extendability.

Assumption 3. *For any quantum system $\mathbf{S}'$ that is described by a C*-algebra $\mathcal{Y}$ and does not interact with an apparatus $\mathbf{A}(\mathbf{x})$ nor $\mathbf{S}$, $\mathbf{A}(\mathbf{x})$ can be extended into an apparatus $\mathbf{A}(\mathbf{x}')$ measuring the composite system $\mathbf{S} + \mathbf{S}'$ with the following statistical properties:*

$$\Pr\{\mathbf{x}' \in \Delta \| \omega \otimes \varphi\} = \Pr\{\mathbf{x} \in \Delta \| \omega\}, \tag{39}$$

$$(\omega \otimes \varphi)_{\{\mathbf{x}' \in \Delta\}} = \omega_{\{\mathbf{x} \in \Delta\}} \otimes \varphi \tag{40}$$

for all $\omega \in \mathcal{V}_{\text{in}} \cap \mathcal{S}(\mathcal{X})$, $\varphi \in \mathcal{W} \cap \mathcal{S}(\mathcal{Y})$ and $\Delta \in \mathcal{F}$, where $\mathcal{W}$ is a central subspace of $\mathcal{Y}^*$.

Let $\mathcal{M}$ and $\mathcal{N}$ be von Neumann algebras. For every $\sigma \in \mathcal{N}_*$, we define a map $\text{id} \otimes \sigma : \mathcal{M} \,\overline{\otimes}\, \mathcal{N} \to \mathcal{M}$ by $\langle \rho \otimes \sigma, X \rangle = \langle \rho, (\text{id} \otimes \sigma)(X) \rangle$ for all $\rho \in \mathcal{M}_*$ and $X \in \mathcal{M} \,\overline{\otimes}\, \mathcal{N}$.

A measuring apparatus that satisfies Assumption 3 is described by a CP instrument. In the von Neumann algebraic setting, a measuring process is defined as follows.

Definition 9 (Measuring process [19] (Definition 3.2))**.** *Let $\mathcal{M}$ be a von Neumann algebra on a Hilbert space $\mathcal{H}$, and $(S, \mathcal{F})$ a measurable space. A 4-tuple $\mathbb{M} = (\mathcal{K}, \sigma, E, U)$ is called a measuring process for $(\mathcal{M}, S)$ if it satisfies the following conditions:*
(1) *$\mathcal{K}$ is a Hilbert space,*
(2) *σ is a normal state on $\mathbf{B}(\mathcal{K})$,*
(3) *$E : \mathcal{F} \to \mathbf{B}(\mathcal{K})$ is a spectral measure,*
(4) *U is a unitary operator on $\mathcal{H} \otimes \mathcal{K}$,*
(5) *$\{\mathcal{I}_{\mathbb{M}}(M, \Delta) \mid M \in \mathcal{M}, \Delta \in \mathcal{F}\} \subset \mathcal{M}$, where $\mathcal{I}_{\mathbb{M}} : \mathbf{B}(\mathcal{H}) \times \mathcal{F} \to \mathbf{B}(\mathcal{H})$ is defined by*

$$\mathcal{I}_{\mathbb{M}}(X, \Delta) = (\text{id} \otimes \sigma)[U^*(X \otimes E(\Delta))U] \tag{41}$$

for all $X \in \mathbf{B}(\mathcal{H})$ and $\Delta \in \mathcal{F}$.

As shown in [18], every CP instrument for $(\mathbf{B}(\mathcal{H}), S)$ is defined by a measuring process. By contrast, in the case where $\mathcal{M}$ is a non-atomic injective von Neumann algebra, it is shown in [19] that there exist CP instruments for $(\mathcal{M}, S)$ which cannot be defined by any measuring processes. Furthermore, a necessary and sufficient condition for a CP instrument to be defined by a measuring process is given in [19].

In the context of measurement, we do not always care about sectors as a macroscopic unit, but we actively utilize the macroscopic distinction based on the disjointness. We introduce two kinds of subcentral lifting property for instruments as follows.

Definition 10. *An instrument $\mathcal{I}$ for $(\mathcal{X}, \mathcal{V}, S)$ is said to have the first subcentral lifting property if there exists a central subspace $\mathcal{W}$ of the dual space of a C*-algebra $\mathcal{Y}(\supset \mathcal{X})$ and an instrument $\widetilde{\mathcal{I}}$ for $(\mathcal{X}, \mathcal{V}, \mathcal{Y}, \mathcal{W}, S)$ satisfying the following two conditions:*
(1) *For every $\omega \in \mathcal{S}(\mathcal{X}) \cap \mathcal{V}$ and $\Delta \in \mathcal{F}$, $\widetilde{\mathcal{I}}(\Delta)\omega \,\natural\, \widetilde{\mathcal{I}}(\Delta^c)\omega$.*
(2) *For every $\omega \in \mathcal{S}(\mathcal{X}) \cap \mathcal{V}$, $X \in \mathcal{X}$ and $\Delta \in \mathcal{F}$, $[\widetilde{\mathcal{I}}(\Delta)\omega](X) = [\mathcal{I}(\Delta)\omega](X)$.*

Definition 11. *An instrument $\mathcal{I}$ for $(\mathcal{X}, \mathcal{V}, S)$ is said to have the second subcentral lifting property if there exists a central subspace $\mathcal{W}$ of the dual space of a C*-algebra $\mathcal{Y}(\supset \mathcal{X})$ and an instrument $\widetilde{\mathcal{I}}$ for $(\mathcal{Y}, \mathcal{W}, S)$ satisfying the following two conditions:*
(1) *For every $\varphi \in \mathcal{S}(\mathcal{Y}) \cap \mathcal{W}$ and $\Delta \in \mathcal{F}$, $\widetilde{\mathcal{I}}(\Delta)\varphi \,\natural\, \widetilde{\mathcal{I}}(\Delta^c)\varphi$.*
(2) *For every $\omega \in \mathcal{S}(\mathcal{X}) \cap \mathcal{V}$, there exists $\widetilde{\omega} \in \mathcal{S}(\mathcal{Y}) \cap \mathcal{W}$ such that $\widetilde{\omega}(X) = \omega(X)$ and $[\widetilde{\mathcal{I}}(\Delta)\widetilde{\omega}](Y) = [\mathcal{I}(\Delta)\omega](Y)$ for all $X, Y \in \mathcal{X}$ and $\Delta \in \mathcal{F}$.*

Both subcentral lifting properties characterize the measurement obtained by restricting a measurement, which realizes the disjointness of states (after the measurement) of a larger system corresponding to different output values, to the target system. On the other hand, the difference between these two properties may be obvious from the definitions.

An instrument $\mathcal{I}$ for $(\mathcal{X}, \mathcal{V}_{\text{in}}, \mathcal{Y}, \mathcal{V}_{\text{out}}, S)$ is said to be finite if there exists a finite subset S_0 of S and a map $T : S_0 \to P(\mathcal{V}_{\text{in}}, \mathcal{V}_{\text{out}})$ such that

$$\mathcal{I}(\Delta) = \sum_{s \in S_0 \cap \Delta} T(s) \tag{42}$$

for all $\Delta \in \mathcal{F}$.

Theorem 13. *Every finite instrument for $(\mathcal{X}, \mathcal{V}, S)$ has the first subcentral lifting property and the second subcentral lifting property.*

Proof. Let $\mathcal{I}$ be a finite instrument for $(\mathcal{X}, \mathcal{V}, S)$, a finite subset S_0 of S, and a map $T : S_0 \to P(\mathcal{V})$ satisfying Equation (42) for all $\Delta \in \mathcal{F}$. For every $\Delta \in \mathcal{F}$, a linear map $\widetilde{\mathcal{I}}(\Delta) : \mathcal{V} \to \mathcal{V} \otimes l^1(S_0)$ is defined by

$$\widetilde{\mathcal{I}}(\Delta)\omega = \sum_{s \in S_0 \cap \Delta} T(s)\omega \otimes \delta_s \tag{43}$$

for all $\omega \in \mathcal{V}$. Then, $\widetilde{\mathcal{I}}$ is a finite instrument for $(\mathcal{X}, \mathcal{V}, \mathcal{X} \otimes_{\min} l^\infty(S_0), \mathcal{V} \otimes l^1(S_0), S)$. Then, $\widetilde{\mathcal{I}}$ satisfies $\widetilde{\mathcal{I}}(\Delta)\omega \, \delta \, \widetilde{\mathcal{I}}(\Delta^c)\omega$ for all $\omega \in \mathcal{S}(\mathcal{X}) \cap \mathcal{V}$ and $\Delta \in \mathcal{F}$. Furthermore, every $\omega \in \mathcal{S}(\mathcal{X}) \cap \mathcal{V}$, $X \in \mathcal{X}$ and $\Delta \in \mathcal{F}$, $[\widetilde{\mathcal{I}}(\Delta)\omega](X \otimes 1) = [\mathcal{I}(\Delta)\omega](X)$. Therefore, $\mathcal{I}$ has the first subcentral lifting property.

Next, we define a finite instrument $\widehat{\mathcal{I}}$ for $(\mathcal{X} \otimes_{\min} l^\infty(S_0), \mathcal{V} \otimes l^1(S_0), S)$ by

$$\widehat{\mathcal{I}}(\Delta)\varphi = \widetilde{\mathcal{I}}(\Delta)(j(\varphi)) \tag{44}$$

for all $\Delta \in \mathcal{F}$ and $\varphi \in \mathcal{V} \otimes l^1(S_0)$, where $j : \mathcal{V} \otimes l^1(S_0) \to \mathcal{V}$ is a linear map defined by

$$[j(\varphi)](X) = \varphi(X \otimes 1) \tag{45}$$

for all $X \in \mathcal{X}$. For every $\varphi \in \mathcal{S}(\mathcal{X} \otimes_{\min} l^\infty(S_0)) \cap (\mathcal{V} \otimes l^1(S_0))$ and $\Delta \in \mathcal{F}, \widehat{\mathcal{I}}(\Delta)\varphi \, \delta \, \widehat{\mathcal{I}}(\Delta^c)\varphi$. For every $\omega \in \mathcal{S}(\mathcal{X}) \cap \mathcal{V}$, $\widetilde{\omega} = \omega \otimes \delta_{s_0}$, where $s_0 \in S_0$ satisfies $\widetilde{\omega}(X \otimes 1) = \omega(X)$ and $[\widetilde{\mathcal{I}}(\Delta)\widetilde{\omega}](Y \otimes 1) = [\mathcal{I}(\Delta)\omega](Y)$ for all $X, Y \in \mathcal{X}$ and $\Delta \in \mathcal{F}$. Therefore, $\mathcal{I}$ has the second subcentral lifting property. □

We conjecture that every CP instrument has both subcentral lifting properties.

6. Discussion and Perspectives

In the study, we have defined instruments by using central subspaces of the dual of a C*-algebra. We have checked its consistency with the definition in the von Neumann algebraic setting. This result means that the extension of the measurement theory to C*-algebra in the paper is valid. Furthermore, we have proposed a unification of the measurement theory and the sector theory: we have defined and characterized the centrality of instruments. In addition, we have discussed the operational characterization and macroscopic nature of quantum measurement. In the context, we have actively used the disjointness of states to distinguish different output values of the meter. Our results are, of course, applicable to systems described by C*-algebras generated from field operators, and the macroscopic aspects of quantum fields can now be discussed in terms of measurement theory.

In the setting of AQFT, we use a local net $\{\mathcal{A}(\mathcal{O})\}_{\mathcal{O} \in \mathcal{R}_1}$ on a space M_1 in order to describe the DP phenomena. In describing the measurement of DPs, only the use of the local net first adopted is not enough. In fact, to detect (the effect of) DPs, we need an operation wherein some probe is brought closer to the spatial scale at which DPs are generated. We introduced an extension of a local net to mathematically describe the operation at the level of observable algebras.

Definition 12. Let $\{\mathcal{A}(\mathcal{O})\}_{\mathcal{O}\in\mathcal{R}_1}$ and $\{\mathcal{B}(\mathcal{O})\}_{\mathcal{O}\in\mathcal{R}_2}$ be local nets on M_1 and M_2, respectively. $\{\mathcal{B}(\mathcal{O})\}_{\mathcal{O}\in\mathcal{R}_2}$ is an extension of $\{\mathcal{A}(\mathcal{O})\}_{\mathcal{O}\in\mathcal{R}_1}$ if it satisfies the following three conditions:
(i) $M_1 \subset M_2$.
(ii) $\mathcal{R}_1 \subset \mathcal{R}_2$.
(iii) For every $\mathcal{O} \in \mathcal{R}_1$, $\mathcal{A}(\mathcal{O}) \subset \mathcal{B}(\mathcal{O})$.

We use the extensions of a local net because the construction of the composite system of the system of interest and a measuring apparatus is not so simple. In particular, the construction of the composite system by the tensor product is not always applicable to quantum fields.

Let $\{\mathcal{B}(\mathcal{O})\}_{\mathcal{O}\in\mathcal{R}_2}$ be a local net on M_2 and an extension of a local net $\{\mathcal{A}(\mathcal{O})\}_{\mathcal{O}\in\mathcal{R}_1}$ on M_1. We suppose that M_1 is bounded. The composite system of the original system and a probe, which is close to the original system on the spatial scale where DPs are generated, is described by $\{\mathcal{B}(\mathcal{O})\}_{\mathcal{O}\in\mathcal{R}_2}$ as a quantum field. Furthermore, the material system, which is a part of the composite system, is assumed to be localized in the neighborhood of M_1. In the composite system, the generation and annihilation of DPs constantly occur near non-uniform materials in the unstable situation where light continues to incident constantly. By measuring the emitted light at regions far from M_1, we check (or estimate) the effect of DPs generated in M_1.

Constructing a concrete model of DPs as a quantum field in order to correlate experiments of DPs with the theory is a future task. We hope to describe the DP phenomena as open systems at the next stage. In the future, clarification of the relationship between this study and the recent trends in DP research [33] is required. Moreover, the mathematical theory of quantum measurement for quantum systems described by C*-algebras should be further developed.

Funding: This research received no external funding.

Acknowledgments: The author thanks anonymous reviewers for their comments to improve the quality of this paper.

Conflicts of Interest: The author declares no conflict of interest.

Abbreviations

Abbreviations

The following abbreviations are used in this manuscript:

AQFT algebraic quantum field theory
CP   completely positive
DP   dressed photon
PVM   projection valued measure

Appendix A. Operator Algebra

We introduce the basic facts on operator algebras. See [26,30,31,34–37] for more details on operator algebras. A set $\mathcal{X}$ is called a C*-algebra if it satisfies the following conditions:
(1) $\mathcal{X}$ is a Banach space over $\mathbb{C}$.
(2) $\mathcal{X}$ is a *-algebra, i.e., it is an algebra with involution. The involution $* : \mathcal{X} \to \mathcal{X}$ satisfies $(aX + bY)^* = \bar{a}X^* + \bar{b}Y^*$, $(XY)^* = Y^*X^*$, and $X^{**} := (X^*)^* = X$ for all $a, b \in \mathbb{C}$ and $X, Y \in \mathcal{X}$.
(3) The norm of $\mathcal{X}$ satisfies $\|X^*X\| = \|X\|^2$ for all $X \in \mathcal{X}$.

We assume that C*-algebras are unital.

Let $\mathcal{X}$ and $\mathcal{Y}$ be C*-algebras. A map $j : \mathcal{X} \to \mathcal{Y}$ is called a *-homomorphism if it satisfies the following conditions:
(i) $j(aX_1 + bX_2) = aj(X_1) + bj(X_2)$ for all $a, b \in \mathbb{C}$ and $X_1, X_2 \in \mathcal{X}$.
(ii) $j(X_1X_2) = j(X_1)j(X_2)$ for all $X_1, X_2 \in \mathcal{X}$.

(iii) $j(X^*) = j(X)^*$ for all $X \in \mathcal{X}$.
(iv) $j(1) = 1$.

A $*$-homomorphims β of $\mathcal{X}$ is called a $*$-automorphism of $\mathcal{X}$ if there exists a $*$-homomorphims γ of $\mathcal{X}$ such that $\beta \circ \gamma = \mathrm{id}_\mathcal{X}$ and $\gamma \circ \beta = \mathrm{id}_\mathcal{X}$. $Aut(\mathcal{X})$ denotes the set of automorphisms of $\mathcal{X}$. A $*$-homomorphism and a $*$-automorphism are simply called a homomorphism and an automorphism, respectively.

Let ω be a linear functional on $\mathcal{X}$.
(i) ω is positive if $\omega(X^*X) \geq 0$ for all $X \in \mathcal{X}$.
(ii) ω is normalized if $\omega(1) = 1$.

$\mathcal{X}^*$ denotes the set of (complex) linear functionals on $\mathcal{X}$. $\mathcal{X}^*_+$ denotes the set of positive linear functionals on $\mathcal{X}$. A linear functional on $\mathcal{X}$ is called a state on $\mathcal{X}$ if it is positive and normalized. $\mathcal{S}(\mathcal{X})$ denotes the set of states on $\mathcal{X}$. A state ω on $\mathcal{X}$ is faithful if $\omega(X^*X) = 0$ implies $X = 0$. A C^*-algebra $\mathcal{W}$ is called a W^*-algebra if it is the dual of a Banach space $\mathcal{W}_*$, called the predual of $\mathcal{W}$. The second dual $\mathcal{X}^{**} = (\mathcal{X}^*)^*$ of a C^*-algebra $\mathcal{X}$ is a W^*-algebra and is called the universal enveloping algebra of $\mathcal{X}$. A W^*-algebra $\mathcal{W}$ is said to be σ-finite if it admits at most countably many orthogonal projections. A positive linear functional φ on $\mathcal{W}$ is said to be normal if $\{\varphi(A_\gamma)\}_{\gamma \in \Gamma}$ converges to $\varphi(A)$ for all non-decreasing nets $\{A_\gamma\}_{\gamma \in \Gamma}$ of positive operators in $\mathcal{W}$ convergent to a positive operator $A \in \mathcal{W}$. A positive linear functional φ on $\mathcal{W}$ is normal if and only if $\varphi \in \mathcal{W}_*$. $B(\mathcal{H})$ denotes the set of bounded linear operators on a Hilbert space $\mathcal{H}$. A W^*-algebra $\mathcal{M}$ is called a von Neumann algebra on a Hilbert space $\mathcal{H}$ if it is a subset of $B(\mathcal{H})$, and the involution of $\mathcal{M}$ coincides with the adjoint operation on $B(\mathcal{H})$. The predual $\mathcal{M}_*$ of a von Neumann algebra $\mathcal{M}$ on a Hilbert space $\mathcal{H}$ satisfies

$$\mathcal{M}_* = \{\varphi \in \mathcal{M}^* | \exists \rho \in T(\mathcal{H}) \text{ s.t. } \varphi(M) = \mathrm{Tr}[M\rho] \text{ for all } M \in \mathcal{M}\}, \tag{A1}$$

where $T(\mathcal{H})$ denotes the set of trace-class operators on $\mathcal{H}$.

For every state ω on $\mathcal{X}$, there exist a Hilbert space $\mathcal{H}_\omega$, a representation π_ω of $\mathcal{X}$ on $\mathcal{H}_\omega$ and a unit vector Ω_ω of $\mathcal{H}_\omega$ such that

$$\omega(X) = \langle \Omega_\omega | \pi_\omega(X) \Omega_\omega \rangle, \quad X \in \mathcal{X}, \tag{A2}$$

and $\mathcal{H}_\omega = \overline{\pi_\omega(\mathcal{X})\Omega_\omega}$. Here, a map $\pi: \mathcal{X} \to B(\mathcal{H})$ is called a representation of $\mathcal{X}$ on a Hilbert space $\mathcal{H}$ if it satisfies $\pi(aX + bY) = a\pi(X) + b\pi(Y)$, $\pi(XY) = \pi(X)\pi(Y)$, and $\pi(X^*) = \pi(X)^*$ for all $a, b \in \mathbb{C}$ and $X, Y \in \mathcal{X}$. The triple $(\pi_\omega, \mathcal{H}_\omega, \Omega_\omega)$ is called the GNS representation of ω and is unique up to unitary equivalence.

For any subset S of $B(\mathcal{H})$, we define the commutant S' of S by $S' = \{A \in B(\mathcal{H}) \mid \forall B \in S, AB = BA\}$ and the double commutant S'' of S by $S'' = (S')'$. $\pi_\omega(\mathcal{X})''$ and $\pi_\omega(\mathcal{X})'$ are then von Neumann algebras on $\mathcal{H}_\omega$.

Appendix B. The Proof of Theorem 1

First, we present theorems used to show Theorem 1.

Theorem A1 ([24–27,31]). *Let $\mathcal{X}$ be a C^*-algebra and $\mathcal{H}$ a Hilbert space. For every CP map $T: \mathcal{X} \to B(\mathcal{H})$, there exist a Hilbert space $\mathcal{K}$, a representation π of $\mathcal{X}$ on $\mathcal{K}$, and $V \in B(\mathcal{H}, \mathcal{K})$ such that*

$$T(X) = V^*\pi(X)V \tag{A3}$$

for all $X \in \mathcal{X}$, and that $\mathcal{K} = \overline{\mathrm{span}}(\pi(\mathcal{X})V\mathcal{H})$. If $\mathcal{X}$ and $\mathcal{H}$ are separable, then so is $\mathcal{K}$.

The triplet $(\pi, \mathcal{K}, V)$ is called a Stinespring representation of T, and is unique up to unitary equivalence.

Theorem A2 ([26] (Chapter IV, Theorem 5.5)). *Let $\mathcal{M}_1$ and $\mathcal{M}_2$ be von Neumann algebras on Hilbert spaces $\mathcal{H}_1$ and $\mathcal{H}_2$, respectively. If π is a normal homomorphism of $\mathcal{M}_1$ onto $\mathcal{M}_2$, then* there exist a Hilbert space $\mathcal{L}$, a projection E of $\mathcal{M}_1' \,\overline{\otimes}\, \mathbf{B}(\mathcal{L})$, and an isometry U of $E(\mathcal{H}_1 \otimes \mathcal{L})$ onto $\mathcal{H}_2$ such that

$$\pi(M) = Uj_E(M \otimes 1)U^* \tag{A4}$$

for all $M \in \mathcal{M}_1$, where $j_E : \mathbf{B}(\mathcal{H}_1 \otimes \mathcal{L}) \to E\mathbf{B}(\mathcal{H}_1 \otimes \mathcal{L})E$ is defined by $j_E(X) = EXE$ for all $X \in \mathbf{B}(\mathcal{H}_1 \otimes \mathcal{L})$. $\mathcal{M}_1 \,\overline{\otimes}\, \mathbb{C}1$ is then a multiplicative domain of j_E.

As a corollary of Theorem A2, the following holds:

Corollary A1. Let $\mathcal{H}_1$ and $\mathcal{H}_2$ be Hilbert spaces. If π is a normal homomorphism of $\mathbf{B}(\mathcal{H}_1)$ onto $\mathbf{B}(\mathcal{H}_2)$, then there exist a Hilbert space $\mathcal{K}$ and a unitary W of $\mathcal{H}_1 \otimes \mathcal{K}$ onto $\mathcal{H}_2$ such that

$$\pi(X) = W(X \otimes 1)W^* \tag{A5}$$

for all $X \in \mathbf{B}(\mathcal{H}_1)$.

Let $\mathcal{X}$ and $\mathcal{Y}$ be C*-algebras. We define a partial order $T_1 \leq T_2$ on $\mathrm{CP}(\mathcal{X}, \mathcal{Y})$ by $T_2 - T_1 \in \mathrm{CP}(\mathcal{X}, \mathcal{Y})$.

Theorem A3 ([25] (Theorem 1.4.2)). *Let T_1, T_2 be elements of $\mathrm{CP}(\mathcal{X}, \mathbf{B}(\mathcal{H}))$ such that $T_1 \leq T_2$, and $(\pi, \mathcal{K}, V)$ is the Stinespring representation of T_2. There exists a positive operator R of $\pi(\mathcal{X})'$ such that*

$$T_1(X) = V^* R \pi(X) V \tag{A6}$$

for all $X \in \mathcal{X}$.

By using the above theorems, we show Theorem 1.

Proof of Theorem 1. Put $P = T(1)$. Suppose $P \neq 0$ without loss of generality. We define a unital normal CP map T' on $\mathbf{B}(\mathcal{H})$ by

$$T'(X) = \frac{1}{\|P\|} T(X) + \left(1 - \frac{P}{\|P\|}\right)^{\frac{1}{2}} X \left(1 - \frac{P}{\|P\|}\right)^{\frac{1}{2}} \tag{A7}$$

for all $X \in \mathbf{B}(\mathcal{H})$. By Theorem A1, there exist a separable Hilbert space $\mathcal{K}'$, a normal representation π' of $\mathcal{X}$ on $\mathcal{K}'$, and an isometry $V' \in \mathbf{B}(\mathcal{H}, \mathcal{K})$ such that $\mathcal{K}' = \overline{\mathrm{span}}(\pi'(\mathcal{X})V'\mathcal{H})$ and that

$$T'(X) = (V')^* \pi'(X) V' \tag{A8}$$

for all $X \in \mathbf{B}(\mathcal{H})$. Since

$$\frac{1}{\|P\|} T(X^*X) \leq T'(X^*X) \tag{A9}$$

for all $X \in \mathbf{B}(\mathcal{H})$, by Theorem A3, there exists a positive operator R' of $\pi'(\mathcal{X})'$ such that

$$\frac{1}{\|P\|} T(X) = (V')^* \pi'(X) R' V' \tag{A10}$$

for all $X \in \mathbf{B}(\mathcal{H})$. By Corollary A1, there exist a separable Hilbert space $\mathcal{L}_1$ and a unitary operator $W \in \mathbf{B}(\mathcal{H} \otimes \mathcal{L}_1, \mathcal{K}')$ such that

$$\pi'(X) = W'(X \otimes 1)W'^* \tag{A11}$$

for all $X \in \mathbf{B}(\mathcal{H})$. There then exists a positive operator R'' on $\mathcal{L}_1$ such that $R'W' = W'(1 \otimes R'')$.

Let $\mathcal{L}_2$ be an infinite-dimensional separable Hilbert space, v a unit vector in $\mathcal{L}_2$, and y a unit vector in $\mathcal{L}_1$. We define an isometry $U : \mathcal{H} \otimes \mathbb{C}y \otimes \mathbb{C}v \to \mathcal{H} \otimes \mathcal{L}_1 \otimes \mathcal{L}_2$ by

$$U_0(x \otimes y \otimes v) = (W')^* V' x \otimes v \tag{A12}$$

for all $x \in \mathcal{H}$. Since $\mathcal{H} \otimes \mathbb{C}y \otimes \mathbb{C}v$ and $U_0(\mathcal{H} \otimes \mathbb{C}y \otimes \mathbb{C}v)$ satisfy $\dim((\mathcal{H} \otimes \mathbb{C}y \otimes \mathbb{C}v)^\perp) = \dim((U_0(\mathcal{H} \otimes \mathbb{C}y \otimes \mathbb{C}v))^\perp)$ as subspaces of $\mathcal{H} \otimes \mathcal{L}_1 \otimes \mathcal{L}_2$, there exists a unitary operator U on $\mathcal{H} \otimes \mathcal{L}_1 \otimes \mathcal{L}_2$ such that $U|_{\mathcal{H} \otimes \mathbb{C}y \otimes \mathbb{C}v} = U_0$. We put $\mathcal{K} = \mathcal{L}_1 \otimes \mathcal{L}_2$ and $\xi = y \otimes v$, and define a positive operator R on $\mathcal{K}$ by $R = \|P\|R'' \otimes 1$. For every $X \in B(\mathcal{H})$ and $x_1, x_2 \in \mathcal{H}$, we obtain

$$\begin{aligned}
\langle x_1 | T(X) x_2 \rangle &= \|P\| \langle x_1 | (V')^* W'(X \otimes R'')(W')^* V' x_2 \rangle \\
&= \|P\| \langle (W')^* V' x_1 \otimes v | (X \otimes R'' \otimes 1)[(W')^* V' x_2 \otimes v] \rangle \\
&= \langle U(x_1 \otimes y \otimes v) | (X \otimes R)[U(x_2 \otimes y \otimes v)] \rangle \\
&= \mathrm{Tr}[U^*(X \otimes R)U(|x_2\rangle\langle x_1| \otimes |\xi\rangle\langle\xi|)] \\
&= \mathrm{Tr}[\mathrm{Tr}_\mathcal{K}[U^*(X \otimes R)U(1 \otimes |\xi\rangle\langle\xi|)]|x_2\rangle\langle x_1|] \\
&= \langle x_1 | \mathrm{Tr}_\mathcal{K}[U^*(X \otimes R)U(1 \otimes |\xi\rangle\langle\xi|)] x_2 \rangle,
\end{aligned} \tag{A13}$$

which completes the proof of (1).

Next, we show (2). By Theorem A1, there exist a separable Hilbert space $\mathcal{K}_1$, a normal representation π of $\mathcal{X}$ on $\mathcal{K}$ and $V \in B(\mathcal{H}, \mathcal{K})$ such that $\mathcal{K}_1 = \overline{\mathrm{span}}(\pi(\mathcal{X}) V \mathcal{H})$ and that

$$T(X) = V^* \pi(X) V \tag{A14}$$

for all $X \in B(\mathcal{H})$. By Corollary A1, there exist a separable Hilbert space $\mathcal{K}_2$ and a unitary operator $W \in B(\mathcal{K}_1, \mathcal{H} \otimes \mathcal{K}_2)$ such that

$$\pi(X) = W(X \otimes 1)W^* \tag{A15}$$

for all $X \in B(\mathcal{H})$. Let $\{y_i\}_{i=1}^{\dim(\mathcal{K}_2)}$ be a complete orthonormal system of $\mathcal{K}_2$. For every $1 \le i \le \dim(\mathcal{K}_2)$, we define $K_i \in B(\mathcal{H})$ by

$$\langle x_1 | K_i x_2 \rangle = \langle x_1 \otimes y_i | W^* V x_2 \rangle \tag{A16}$$

for all $x_1, x_2 \in \mathcal{H}$. For every $1 \le i \le \dim(\mathcal{K}_2)$, $X \in B(\mathcal{H})$ and $x_1, x_2 \in \mathcal{H}$, we have

$$\begin{aligned}
\langle x_1 | K_i^* X K_i x_2 \rangle &= \langle K_i x_1 | X K_i x_2 \rangle = \sum_{j=1}^{\dim(\mathcal{H})} \langle K_i x_1 | z_j \rangle \langle z_j | X K_i x_2 \rangle \\
&= \sum_{j=1}^{\dim(\mathcal{H})} \langle K_i x_1 | z_j \rangle \langle X^* z_j | K_i x_2 \rangle \\
&= \sum_{j=1}^{\dim(\mathcal{H})} \langle W^* V x_1 | z_j \otimes y_i \rangle \langle X^* z_j \otimes y_i | W^* V x_2 \rangle \\
&= \sum_{j=1}^{\dim(\mathcal{H})} \langle W^* V x_1 | (|z_j\rangle\langle z_j| \otimes |y_i\rangle\langle y_i|)(X \otimes 1) W^* V x_2 \rangle \\
&= \langle W^* V x_1 | (X \otimes |y_i\rangle\langle y_i|) W^* V x_2 \rangle = \langle x_1 | V^* W (X \otimes |y_i\rangle\langle y_i|) W^* V x_2 \rangle.
\end{aligned} \tag{A17}$$

Therefore, for every $X \in B(\mathcal{H})$ and $x_1, x_2 \in \mathcal{H}$, we obtain

$$\begin{aligned}\langle x_1|T(X)x_2\rangle &= \langle x_1|V^*W(X\otimes 1)W^*Vx_2\rangle \\ &= \sum_{i=1}^{\dim(\mathcal{K}_2)} \langle x_1|V^*W(X\otimes |y_i\rangle\langle y_i|)W^*Vx_2\rangle \\ &= \sum_{i=1}^{\dim(\mathcal{K}_2)} \langle x_1|K_i^*XK_ix_2\rangle = \langle x_1|\left(\sum_{i=1}^{\dim(\mathcal{K}_2)} K_i^*XK_i\right)x_2\rangle,\end{aligned} \qquad (A18)$$

which completes the proof of (2). □

The proof of (1) in the above theorem refers to that of [18] (Theorem 5.1). The results of this appendix are related to the theory of Hilbert modules [38–43].

References

1. Ohtsu, M. *Dressed Photons*; Springer: Berlin, Germany, 2014.
2. Haag, R.; Kastler, D. An algebraic approach to quantum field theory. *J. Math. Phys.* **1964**, *5*, 848–861. [CrossRef]
3. Araki, H. *Mathematical Theory of Quantum Fields*; Oxford UP: Oxford, UK, 1999.
4. Haag, R. *Local Quantum Physics: Fields, Particles, Algebras*, 2nd ed.; Springer: Berlin, Germany, 2012.
5. Doplicher, S.; Haag, R.; Roberts, J.E. Fields, observables and gauge transformations I. *Comm. Math. Phys.* **1969**, *13*, 1–23. [CrossRef]
6. Doplicher, S.; Haag, R.; Roberts, J.E. Fields, observables and gauge transformations II. *Comm. Math. Phys.* **1969**, *15*, 173–200. [CrossRef]
7. Doplicher, S.; Haag, R.; Roberts, J.E. Local observables and particle statistics, I. *Comm. Math. Phys.* **1971**, *23*, 199–230. [CrossRef]
8. Doplicher, S.; Haag, R.; Roberts, J.E. Local observables and particle statistics, II. *Comm. Math. Phys.* **1974**, *35*, 49–85. [CrossRef]
9. Doplicher, S.; Roberts, J.E. Why there is a field algebra with a compact gauge group describing the superselection structure in particle physics. *Comm. Math. Phys.* **1990**, *131*, 51–107. [CrossRef]
10. Umezawa, H.; Matsumoto, H.; Tachiki, M. *Thermo Field Dynamics and Condensed States*; North-Holland: Amsterdam, The Netherlands, 1982.
11. Umezawa, H. *Advanced Field Theory: Micro, Macro, and Thermal Physics*; AIP: New York, NY, USA, 1993.
12. Blasone, M.; Jizba, P.; Vitiello, G. *Quantum Field Theory and Its Macroscopic Manifestations*; World Scientific: London, UK, 2011.
13. Blasone, M.; Jizba, P.; Smaldone, L. Functional integrals and inequivalent representations in Quantum Field Theory. *Ann. Phys.* **2017**, *383*, 207–238. [CrossRef]
14. Ojima, I. A unified scheme for generalized sectors based on selection criteria—Order parameters of symmetries and of thermality and physical meanings of adjunctions. *Open Syst. Inform. Dyn.* **2003**, *10*, 235–279. [CrossRef]
15. Ojima, I. Temperature as order parameter of broken scale invariance. *Publ. Res. Inst. Math. Sci.* **2004**, *40*, 731–756. [CrossRef]
16. Ojima, I. Micro-Macro Duality in Quantum Physics. In *Proceedings International Conference on Stochastic Analysis, Classical and Quantum*; World Scientific: Singapore, 2005; pp. 143–161.
17. Davies, E.B.; Lewis, J.T. An operational approach to quantum probability. *Commun. Math. Phys.* **1970**, *17*, 239–260. [CrossRef]
18. Ozawa, M. Quantum measuring processes of continuous observables. *J. Math. Phys.* **1984**, *25*, 79–87. [CrossRef]
19. Okamura, K.; Ozawa, M. Measurement theory in local quantum physics. *J. Math. Phys.* **2016**, *57*, 015209. [CrossRef]
20. Okamura, K. Measuring processes and the Heisenberg picture. In *Reality and Measurement in Algebraic Quantum Theory: NWW 2015, Nagoya, Japan, 9–13 March*; Ozawa, M., Butterfield, J., Halvorson, H., Rédei, M., Kitajima, Y., Buscemi, F., Eds.; Springer: Singapore, 2018; pp. 361–396.
21. Ojima, I.; Okamura, K.; Saigo, H. Derivation of Born Rule from Algebraic and Statistical Axioms. *Open Sys. Inform. Dyn.* **2014**, *21*, 1450005. [CrossRef]
22. Hora, A.; Obata, N. *Quantum Probability and Spectral Analysis of Graphs*; Springer: Berlin, Germany, 2007.
23. Ojima, I.; Okamura, K.; Saigo, H. Local state and sector theory in local quantum physics. *Lett. Math. Phys.* **2016**, *106*, 741–763. [CrossRef]
24. Stinespring, W.F. Positive functions on C*-algebras. *Proc. Am. Math. Soc.* **1955**, *6*, 211–216.
25. Arveson, W. Subalgebras of C*-algebras. *Acta Math.* **1969**, *123*, 141–224. [CrossRef]
26. Takesaki, M. *Theory of Operator Algebras I*; Springer: Berlin, Germany, 1979.
27. Paulsen, V. *Completely Bounded Maps and Operator Algebras*; Cambridge UP: Cambridge, UK, 2002.
28. Accardi, L.; Frigerio, L.; Lewis, J.T. Quantum stochastic processes. *Publ. Res. Inst. Math. Sci.* **1982**, *18*, 97–133. [CrossRef]
29. Belavkin, V.P. Reconstruction Theorem for Quantum Stochastic Processes. *Theoret. Math. Phys.* **1985**, *3*, 409–431.
30. Dixmier, J. *C*-Algebras*; North-Holland: Amsterdam, The Netherlands, 1977.
31. Bratteli, O.; Robinson, D.W. *Operator Algebras and Quantum Statistical Mechanics*, 2nd ed.; Springer: Berlin, Germany, 2002; Volume 1.
32. Ozawa, M. Uncertainty relations for noise and disturbance in generalized quantum measurements. *Ann. Phys. (N. Y.)* **2004**, *331*, 350–416. [CrossRef]

33. Ohtsu, M. History, current developments, and future directions of near-field optical science. *Opto-Electron. Adv.* **2020**, *3*, 190046. [CrossRef]
34. Arveson, W. *An Invitation to C*-Algebras*; Springer: New York, NY, USA, 2012.
35. Dixmier, J. *Von Neumann Algebras*; North-Holland: Amsterdam, The Nederlands, 1981.
36. Takesaki, M. *Theory of Operator Algebras II*; Springer: Berlin, Germany, 2003.
37. Takesaki, M. *Theory of Operator Algebras III*; Springer: Berlin, Germany, 2003.
38. Paschke, W.L. Inner product modules over B*-algebras. *Trans. Am. Math. Soc.* **1973**, *182*, 443–468. [CrossRef]
39. Rieffel, M.A. Morita equivalence for C*-algebras and W*-algebras. *J. Pure Appl. Algebra* **1974**, *5*, 51–96. [CrossRef]
40. Rieffel, M.A. Induced representations of C*-algebras. *Adv. Math.* **1974**, *13*, 176–257. [CrossRef]
41. Lance, E.C. *Hilbert C*-Modules: A Toolkit for Operator Algebraists*; Cambridge UP: Cambridge, UK, 1995.

42. Skeide, M. Generalized matrix C*-algebras and representations of Hilbert modules. *Math. Proc. Royal Irish Acad.* **2000**, *100A*, 11–38.
43. Skeide, M. *Hilbert Modules and Applications in Quantum Probability*; Habilitationsschrift: Cottbus, Germany, 2001.

Article

Category Algebras and States on Categories

Hayato Saigo

Nagahama Institute of Bio-Science and Technology, 1266 Tamura, Nagahama, Shiga 526-0829, Japan; h_saigoh@nagahama-i-bio.ac.jp

Abstract: The purpose of this paper is to build a new bridge between category theory and a generalized probability theory known as noncommutative probability or quantum probability, which was originated as a mathematical framework for quantum theory, in terms of states as linear functional defined on category algebras. We clarify that category algebras can be considered to be generalized matrix algebras and that the notions of state on category as linear functional defined on category algebra turns out to be a conceptual generalization of probability measures on sets as discrete categories. Moreover, by establishing a generalization of famous GNS (Gelfand–Naimark–Segal) construction, we obtain a representation of category algebras of †-categories on certain generalized Hilbert spaces which we call semi-Hilbert modules over rigs. The concepts and results in the present paper will be useful for the studies of symmetry/asymmetry since categories are generalized groupoids, which themselves are generalized groups.

Keywords: category; algebra; state; category algebra; state on category; noncommutative probability; quantum probability; GNS representation

Citation: Saigo, H. Category Algebras and States on Categories. *Symmetry* **2021**, *13*, 1172. https:// doi.org/10.3390/sym13071172

Academic Editors: Motoichi Ohtsu and Alexey Kanel-Belov

Received: 28 May 2021
Accepted: 26 June 2021
Published: 29 June 2021

Publisher's Note: MDPI stays neutral with regard to jurisdictional claims in published maps and institutional affiliations.

Copyright: © 2021 by the authors. Licensee MDPI, Basel, Switzerland. This article is an open access article distributed under the terms and conditions of the Creative Commons Attribution (CC BY) license (https:// creativecommons.org/licenses/by/ 4.0/).

1. Introduction

In the present paper, we study category algebras and states defined on arbitrary small categories to build a new bridge between category theory (see [1–4] and references therein, for example) and noncommutative probability or quantum probability (see [5–7] and references therein, for example), a generalized probability theory which was originated as a mathematical framework for quantum theory.

A category algebra is, in short, a convolution algebra of functions on a category. For example, on certain categories called finely finite category [8], which is a categorical generalization of locally finite poset, the convolution operation can be defined on the set of arbitrary functions and it becomes a unital algebra called incidence algebra. Many authors have studied the notions of Möbius inversion, which has been one of fundamental part of combinatorics since the pioneering work by Rota [9] on posets, in the context of incidence algebras on categories ([8,10–14], for example).

There is another approach to obtain the notion of category algebra. As is well known, a group algebra is defined as a convolution algebra consisting of finite linear combinations of elements. By generalization with replacing "elements" by "arrows", one can obtain another notion of category algebra (see [13], for example), which also includes monoid algebra (in particular polynomial algebras) and groupoid algebras as examples. Please note that for a category with infinite number of objects, the algebra is not unital.

The category algebras we focus on in the present paper are unital algebras defined on arbitrary small categories, which are slightly generalized versions of algebras studied under the name of the ring of an additive category [15]. These category algebras include the ones studied in [13] as subalgebras in general, and they coincide for categories with finite number of objects. Moreover, one of the algebras we study, called "backward finite category algebra", coincides with incidence algebras for combinatorially important cases originally studied in [9].

The purpose of this paper is to provide a new framework for the interplay between regions of mathematical sciences such as algebra, probability and physics, in terms of states as linear functional defined on category algebras. As is well known, quantum theory can be considered to be a noncommutative generalization of probability theory. At the beginning of quantum theory, matrix algebras played a crucial role (see [16] for example). In the present paper, we clarify that category algebras can be considered to be generalized matrix algebras and that the notions of states on categories as linear functionals defined on category algebras turns out to be a conceptual generalization of probability measures on sets as discrete categories (For the case of states on groupoid algebras over the complex field $\mathbb{C}$ it is already studied [17]).

Moreover, by establishing a generalization of famous GNS (Gelfand–Naimark–Segal) construction [18,19] (as for the studies in category theoretic context, see [20–22] for example), we obtain a representation of category algebras of †-categories on certain generalized Hilbert spaces (semi-Hilbert modules over rigs), which can be considered to be an extension of the result in [17] for groupoid algebras over $\mathbb{C}$. This construction will provide a basis for the interplay between category theory, noncommutative probability and other related regions such as operator algebras or quantum physics.

Notation 1. *In the present paper, categories are always supposed to be small (This assumption may be relaxed by applying some appropriate foundational framework). The set of all arrows in a category $\mathcal{C}$ is also denoted as $\mathcal{C}$. $|\mathcal{C}|$ denotes the set of all objects, which are identified with corresponding identity arrows, in $\mathcal{C}$. We also use the following notations:*

$$^{C'}\mathcal{C}_C := \mathcal{C}(C,C'), \quad \mathcal{C}_C := \sqcup_{C' \in |\mathcal{C}|} \mathcal{C}(C,C'), \quad ^{C'}\mathcal{C} := \sqcup_{C \in |\mathcal{C}|} \mathcal{C}(C,C'),$$

where $\mathcal{C}(C,C')$ denotes the set of all arrows from C to C'.

2. Category Algebras

We introduce the notion of rig, module over rig, and algebra over rig in order to study category algebras in sufficient generality for various future applications in noncommutative probability, quantum physics and other regions of mathematical sciences such as tropical mathematics.

Definition 1 (Rig). *A rig R is a set with two binary operations called addition and multiplication such that*

1. *R is a commutative monoid with respect to addition with the unit 0,*
2. *R is a monoid with respect to multiplication with the unit 1,*
3. *$r''(r' + r) = r''r' + r''r$, $(r'' + r')r = r''r + r'r$ holds for any $r, r', r'' \in R$ (Distributive law),*
4. *$0r = 0$, $r0 = 0$ holds for any $r \in R$ (Absorption law).*

Definition 2 (Module over Rig). *A commutative monoid M under addition with unit 0 together with a left action of R on M $(r,m) \mapsto rm$ is called a left module over R if the action satisfies the following:*

1. *$r(m' + m) = rm' + rm$, $(r' + r)m = r'm + rm$ for any $m, m' \in M$ and $r, r' \in R$.*
2. *$0m = 0$, $r0 = 0$ for any $m \in M$ and $r \in R$.*

Dually we can define the notion of right module over R.

Let M is left and right module over R. M is called R-bimodule if

$$r'(mr) = (r'm)r$$

holds for any $r, r' \in R$ and $m \in M$.

The left/right action above is called the scalar multiplication.

Definition 3 (Algebra over Rig). *A bimodule A over R is called an algebra over R if it is also a rig with respect to its own multiplication which is compatible with scalar multiplication, i.e.,*

$$(r'a')(ar) = r'(a'a)r, \ (a'r)a = a'(ra)$$

for any $a, a' \in A$ and $r, r' \in R$.

Usually the term "algebra" is defined on rings and algebras are supposed to have negative elements. In this paper, we use the term algebra to mean the module over rig with multiplication.

Definition 4 (Category Algebra). *Let $\mathcal{C}$ be a category and R be a rig. An R-valued function α defined on $\mathcal{C}$ is said to be of backward (resp. forward) finite propagation if for any object C there are at most finite number of arrows in the support of α whose codomain (resp. domain) is C. The module over R consisting of all R-valued functions of backward (resp. forward) finite propagation together with the multiplication defined by*

$$(\alpha'\alpha)(c'') = \sum_{\{(c',c)\mid c''=c'\circ c\}} \alpha'(c')\alpha(c), \ c, c', c'' \in \mathcal{C}$$

becomes an algebra over R with unit ϵ defined by

$$\epsilon(c) = \begin{cases} 1 & (c \in |\mathcal{C}|) \\ 0 & (otherwise) \end{cases},$$

and is called the category algebra of backward (resp. forward) finite propagation $R_0[\mathcal{C}]$ (resp. $^0R[\mathcal{C}]$) of $\mathcal{C}$ over R. The algebra $^0R_0[\mathcal{C}]$ over R defined as the intersection $R_0[\mathcal{C}] \cap {}^0R[\mathcal{C}]$ is called the category algebra of finite propagation of $\mathcal{C}$ over R.

Remark 1. $^0R_0[\mathcal{C}]$ *coincide with the algebra studied in [15] if R is a ring.*

In the present paper, we focus on the category algebras $R_0[\mathcal{C}], {}^0R[\mathcal{C}]$ and $^0R_0[\mathcal{C}]$ which are the same if $|\mathcal{C}|$ is finite, although other extensions or subalgebras of $^0R_0[\mathcal{C}]$ are also of interest (see Examples 4 and 7).

Notation 2. *In the following we use the term category algebra and the notation $R[\mathcal{C}]$ to denote either of category algebras $R_0[\mathcal{C}], {}^0R[\mathcal{C}]$ and $^0R_0[\mathcal{C}]$.*

Definition 5 (Indeterminates). *Let $R[\mathcal{C}]$ be a category algebra and $c \in \mathcal{C}$. The function $\chi^c \in R[\mathcal{C}]$ defined as*

$$\chi^c(c') = \begin{cases} 1 & (c' = c) \\ 0 & (otherwise) \end{cases}$$

is called the indeterminate (See Example 2) corresponding to c.

For indeterminates, it is easy to obtain the following:

Theorem 1 (Calculus of Indeterminates). *Let $c, c' \in \mathcal{C}$, $\chi^c, \chi^{c'}$ be the corresponding indeterminates and $r \in R$. Then*

$$\chi^{c'}\chi^c = \begin{cases} \chi^{c'\circ c} & (\mathrm{dom}(c') = \mathrm{cod}(c)) \\ 0 & (otherwise), \end{cases}$$

$$r\chi^c = \chi^c r.$$

51

In short, a category algebra $R[\mathcal{C}]$ is an algebra of functions on $\mathcal{C}$ equipped with the multiplication which reflects the compositionality structure of $\mathcal{C}$. By the identification of $c \in \mathcal{C} \mapsto \chi^c \in R[\mathcal{C}]$, categories are included in category algebras.

Let us establish the basic notions for calculation in category algebras:

Definition 6 (Column, Row, Entry). *Let $\alpha \in R[\mathcal{C}]$ and $C, C' \in |\mathcal{C}|$. The elements α_C, $^{C'}\alpha$, $^{C'}\alpha_C \in R[\mathcal{C}]$ defined as*

$$\alpha_C(c) = \begin{cases} \alpha(c) & (c \in \mathcal{C}_C) \\ 0 & (otherwise), \end{cases}$$

$$^{C'}\alpha(c) = \begin{cases} \alpha(c) & (c \in {}^{C'}\mathcal{C}) \\ 0 & (otherwise), \end{cases}$$

$$^{C'}\alpha_C(c) = \begin{cases} \alpha(c) & (c \in {}^{C'}\mathcal{C}_C) \\ 0 & (otherwise), \end{cases}$$

are called the C-column, C'-row and (C', C)-entry of α, respectively.

Please note that either of the data $\alpha_C (C \in |\mathcal{C}|)$, $^{C'}\alpha (C' \in |\mathcal{C}|)$ or $^{C'}\alpha_C (C, C' \in |\mathcal{C}|)$ determine α. Moreover, if $|\mathcal{C}|$ is finite,

$$\alpha = \sum_{C, C' \in |\mathcal{C}|} {}^{C'}\alpha_C.$$

By definition, the following theorem holds:

Theorem 2 (Polynomial Expression). *For any $\alpha \in R[\mathcal{C}]$*

$$^{C'}\alpha_C = \sum_{c \in {}^{C'}\mathcal{C}_C} \alpha(c) \chi^c = \sum_{c \in {}^{C'}\mathcal{C}_C} \chi^c \alpha(c).$$

If $|\mathcal{C}|$ is finite,

$$\alpha = \sum_{c \in \mathcal{C}} \alpha(c) \chi^c = \sum_{c \in \mathcal{C}} \chi^c \alpha(c).$$

The formulae above clarify that category algebras are generalized polynomial algebra (see Example 2). On the other hand, the following theorem, which shows that category algebras are generalized matrix algebras (see Example 7), also follows by definition:

Theorem 3 (Matrix Calculus). *For any $\alpha, \alpha' \in R[\mathcal{C}]$, $C, C' \in |\mathcal{C}|$ and $r \in R$, the followings hold:*

$$(\alpha' + \alpha)_C = \alpha'_C + \alpha_C, \quad {}^{C'}(\alpha' + \alpha) = {}^{C'}\alpha' + {}^{C'}\alpha,$$

$$^{C'}(\alpha' + \alpha)_C = {}^{C'}\alpha'_C + {}^{C'}\alpha_C$$

$$(r'\alpha r)_C = r' \alpha_C r, \quad {}^{C'}(r'\alpha r) = r' {}^{C'}\alpha r, \quad {}^{C'}(r'\alpha r)_C = r' {}^{C'}\alpha_C r$$

$$(\alpha'\alpha)_C = \alpha' \alpha_C = \sum_{C'' \in |\mathcal{C}|} \alpha'_{C''} {}^{C''}\alpha_C$$

$$^{C'}(\alpha'\alpha) = {}^{C'}\alpha' \alpha = \sum_{C'' \in |\mathcal{C}|} {}^{C'}\alpha'_{C''} {}^{C''}\alpha$$

$$^{C'}(\alpha'\alpha)_C = {}^{C'}\alpha' \alpha_C = \sum_{C'' \in |\mathcal{C}|} {}^{C'}\alpha'_{C''} {}^{C''}\alpha_C.$$

The theorem above implies the following:

Theorem 4. $\alpha \in R[\mathcal{C}]$ *is determined by its action on columns ϵ_C/ rows $^{C'}\epsilon$ of the unit ϵ for all $C, C' \in |\mathcal{C}|$.*

Proof. Let $\alpha \in R[\mathcal{C}]$ and ϵ be the unit of $R[\mathcal{C}]$. Then by definition

$$\alpha = \alpha\epsilon, \; \alpha = \epsilon\alpha$$

holds and it implies $\alpha_C = \alpha\epsilon_C$, $^{C'}\alpha = {}^{C'}\epsilon\,\alpha$, which determines α. □

Remark 2. *It is convenient to make use of a kind of "Einstein convention" in physics: Double appearance of object indices which do not appear elsewhere means the sum over all objects in the category. For instance,*

$$^{C'}(\alpha'\alpha)_C = {}^{C'}\alpha'_{C''}\,{}^{C''}\alpha_C$$

means

$$^{C'}(\alpha'\alpha)_C = \sum_{C'' \in |\mathcal{C}|} {}^{C'}\alpha'_{C''}\,{}^{C''}\alpha_C.$$

The notation is quite useful especially for category algebra $R[\mathcal{C}]$ where $|\mathcal{C}|$ is finite. In that case it is easy to show the decomposition of unit:

$$\epsilon = \epsilon_C\,{}^C\epsilon.$$

As a corollary,

$$\alpha'\alpha = \alpha'\epsilon\alpha = \alpha'\epsilon_C\,{}^C\epsilon\alpha = \alpha'_C\,{}^C\alpha,$$

holds, which means that the multiplication can be interpreted as inner product of columns and rows. Hence, you can insert $_C{}^C$ in formulae when C does not appear elsewhere.

3. Example of Category Algebras

Let us see some important examples of category algebras.

Example 1 (Function Algebra). *Let $\mathcal{C}$ be a set as discrete category, i.e., a category whose arrows are all identities. Then $R[\mathcal{C}]$ is nothing but the R-valued function algebra on $|\mathcal{C}|$, where the operations are defined pointwise.*

When the rig R is commutative such as $R = \mathbb{C}$, the function algebra is also commutative. On the other hand, a category algebra is in general noncommutative even if the rig is commutative. In this sense, category algebras can be considered to be generalized (noncommutative) function algebras.

As we have noted, category algebras can also be considered to be generalized polynomial algebras:

Example 2 (Monoid Algebra). *Let $\mathcal{C}$ be a monoid, i.e., a category with only one object. Then $R[\mathcal{C}]$ is the monoid algebra of $\mathcal{C}$. For example, in the case of $\mathcal{C} = \mathbb{N}$ as additive monoid, $R[\mathcal{C}]$ is the polynomial algebra over R.*

Since a monoid $\mathcal{C}$ has only one object, any $\alpha \in R[\mathcal{C}]$ can be presented as,

$$\alpha = \sum_{c \in \mathcal{C}} \alpha(c)\chi^c$$

by Theorem 2 which make it clear that $R[\mathcal{C}]$ is a generalized polynomial algebra.

As special cases of Example 2, we have group algebras.

Example 3 (Group Algebra). *Let $\mathcal{C}$ be a group, i.e., a monoid whose arrows are all invertible. Then $R[\mathcal{C}]$ coincides with the group algebra of $\mathcal{C}$. For example, in the case of $\mathcal{C} = \mathbb{Z}$, $R[\mathcal{C}]$ is the Laurent polynomial algebra over R.*

By another generalization of Example 3 other than Example 2, we have groupoid algebras.

Example 4 (Groupoid Algebra). *Let $\mathcal{C}$ be a groupoid, i.e., a category whose arrows are all invertible. When $|\mathcal{C}|$ is finite, $R[\mathcal{C}]$ is nothing but the groupoid algebra of $|\mathcal{C}|$. Otherwise $R[\mathcal{C}]$ is a unital extension of the groupoid algebra in conventional sense which is nonunital. $R[\mathcal{C}]$ is quite useful to treat certain algebras which appeared in quantum physics [17]. (See Example 5 also.)*

As special cases of the Example 4 we have matrix algebras:

Example 5 (Matrix Algebra). *Let $\mathcal{C}$ be an indiscrete category, i.e., a category such that for every pair of objects C, C' there is exactly one arrow from C to C'. Denote the cardinal of $|\mathcal{C}|$ is n. Then $R[\mathcal{C}]$ is isomorphic to the matrix algebra $M_n(R)$.*

Example 5 above shows that matrix algebras are category algebras. Conversely, any category algebra can be considered to be generalized matrix algebra (see Theorem 3). This point of view is also useful to study quivers [23], i.e., directed graphs with multiple edges and loops.

Example 6 (Path Algebra). *Let $\mathcal{C}$ be the free category of a quiver Q. $R[\mathcal{C}]$ coincides with the notion of path algebra when the quiver Q has finite number of vertices. Otherwise, the former includes the latter as a subalgebra.*

Another important origin of the notion of category algebra is that of incidence algebra ([8,10–14], for example) originally studied on posets [9].

Example 7 (Incidence Algebra). *Let $\mathcal{C}$ be a finely finite category [8], i.e., a category such that for any $c \in \mathcal{C}$ there exist finite number of pairs of arrows $c', c'' \in \mathcal{C}$ satisfying $c = c' \circ c''$. Then $R^{\mathcal{C}}$, the set of all functions from $\mathcal{C}$ to R, becomes a unital algebra and called the incidence algebra of $\mathcal{C}$ over R.*

Let $\mathcal{C}$ be a category such that for any $C \in \mathcal{C}$ there exist at most finitely many arrows whose codomain is C. Then $R_0[\mathcal{C}]$ coincides with the incidence algebra on $\mathcal{C}$. (One of the most classical examples is the poset consisting of all positive integers ordered by divisibility). For the category satisfying the condition above, $R[\mathcal{C}]$ includes the zeta function ζ defined as

$$\zeta(c) = 1$$

for all c. The multiplicative inverse of ζ is denoted as μ and called Möbius function. The relation $\mu\zeta = \zeta\mu = \epsilon$ is a generalization of the famous Möbius inversion formula, which has been considered to be the foundation of combinatorial theory since one of the most important papers in modern combinatorics [9].

4. States on Categories

We will introduce the notion of states on categories to provide a foundation for stochastic theories on categories. As we will see, we can construct noncommutative probability space, a generalized notion of measure theoretic probability space based on category algebras. The key insight is that what we need to establish statistical law is the expectation functional, which is the functional which maps each random variable (or "observable" in the quantum physical context) to its expectation value. Considering a functional on $R[\mathcal{C}]$ as expectation functional, we can interpret $R[\mathcal{C}]$ as an algebra of noncommutative random variables, such as observables of quanta.

Definition 7 (Linear Functional). *Let A be an algebra over a rig R. An R-valued linear function on A, i.e., a function preserving addition and scalar multiplication, is called a linear functional on*

A. A linear functional on A is said to be unital if $\varphi(\epsilon) = 1$ where ϵ and 1 denote the multiplicative unit in A and R, respectively.

Definition 8 (Linear Functional on Category). *Let R be a rig and $\mathcal{C}$ be a category. A (unital) linear functional on $R[\mathcal{C}]$ is said to be an R-valued (unital) linear functional on the category $\mathcal{C}$.*

Although the main theme here is stochastic theory making use of positivity structure defined later, linear functionals on category algebras are used not only in the context with positivity. A very interesting example is "umbral calculus" [24], an interesting tool in combinatorics, which can be interpreted as the theory of linear functionals on certain monoid algebras. Hence, studying the linear functionals on a category will lead to a generalization of umbral calculus.

Given a linear functional on a category, we obtain a function on the set of arrows. For categories with a finite number of objects, we can characterize the former in terms of the latter:

Theorem 5 (Linear Function and Function). *Let φ be a R-valued linear functional on $\mathcal{C}$. Then the function $\hat{\varphi}$ defined as*

$$\hat{\varphi}(c) = \varphi(\chi^c)$$

becomes a $Z(R)$-valued function on $\mathcal{C}$, i.e., an R-valued function satisfying $r\hat{\varphi}(c) = \hat{\varphi}(c)r$ for any $c \in \mathcal{C}$ and $r \in R$. Conversely, when $|\mathcal{C}|$ is finite, any $Z(R)$-valued function ϕ on $\mathcal{C}$ gives R-valued linear functional $\check{\phi}$ defined as

$$\check{\phi}(\alpha) = \sum_{c \in \mathcal{C}} \alpha(c)\phi(c) = \sum_{c \in \mathcal{C}} \phi(c)\alpha(c)$$

and the correspondence is bijective.

Proof. Let φ be a R-valued linear functional. Since $r\chi^c = \chi^c r$ for any $r \in R$ and $c \in \mathcal{C}$, we have $r\varphi(\chi^c) = \varphi(\chi^c)r$ which means $r\hat{\varphi}(c) = \hat{\varphi}(c)r$. The converse direction and bijectivity directly follows from definitions and Theorem 2. □

As a corollary we also have the following:

Theorem 6 (Unital Linear Functional and Normalized Function). *Let $\mathcal{C}$ be a category such that $|\mathcal{C}|$ is finite. Then there is one to one correspondence between R-valued unital linear functionals φ and normalized $Z(R)$-valued functions ϕ on $\mathcal{C}$, i.e., $Z(R)$-valued functions ϕ satisfying*

$$\sum_{C \in |\mathcal{C}|} \phi(C) = 1.$$

(Please note that we identify objects and identity arrows.)

To define the notion of state as generalized probability measure which can be applied in noncommutative contexts such as stochastic theory on category algebras, we need the notions of involution and positivity structure.

Definition 9 (Involution on Category). *Let $\mathcal{C}$ be a category. A covariant/contravariant endofunctor $(\cdot)^{\dagger}$ on $\mathcal{C}$ is said to be a covariant/contravariant involution on $\mathcal{C}$ when $(\cdot)^{\dagger} \circ (\cdot)^{\dagger}$ is equal to the identity functor on $\mathcal{C}$. A category with contravariant involution which is identity on objects is called a †-category.*

Remark 3. *For the studies on involutive categories, which are categories with involution satisfying certain conditions, see [20,22] for example.*

Definition 10 (Involution on Rig). *Let R be a rig. An operation $(\cdot)^*$ on R preserving addition and covariant/contravariant with respect to multiplication is said to be a covariant/contravariant involution on R when $(\cdot)^* \circ (\cdot)^*$ is equal to the identity function on R. A rig with contravariant involution is called a *-rig.*

Definition 11 (Involution on Algebra). *Let A be an algebra over a rig R with a covariant (resp. contravariant) involution $\overline{(\cdot)}$. A covariant (resp. contravariant) involution $(\cdot)^*$ on A as a rig is said to be a covariant (resp. contravariant) involution on A as an algebra over R if it is compatible with scalar multiplication, i.e.,*

$$(r'ar)^* = \overline{r'}a^*\overline{r} \text{ (covariant case)}, \quad (r'ar)^* = \overline{r}a^*\overline{r'} \text{ (contravariant case)}.$$

*An algebra A over a *-rig R with contravariant involution is called a *-algebra over R.*

Theorem 7 (Category Algebra as Algebra with Involution). *Let $\mathcal{C}$ be a category with a covariant (resp. contravariant) involution $(\cdot)^\dagger$ and R be a rig with a covariant (resp. contravariant) involution $\overline{(\cdot)}$. Then the category algebra $^0R_0[\mathcal{C}]$ becomes an algebra with covariant involution (resp. *-algebra) over R.*

Proof. The operation $(\cdot)^*$ defined as $\alpha^*(c) = \overline{\alpha(c^\dagger)}$ becomes a covariant (resp. contravariant) involution on $^0R_0[\mathcal{C}]$. For the contravariant case,

$$(\alpha\beta)^*(c) = \overline{\alpha\beta(c^\dagger)} = \overline{\sum_{c^\dagger=c'\circ c''} \alpha(c')\beta(c'')} = \sum_{c^\dagger=c'\circ c''} \overline{\alpha(c')\beta(c'')} = \sum_{c^\dagger=c'\circ c''} \overline{\beta(c'')}\, \overline{\alpha(c')}$$

which is equal to $\sum_{c=c''^\dagger \circ c'^\dagger} \overline{\beta(c'')}\, \overline{\alpha(c')}$. By changing the labels of arrows, it can be rewritten as

$$\sum_{c=c''^\dagger \circ c'^\dagger} \overline{\beta(c'')}\, \overline{\alpha(c')} = \sum_{c=c'\circ c''} \overline{\beta(c'^\dagger)}\, \overline{\alpha(c''^\dagger)} = \sum_{c=c'\circ c''} \beta^*(c')\alpha^*(c'') = \beta^*\alpha^*(c).$$

The proof for the covariant case is similar and more straightforward. □

Every category/rig has a trivial involution (identity). Thus, any category algebra $^0R_0[\mathcal{C}]$ can be considered to be algebra with involution. In physics, especially quantum theory, the *-algebra $^0R_0[\mathcal{C}]$ where $\mathcal{C}$ is a groupoid as †-category with inversion as involution and $R = \mathbb{C}$ as *-rig with complex conjugate as involution. (For the importance of groupoid algebra in physics, see [17] and references therein, for example).

Based on the involutive structure we can define the positivity structure on algebras:

Definition 12 (Positivity). *A pair of rigs with involution (R, R_+) is called a positivity structure on R if R_+ is a subring such that $r, s \in R_+$ and $r + s = 0$ implies $r = s = 0$, and that $a^*a \in R_+$ for any $a \in R$.*

The most typical examples are $(\mathbb{C}, \mathbb{R}_{\geq 0})$, $(\mathbb{R}, \mathbb{R}_{\geq 0})$, and $(\mathbb{R}_{\geq 0}, \mathbb{R}_{\geq 0})$. Another interesting example is the tropical algebraic one $(\mathbb{R} \cup \{\infty\}, \mathbb{R} \cup \{\infty\})$ where $\mathbb{R} \cup \{\infty\}$ is considered to be a rig with respect to min and $+$.

Definition 13 (State). *Let R be a rig with involution and (R, R_+) be a positivity structure on R. A state φ on an algebra A with involution over R with respect to (R, R_+) is a unital linear functional $\varphi : A \longrightarrow R$ which satisfies $\varphi(a^*a) \in R_+$ and $\varphi(a^*) = \overline{\varphi(a)}$ for any $a \in R$, where $(\cdot)^*$ and $\overline{(\cdot)}$ denotes the involution on A and R, respectively.*

Remark 4. *The last condition $\varphi(a^*) = \overline{\varphi(a)}$ follows from other conditions if $R = \mathbb{C}$.*

Definition 14 (Noncommutative Probability Space). *A pair (A, φ) consisting of an algebra A with involution over a rig R with involution and an R-valued state φ is called a noncommutative probability space.*

There are many studies on noncommutative probability spaces where the algebra A is a $*$-algebra over $\mathbb{C}$. As is well known, the notion of noncommutative probability space essentially includes the one of probability spaces in conventional sense, which corresponds to the cases that algebras A are commutative $*$-algebras (with certain topological structure). On the other hand, when the algebras are noncommutative, noncommutative probability spaces provide many examples which cannot be reduced to conventional probability spaces, such as models for quantum systems.

Definition 15 (State on Category). *Let R be a rig with involution and (R, R_+) be a positivity structure on R. A state on the category algebra $^0R_0[\mathcal{C}]$ over R with respect to (R, R_+) is said to be a state on a category $\mathcal{C}$ with respect to (R, R_+).*

As category algebras are in general noncommutative, states on categories provide many concrete noncommutative probability spaces generalizing such simplest examples as interacting Fock spaces [25] which are generalized harmonic oscillators, where the categories are indiscrete categories corresponding to certain graphs.

The notion of state can be characterized for the categories with finite number of objects as follows:

Theorem 8 (State and Normalized Positive Semidefinite Function). *Let $\mathcal{C}$ be a category such that $|\mathcal{C}|$ is finite. Then there is one to one correspondence between states φ with respect to (R, R_+) and normalized positive semidefinite $Z(R)$-valued functions ϕ with respect to (R, R_+), i.e., normalized functions such that*

$$\sum_{\{(c,c')|\mathrm{dom}((c')^\dagger)=\mathrm{cod}(c)\}} \overline{\xi(c')} \phi((c')^\dagger \circ c) \xi(c)$$

is in R_+ for any function ξ on $\mathcal{C}$ with finite support and that $\phi(c^\dagger) = \overline{\phi(c)}$, where $(\cdot)^*$ and $\overline{(\cdot)}$ denotes the involution on A and R, respectively.

Proof. Please note that a function ξ on $\mathcal{C}$ with finite support can be considered to be an element in $^0R_0[\mathcal{C}]$ and vice versa when $|\mathcal{C}|$ is finite. Then the theorem follows from the identity

$$\xi^*\xi = (\sum_{c' \in \mathcal{C}} \overline{\xi((c')^\dagger)} \chi^{c'})(\sum_{c \in \mathcal{C}} \chi^c \xi(c))$$
$$= (\sum_{c' \in \mathcal{C}} \overline{\xi(c')} \chi^{(c')^\dagger})(\sum_{c \in \mathcal{C}} \chi^c \xi(c))$$
$$= \sum_{\{(c,c')|\mathrm{dom}((c')^\dagger)=\mathrm{cod}(c)\}} \overline{\xi(c')} \chi^{(c')^\dagger \circ c} \xi(c).$$

and the condition corresponding to $\varphi(\xi^*) = \overline{\varphi(\xi)}$. □

The theorem above is a generalization of the result stated in Section 2.2.2 in [17] for groupoid algebras over $\mathbb{C}$. For the case of discrete category, the notion coincides with the notion of probability measure on objects (identity arrows). Hence, the notion of state on category can be considered to be noncommutative generalization of probability measure which is associated with the transition from set as discrete category (0-category) to general category (1-category).

Given a state on a †-category, we can construct a kind of GNS (Gelfand–Naimark–Segal) representation [18,19] (as for generalized constructions, see [20–22,26,27] for example) in a semi-Hilbert module defined below, a generalization of Hilbert space:

Definition 16 (Semi-Hilbert Module over Rig). *Let R be a rig with involution $\overline{(\cdot)}$. A right module E over R equipped with a positive semidefinite sesquilinear form, i.e., a function $\langle \cdot | \cdot \rangle : E \times E \longrightarrow R$ satisfying*

$$\langle v'' | v'r' + vr \rangle = \langle v'' | v' \rangle r' + \langle v'' | v \rangle r$$

$$\langle v' | v \rangle = \overline{\langle v | v' \rangle}$$

$$\langle v | v \rangle \in R_+$$

for any $v, v', v'' \in E$ and $r, r' \in R$ is called a semi-Hilbert module over R.

When a semi-Hilbert module over E is also a left module over R, the set $\mathrm{End}(E)$ consisting of module endomorphisms over R on E becomes an algebra over R: The bimodule structure is given by $(r'Tr)(v) = r'T(rv)$, where $T \in \mathrm{End}(E)$ and $r, r' \in R$.

Theorem 9 (Generalized GNS Representation). *Let A be an *-algebra over a rig R with involution $(\cdot)^*$. For any state φ on A with respect to (R, R_+), there exist a semi-Hilbert module E^φ over R which is also a left R module equipped with a positive semidefinite sesquilibear form $\langle \cdot | \cdot \rangle^\varphi$, an element $e^\varphi \in E^\varphi$ such that $\langle e^\varphi | e^\varphi \rangle^\varphi = 1$, and a homomorphism $\pi^\varphi : A \longrightarrow \mathrm{End}(E^\varphi)$ between algebras over R such that*

$$\varphi(\alpha) = \langle e^\varphi | \pi^\varphi(\alpha) e^\varphi \rangle^\varphi$$

and

$$\langle v' | \pi^\varphi(\alpha) v \rangle^\varphi = \langle \pi^\varphi(\alpha^*) v' | v \rangle^\varphi$$

hold for any $\alpha \in A$ and $v, v' \in E^\varphi$.

Proof. Let E^φ be the algebra A itself as a module over R equipped with $\langle \cdot | \cdot \rangle^\varphi$ defined by $\langle \alpha' | \alpha \rangle^\varphi = \varphi((\alpha')^* \alpha)$. It is easy to show that $\langle \cdot | \cdot \rangle^\varphi$ is a positive semidefinite sesquilinear form and satisfies $\varphi(\alpha) = \langle e^\varphi | \pi^\varphi(\alpha) e^\varphi \rangle^\varphi$, and $\langle v' | \pi^\varphi(\alpha) v \rangle^\varphi = \langle \pi^\varphi(\alpha^*) v' | v \rangle^\varphi$ where π^φ denotes the homomorphism $\pi^\varphi : A \longrightarrow \mathrm{End}(E^\varphi)$ defined by $\pi^\varphi(\alpha) = \alpha(\cdot)$, the left multiplication by α, and e^φ denotes the unit ϵ of A as an element of E^φ. □

Remark 5. *When the rig R is actually a ring, we can construct *-representation of A as follows (This idea is due to Malte Gerhold): We call an endomorphism T on a semi-Hilbert module E adjointable if there is a (not necessarily unique) adjoint, i.e., an endomorphism T^* with $\langle v' | Tv \rangle = \langle T^*v' | v \rangle$ for any $v, v' \in E$. When E is also a left R module, the set of adjointable endomorphisms $\mathrm{Adj}(E)$ becomes a subalgebra over R of $\mathrm{End}(E)$. The set $\mathrm{Nul}(E) = \{T | \langle v' | Tv \rangle = 0, \forall v, v' \in E\}$ becomes a two-sided ideal in $\mathrm{Adj}(E)$. When R is a ring, the quotient of $\mathrm{Adj}(E)$ by $\mathrm{Nul}(E)$ becomes a *-algebra and we can construct the *-representation of A, since we can show that the two "adjoints" of an endomorphism coincide up to some element of $\mathrm{Nul}(E)$ by taking subtraction of endomophisms and can define the "taking adjoint" as involution operation in the quotient. In more general cases (especially for the rigs such that the cancellation law for addition does not hold), the GNS construction might not necessarily lead to a *-representations by adjointable endomorphisms.*

When A is a *-algebra over $\mathbb{C}$, we can prove Cauchy-Schwarz inequality for semi-Hilbert space. Then the set $N^\varphi = \{\alpha \in A | \langle \alpha | \alpha \rangle^\varphi = 0\}$ becomes a subspace of A. By taking the quotient $E^\varphi = A/N^\varphi$, which becomes a pre-Hilbert space, we obtain the following "GNS (Gelfand–Naimark–Segal)" representation of A.

Theorem 10 (GNS Representation). *Let A be a *-algebra over $\mathbb{C}$. For any state φ on A with respect to $(\mathbb{C}, \mathbb{R}_{\geq 0})$, there exist a pre-Hilbert space E^φ over $\mathbb{C}$ equipped with an inner product*

$\langle \cdot | \cdot \rangle^\varphi$, an element $e^\varphi \in E^\varphi$ such that $\langle e^\varphi | e^\varphi \rangle^\varphi = 1$, and a homomorphism $\pi^\varphi : A \longrightarrow \text{End}(E^\varphi)$ between algebras over R such that

$$\varphi(\alpha) = \langle e^\varphi | \pi^\varphi(\alpha) e^\varphi \rangle^\varphi$$

and

$$\langle v' | \pi^\varphi(\alpha) v \rangle^\varphi = \langle \pi^\varphi(\alpha^*) v' | v \rangle^\varphi$$

hold for any $\alpha \in A$ and $v, v' \in E^\varphi$.

By taking completion we have usual Hilbert space formulation popular in the context of quantum mechanics.

Remark 6. *If the state φ is fixed as "standard" one, such as "vacuum", the Dirac bracket notation becomes valid if we interpret as follows:*
$|\alpha\rangle = \pi^\varphi(\alpha)$, $\langle \alpha | = \varphi(\alpha^*(\cdot))$, $\langle \alpha' | \alpha \rangle = \varphi(a^*b)$, $|0\rangle = |\epsilon\rangle$ *(vacuum).*

As corollaries of theorems above, we have the following results, which are extensions of the Theorem 1 in [17]. :

Theorem 11 (Generalized GNS Representation of †-Category). *Let $\mathcal{C}$ be a †-category and R be a $*$-rig. For any φ be a state on $\mathcal{C}$ with respect to (R, R_+), there exist a semi-Hilbert module E^φ over R which is also a left R module equipped with a sesquilinear form $\langle \cdot | \cdot \rangle^\varphi$, an element $e^\varphi \in E^\varphi$ such that $\langle e^\varphi | e^\varphi \rangle^\varphi = 1$, and a homomorphism $\pi^\varphi : {}^0R_0[\mathcal{C}] \longrightarrow \text{End}(E^\varphi)$ between algebras over R such that*

$$\varphi(\alpha) = \langle e^\varphi | \pi^\varphi(\alpha) e^\varphi \rangle^\varphi$$

and

$$\langle v' | \pi^\varphi(\alpha) v \rangle^\varphi = \langle \pi^\varphi(\alpha^*) v' | v \rangle^\varphi$$

hold for any $\alpha \in A$ and $v, v' \in E^\varphi$.

Theorem 12 (GNS Representation of †-Category). *Let $\mathcal{C}$ be a †-category. For any φ be a state on $\mathcal{C}$ with respect to $(\mathbb{C}, \mathbb{R}_{\geq 0})$, there exist a pre-Hilbert space E^φ over $\mathbb{C}$ equipped with an inner product $\langle \cdot | \cdot \rangle^\varphi$, an element $e^\varphi \in E^\varphi$ such that $\langle e^\varphi | e^\varphi \rangle^\varphi = 1$, and a homomorphism $\pi^\varphi : {}^0R_0[\mathcal{C}] \longrightarrow \text{End}(E^\varphi)$ between algebras over $\mathbb{C}$ such that*

$$\varphi(\alpha) = \langle e^\varphi | \pi^\varphi(\alpha) e^\varphi \rangle^\varphi$$

and

$$\langle v' | \pi^\varphi(\alpha) v \rangle^\varphi = \langle \pi^\varphi(\alpha^*) v' | v \rangle^\varphi$$

hold for any $\alpha \in A$ and $v, v' \in E^\varphi$.

Funding: This work was partially supported by Research Origin for Dressed Photon, JSPS KAKENHI (grant number 19K03608 and 20H00001) and JST CREST (JPMJCR17N2).

Institutional Review Board Statement: Not applicable.

Informed Consent Statement: Not applicable.

Acknowledgments: The author is grateful to Hiroshi Ando, Soichiro Fujii and Misa Saigo for fruitful discussions and comments.

Conflicts of Interest: The author declares no conflict of interest.

References

1. Eilenberg, S.; MacLane, S. General Theory of Natural Equivalences. *Trans. Am. Math. Soc.* **1945**, *58*, 231–294. [CrossRef]
2. Mac Lane, S. *Categories for the Working Mathematician*, 2nd ed.; Springer: New York, NY, USA, 1998.

3. Awodey, S. *Category Theory*, 2nd ed.; Oxford University Press: New York, NY, USA, 2010.
4. Leinster, T. *Basic Category Theory*; Cambridge University Press: Cambridge, UK, 2014.
5. Accardi, L. Quantum Probability: An Historical Survey. *Contemp. Math.* **2000**, *261*, 145–159.
6. Hora, A.; Obata, N. *Quantum Probability and Spectral Analysis of Graphs*; Springer: Berlin/Heidelberg, Germany, 2007.
7. Biane, P.; Guionnet, A.; Voiculescu, D.-V. *Noncommutative Probability and Random Matices at Saint-Flour*; Springer: Berlin/Heidelberg, Germany, 2012.
8. Leinster, T. Notions of Möbius inversion. *Bull. Belg. Math. Soc. Simon Stevin* **2012**, *19*, 909–933. [CrossRef]
9. Rota, G.-C. On the foundations of combinatorial theory I: theory of Möbius functions. *Z. Wahrscheinlichkeitstheorie Verw. Gebiete* **1964**, *2*, 340–368. [CrossRef]
10. Cartier, P.; Foata, D. *Problèmes Combinatoires de Commutation et Réarrangements*; No. 85 in Springer Lecture Notes in Mathematics; Springer: Berlin New York, NY, USA, 1969.
11. Leroux, P. Les catégories des Möbius. *Cah. Topol. Géom. Différ. Catégor.* **1975**, *16*, 280–282.
12. Content, M.; Lemay, F.; Leroux, P. Catégories de Möbius et fonctorialités: un cadre général pour l'inversion de Möbius. *J. Combin. Theory Ser.* **1980**, *10*, 142–149. [CrossRef]
13. Haigh, J. On the Möbius algebra and the Grothendieck ring of a finite category. *J. Lond. Math. Soc.* **1980**, *21*, 81–92. [CrossRef]
14. Lawvere, F.W.; Mehni, M. The Hopf algebra of Möbius intervals. *Theory Appl. Categ.* **2010**, *24*, 221–265.
15. Mitchel, B. Rings with several objects. *Adv. Math.* **1972**, *8*, 1–161. [CrossRef]
16. Born, M. *Natural Philosophy of Cause and Chance*; Clarendon: Oxford, UK, 1949.
17. Ciaglia, F.M.; Ibort, A.; Marmo, G. Schwinger's Picture of Quantum Mechanics III: The statistical Interpretation. *Int. J. Geom. Meth. Modern Phys.* **2019**, *16*, 1950165. [CrossRef]
18. Gelfand, I.; Neumark, M. On the imbedding of normed rings into the ring of operators in Hilbert space. *Mat. Sb.* **1943**, *12*, 187-217.
19. Segal, I. Irreducible representations of operator algebras. *Bull. Am. Math. Soc.* **1947**, *53*, 73–88. [CrossRef]
20. Jacobs, B. Involutive Categories and Monoids, with a GNS-Correspondence. *Found. Phys.* **2012**, *42*, 874–895. [CrossRef]
21. Parzygnat, A.J. From Observables and States to Hilbert Space and Back: A 2-Categorical Adjunction. *Appl. Categ. Struct.* **2018**, *26*, 1123–1157. [CrossRef]
22. Yau, D. *Involutive Category Theory*; No. 2279 in Springer Lecture Notes in Mathematics; Springer: Cham, Switzerland, 2020.
23. Gabriel, P. Unzerlegbare Darstellungen. I. *Manuscripta Math.* **1972**, *6*, 71–103. [CrossRef]
24. Roman, S.; Rota, G.-C. The umbral calculus. *Adv. Math.* **1978**, *27*, 95–188. [CrossRef]
25. Accardi, L.; Bożejko, M. Interacting Fock spaces and gaussianization of probability measures. *Infin. Dimens. Anal. Quantum Probab. Relat. Top.* **1998**, *1*, 663–670. [CrossRef]
26. Steinspring, W.F. Positive functions on C*-algebras. *Proc. Amer. Math. Sci.* **1955**, *6*, 211–216.
27. Paschke, W.L. Inner product modules over B* -algebras. *Trans. Amer. Math. Soc.* **1973**, *182*, 443–468. [CrossRef]

Article

Categorical Nonstandard Analysis

Hayato Saigo [1,*] and Juzo Nohmi [2]

[1] Nagahama Institute of Bio-Science and Technology, Shiga 526-0829, Japan
[2] Independent Reseacher, Tokyo 103-0008, Japan; xyzzy413@gmail.com
* Correspondence: h_saigoh@nagahama-i-bio.ac.jp

Abstract: In the present paper, we propose a new axiomatic approach to nonstandard analysis and its application to the general theory of spatial structures in terms of category theory. Our framework is based on the idea of internal set theory, while we make use of an endofunctor $\mathcal{U}$ on a topos of sets $\mathcal{S}$ together with a natural transformation v, instead of the terms as "standard", "internal", or "external". Moreover, we propose a general notion of a space called $\mathcal{U}$-space, and the category $\mathcal{U}Space$ whose objects are $\mathcal{U}$-spaces and morphisms are functions called $\mathcal{U}$-spatial morphisms. The category $\mathcal{U}Space$, which is shown to be Cartesian closed, gives a unified viewpoint toward topological and coarse geometric structure. It will also be useful to further study symmetries/asymmetries of the systems with infinite degrees of freedom, such as quantum fields.

Keywords: category theory; nonstandard analysis; coarse geometry

1. Introduction

Nonstandard analysis and category theory are two of the great inventions in foundation (or organization) of mathematics. Both of these have provided productive viewpoints to organize many kinds of topics in mathematics or related fields [1,2]. On the other hand, a unification of the two theories is yet to be developed, although there are some pioneering works, such as [3].

In the present paper, we propose a new axiomatic framework for nonstandard analysis in terms of category theory. Our framework is based on the idea of internal set theory [4], while we make use of an endofunctor $\mathcal{U}$ on a topos of sets $\mathcal{S}$ together with a natural transformation v, instead of the terms as "standard", "internal", or "external".

The triple $(\mathcal{S}, \mathcal{U}, v)$ is supposed to satisfy two axioms. The first axiom ("elementarity axiom") introduced in Section 2 states that the endofunctor $\mathcal{U}$ should preserve all finite limits and finite coproducts. Then, the endofunctor $\mathcal{U}$ is viewed as some kind of extension of functions preserving all elementary logical properties. In Section 3, we introduce another axiom ("idealization axiom"), which is the translation of "the principle of idealization" in internal set theory and proves the appearance of useful entities, such as infinitesimals or relations, such as "infinitely close", in the spirit of Nelson's approach to nonstandard analysis [4].

Section 4 is devoted to provide a few examples of applications on topology (on metric spaces, for simplicity). Although the characterizations of continuous maps or uniform continuous maps in terms of nonstandard analysis are well known, we prove them from our framework for the reader's convenience. In Section 5, we characterize the notion of a bornologous map, which is a fundamental notion in coarse geometry [5].

In Section 6, we introduce the notion of $\mathcal{U}$-space and $\mathcal{U}$-morphism, which are the generalizations of examples in the previous two sections. We introduce the category $\mathcal{U}Space$ consisting of $\mathcal{U}$-spaces and $\mathcal{U}$-morphisms, which is shown to be Cartesian closed. This will give a unified viewpoint toward topological and coarse geometric structure, and will be useful to study symmetries/asymmetries of the systems with infinite degrees of freedom, such as quantum fields.

Citation: Saigo, H.; Nohmi, J. Categorical Nonstandard Analysis. *Symmetry* **2021**, *13*, 1573. https://doi.org/10.3390/sym13091573

Academic Editor: Stefano Profumo

Received: 30 July 2021
Accepted: 23 August 2021
Published: 26 August 2021

Publisher's Note: MDPI stays neutral with regard to jurisdictional claims in published maps and institutional affiliations.

Copyright: © 2021 by the authors. Licensee MDPI, Basel, Switzerland. This article is an open access article distributed under the terms and conditions of the Creative Commons Attribution (CC BY) license (https://creativecommons.org/licenses/by/4.0/).

2. Elementarity Axiom

Let $\mathcal{S}$ be a topos of sets, i.e., an elementary topos with a natural number object satisfying well-pointedness and the axiom of choice (See [1], which is based on the idea in [6]). We make use of an endofunctor $\mathcal{U} : \mathcal{S} \longrightarrow \mathcal{S}$ with a natural transformation $v : Id_{\mathcal{S}} \longrightarrow \mathcal{U}$ satisfying two axioms, "elementarity axiom", and "idealization axiom".

Elementarity Axiom: $\mathcal{U}$ preserves all finite limits and finite coproducts.

Remark 1. $\mathcal{U}$ *does not necessarily preserve power sets. This is the reason for the name of "elementarity".*

It is easy to see that "elementarity axiom" implies the preservation of many basic notions, such as elements, subsets, finite cardinals (in particular, the subobject classifier 2), and propositional calculi. Moreover, the following theorem holds.

Theorem 1. $\mathcal{U}$ *is faithful.*

Proof. It preserves diagonal morphisms and complements. □

Theorem 2. *For any element* $x : 1 \longrightarrow X$, $v_X(x) = \mathcal{U}(x) \circ v_1$.

Proof. By naturality of v. □

Corollary 1. *All components of v are monic.*

From the discussion above, a set X in $\mathcal{S}$ is to be considered as a canonical subset of $\mathcal{U}(X)$ through $v_X : X \longrightarrow \mathcal{U}(X)$. Hence, $\mathcal{U}(f) : \mathcal{U}(X_0) \longrightarrow \mathcal{U}(X_1)$ can be considered as "the function induced from $f : X_0 \longrightarrow X_1$ through v."

Definition 1. *Let A, B be objects in $\mathcal{S}$. The function* $ev_{A,B} : A \times B^A \longrightarrow B$ *satisfying*

$$ev_{A,B}(a,f) = f(a)$$

for all $(a, f) \in A \times B^A$ *is called the evaluation (for A, B). The lambda conversion* $\hat{g} : Z \longrightarrow Y^X$ *of* $g : X \times Z \longrightarrow Y$ *is the function satisfying*

$$g = ev_{X,Y} \circ (1_X \times \hat{g}),$$

where $1_X \times \hat{g}$ *denotes the function satisfying*

$$(1_X \times \hat{g})(x,z) = (x, \hat{g}(z)).$$

We define a family of functions $\kappa_{A,B} : \mathcal{U}(B^A) \longrightarrow \mathcal{U}(B)^{\mathcal{U}(A)}$ in $\mathcal{S}$ by the lambda conversion of $\mathcal{U}(ev_{A,B}) : \mathcal{U}(A \times B^A) \cong \mathcal{U}(A) \times \mathcal{U}(B^A) \longrightarrow \mathcal{U}(B)$.

The theorem below means that $\kappa_{A,B} \circ v_{B^A}$ represents "inducing $\mathcal{U}(f)$ from f through v" in terms of exponentials.

Theorem 3. *Let* $f : A \longrightarrow B$ *be any function in $\mathcal{S}$. Then,*

$$\kappa_{A,B} \circ v_{B^A}(\hat{f}) = \widehat{\mathcal{U}(f)}.$$

(Here, $\hat{}$ denotes the lambda conversion operation.)

Proof. Take the (inverse) lambda conversion of the left hand side of the equality to be proved. It is $ev_{\mathcal{U}(A),\mathcal{U}(B)} \circ (id_{\mathcal{U}(A)} \times \kappa_{A,B}) \circ (id_{\mathcal{U}(A)} \times v_{B^A}) \circ (id_{\mathcal{U}(A)} \times \widehat{f})$. By the naturality of v and functorial properties of $\mathcal{U}$, it is calculated as follows:

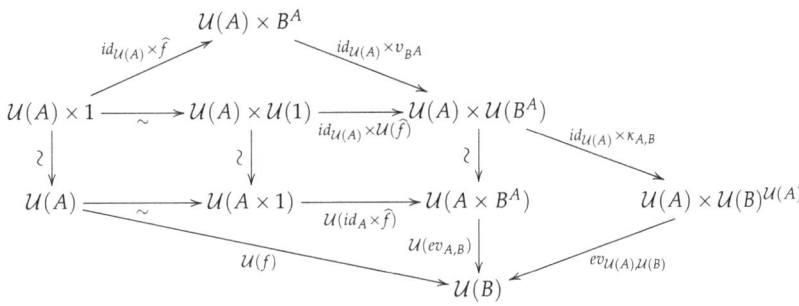

Corollary 2. $\kappa_{A,B} \circ v_{B^A}$ is monic.

Notation 1. *From here, we omit v and κ. $\mathcal{U}(f) : \mathcal{U}(X) \longrightarrow \mathcal{U}(Y)$ will be often identified with $f : X \longrightarrow Y$ and denoted simply as f instead of $\mathcal{U}(f)$.*

Theorem 4. *Let $P : X \longrightarrow 2$ be any proposition (function in $\mathcal{S}$). Then,*

$$\forall_{x \in X} P(x) \iff \forall_{x \in \mathcal{U}(X)} P(x).$$

Proof. $P : X \longrightarrow 2$ factors through "true" $: 1 \longrightarrow 2$ if and only if $P : \mathcal{U}(X) \longrightarrow 2$ factors thorough "true" $: 1 \longrightarrow 2$. □

Dually, we obtain the following:

Theorem 5. *Let $P : X \longrightarrow 2$ be any proposition (function in $\mathcal{S}$). Then,*

$$\exists_{x \in X} P(x) \iff \exists_{x \in \mathcal{U}(X)} P(x).$$

The two theorems above are considered as the simplest versions of "transfer principle". To treat with free variables and quantification, the theorem below is important. (The author thanks Professor Anders Kock for indicating this crucial point.)

Theorem 6. *$\mathcal{U}$ preserves images.*

Proof. As $\mathcal{U}$ preserves all finite limits, it preserves monics. On the other hand, it also preserves epics since every functor preserves split epics and every epic in $\mathcal{S}$ is split epic (axiom of choice). Hence, the image, which is nothing but the epi-mono factorization, is preserved. □

3. Idealization Axiom

From our viewpoint, nonstandard Analysis is nothing but a method of using an endofunctor, which satisfies the "elementarity axiom" and the following "idealization axiom". The name is after "the principle of idealization" in Nelson's internal set theory [4]. Most of the basic ideas in this section have much in common with [4], although the functorial approach is not taken in internal set theory.

Remark 2. *Internal set theory (IST) is a syntactical approach to nonstandard analysis consisting of the "principle of Idealization (I)" and the two more basic principles, called "principle of Standard-*

ization (S)" and "Transfer principle (T)". In our framework, the role of (S) is played by the axiom of choice for $\mathcal{S}$, and (T) corresponds to the contents of Section 2.

Notation 2. *For any set X, $\tilde{X}$ denotes the set of all finite subsets of X.*

Idealization Axiom: Let P be an element of $\mathcal{U}(2^{X \times Y})$. Then,

$$\forall_{x' \in \tilde{X}} \exists_{y \in \mathcal{U}(Y)} \forall_{x \in x'} P(x,y) \iff \exists_{y \in \mathcal{U}(Y)} \forall_{x \in X} P(x,y).$$

Or dually,

Idealization Axiom, dual form: Let P be an element of $\mathcal{U}(2^{X \times Y})$ Then,

$$\exists_{x' \in \tilde{X}} \forall_{y \in \mathcal{U}(Y)} \exists_{x \in x'} P(x,y) \iff \forall_{y \in \mathcal{U}(Y)} \exists_{x \in X} P(x,y).$$

When X is a directed set with an order $\leq$ and $P \in \mathcal{U}(2^{X \times Y})$ satisfies the "filter condition", i.e.,

$$\forall_{x_0 \in X}(P(x_0, y) \implies \forall_{x \in X}(x \leq x_0 \implies P(x,y))),$$

or dually, the "cofilter condition", i.e.,

$$\forall_{x_0 \in X}(P(x_0, y) \implies \forall_{x \in X}(x_0 \leq x \implies P(x,y))),$$

then "idealization axiom" is simplified as the "commutation principle":

Theorem 7 (Commutation Principle). *If $P \in \mathcal{U}(2^{X \times Y})$ satisfies the "filter condition" and "cofilter condition" above, respectively, and then*

$$\forall_{x \in X} \exists_{y \in \mathcal{U}(Y)} P(x,y) \iff \exists_{y \in \mathcal{U}(Y)} \forall_{x \in X} P(x,y)$$

and

$$\exists_{x \in X} \forall_{y \in \mathcal{U}(Y)} P(x,y) \iff \forall_{y \in \mathcal{U}(Y)} \exists_{x \in X} P(x,y)$$

holds, respectively.

By the principle above, we can easily prove the existence of "unlimited numbers" in $\mathcal{U}(\mathbb{N})$, where all arithmetic operations and order structure on $\mathbb{N}$ are naturally extended.

Theorem 8 (Existence of "unlimited numbers"). *There exists some $\omega \in \mathcal{U}(\mathbb{N})$ such that $n \leq \omega$ for any $n \in \mathbb{N}$.*

Proof. It is obvious that, for any $n \in \mathbb{N}$, there exists some $\omega \in \mathbb{N} \subset \mathcal{U}(\mathbb{N})$ such that $n < \omega$. □

As in $\mathcal{S}$, we can construct rational numbers and the completion of them as usual, we have the object $\mathbb{R}$, the set of real numbers. Then, we obtain the following:

Corollary 3. *"Infinitesimals" do exist in $\mathcal{U}(\mathbb{R})$. That is, there exists some $r \in \mathcal{U}(\mathbb{R})$ such that $|r| < R$ for any positive $R \in \mathbb{R}$.*

4. Topological Structure: Continuous Map and Uniform Continuous Map

We will take an example of basic applications of nonstandard analysis within our framework, i.e., the characterization of continuity and uniform continuity in terms of a relation $\approx$ ("infinitely close") on $\mathcal{U}(X)$, which is based on essentially the same arguments that are well-known in nonstandard analysis—particularly, internal set theory [4]. For simplicity, we will discuss only for metric spaces here. (For more general topological spaces, we can define $\approx$ in terms of the system of open sets. See [4] for example.)

Definition 2 (Infinitely close). *Let (X,d) be a metric space. We call the relation $\approx$ on $\mathcal{U}(X)$ defined below as "infinitely close":*

$$x \approx x' \iff \forall_{\epsilon \in \mathbb{R}} d(x,x') < \epsilon.$$

That is, $d(x,x')$ is infinitesimal. It is easy to see that $\approx$ is an equivalence relation on $\mathcal{U}(X)$.

Theorem 9 (Characterization of continuity). *Let $(X_0,d_0), (X_1,d_1)$ be metric spaces and $\approx_0, \approx_1$ be infinitely close relations on them, respectively. A map $f : X_0 \longrightarrow X_1$ is continuous if and only if*

$$\forall_{x \in X_0} \forall_{x' \in \mathcal{U}(X_0)} \, (\, x \approx_0 x' \Rightarrow f(x) \approx_1 f(x') \,)$$

holds.

Proof. We can translate the condition for f by using the usual logic, "commutation principle", and "transfer principle" as follows:

$$\forall_{x \in X_0} \forall_{x' \in \mathcal{U}(X_0)} \, (\, x \approx_0 x' \Rightarrow f(x) \approx_1 f(x') \,)$$
$$\iff \forall_{x \in X_0} \forall_{x' \in \mathcal{U}(X_0)} \, (\, \forall_{\delta \in \mathbb{R}} d_0(x,x') < \delta \Rightarrow \forall_{\epsilon \in \mathbb{R}} d_1(f(x),f(x')) < \epsilon \,)$$
$$\iff \forall_{x \in X_0} \forall_{x' \in \mathcal{U}(X_0)} \forall_{\epsilon \in \mathbb{R}} \exists_{\delta \in \mathbb{R}} \, (\, d_0(x,x') < \delta \Rightarrow d_1(f(x),f(x')) < \epsilon \,)$$
$$\iff \forall_{x \in X_0} \forall_{\epsilon \in \mathbb{R}} \forall_{x' \in \mathcal{U}(X_0)} \exists_{\delta \in \mathbb{R}} \, (\, d_0(x,x') < \delta \Rightarrow d_1(f(x),f(x')) < \epsilon \,)$$
$$\iff \forall_{x \in X_0} \forall_{\epsilon \in \mathbb{R}} \exists_{\delta \in \mathbb{R}} \forall_{x' \in \mathcal{U}(X_0)} \, (\, d_0(x,x') < \delta \Rightarrow d_1(f(x),f(x')) < \epsilon \,)$$
$$\iff \forall_{x \in X_0} \forall_{\epsilon \in \mathbb{R}} \exists_{\delta \in \mathbb{R}} \forall_{x' \in X_0} \, (\, d_0(x,x') < \delta \Rightarrow d_1(f(x),f(x')) < \epsilon \,).$$

□

Theorem 10 (Characterization of uniform continuity). *Let $(X_0,d_0), (X_1,d_1)$ be metric spaces and $\approx_0, \approx_1$ be infinitely close relations on them, respectively. A map $f : X_0 \longrightarrow X_1$ is uniformly continuous if and only if*

$$\forall_{x \in \mathcal{U}(X_0)} \forall_{x' \in \mathcal{U}(X_0)} \, (\, x \approx_0 x' \Rightarrow f(x) \approx_1 f(x') \,)$$

holds.

Proof. We can translate the condition for f by using usual logic, "commutation principle" and "transfer Principle" as follows:

$$\forall_{x \in \mathcal{U}(X_0)} \forall_{x' \in \mathcal{U}(X_0)} \, (\, x \approx_0 x' \Rightarrow f(x) \approx_1 f(x') \,)$$
$$\iff \forall_{x \in \mathcal{U}(X_0)} \forall_{x' \in \mathcal{U}(X_0)} \, (\, \forall_{\delta \in \mathbb{R}} d_0(x,x') < \delta \Rightarrow \forall_{\epsilon \in \mathbb{R}} d_1(f(x),f(x')) < \epsilon \,)$$
$$\iff \forall_{x \in \mathcal{U}(X_0)} \forall_{x' \in \mathcal{U}(X_0)} \forall_{\epsilon \in \mathbb{R}} \exists_{\delta \in \mathbb{R}} \, (\, d_0(x,x') < \delta \Rightarrow d_1(f(x),f(x')) < \epsilon \,)$$
$$\iff \forall_{\epsilon \in \mathbb{R}} \forall_{x \in \mathcal{U}(X_0)} \forall_{x' \in \mathcal{U}(X_0)} \exists_{\delta \in \mathbb{R}} \, (\, d_0(x,x') < \delta \Rightarrow d_1(f(x),f(x')) < \epsilon \,)$$
$$\iff \forall_{\epsilon \in \mathbb{R}} \exists_{\delta \in \mathbb{R}} \forall_{x \in \mathcal{U}(X_0)} \forall_{x' \in \mathcal{U}(X_0)} \, (\, d_0(x,x') < \delta \Rightarrow d_1(f(x),f(x')) < \epsilon \,)$$
$$\iff \forall_{\epsilon \in \mathbb{R}} \exists_{\delta \in \mathbb{R}} \forall_{x \in X_0} \forall_{x' \in X_0} \, (\, d_0(x,x') < \delta \Rightarrow d_1(f(x),f(x')) < \epsilon \,).$$

□

As we have seen, a morphism between metric spaces is characterized as "a morphism with respect to $\approx$". This suggests the possibility for considering other kinds of "equivalence relations on (some subset of) $\mathcal{U}(X)$" as generalized spatial structures on X. In the next section, we will take one example related to large scale geometric structure.

5. Coarse Structure: Bornologous Map

Let us consider another kind of equivalence relation $\sim$ ("finitely remote") defined below. For simplicity, we will discuss only for metric spaces here.

Definition 3 (Finitely remote). *Let (X, d) be a metric space. We call the relation $\sim$ on $\mathcal{U}(X)$ defined below as "finitely remote":*

$$x \sim x' \iff \exists_{R \in \mathbb{R}} d(x, x') < R.$$

Note that we use $\exists$ instead of $\forall$, in contrast to "infinitely close". This kind of dual viewpoint will be proven to be useful in the geometric study of large scale structures, such as coarse geometry [5].

In fact, we can prove that a "bornologous map", a central notion of a morphism for coarse geometry, can be characterized as "a morphism with respect to $\sim$", similar to how (uniform) continuity can be viewed as "a morphism with respect to $\approx$".

Definition 4 (Bornologous map). *Let (X_0, d_0) and (X_1, d_1) be metric spaces. A map $f : X_0 \longrightarrow X_1$ is called a bornologous map when*

$$\forall_{R \in \mathbb{R}} \exists_{S \in \mathbb{R}} \forall_{x \in X_0} \forall_{x' \in X_0} (\, d_0(x, x') < R \Rightarrow d_1(f(x), f(x')) < S \,)$$

holds.

Theorem 11 (Characterization of bornologous map). *Let $(X_0, d_0), (X_1, d_1)$ be metric spaces and $\sim_0, \sim_1$ be finitely remote relations on them, respectively. A map $f : X_0 \longrightarrow X_1$ is bornologous if and only if*

$$\forall_{x \in \mathcal{U}(X_0)} \forall_{x' \in \mathcal{U}(X_0)} (\, x \sim_0 x' \Rightarrow f(x) \sim_1 f(x') \,)$$

holds.

Proof. We can translate the condition for f by using the usual logic, "commutation principle", and "transfer principle" as follows:

$$\forall_{x \in \mathcal{U}(X_0)} \forall_{x' \in \mathcal{U}(X_0)} (\, x \sim_0 x' \Rightarrow f(x) \sim_1 f(x') \,)$$
$$\iff \forall_{x \in \mathcal{U}(X_0)} \forall_{x' \in \mathcal{U}(X_0)} (\exists_{R \in \mathbb{R}} d_0(x, x') < R \Rightarrow \exists_{S \in \mathbb{R}} d_1(f(x), f(x')) < S)$$
$$\iff \forall_{x \in \mathcal{U}(X_0)} \forall_{x' \in \mathcal{U}(X_0)} \forall_{R \in \mathbb{R}} \exists_{S \in \mathbb{R}} (\, d_0(x, x') < R \Rightarrow d_1(f(x), f(x')) < S \,)$$
$$\iff \forall_{R \in \mathbb{R}} \forall_{x \in \mathcal{U}(X_0)} \forall_{x' \in \mathcal{U}(X_0)} \exists_{S \in \mathbb{R}} (\, d_0(x, x') < R \Rightarrow d_1(f(x), f(x')) < S \,)$$
$$\iff \forall_{R \in \mathbb{R}} \exists_{S \in \mathbb{R}} \forall_{x \in \mathcal{U}(X_0)} \forall_{x' \in \mathcal{U}(X_0)} (\, d_0(x, x') < R \Rightarrow d_1(f(x), f(x')) < S \,)$$
$$\iff \forall_{R \in \mathbb{R}} \exists_{S \in \mathbb{R}} \forall_{x \in X_0} \forall_{x' \in X_0} (\, d_0(x, x') < R \Rightarrow d_1(f(x), f(x')) < S \,).$$

□

6. The Notion of $\mathcal{U}$-Space and the Category $\mathcal{U}Space$

Based on the characterizations of topological and coarse geometrical structure, we introduce the notion of $\mathcal{U}$-space.

Definition 5 ($\mathcal{U}$-space). *A $\mathcal{U}$-space is a triple $(X, K, \rightsquigarrow)$ consisting of a set X, a subset K of $\mathcal{U}(X)$, which includes X as a subset, and a preorder $\rightsquigarrow$ defined on K.*

When the preorder $\rightsquigarrow$ is an equivalence relation, i.e., a preorder satisfying symmetry, we call the $\mathcal{U}$-space symmetric. A symmetric $\mathcal{U}$-space $(X, K, \rightsquigarrow)$ is called uniform if $K = \mathcal{U}(X)$. The "infinitely close" relation and the "finitely remote" relation provide the simplest examples of uniform $\mathcal{U}$-space structure.

Actually, any topological space X with the set of open sets T can be viewed as $\mathcal{U}$-space $(X, \mathcal{U}(X), \rightharpoonup)$ where $x \rightharpoonup x'$ denotes the preorder "$\forall O \in T \; x \in \mathcal{U}(O) \Longrightarrow x' \in \mathcal{U}(O)$". If (X, T) is a Hausdorff space, we can construct the symmetric $\mathcal{U}$-space $(X, K, \rightsquigarrow)$, where K denotes

$$K = \{x \in \mathcal{U}(X) | \exists x_0 \in X \; x \rightharpoonup x'\}$$

and $x \rightsquigarrow x'$ is defined as the relation "$\exists x_0 \in X \; x_0 \rightharpoonup x \& x_0 \rightharpoonup x'$." The transitivity of $\rightharpoonup$ follows from the fact that if (X, T) is Hausdorff, $x_0 \rightharpoonup x$ and $x'_0 \rightharpoonup x$ imply $x_0 = x'_0$ for all $x_0, x'_0 \in X$. In fact, the preorder $\rightsquigarrow$ becomes an equivalence relation.

The concept of $\mathcal{U}$-space will provide a general framework to unify various spatial structure, such as topological structure and coarse structure. The notion of morphism between $\mathcal{U}$-spaces is defined as follows:

Definition 6 ($\mathcal{U}$-spatial morphism). *Let $(X_0, K_0, \rightsquigarrow_0)$ and $(X_1, K_1, \rightsquigarrow_1)$ be $\mathcal{U}$-spaces. A function $f : X_0 \to X_1$ is called a $\mathcal{U}$-spatial morphism from $(X_0, K_0, \rightsquigarrow_0)$ to $(X_1, K_1, \rightsquigarrow_1)$ when $f(K_0) \subset K_1$ and*

$$x \rightsquigarrow_0 x' \implies f(x) \rightsquigarrow_1 f(x')$$

holds for any $x, x' \in K_0$.

The uniform continuous maps and bornologous maps between metric spaces are nothing but $\mathcal{U}$-spatial morphisms between corresponding uniform $\mathcal{U}$-spaces. The notion of continuous maps between Hausdorff spaces can be characterized as $\mathcal{U}$-spatial morphisms between the corresponding symmetric $\mathcal{U}$-spaces.

Definition 7 (Category $\mathcal{U}Space$). *The category $\mathcal{U}Space$ is a category whose objects are $\mathcal{U}$-spaces and whose morphisms are $\mathcal{U}$-spatial morphisms.*

Definition 8. *Let $(X_0, K_0, \rightsquigarrow_0)$ and $(X_1, K_1, \rightsquigarrow_1)$ be $\mathcal{U}$-spaces. The $\mathcal{U}$-space $(X_0 \times X_1, K_0 \times K_1, \rightsquigarrow)$, where the preorder $\rightsquigarrow$ is defined as*

$$(x_0, x_1) \rightsquigarrow (x'_0, x'_1) \iff x_0 \rightsquigarrow_0 x'_0 \& x_1 \rightsquigarrow_1 x'_1,$$

is called the product $\mathcal{U}$-space of $(X_0, K_0, \rightsquigarrow_0)$ and $(X_1, K_1, \rightsquigarrow_1)$.

Theorem 12. *The projections become $\mathcal{U}$-spatial morphisms. The diagram consisting of two $\mathcal{U}$-spaces, the product space of them, and projections becomes a product in $\mathcal{U}Space$.*

Proof. Easy. □

Definition 9 (Exponential $\mathcal{U}$-space). *Let $(X_0, K_0, \rightsquigarrow_0)$ and $(X_1, K_1, \rightsquigarrow_1)$ be $\mathcal{U}$-spaces. We denote the set of all $\mathcal{U}$-spatial morphisms from X_0 to X_1 as $[X_1^{X_0}]$, which is the subset of $X_1^{X_0}$. The restriction of $ev_{X_0, X_1} : X_0 \times X_1^{X_0} \longrightarrow X_1$ onto $X_0 \times [X_1^{X_0}] \longrightarrow X_1$ is denoted as $[ev_{X_0, X_1}]$. The $\mathcal{U}$-space $([X_1^{X_0}], K, \rightsquigarrow)$, where K is defined as the subset of $\mathcal{U}([X_1^{X_0}])$,*

$$K = \{f | \forall x \in K_0 [ev_{X_0, X_1}](x, f) \in K_1 \text{ and } x \rightsquigarrow_0 x' \implies [ev_{X_0, X_1}](x, f) \rightsquigarrow_1 [ev_{X_0, X_1}](x, f')\}$$

and $\rightsquigarrow$ is defined as

$$f \rightsquigarrow f' \iff \forall x \in K_0 \; [ev_{X_0, X_1}](x, f) \rightsquigarrow_1 [ev_{X_0, X_1}](x, f'),$$

is called the exponential $\mathcal{U}$-space from $(X_0, K_0, \rightsquigarrow_0)$ to $(X_1, K_1, \rightsquigarrow_1)$.

Theorem 13. *Let $(X_0, K_0, \rightsquigarrow_0)$ and $(X_1, K_1, \rightsquigarrow_1)$ be $\mathcal{U}$-spaces and $([X_1^{X_0}], K, \rightsquigarrow)$ be the exponential $\mathcal{U}$-space from $(X_0, K_0, \rightsquigarrow_0)$ to $(X_1, K_1, \rightsquigarrow_1)$. The morphism $[ev_{X_0, X_1}] : X_0 \times [X_1^{X_0}] \longrightarrow X_1$, the restriction of ev_{X_0, X_1}, is a $\mathcal{U}$-spatial morphism. Moreover, it becomes an evaluation in $\mathcal{U}Space$ and $[X_1^{X_0}]$ is an exponential in $\mathcal{U}Space$.*

Proof. First, we prove that $[ev_{X_0,X_1}]$ is a $\mathcal{U}$-spatial morphism: For any $(x, f) \in K_0 \times K$, $[ev_{X_0,X_1}](x, f)$ is in K_1 since $x \in K_0$ and $f \in K$. Suppose that $(x, f), (x', f') \in K_0 \times K$ and $(x, f) \rightsquigarrow (x', f')$, that is, $x, x' \in K_0$, $f, f' \in K$, $x \rightsquigarrow x'$ and $f \rightsquigarrow f'$. Then, we have

$$[ev_{X_0,X_1}](x, f) \rightsquigarrow [ev_{X_0,X_1}](x, f')$$

since $f \rightsquigarrow f'$. We also have

$$[ev_{X_0,X_1}](x, f') \rightsquigarrow [ev_{X_0,X_1}](x', f')$$

since $f' \in K$. Hence, $[ev_{X_0,X_1}](x, f) \rightsquigarrow [ev_{X_0,X_1}](x', f')$.

Next, we prove that $[ev_{X_0,X_1}]: X_0 \times [X_1^{X_0}] \longrightarrow X_1$ becomes an evaluation in $\mathcal{U}Space$, and $[X_1^{X_0}]$ is an exponential in $\mathcal{U}Space$: Let $(X_2, K_2, \rightsquigarrow_2)$ be any $\mathcal{U}$-space and $f : X_0 \times X_2 \longrightarrow X_1$ be any $\mathcal{U}$-spatial morphism. Consider the lambda conversion $\hat{f} : X_2 \longrightarrow X_1^{X_0}$. By assumption that f is $\mathcal{U}$-spatial,

$$(x, c), (x', c') \in K_0 \times K_2 \ \& \ (x, c) \rightsquigarrow (x', c') \Longrightarrow f(x, c), f(x', c') \in K_1 \ \& \ f(x, c) \rightsquigarrow_1 f(x', c')$$

holds, where $\rightsquigarrow$ denote the preorder on $K_0 \times K_2$. It is equivalent to the statement that $c, c' \in K_2$ and $c \rightsquigarrow_2 c'$ implies that

$$x, x' \in K_0 \ \& \ x \rightsquigarrow_0 x' \Longrightarrow \hat{f}(c)(x), \hat{f}(c')(x') \in K_1 \ \& \ \hat{f}(c)(x) \rightsquigarrow_1 \hat{f}(c')(x').$$

Applying the implication above for the case $c = c' \in X_2$, we have $\hat{f}(c) \in [X_1^{X_0}]$. Hence, we can replace $\hat{f} : X_2 \longrightarrow X_1^{X_0}$ with $[\hat{f}] : X_2 \longrightarrow [X_1^{X_0}]$ by restricting the codomain to the image of $\hat{f}$. Moreover, we can also prove that $[\hat{f}]$ is $\mathcal{U}$-spatial from the implication: By the implication above, we have $[\hat{f}](c), [\hat{f}](c') \in K$ and $[\hat{f}](c) \rightsquigarrow [\hat{f}](c')$ when $c, c' \in K_2$ and $c \rightsquigarrow_2 c'$. This means that $[\hat{f}]$ is $\mathcal{U}$-spatial.

It is easy to show that this $[\hat{f}]$ is the unique $\mathcal{U}$-spatial morphism from X_2 to $[X_1^{X_0}]$ satisfying $[ev_{X_0,X_1}] \circ (1_{X_0} \times [\hat{f}]) = f$. This completes the proof. □

Combining the two theorems above, we have:

Theorem 14. *The category $\mathcal{U}Space$ is a Cartesian closed category.*

Author Contributions: Conceptualization, H.S. and J.N.; Investigation, H.S. and J.N.; Methodology, H.S.; Writing—original draft, H.S.; Writing—review & editing, J.N. All authors have read and agreed to the published version of the manuscript.

Funding: This work was partially supported by Research Origin for Dressed Photon, JSPS KAKENHI (grant number 19K03608 and 20H00001) and JST CREST (JPMJCR17N2).

Institutional Review Board Statement: Not applicable.

Informed Consent Statement: Not applicable.

Acknowledgments: The authors would like to express their sincere thanks to Anders Kock and Edward Nelson for their encouragements. They are grateful to Hiroshi Ando, Izumi Ojima, Kazuya Okamura, Misa Saigo, Hiroki Sako, and Ryokichi Tanaka for the fruitful discussions and comments.

Conflicts of Interest: The authors declare no conflict of interest.

References

1. MacLane, S. *Categories for the Working Mathematician*, 2nd ed.; Springer: Berlin/Heidelberg, Germany; New York, NY, USA, 1998.
2. Robinson, A. *Non-Standard Analysis*; North Holland: Amsterdam, The Netherlands, 1966.
3. Kock, A.; Mikkelsen, J. Topos-theoretic factorization of nonstandard extensions. In *Victoria Symposium on Nonstandard Analysis*; Lecture Notes in Mathematics; Springer: Berlin/Heidelberg, Germany, 1974; Volume 369, pp. 122–143.
4. Nelson, E. Internal set theory: A new approach to nonstandard analysis. *Bull. Am. Math. Soc.* **1977**, *83*, 1165–1198. [CrossRef]

5. Roe, J. *Lectures on Coarse Geometry*; University Lecture Series; American Mathematical Society: Providence, RI, USA, 2003; Volume 31.
6. Lawvere, W. Elementary Theory of the Category of Sets. *Proc. Nat. Acad. Sci. USA* **1964**, *52*, 1506–1511. [CrossRef] [PubMed]

Article
Quantum Fields as Category Algebras

Hayato Saigo

Department of Bioscience, Nagahama Institute of Bio-Science and Technology, Nagahama 526-0829, Japan; h_saigoh@nagahama-i-bio.ac.jp

Abstract: In the present paper, we propose a new approach to quantum fields in terms of category algebras and states on categories. We define quantum fields and their states as category algebras and states on causal categories with partial involution structures. By utilizing category algebras and states on categories instead of simply considering categories, we can directly integrate relativity as a category theoretic structure and quantumness as a noncommutative probabilistic structure. Conceptual relationships with conventional approaches to quantum fields, including Algebraic Quantum Field Theory (AQFT) and Topological Quantum Field Theory (TQFT), are also be discussed.

Keywords: quantum field; category; category algebra; state on category

Citation: Saigo, H. Quantum Fields as Category Algebras. *Symmetry* **2021**, *13*, 1727. https://doi.org/10.3390/sym13091727

Academic Editor: Alexei Kanel-Belov

Received: 30 August 2021
Accepted: 14 September 2021
Published: 17 September 2021

Publisher's Note: MDPI stays neutral with regard to jurisdictional claims in published maps and institutional affiliations.

Copyright: © 2021 by the authors. Licensee MDPI, Basel, Switzerland. This article is an open access article distributed under the terms and conditions of the Creative Commons Attribution (CC BY) license (https://creativecommons.org/licenses/by/4.0/).

1. Introduction

Quantum fields are the most fundamental entities in modern physics. Intuitively, the notion of quantum field is the unification of relativity theory and quantum theory. However, the existence of a non-trivial interacting quantum field model defined on a four-dimensional Minkowski spacetime, which is a covariant with respect to the Poincaré group, has not yet been proven. In axiomatic approaches to the quantum field theory, there have been shown many fundamental theorems including no-go theorems such as Haag's theorem [1,2], which implies that the "interaction picture exists only if there is no interaction" [3] through the clarification of the concept of the quantum field (see [3,4] and references therein). To put it roughly, we cannot go beyond the free fields if we remain at the axioms that we take for granted in conventional quantum field theories.

In this paper, we propose a new approach to quantum fields: The core idea is to investigate quantum fields in terms of category algebra, which is noncommutative, in general, over a rig ("ring without negatives"), i.e., an algebraic system equipped with addition and multiplication, in which the category and rig correspond to the "relativity" aspect and the "quantum" aspect of nature, respectively. By utilizing category algebra and states on categories instead of simply considering categories, we can directly integrate relativity as a category theoretic structure and quantum nature as a noncommutative probabilistic structure. The cases in which the rig is an algebra over $\mathbb{C}$, the field of complex numbers become especially important for our approach to quantum fields. For other regions of physics, such as classical variational contexts, the tropical semiring (originally introduced in [5]), i.e., a rig with "min" and "plus" as addition and multiplication, will be useful. The author believes that it is quite interesting to see the quantum–classical correspondence from the unified viewpoint of the category algebras over rigs.

As is well known, the essence of the relativity is nothing but the structure of the possible relationships between possible events. If we assume the structure of the relationships between events, we can essentially reconstruct the relativity structure. More concretely, in [6], it is shown that two future-and-past-distinguishing Lorentzian manifolds are conformally equivalent if and only if the associated posets are isomorphic, where the poset consists of events and of the order relation defined by the existence of future-directed causal curves, based on [7]; what really matters are the causal relationships (for details, see [8] and reference therein). This viewpoint is quite essential and there is an interesting order-theoretic approach to spacetime (for example, the "causal set" approach [9]). However, to investigate the off-shell nature of quantum fields, which seems to be essential in modeling interacting fields on the spacetime, we need to take not only causal relationships but also more general relationships between spacelike events into consideration. Then, the question arises: how should we generalize a framework of previous approaches?

The strategy we propose is to think categories, which are generalizations of both of ordered sets (causality structures) and groups (symmetry structures), "as" relativity in a generalized sense. More concretely, we identify the notion of causal category equipped with partial involution structure, introduced in Section 2, as the generalized relativity structure. To combine this relativity structure with quantum theory, which can be modeled by noncommutative rigs, especially effectively by noncommutative algebras over $\mathbb{C}$ as history has shown, we need noncommutative algebras that reflect the structures of categories. Category algebras are just such algebras. As categories are generalized groups, category algebras are generalized group algebras.

The above discussion intuitively explains why we use category algebras to model quantum fields. For simplicity, in this paper, we focus on a category algebra which satisfies a suitable finiteness condition. Importantly, the category algebras can be considered as generalized matrix algebras over R as well as generalized polynomial algebras [10], which provides a platform for concrete and flexible studies as well as calculations. The extension to larger algebras is, of course, of interest but the category algebras we focus on already have rich structures as covariance and local structures of subalgebras reflect the causal and partial involution structure of the category, as we will see in Section 3. By focusing on these structures, we can also see the conceptual relationship between our approach and the preceding approaches such as Algebraic Quantum Field Theory (AQFT) [4,11] and Topological Quantum Field Theory (TQFT) [12,13].

Identifying a quantum field to be a category algebra over a rig, the next problem, which is treated in Section 4, concerns how to define a state of it. In general, the notion of state on *-algebra over $\mathbb{C}$ is defined as positive normalized linear functional. We can naturally extend the notion in the context of algebras with involution over rigs ([10] for details). We call the states on category algebras as states on categories. If the number of objects in the category is finite, states can be characterized by functions on arrows satisfying certain conditions [10], which is a generalization of the result in [14] for groupoids with finite numbers of objects. More generally, to define a state on a category whose support is contained in a subcategory with finite numbers of objects is equivalent to defining the corresponding function which assigns the weight to each arrow. By considering such states, we can see a quantum mechanical system as an aspect of the quantum field. This viewpoint will shed light on the foundation of quantum theory.

For the study of quantum fields, a localized notion of state, or a "local state" [15,16], is important. We can define the counterpart of the notion, originally studied in the AQFT approach, as the system of states on certain subalgebras of category algebras called local algebras, introduced in Section 3. These matters will be explained in Section 4 with more clarification of the conceptual relationship with AQFT and TQFT. The discussion in Section 4 will provide a new basis for generalizing the DHR (Doplicher–Haag–Roberts)–DR (Doplicher–Roberts) sector theory [17–23] as well as for developing Ojima's micro–macro duality [24,25] and quadrality scheme [26] from the viewpoint of category algebras and states on categories.

In the last section, we will discuss the prospect of research directions based on our framework. In addition to the importance of mathematical research, such as taking topological or differential structures into account, there is the challenge of integrating various approaches to quantum fields and of conducting research on quantum foundations based on our framework. These are where new concepts such as quantum walks on categories will be useful. One of the most exciting problems is, of course, to construct a model of a non-trivial quantum field with interactions. The author hopes that the present paper will be a small, new step towards these big problems.

2. Structure of Dynamics as Category

In this section, the "relativistic structure" as the basic structure of dynamics, consisting of possible events and relations (or "processes") between them, is formulated in terms of category theory.

2.1. Definition of Category

A category is a mathematical system composed of entities called objects and arrows (or morphisms) satisfying the following four conditions.

Condition 1. *For any arrow f, there exist an object called $\mathrm{dom}(f)$ and another object called $\mathrm{cod}(f)$, which are called the domain of f and the codomain of f, respectively.*

When $\mathrm{dom}(f) = X$ and $\mathrm{cod}(f) = Y$, we denote it as

$$f : X \longrightarrow Y$$

or

$$X \xrightarrow{f} Y.$$

Arrows are also denoted in any direction, not only from left to right, as above.

Condition 2. *For any pair of morphism f, g satisfying $\mathrm{dom}(g) = \mathrm{cod}(f)$*

$$Z \xleftarrow{g} Y \xleftarrow{f} X,$$

there exist an arrow $g \circ f$

$$Z \xleftarrow{g \circ f} X$$

called the composition of f, g.

For the composition of arrows, we assume the following conditions:

Condition 3 (associative law). *For any triple f, g, h of arrows satisfying $\mathrm{dom}(h) = \mathrm{cod}(g)$ and $\mathrm{dom}(g) = \mathrm{cod}(f)$,*

$$(h \circ g) \circ f = h \circ (g \circ f)$$

holds.

Condition 4 (identity law). *For any object X, there exists an arrow called **identity arrow** $1_X : X \longrightarrow X$. For any arrow $f : X \longrightarrow Y$*

$$f \circ 1_X = f = 1_Y \circ f$$

holds.

By the correspondence from objects to their identity arrows, objects can be considered as special kinds of arrows by identifying each object X with its identity arrow 1_X.

In sum, the definition of a category is as follows.

Definition 1 (category). *A category is a system composed of two kinds of entities called objects and arrows, equipped with domain/codomain, composition, and identity, satisfying the associative law and the identity law.*

In a category, we can define the "essential sameness" between objects via the notion of invertible arrows (isomorphism).

Definition 2 (invertible arrow (isomorphism)). *Let $\mathcal{C}$ be a category. An arrow $f : X \longrightarrow Y$ in $\mathcal{C}$ is said to be invertible in $\mathcal{C}$ if there exists some arrow $g : Y \longrightarrow X$ such that*

$$g \circ f = 1_X, \ f \circ g = 1_Y.$$

An invertible arrow in $\mathcal{C}$ is also called an isomorphism in $\mathcal{C}$.

There are many categories whose collection of arrows is too large to be a set. In the present paper, we focus on small categories:

Definition 3 (small category). *A category $\mathcal{C}$ is called small if the collection of arrows is a set.*

Let us see the examples of small categories which are used in the present paper.

Definition 4 (preorder). *A pair $(P, \rightsquigarrow)$ of a set P and a relation $\rightsquigarrow$ on P satisfying $p \rightsquigarrow p$ for any $p \in P$ and*

$$p \rightsquigarrow q \text{ and } q \rightsquigarrow r \Longrightarrow p \rightsquigarrow r$$

for any $p, q, r \in P$ is called a preordered set. The relation $\rightsquigarrow$ on P is called a preorder on P. The preordered set $(P, \rightsquigarrow)$ can be viewed as a category whose objects are elements of P when we define the relation $p \rightsquigarrow q$ between p, q as the unique arrow from p to q. Conversely, we can define a preordered set as a small category such that for any pair of objects p, q, there exists at most one arrow from p to q.

Note that the notion of preorder is a generalization of a partial order and an equivalence relation. As a special extreme case of the concept of preordered sets, we have the following.

Definition 5 (indiscrete category and discrete category). *An indiscrete category is a small category such that for any pair of objects C, C', there exists exactly one morphism from C to C'. A discrete category is a small category such that all arrows are identity arrows.*

Note that an indiscrete category corresponds to a complete graph and that any set can be considered as a discrete category.

Additionally, the notion of group, which is essential in the study of symmetry, can also be defined as a small category as follows.

Definition 6 (monoid and group). *A small category with only one object is called a monoid. A monoid is called a group if all arrows are invertible.*

To see the equivalence between the definition of the group as a category, define the arrows as the elements and the unique identity arrow (which can be identified with the unique object) as the identity element.

By definition, the concept of monoid is a generalization of that of a group, allowing for the existence of non-invertible arrows. the concept of groupoid is another generalization of that of a group:

Definition 7 (groupoid). *A small category is said to be a groupoid if all arrows are invertible.*

As for the importance of groupoids in physics, see [14] and references therein, for example. From the mathematical point of view, the present paper is based on an extension of the previous work [14] on groupoid algebras over $\mathbb{C}$ into category algebras of an arbitrary (small) category over a (in general, noncommutative) rig R, i.e., "ring without negatives" (algebraic system with addition and multiplication), which will be introduced in the next section. Even in the case of $R = \mathbb{C}$, this extension physically means allowing for irreversible processes considering a category can be seen as a generalized groupoid allowing for invertible arrows in general. The involution structure of the category algebra is provided by the partial involution structure of the category, as we will see in the next section ($\dagger$-category introduced later can be seen as a generalization of groupoid).

A functor is defined as a structure-preserving correspondence between two categories, as follows.

Definition 8 (functor (covariant functor)). *Let $\mathcal{C}$ and $\mathcal{C}'$ be categories. A correspondence F from $\mathcal{C}$ to $\mathcal{C}'$, which maps objects and arrows in $\mathcal{C}$ to objects and arrows in $\mathcal{C}'$, is said to be a covariant functor or simply a functor from $\mathcal{C}$ to $\mathcal{C}'$ if it satisfies the following conditions:*

1. *It maps $f : X \longrightarrow Y$ in $\mathcal{C}$ to $F(f) : F(X) \longrightarrow F(Y)$ in $\mathcal{C}'$.*
2. *$F(g \circ f) = F(g) \circ F(f)$ for any (compositable) pair of f, g in $\mathcal{C}$.*
3. *For each X in $\mathcal{C}$, $F(1_X) = 1_{F(X)}$.*

Definition 9 (contravariant functor). *Let $\mathcal{C}$ and $\mathcal{C}'$ be categories. A correspondence F from $\mathcal{C}$ to $\mathcal{C}'$, which maps objects and arrows in $\mathcal{C}$ to objects and arrows in $\mathcal{C}'$ is said to be a contravariant functor from $\mathcal{C}$ to $\mathcal{C}'$ if it satisfies the following conditions:*

1. *It maps $f : X \longrightarrow Y$ in $\mathcal{C}$ to $F(f) : F(X) \longleftarrow F(Y)$ in $\mathcal{C}'$.*
2. *$F(g \circ f) = F(f) \circ F(g)$ for any (compositable) pair of f, g in $\mathcal{C}$.*
3. *For each X in $\mathcal{C}$, $F(1_X) = 1_{F(X)}$.*

Definition 10 (composition of functors). *Let F be a functor from $\mathcal{C}$ to $\mathcal{C}'$ and G be a functor from $\mathcal{C}'$ to $\mathcal{C}''$. The composition functor $G \circ F$ is a functor from $\mathcal{C}$ to $\mathcal{C}''$, defined as $(G \circ F)(c) = G(F(c))$ for any arrow c in $\mathcal{C}$.*

Definition 11 (identity functor). *Let $\mathcal{C}$ be a category. A functor from $\mathcal{C}$ to $\mathcal{C}$, which maps any arrow to itself, is called the identity functor.*

We can consider categories consisting of (certain kind of) categories as objects and (certain kind of) functors as arrows.

The concept of involution on the category is important throughout the present paper.

Definition 12 (involution on category). *Let $\mathcal{C}$ be a category. A covariant/contravariant endofunctor $(\cdot)^{\dagger}$ from $\mathcal{C}$ to $\mathcal{C}$ is said to be a covariant/contravariant involution on $\mathcal{C}$ when $(\cdot)^{\dagger} \circ (\cdot)^{\dagger}$ is equal to the identity functor on $\mathcal{C}$. A category with contravariant involution, which is the identity on objects, is called a $\dagger$-category.*

We conclude this subsection by defining the concept of natural transformation and the related concepts. The concept of natural transformation can be seen as a generalization of the various concepts of transformations in mathematics and other sciences, including physics.

Definition 13 (natural transformation). *Let $\mathcal{C}, \mathcal{D}$ be categories and F, G be functors from a category $\mathcal{C}$ to a category $\mathcal{D}$. A correspondence t is said to be a natural transformation from F to G if it satisfies the following conditions:*

1. *t maps each object X in $\mathcal{C}$ to the corresponding arrow $t_X : F(X) \longrightarrow G(X)$ in $\mathcal{D}$.*
2. *For any $f : X \longrightarrow Y$ in $\mathcal{C}$,*

$$t_Y \circ F(f) = G(f) \circ t_X.$$

The arrow t_X is called the X component of t.

Definition 14 (functor category). *Let $\mathcal{C}$ and $\mathcal{C}'$ be categories. The functor category $\mathcal{C}'^{\mathcal{C}}$ is a category consisting of functors from $\mathcal{C}$ to $\mathcal{C}'$ as objects and natural transformations as arrows (domain, codomain, composition, and identity are defined in a natural way).*

Definition 15 (natural equivalence). *An isomorphism in a functor category, i.e., an invertible natural transformation, is said to be a natural equivalence.*

Notation 1. *In the rest of the present paper, categories are always supposed to be small. The set of all arrows in a category $\mathcal{C}$ is also denoted as $\mathcal{C}$. $|\mathcal{C}|$ denotes the set of all objects, which are identified with corresponding identity arrows in $\mathcal{C}$.*

2.2. Relativistic Structure as Category

If we intuitively consider the spacetime degrees of freedom with the geometric notion of the "set" of possible events, it is natural to think that the structure of dynamics of quantum can be modeled with "category" as the total system structure of relationships.

Definition 16 (causal category). *A category $\mathcal{C}$ equipped with a subcategory $\mathcal{C}^{cau}$ satisfying $|\mathcal{C}| = |\mathcal{C}^{cau}|$ is called a causal category. Arrows in $\mathcal{C}^{cau}$ are said to be causal.*

Any category can be considered as a causal category by taking $\mathcal{C} = \mathcal{C}^{cau}$. Note that $|\mathcal{C}|$ is equipped with preorder $\rightsquigarrow$, defined as the existence of causal arrows between objects.

A typical example of causal categories is constructed as follows. For a spacetime (with inner degrees of freedom) E, usually modeled by a manifold and sometimes by a symmetric directed graph (as in the lattice gauge theory [27]), we can construct a category $\mathcal{C} = \mathcal{M}[E]$ whose objects and arrows are points and paths between them. More precisely, we consider $\mathcal{M}(E)$ as a subcategory of the "Moore path category" [28] of E, consisting of smooth paths in the manifold case and as the free category of E in the discrete case. Then, we can define $\mathcal{C}^{cau}$ as the subcategory consisting of "causal paths". For the manifold case, the notion of causal paths can be defined as the paths whose tangent vectors are all in the future light cone. For the graph case, a path (i.e., an arrow in the free category) c is said to be causal if $c = c' \circ c''$ implies $\text{dom}(c') \rightsquigarrow \text{cod}(c')$ and $\text{dom}(c'') \rightsquigarrow \text{cod}(c'')$, where $\rightsquigarrow$ denotes a preorder previously defined on the set of vertices.

Definition 17 (relevant category). *Let $\mathcal{C}$ be a causal category and $\mathcal{O}$ be a subset of $|\mathcal{C}|$. The subcategory of $\mathcal{C}$ generated by*

arrows whose domain and codomain are in $\mathcal{O}$;
causal arrows whose domain is in $\mathcal{O}$ and whose codomain is in $|\mathcal{C}| \setminus \mathcal{O}$;
causal arrows whose codomain is in $\mathcal{O}$ and whose domain is in $|\mathcal{C}| \setminus \mathcal{O}$; and
identity arrows (identified with objects) in $|\mathcal{C}| \setminus \mathcal{O}$,

is called the relevant category for $\mathcal{O}$ and denoted as $\mathcal{O}^{rel}$.

By the definition of relevant categories, the following structure theorem holds.

Theorem 1 (structure theorem for relevant category). *Let $\mathcal{C}$ be a causal category and $\mathcal{O}$ be a subset of $|\mathcal{C}|$. Any arrow in the relevant category $\mathcal{O}^{rel}$ can be written in either of the following forms:*

$$c, c^{out} \circ c, c \circ c^{in}, c^{out} \circ c \circ c^{in}, i,$$

where c denotes an arrow whose domain and codomain is in $\mathcal{O}$; c^{out} denotes a causal arrow whose domain is in $\mathcal{O}$ and whose codomain is in $|\mathcal{C}| \setminus \mathcal{O}$; c^{in} denotes a causal arrow whose codomain is in $\mathcal{O}$ and whose domain is in $|\mathcal{C}| \setminus \mathcal{O}$; and i denotes an identity arrow in $|\mathcal{C}| \setminus \mathcal{O}$.

The notion below is quite important to see the essence of the relativistic structure.

Definition 18 (spacelike separated). *Let $\mathcal{C}$ be a causal category and $\mathcal{O}, \mathcal{O}'$ be a subset of $|\mathcal{C}|$. $\mathcal{O}$ and $\mathcal{O}'$ are said to be spacelike separated if there is no causal arrow between their objects.*

By definition, two spacelike separated subsets are disjoint considering the identity arrows are causal. Moreover, we have the following directly from the structure theorem of the relevant category.

Theorem 2 (non-existence of non-trivial compositable pair). *Let $\mathcal{C}$ be a causal category and $\mathcal{O}, \mathcal{O}'$ be a pair of spacelike separated subsets of $|\mathcal{C}|$. There is no pair of arrows $(c, c') \notin |\mathcal{C}| \times |\mathcal{C}|$ satisfying $c \in \mathcal{O}^{rel}$, $c' \in (\mathcal{O}')^{rel}$ and $\mathrm{cod}(c) = \mathrm{dom}(c')$.*

For the application to quantum theory, the involution structure is important. From now on, we consider a causal category with partial involution structures as defined below.

Definition 19 (partial involution structure on category). *Let $\mathcal{C}$ be a category. A partial involution structure on $\mathcal{C}$ is a subcategory $\mathcal{C}^\sim$ equipped with an involution such that $|\mathcal{C}| = |\mathcal{C}^\sim|$.*

Note that any category $\mathcal{C}$ has the trivial partial involution structure, since $\mathcal{C}$ is equipped with the involution structure $|\mathcal{C}|$, defined as $C^\dagger = C$.

The notion is important because the category $\mathcal{C}^\sim$ physically means the category consisting of "bidirectional" processes. Although this notion is a generalization of the core (i.e., the maximal groupoid in a category consisting of isomorphisms), it does not require the reversibility of the process in the meaning of invertible arrows as isomorphisms. The author believes that this generalization from groupoids to categories and from cores to partial involution structures is quite important for the application to physical phenomena, which include irreversibility.

Based on the partial involution structure, we define the notion of relevant category with involution.

Definition 20 (relevant category with involution). *Let $\mathcal{C}$ be a causal category with the partial involution structure $\mathcal{C}^\sim$. The maximal subcategory $\mathcal{O}^{rel\sim}$ of $\mathcal{C}^\sim$ closed under the involution is called the relevant category with involution on $\mathcal{O}$.*

The importance of the relevant categories with involution concerns the fact that we can naturally define algebras with involution from them. We will see the details of this in the next section.

3. Quantum Fields as Category Algebras

In the previous section, we introduced the notion of causal category equipped with partial involution structures as a generalized "relativity" structure. To combine this structure with the "quantum" structure, which can be modeled by noncommutative algebras, especially effectively by noncommutative algebras over $\mathbb{C}$ as history has shown, we need noncommutative algebras that reflect the structures of categories: category algebra is just the right concept.

3.1. Category Algebra

We introduce the notion of category algebra in this subsection, which is based on [10].

Definition 21 (rig). *A rig R is a set with two binary operations called addition and multiplication, such that*

1. *R is a commutative monoid with respect to addition with the unit 0;*
2. *R is a monoid with respect to multiplication with the unit 1;*
3. *$r''(r' + r) = r''r' + r''r$, $(r'' + r')r = r''r + r'r$ holds for any $r, r', r'' \in R$ (distributive law); and*
4. *$0r = 0$, $r0 = 0$ holds for any $r \in R$ (absorption law).*

Note that, in general, a rig can be noncommutative. The notion of center is important for noncommutative rigs.

Definition 22 (center). *A subrig $Z(R)$ of a rig R defined as the set of elements, which are commutative with all the elements in R, is called the center of R.*

A rig R is commutative if and only if $Z(R) = R$.

Based on the notion of rigs, we define the notion of modules and algebras over rigs.

Definition 23 (module over rig). *A commutative monoid M under addition with unit 0 together with a left action of R on M $(r, m) \mapsto rm$ is called a left module over R if the action satisfies the following conditions:*

1. $r(m' + m) = rm' + rm$, $(r' + r)m = r'm + rm$ for any $m, m' \in M$ and $r, r' \in R$; and
2. $0m = 0$, $r0 = 0$ for any $m \in M$ and $r \in R$.

Dually, we can define the notion of right module over R.

Let M be the left and right module over R. M is called an R-bimodule if

$$r'(mr) = (r'm)r$$

holds for any $r, r' \in R$ and $m \in M$. The left/right action above is called the scalar multiplication.

Definition 24 (algebra over rig). *A bimodule A over R is called an algebra over R if it is also a rig with respect to its own multiplication, which is compatible with scalar multiplication, i.e.,*

$$(r'a')(ar) = r'(a'a)r, \ (a'r)a = a'(ra)$$

for any $a, a' \in A$ and $r, r' \in R$.

We define the principal notion of the present paper:

Definition 25 (category algebra). *Let $\mathcal{C}$ be a category and R be a rig. An R-valued function α defined on $\mathcal{C}$ is said to be of finite propagation if for any object C there are, at most, a finite number of arrows whose codomain or domain is C. The module over R consisting of all R-valued functions of finite propagation together with the multiplication defined by*

$$(\alpha'\alpha)(c'') = \sum_{\{(c',c)|\ c''=c'\circ c\}} \alpha'(c')\alpha(c), \ c, c', c'' \in \mathcal{C}$$

becomes an algebra over R with unit ϵ. This is defined by

$$\epsilon(c) = \begin{cases} 1 & (c \in |\mathcal{C}|) \\ 0 & (otherwise), \end{cases}$$

and is called the category algebra of finite propagation, which is denoted as $R[\mathcal{C}]$. In the present paper, we simply call $R[\mathcal{C}]$ the category algebra of $\mathcal{C}$.

The multiplication defined above is nothing but the "convolution" operation on the category $\mathcal{C}$. $R[\mathcal{C}]$ coincides with the algebra studied in [29] if R is a ring. In [10], it is denoted as $^0R_0[\mathcal{C}]$ to distinguish them from other kinds of category algebras.

A functor from one category to another induces a homomorphism between the corresponding category algebras if the functor is bijective on objects. If the bijective-on-objects functor is also injective on arrows, the induced morphism becomes injective. Hence, the category algebra $R[\mathcal{C}^\circ]$ of a subcategory $\mathcal{C}^\circ$ of a category $\mathcal{C}$ becomes a subalgebra of $R[\mathcal{C}]$.

Definition 26 (indeterminate). *Let $R[\mathcal{C}]$ be a category algebra and $c \in \mathcal{C}$. The function $\iota^c \in R[\mathcal{C}]$ defined as*
$$\iota^c(c') = \begin{cases} 1 & (c' = c) \\ 0 & (otherwise) \end{cases}$$
is called the indeterminate corresponding to c.

In the previous work [10], we denoted the indeterminate ι^c as χ^c. We change the notation to avoid confusion with "character" in representation theory.

For indeterminates, it is easy to obtain the following.

Theorem 3 (calculus of indeterminates). *Let $c, c' \in \mathcal{C}$, $\iota^c, \iota^{c'}$ be the corresponding indeterminates and $r \in R$. Then,*
$$\iota^{c'} \iota^c = \begin{cases} \iota^{c' \circ c} & (\text{dom}(c') = \text{cod}(c)) \\ 0 & (otherwise), \end{cases}$$
$$r\iota^c = \iota^c r.$$

In short, a category algebra $R[\mathcal{C}]$ is an algebra of functions on $\mathcal{C}$, equipped with the multiplication which reflects the compositionality structure of $\mathcal{C}$. By the identification of $c \in \mathcal{C} \mapsto \iota^c \in R[\mathcal{C}]$, categories are included in category algebras.

A category algebra can be considered as a generalized matrix algebra. In fact, matrix algebras are isomorphic to category algebras of indiscrete categories. For the basic notions and rules for matrix-like calculations in category algebras, see [10].

For the main application of the present paper, we need the involution structure on algebras.

Definition 27 (involution on rig). *Let R be a rig. An operation $(\cdot)^*$ on R preserving addition and covariant (resp. contravariant) with respect to multiplication is said to be a covariant (resp. contravariant) involution on R when $(\cdot)^* \circ (\cdot)^*$ is equal to the identity function on R. A rig with contravariant involution is called a *-rig.*

Definition 28 (involution on algebra). *Let A be an algebra over a rig R with a covariant (resp. contravariant) involution $\overline{(\cdot)}$. A covariant (resp. contravariant) involution $(\cdot)^*$ on A as a rig is said to be a covariant (resp. contravariant) involution on A as an algebra over R if it is compatible with scalar multiplication, i.e.,*
$$(r'ar)^* = \overline{r'}a^*\overline{r} \text{ (covariant case)}, \quad (r'ar)^* = \overline{r}a^*\overline{r'} \text{ (contravariant case)}.$$

*An algebra A over a *-rig R with contravariant involution is called a *-algebra over R.*

Theorem 4 (category algebra as algebra with involution). *Let $\mathcal{C}$ be a category with a covariant (resp. contravariant) involution $(\cdot)^\dagger$ and R be a rig with a covariant (resp. contravariant) involution $\overline{(\cdot)}$. Then, the category algebra $R[\mathcal{C}]$ becomes an algebra with covariant involution (resp. *-algebra) over R.*

3.2. Quantum Fields as Category Algebras

In this section, we will show that category algebras provide appropriate models for quantum fields. As already mentioned in the introduction, a quantum field is intuitively a synthesis of relativistic and quantum structures. In the previous section, we argued that the relativistic structure as the basic structure of possible dynamics can be understood from a general point of view by the causal category. The next problem is to construct a noncommutative algebra which is consistent with relativistic covariance as well as with causality. The category algebra $R[\mathcal{C}]$, where $\mathcal{C}$ is a causal category equipped with partial involution structure, is just such an algebra.

Note that by generalizing groupoid algebras to category algebras, we can naturally incorporate processes that are not necessarily reversible. If we focus on the core of the category, i.e., the subcategory consisting of all invertible arrows, we have the corresponding groupoid algebra, which is a subalgebra of $R[\mathcal{C}]$.

Definition 29 (quantum field). *Let $\mathcal{C}$ be a causal category with partial involution structure $\mathcal{C}^\sim$ and R be a rig with involution. The category algebra $R[\mathcal{C}]$ is called the quantum field on $\mathcal{C}$ over R.*

For quantum physics, the cases in which R is some *-algebra over $\mathbb{C}$ are important. The category $\mathcal{C}$ is considered as "spacetime with inner degrees of freedom of the field". Note that a quantum field on a causal category $\mathcal{C}$ over a rig R might be isomorphic to or embedded into another quantum field on another causal category $\tilde{\mathcal{C}}$ over another $\tilde{R}$. Hence, even if we focus on the case that $R = \mathbb{C}$, we might cover many kinds of quantum fields. Nevertheless, we maintain letting R be a general rig R with involution when we can in the present paper for future applications.

Let us see how a quantum field, as a category algebra, incorporates the relativistic covariance structure. To begin, let us assume that a group G (say, the Poincaré group) acts on $|\mathcal{C}|$ and there is a map $u^{(\cdot,\cdot)}$ sending a pair $(g, C) \in G \times \mathcal{C}$ to the arrow $u^{(g,C)} : C \longrightarrow gC$ in $\mathcal{C}$, satisfying $u^{(g'g,C)} = u^{(g',gC)} \circ u^{(g,C)}$ and $u^{(e,C)} = C$, where e denotes the unit of G and C denotes the identity arrow on C in the last equation. Note that each $u^{(g,C)}$ is an invertible arrow. Then, we can define the endfunctor $\widetilde{u^g} : \mathcal{C} \longrightarrow \mathcal{C}$ by

$$\widetilde{u^g}(c) = u^{(g,\operatorname{cod}(c))} \circ c \circ (u^{(g,\operatorname{dom}(c))})^{-1}$$

which becomes invertible and induces the corresponding isomorphism on the category algebra $R[\mathcal{C}]$. Note also that $u^{(g,\cdot)}$ becomes a natural equivalence from $\mathcal{C}$ (identity functor on $\mathcal{C}$) to $\widetilde{u^g}$.

In general, given a natural equivalence u from the identity functor $\mathcal{C}$ to an invertible functor $\hat{u}$ from $\mathcal{C}$ to $\mathcal{C}$, we can define an invertible element $\iota^u \in R[\mathcal{C}]$ as

$$\iota^u(c) = \begin{cases} 1 & (c \text{ is a component of } u) \\ 0 & (\text{otherwise}), \end{cases}$$

and isomorphism $\widetilde{\iota^u}$ on $R[\mathcal{C}]$ as

$$\widetilde{\iota^u}(\alpha) = \iota^u \alpha (\iota^u)^{-1}.$$

This kind of transformation will be useful to study flows, generators, and symmetries such as the local gauge invariance from the viewpoint of category algebras. In sum, the category algebra intrinsically incorporates covariance structures coherent with the structure of "spacetime" category $\mathcal{C}$.

In order to consider the essential features of relativity, it is necessary to consider the structure of causal categories. For this purpose, let us consider the category algebras on relevant categories and relevant categories with involution.

Definition 30 (relevant algebra and local algebra). *Let R be a rig and $\mathcal{C}$ be a causal category. The category algebra $R[\mathcal{O}^{rel}]$ is called the relevant algebra on $\mathcal{O}$ over R. The subrig $R^{loc}[\mathcal{O}]$ of $R[\mathcal{O}^{rel}]$ whose elements are in the form of $\alpha + \delta$, where α denotes an element in $R[\mathcal{O}^{rel}]$, satisfying $\alpha(C) = 0$ for any $C \in |\mathcal{C}| \setminus \mathcal{O}$, and δ denotes an element in $R[\mathcal{O}^{rel}] \cap Z(R[\mathcal{C}])$, becomes an algebra over $Z(R)$ and is called the local algebra on $\mathcal{O}$.*

Definition 31 (relevant algebra with involution and local algebra with involution). *Let R be a rig with involution and $\mathcal{C}$ be a causal category with partial involution structure. The category algebra $R[\mathcal{O}^{rel\sim}]$ is called the relevant algebra with involution on $\mathcal{O}$ over R. The subrig $R^{loc\sim}[\mathcal{O}]$ of $R[\mathcal{O}^{rel\sim}]$, whose elements are in the form of $\alpha + \delta$, where α denotes an element in $R[\mathcal{O}^{rel\sim}]$,* satisfying $\alpha(C) = 0$ for any $C \in |\mathcal{C}| \setminus \mathcal{O}$, and δ denotes an element in $R[\mathcal{O}^{rel\sim}] \cap Z(R[\mathcal{C}])$, becomes an algebra with involution over $Z(R)$ and is called the local algebra with involution on $\mathcal{O}$.

The family of local algebras with involution $\{R^{loc}[\mathcal{O}]\}$, especially when R is a *-algebra over $\mathcal{C}$, is the counterpart of $\{\mathcal{A}(\mathcal{O})\}$ in AQFT [4], where $\mathcal{A}(\mathcal{O})$ denotes the observable algebra defined on the bounded region $\mathcal{O}$ in the spacetime. So far, our framework does not focus on the topological aspect of algebras but the conceptual correspondence between our framework and AQFT is remarkable, as we will see below.

Note that our "local" algebras in general contain a certain kind of information of the "outside" of the regions. Nevertheless, they contain no information of the local algebras corresponding to spacelike separated regions. From the structure theorem of the relevant category and the definition of local algebras, we have the following concepts.

Theorem 5 (commutativity of spacelike separated local algebras). *Local algebras $R^{loc}[\mathcal{O}]$ and $R^{loc}[\mathcal{O}']$ are commutative with each other if the regions $\mathcal{O}$ and $\mathcal{O}'$ are spacelike separated from each other.*

As a collorary, we have the following.

Theorem 6 (commutativity of spacelike separated local algebras with involution). *Local algebras $R^{loc\sim}[\mathcal{O}]$ and $R^{loc\sim}[\mathcal{O}']$ with involution are commutative with each other if the regions $\mathcal{O}$ and $\mathcal{O}'$ are spacelike separated from each other.*

The theorem above is the conceptual counterpart of one of the axioms called the "Einstein causality" ("Axiom E" in [4]).

3.3. Remarks on the Comparison to TQFT

Our category algebraic framework of quantum field theory can also be compared to the conceptual ideas in other axiomatic approaches to quantum fields, such as Topological Quantum Field Theory (TQFT) [12,13]. In the axiomatization of TQFT, a quantum field theory is considered as a certain functor from the category of n-cobordism $nCob$ into the category $Mod(R)$ of modules over some unital commutative ring R (the typical case is $R = \mathbb{C}$ and $Mod(R) = Vect$, where $Vect$ denotes the category of vector spaces over $\mathbb{C}$).

We can construct such a functor in a generalized setting based on our framework. Let C be an object in a †-category $\mathcal{C}$ and R be a rig. We define the submodule $^C R[\mathcal{C}]$ of $R[\mathcal{C}]$, consisting of elements whose support is included in the set of arrows whose codomain is C. Then, we can define a functor $^{(\cdot)}R : \mathcal{C} \longrightarrow Mod(R)$ by $^C R = \iota^c(\cdot)$, the multiplication of ι^c, i.e., a module homomorphism sending each $\alpha \in {}^{\text{dom}(c)}R[\mathcal{C}]$ to $\iota^c \alpha \in {}^{\text{cod}(c)}R[\mathcal{C}]$, for any $c \in \mathcal{C}$.

Since $nCob$ is a †-category, the above construction works and we obtain a canonical functor from $nCob$ to $Mod(R)$. Although this functor does not satisfy all the technical parts of the axioms proposed in TQFT, it is coherent with the physical ideas of relativistic covariance and quantum properties behind the axioms. This coherence will become more clear after introducing the notion of states on categories in the next section.

4. States of Quantum Fields as States on Categories

4.1. State on Category

While an algebra embodies the intrinsic structure of a system, a state embodies the interface between that system and its environment. This view, which has been advocated by Ojima [30], is consistent with the mathematical framework of algebraic quantum field theory and quantum probability theory: states provide concrete representations of an algebra.

In general, a representation refers to an expression of intrinsic structures in a certain way, which corresponds to the concrete realization of the intrinsic properties of a system in the way it interacts with its environment. To be more specific, a state is a mapping which sends elements of an algebra to scalar values as "expectation values". In short, states define the statistical laws, which generalize the notion of probability measures to the noncommutative context. Conversely, if the algebra is a unital commutative C^*-algebra, we have the Radon measure on a compact Hausdorff space by the Riesz–Markov–Kakutani theorem [31]. In other words, a pair of an algebra and state on it is a generalized probability space: a noncommutative probability space.

As for the category algebras that reflect the structure of the possible dynamics, defining a state on it means evaluating arrows corresponding to the individual processes with expectation values. Conversely, for a category with a finite number of objects, the weighting of the arrows gives a state. Based on this fact, we call a state on a category algebra, a state on category by abuse of terminology.

The rest of this subsection is based on [10].

Definition 32 (linear functional). *Let A be an algebra over a rig R. An R-valued linear function on A, i.e., a function preserving addition and scalar multiplication, is called a linear functional on A. A linear functional on A is said to be unital if $\varphi(\epsilon) = 1$, where ϵ and 1 denote the multiplicative units in A and R, respectively.*

Definition 33 (positivity). *A pair of rigs with involution (R, R_+) is called a positivity structure on R if R_+ is a subrig with involution such that $r, s \in R_+$ and $r + s = 0$ imply $r = s = 0$, and that $a^*a \in R_+$ for any $a \in R$.*

Definition 34 (state). *Let R be a rig with involution and (R, R_+) be a positivity structure on R. A state φ on an algebra A with involution over R with respect to (R, R_+) is a unital linear functional $\varphi : A \longrightarrow R$, which satisfies $\varphi(a^*a) \in R_+$ and $\varphi(a^*) = \overline{\varphi(a)}$ for any $a \in R$, where $(\cdot)^*$ and $\overline{(\cdot)}$ denote the involutions on A and R, respectively (the last condition $\varphi(a^*) = \overline{\varphi(a)}$ follows from other conditions if $R = \mathbb{C}$).*

Definition 35 (noncommutative probability space). *A pair (A, φ) consisting of an algebra A with involution over a rig R with involution and a state φ is called a noncommutative probability space.*

Definition 36 (state on category). *Let R be a rig with involution and (R, R_+) be a positivity structure on R. A state on the category algebra $R[\mathcal{C}]$ over R with respect to (R, R_+) is said to be a state on a category $\mathcal{C}$ with respect to (R, R_+).*

Given a state φ on a category $\mathcal{C}$ with involution, we have a function $\hat{\varphi} : \mathcal{C} \longrightarrow R$ defined as $\hat{\varphi}(c) = \varphi(\iota^c)$. For the category with a finite number of objects, we can obtain the following theorem [10], which is a generalization of the result in [14] for groupoids.

Theorem 7 (state and normalized positive semidefinite function). *Let $\mathcal{C}$ be a category such that $|\mathcal{C}|$ is finite. Then, there is a one-to-one correspondence between states φ with respect to (R, R_+) and normalized positive semidefinite $Z(R)$-valued functions ϕ with respect to (R, R_+), i.e., normalized functions such that*

$$\sum_{\{(c,c')|\mathrm{dom}((c')^\dagger)=\mathrm{cod}(c)\}} \overline{\xi(c')}\phi((c')^\dagger \circ c)\xi(c)$$

is in R_+ for any R-valued function ξ on $\mathcal{C}$ with finite support and that $\phi(c^\dagger) = \overline{\phi(c)}$, where $(\cdot)^*$ and $\overline{(\cdot)}$ denote the involutions on $\mathcal{C}$ and R, respectively.

Conceptually, the theorem above means that states on a category with involution (with finite objects) are nothing but the weights on arrows, which are generalizations of probability distributions on a (finite) set as the discrete category (with finite objects). More generally, we can say that to define a state on a category whose support is contained in a subcategory with finite numbers of objects is equivalent to defining the corresponding function which assigns the weight to each arrow.

For a state on a category whose support is not contained in a subcategory with finite number of objects, we will need some topological structures (or coarse geometric structures [32]). Nonstandard-analytical methods (see [33], for example) will provide useful tools.

4.2. States of Quantum Fields as States on Categories

As we see quantum fields as category algebras, it is quite natural to model physical states of quantum fields as states on category algebras.

Definition 37 (state of quantum field). *Let $\mathcal{C}$ be a causal category with partial involution structure $\mathcal{C}^\sim$ and (R, R_+) be a positivity structure on a rig R with involution. A unital linear functional on $\mathcal{C}$, which is also a state on $\mathcal{C}^\sim$ with respect to (R, R_+), whose image is contained in a subrig R' with involution of R, is said to be an R'-valued state of the quantum field on $\mathcal{C}$ over R with respect to (R, R_+).*

In conventional cases, R is supposed to be a *-algebra over $\mathbb{C}$ and $R' = \mathbb{C}$. The phrase "with respect to (R, R_+)" will be omitted if it is clear in the context. In general, given a state φ on *-algebra A over a *-rig R with involution, we can construct the representation of the algebra into the algebra consisting of endomorphism on a certain module (generalized GNS representation [10]). In particular, when R is a *-rig over $\mathbb{C}$ and φ is $\mathbb{C}$-valued, we have a representation called the GNS (Gelfand–Naimar–Segal) representation [34,35] into a pre-Hilbert space consisting of the equivalence class of the elements in A, equipped with the inner product structure induced by the sesquilinear form $\langle a', a \rangle = \varphi((a')^*a)$ $(a, a' \in A)$. The unit of the algebra plays a role of a "vacuum" vector (see [10] and reference therein, for example).

In sum, a noncommutative probability space, i.e., a pair (A, φ) of a *-algebra over $\mathbb{C}$ and a $\mathbb{C}$-valued state on it, is sufficient to reconstruct the ingredients in conventional quantum physics based on the Hilbert spaces. In fact, the approach based on the noncommutative probability space is more general than the conventional approach: if we focus onto the local structures of quantum fields, it is known that we cannot use one a priori Hilbert space as a starting point of the theory (actually, this fact itself was one of the historical motivations of AQFT, the pioneer of noncommutative probabilistic approach; see [4], for example).

Our category algebraic approach is a new unification of the noncommutative probabilistic approach and the category theoretic viewpoint. As we observed in the previous section, for †-category (or in general, categories with involution), its category algebra is a *-algebra (or in general, an algebra with involution). Note that our algebra is unital, even if $\mathcal{C}$ has infinitely many objects. Then, the construction above holds and we can see the unit ϵ as a "vacuum" in our theory.

The concept of states on categories also shed light on the foundation of quantum mechanics as a part of the quantum field theory. From our viewpoint, a quantum mechanical system of finite degrees of freedom can be defined as a noncommutative probability space whose algebra is a subalgebra of a category algebra on a causal category with partial involution and whose state satisfies the condition that the support is contained in a subcategory with finite numbers of objects.

In general, quantum fields as category algebras together with states "contain" vast numbers of quantum mechanical systems, or, more precisely, considering a state whose support is contained in some subcategory with finite numbers of objects, is focusing on a quantum mechanical system as an aspect of the quantum field. Note that quantum mechanical systems in the above meaning are not necessarily contained in a single point but can have spatial degrees of freedom, e.g., a system in the double slit experiment, in which the support of the state can be considered to be contained in a subcategory with finite objects. Understanding the situation in which multiple observers are involved in a single quantum field—such as the EPR (Einstein–Podolsky–Rosen) situation [36]—through the concepts of local algebra and local states also seems to be an important research topic.

The idea at the heart of the above discussions is that we are free to think of "localized states" (not just "global" states such as vacuum states). The concept corresponding to these kinds of states is particularly important in the context of AQFT and is called "local states" [15,16]. We can define the local states in our framework, which is a conceptual counterpart of the local states in AQFR, as follows.

Definition 38 (local state). *Let $\mathcal{C}$ be a causal category equipped with partial involution structure $\mathcal{C}^\sim$ and R be a rig with involution. A state on $R[\mathcal{C}^\sim(\mathcal{O})]$ for a subset $\mathcal{O}$ of $|\mathcal{C}|$ is called a local state of the quantum field $R[\mathcal{C}]$ on $\mathcal{O}$.*

From a physical point of view, the notion of local state is quite natural. A macroscopic setting of the environment for the quantum field basically concerns only a bounded space-time domain and the global state should be seen as an idealization of it. Considering a family of local states, instead of a single state, can be seen as a sheaf theoretic extension of the conventional quantum field theory. The extension will lead to the notion of consistent families of Hilbert spaces and operators on them through the GNS construction, which will be mathematically interesting.

By translating the previous study of [15] into our context, we will be able to construct the generalized sector theory, which is the generalization of DHR (Doplicher–Haag–Roberts)–DR (Doplicher–Roberts) Theory [17–23], as well as develop Ojima's micro–macro duality [24,25] and quadrality scheme [26] from the viewpoint of category algebras and states on categories.

4.3. Remarks on the Comparison to TQFT (Continued)

In Section 3, we constructed for any †-category $\mathcal{C}$ a functor $^{(\cdot)}R : \mathcal{C} \longrightarrow Mod(R)$ by $^cR = \iota^c(\cdot)$ for $c \in \mathcal{C}$. For quantum physical studies, we need to induce a functor into $Hilb$, which is a category of Hilbert spaces over $\mathbb{C}$. Let us explain the role of states in this induction.

Given any state φ on the †-category $\mathcal{C}$, $^C R := {}^C R[\mathcal{C}]$ for each object $C \in \mathcal{C}$ can be equipped with the "almost inner product" (semi-Hilbert space structure) by defining the sesquilinear form $\langle \cdot | \cdot \rangle^\varphi$ by $\langle \alpha' | \alpha \rangle^\varphi := \varphi((\alpha')^* \alpha)$ (generalized GNS construction, see [10] and references therein). When R is a $*$-algebra over $\mathbb{C}$ and φ is a $\mathbb{C}$-valued "good" state φ on the category given, this functor induces a functor into $Hilb$. More precisely, suppose that R is a $*$-algebra over $\mathbb{C}$ and the $\mathbb{C}$-valued state φ satisfies the condition

$$\varphi(\alpha^* \alpha) \geq \varphi((\iota^c \alpha)^* (\iota^c \alpha))$$

for any $\alpha \in R[\mathcal{C}]$ and $c \in \mathcal{C}$. Then, the functor $^{(\cdot)}R : \mathcal{C} \longrightarrow Mod(R)$ induces the functor $^{(\cdot)}R^\varphi : \mathcal{C} \longrightarrow preHilb$, where $preHilb$ denotes the category of the pre-Hilbert spaces, taking the quotient of $^C R$ equipped with $\langle \cdot | \cdot \rangle^\varphi$ by $N^\varphi = \{\alpha \in {}^C R | \varphi(\alpha^* \alpha) = 0\}$, which can be shown as a submodule of $^C R$ (note that by the assumption $\varphi(\alpha^* \alpha) = 0 \Longrightarrow \varphi((\iota^c \alpha)^* (\iota^c \alpha)) = 0$ holds; this kind of construction itself has a certain generalization to a more general R by using this condition directly). Then, by the assumption of φ, $^{(c)}R^\varphi$ extends uniquely to the morphism in $Hilb$ by completion and we have the corresponding functor from $\mathcal{C}$ to $Hilb$, which sends c to the unique bounded extension of $^{(c)}R^\varphi$ (note that a bounded operator between pre-Hilbert spaces extends to the unique bounded operator between Hilbert spaces). By applying this construction for $\mathcal{C} = nCob$, we have a version of TQFT. Note that our framework is naturally incorporated with the causal structure and it is quite interesting to the counterpart of the structure in TQFT.

5. Prospects

As we have seen, our new approach to quantum fields is conceptually related to conventional approaches such as AQFT and TQFT. Elucidating this relationship at a deeper level will be important in the study of quantum fields. In order to carry out such research, we will need to include more detailed structures such as topological or differential structures in addition to the algebraic and noncommutative probabilistic structures that we have discussed in this paper.

Additionally, it should be emphasized that our approach is directly applicable to the lattice gauge theory [27] and other discrete spacetime approaches, as can be seen from the fact that our approach works on general categories. Its applicability extends to the context of unifying general relativity and quantum theory.

Needless to say, the relationship with categorical approaches to quantum theory, such as "categorical quantum mechanics" [37,38] based on the †-category, should also be explored. The categorical structure of the submodules of the category algebra, as a generalized matrix algebra and regarding the computations based on it, will play an important role. It is also interesting to clarify the relationship between our framework and the approach in a recently published article [8], which also investigates the AQFT and Quantum Cellular Automata (QCA) approach [39,40] from a general categorical viewpoint.

The notion of quantum walk (see [41,42] and references therein, for example), which is closely related to the QCA approach, can also be formulated from our standpoint. Based on our framework, we can model a concrete dynamics of quantum fields as a sequence or flow of the states on a category. In general, the dynamics can be irreversible. The typical examples of reversible dynamics are called quantum walks. The notion of quantum walks on general *-algebras and quantum walks on †-categories can be defined as follows:

Definition 39 (quantum walk). *Let A be a *-algebra. A sequence of states given by*

$$\varphi^t(\alpha) = \varphi((\omega^*)^t \alpha \omega^t) \quad t = 0, 1, 2, 3, \ldots$$

generated by a unitary element $\omega \in R[\mathcal{C}]$, i.e., an element satisfying $\omega^* \omega = \omega \omega^* = \epsilon$, is called a quantum walk on A.

Definition 40 (quantum walk on †-category). *Let $\mathcal{C}$ be a †-category and R be a *-rig. A quantum walk on $R[\mathcal{C}]$ is said to be a quantum walk on a †-category $\mathcal{C}$.*

A quantum walk can be considered as a sequence of "state vectors" through the GNS construction. the notion of quantum walk defined on †-category includes the various concrete dynamical models under the name of quantum walks. For example, this includes quantum walks on simple undirected graphs as a certain sequence of states on an indiscrete category. The category algebraic approach will play a fundamental role for the quantum walks on graphs with multiple edges and loops. Quantum walks on graphs have been used in the modeling of the "dressed photon" [43], which cannot be understood without focusing on the off-shell nature of quantum fields [44], i.e., the aspect of quantum fields which cannot be described as the collection of the modes satisfying the on-shell conditions, and quantum walks on categories may become important in quantum field theory in general. They will also connect the QCA approach to quantum fields and other approaches to quantum fields.

One of the most exciting problems is, of course, to construct a model of a non-trivial quantum field with interactions. We believe we can approach such problems. In particular, it seems that the fact that relevant categories have arrows that go through objects in very distant regions, while the local algebras defined on them satisfy commutativity, may be the key to avoiding various no-go theorems. Note also that our approach extends the coefficients to general (commutative or noncommutative) rigs, which greatly expands the possibilities of investigating interactions. Finally, it should be emphasized that our approach is not limited to quantum fields but can be extended to give a very general noncommutative statistical models with causal structures. The author hopes that the present paper will be a small, new step towards these big problems.

Funding: This work was partially supported by Research Origin for Dressed Photon, JSPS KAKENHI (grant number 19K03608 and 20H00001), and JST CREST (JPMJCR17N2).

Institutional Review Board Statement: Not applicable.

Informed Consent Statement: Not applicable.

Acknowledgments: The author is grateful to Hiroshi Ando, Takahiro Hasebe, Soichiro Fujii, Izumi Ojima, Kazuya Okamura, Misa Saigo, and Juzo Nohmi for the fruitful discussions and comments.

Conflicts of Interest: The author declares no conflict of interest.

References

1. Haag, R. On Quantum Field Theory. *Dan. Mat. Fys. Medd.* **1955**, *29*, 12.
2. Hall, D.; Wightman, A.S. A Theorem on Invariant Analytic Functions with Applications to Relativistic Quantum Field Theory. *Mat. Fys. Medd. Dan. Vid. Selsk.* **1957**, *31*, 5.
3. Streater, R.F.; Wightman, A.S. *PCT, Spin and Statistics, and All That*; Princeton University Press: Princeton, NJ, USA, 2000.
4. Haag, R. *Local Quantum Physics*, 2nd ed.; Springer: Berlin/Heidelberg, Germany, 1996.
5. Simon, I. Limited subsets of a free monoid. In *19th Annual Symposium on Foundations of Computer Science*; IEEE: Piscataway, NJ, USA, 1978; pp. 143–150.
6. Malament, D.B. The class of continuous timelike curves determines the topology of spacetime. *J. Math. Phys.* **1977**, *18*, 1399–1404. [CrossRef]
7. Hawking, S.W.; King, A.R.; McCarthy, P.J. A New Topology for Curved Space-Time Which Incorporates the Causal, Differential, and Conformal Structures. *J. Math. Phys.* **1976**, *17*, 174–181. [CrossRef]
8. Gogioso, S.; Stasinou, E.; Coecke, B. Functorial Evolution of Quantum Fields. *Front. Phys.* **2021**, *9*, 534265. [CrossRef]
9. Bombelli, L.; Lee, J.; Meyer, D.; Sorkin, R.D. Space-time as a causal set. *Phys. Rev. Lett.* **1987**, *59*, 521. [CrossRef]
10. Saigo, H. Category Algebras and States on Categories. *Symmetry* **2021**, *13*, 1172. [CrossRef]
11. Haag, R.; Kastler, D. An algebraic approach to quantum field theory. *J. Math. Phys.* **1964**, *5*, 848–861. [CrossRef]
12. Atiyah, M. Topological Quantum Field Theories. *Publ. Math. de l'Institut des Hautes Sci.* **1988**, *68*, 175–186. [CrossRef]
13. Witten, E. Topological Quantum Field Theory. *Commun. Math. Phys.* **1988**, *117*, 353–386. [CrossRef]
14. Ciaglia, F.M.; Ibort, A.; Marmo, G. Schwinger's Picture of Quantum Mechanics III: The statistical Interpretation. *Int. J. Geom. Meth. Modern Phys.* **2019**, *16*, 1950165. [CrossRef]
15. Ojima, I.; Okamura, K.; Saigo, H. Local State and Sector Theory in Local Quantum Physics. *Lett. Math. Phys.* **2016**, *106*, 741–763. [CrossRef]
16. Werner, R.F. Local preparability of states and the split property in quantum field theory. *Lett. Math. Phys.* **1987**, *13*, 325–329. [CrossRef]
17. Doplicher, S.; Haag, R.; Roberts, J.E. Fields, observables and gauge transformations I. *Commun. Math. Phys.* **1969**, *13*, 1–23. [CrossRef]
18. Doplicher, S.; Haag, R.; Roberts, J.E. Fields, observables and gauge transformations II. *Commun. Math. Phys.* **1969**, *15*, 173–200. [CrossRef]
19. Doplicher, S.; Haag, R.; Roberts, J.E. Local observables and particle statistics, I. *Commun. Math. Phys.* **1971**, *23*, 199–230. [CrossRef]
20. Doplicher, S.; Haag, R.; Roberts, J.E. Local observables and particle statistics, II. *Commun. Math. Phys.* **1974**, *35*, 49–85. [CrossRef]
21. Doplicher, S.; Roberts, J.E. Endomorphism of C*-algebras, cross products and duality for compact groups. *Ann. Math.* **1989**, *130*, 75–119. [CrossRef]
22. Doplicher, S.; Roberts, J.E. A new duality theory for compact groups. *Invent. Math.* **1989**, *98*, 157–218. [CrossRef]
23. Doplicher, S.; Roberts, J.E. Why there is a field algebra with a compact gauge group describing the superselection structure in particle physics. *Commun. Math. Phys.* **1990**, *131*, 51–107. [CrossRef]
24. Ojima, I. A unified scheme for generalized sectors based on selection criteria—Order parameters of symmetries and of thermality and physical meanings of adjunctions. *Open Syst. Inf. Dyn.* **2003**, *10*, 235–279. [CrossRef]
25. Ojima, I. Micro-Macro Duality in Quantum Physics. In *Proceedings in International Conference on Stochastic Analysis, Classical and Quantum*; World Scientific: Singapore, 2005; pp. 143–161.
26. Ojima, I. Meaning of Non-Extensive Entropies in Micro-Macro Duality. *J. Phys. Conf. Ser.* **2010**, *201*, 012017. [CrossRef]
27. Wilson, K.G. Confinement of quarks. *Phys. Rev. D* **1974**, *10*, 2445. [CrossRef]
28. Brown, R. Moore hyperrectangles on a space form a strict cubical omega-category. *arXiv* **2009**, arXiv:0909.2212v2.
29. Mitchel, B. Rings with several objects. *Adv. Math.* **1972**, *8*, 1–161. [CrossRef]
30. Ojima, I. Fundamental Concepts in Quantum Physics. In *Quantum Information and Evolution Dynamics*; Makino-Shoten: Tokyo, Japan, 1996. (In Japanese)
31. Hora, A.; Obata, N. *Quantum Probability and Spectral Analysis of Graphs*; Springer: Berlin/Heidelberg, Germany, 2007.
32. Roe, J. *Lectures on Coarse Geometry*; University Lecture Series 31; American Mathematical Society: Providence, RI, USA, 2003.
33. Saigo, H.; Nohmi, J. Categorical Nonstandard Analysis. *Symmetry* **2021**, *13*, 1573. [CrossRef]
34. Gelfand, I.; Neumark, M. On the imbedding of normed rings into the ring of operators in Hilbert space. *Mat. Sb.* **1943**, *12*, 187–217.

35. Segal, I.E. Irreducible representations of operator algebras. *Bull. Am. Math. Soc.* **1947**, *53*, 73–88. [CrossRef]
36. Einstein, A.; Podolsky, B.; Rosen, N. Can Quantum-Mechanical Description of Physical Reality Be Considered Complete? *Phys. Rev.* **1935**, *47*, 777–780. [CrossRef]
37. Abramsky, S.; Coecke, B. A categorical semantics of quantum protocols. In Proceedings of the 19th Annual IEEE Symposium on Logic in Computer Science, Turku, Finland, 17 July 2004; pp. 415–425
38. Abramsky, S.; Coecke, B. Categorical quantum mechanics. In *Handbook of Quantum Logic and Quantum Structures*; Engesser, K., Gabbay, D.M., Lehmann, D., Eds.; Elsevier: Amsterdam, The Netherlands, 2008; pp. 261–323.
39. Arrighi, P. An Overview of Quantum Cellular Automata. *Nat. Comput.* **2019**, *18*, 885–899. [CrossRef]
40. D'Ariano, G.M.; Perinotti, P. Quantum Cellular Automata and Free Quantum Field Theory. *Front. Phys.* **2016**, *12*, 120301. [CrossRef]
41. Ambainis, A. Quantum walk algorithm for element distinctness. In Proceedings of the 45th IEEE Symposium on Foundations of Computer Science (FOCS), Washington, DC, USA, 17–19 October 2004; pp. 22–31.
42. Konno, N. Quantum Walks. In *Quantum Potential Theory*; Franz, U., Schürmann, M., Eds.; Lecture Notes in Mathematics, 1954; Springer: Heidelberg, Germany, 2008; pp. 309–452.
43. Ohtsu, M. *Dressed Photons*; Springer: Berlin/Heidelberg, Germany, 2014.
44. Hamano, M.; Saigo, H. Quantum Walk and Dressed Photon. *Electron. Proc. Theor. Comput. Sci.* **2020**, *315*, 93–99. [CrossRef]

Article

Description of Dressed-Photon Dynamics and Extraction Process

Suguru Sangu [1,*] and Hayato Saigo [2]

[1] Advanced Technology R&D Division, Ricoh Company, Ltd., Ebina 243-0460, Japan
[2] Department of Bioscience, Nagahama Institute of Bio-Science and Technology, Nagahama 526-0829, Japan; h_saigoh@nagahama-i-bio.ac.jp
* Correspondence: suguru.sangu@jp.ricoh.com

Abstract: Several interesting physical phenomena and industrial applications explained by the dressed photon have been reported in recent years. These require a novel concept in an off-shell science that deviates from the conventional optics, satisfying energy and momentum conservation laws. In this paper, starting from an original model that captures dressed-photon characteristics phenomenologically, the dynamics of the dressed photon in a nanomatter system and the mechanism for extracting internal degrees of freedom of the dressed photon to an external space have been examined by theoretical and numerical approaches. Our proposal is that basis states of the dressed photon can be transformed to the form that reflects the spatial distribution of the dressed-photon steady state in the system, and some of basis states with predetermined spatial distribution can relate to the dissipation components in the external space by means of the renormalization technique. From the results of numerical simulation, it is found that quasi-static states are regarded as the photon with light mass or massless, and the extraction of active states strongly affects the spatial distribution in a new steady state. The concept for extracting dressed-photon energy to an external space will contribute to a detailed understanding of dressed-photon physics and future industrial applications.

Keywords: dressed photon; localization; dissipation; off-shell science; non-equilibrium open system; quantum master equation; quantum density matrix; projection operator; renormalization

Citation: Sangu, S.; Saigo, H. Description of Dressed-Photon Dynamics and Extraction Process. *Symmetry* **2021**, *13*, 1768. https://doi.org/10.3390/sym13101768

Academic Editor: Motoichi Ohtsu

Received: 3 September 2021
Accepted: 20 September 2021
Published: 23 September 2021

Publisher's Note: MDPI stays neutral with regard to jurisdictional claims in published maps and institutional affiliations.

Copyright: © 2021 by the authors. Licensee MDPI, Basel, Switzerland. This article is an open access article distributed under the terms and conditions of the Creative Commons Attribution (CC BY) license (https://creativecommons.org/licenses/by/4.0/).

1. Introduction

In recent years, some novel and fundamental experimental studies have been reported that originate from the photon localized at a nanometer scale. For example, a Si light emitter with a nanostructure of boron dopants has been demonstrated, where Si is an indirect semiconductor and such an optical transition is forbidden in the conventional optics [1,2]. For microfabrication techniques, size-selective and non-adiabatic photochemical reactions (etching [3] and deposition [4]) have been observed on rough surfaces with nanostructures and under nanometrically tapered optical fiber probes. Furthermore, a giant magneto-optical effect using a ZnO single crystal with a nanostructure of the dopant has been confirmed as a surprising experimental result [5]. To explain these experimental facts, it is necessary to step into an off-shell science [6,7], which is a concept that overcomes the conventional optics limited by energy and momentum conservation laws. The origin of the appearance of strange optical phenomena in the off-shell region is considered to be environmental effects of background materials, such as the electronic excitation field and the phonon field, on the internal photon field, which is called the dressed photon. However, it is a challenging task to build a complete theory, since this would require incorporating an unknown contribution of infinite degrees of freedom. Thus, a simple theoretical expression without losing the essence of the dressed photon is strongly desired.

In this paper, a phenomenological model of the dressed photon is proposed without touching on the specific generation process of the dressed photon. At first glance, such a model may resemble an exciton–polariton picture, but the dressed photon is considered to be a quasi-particle bounded in a finite distance with the help of the surrounding electronic and phononic excitations, and the energy transfer of the dressed photon via the off-shell region or non-resonant region is allowed. This is the difference between the dressed photon and the exciton polariton. A numerical simulation is also demonstrated for expressing the dressed photon dynamics, and discussing the extraction of energy from the internal dressed-photon system to the external field.

The logical flow in this paper is summarized as follows. The spatial distribution of the dressed photon has been decomposed into plural characteristic basis states reflecting a certain steady state. At this time, the basis states can be distinguished into strong and weak contributions to the system dynamics by referring to the formula for renormalizing the weak interaction into the strong one. The weak-interacting basis states can be regarded as quasi-particle states with a light mass that resemble a photon reservoir system. In this way, the influence of a microscopic system on a macroscopic one can be formulated, and the microscopic system can be controlled from the macroscopic one. It will be a clue to explain the emergence of optical functions via the dressed photon, such as the light emission from indirect semiconductors.

The following sections are constructed to evaluate the above concept as follows. Section 2 describes the formulation of dressed-photon dynamics. Here, in addition to providing the equation of motion in a non-equilibrium system, dressed-photon basis states characterized by the spatial distribution is introduced for the subsequent discussions. In Section 3, a method for dividing a dressed-photon system into the systems with strong and weak contributions is proposed using the renormalization technique. Section 4 gives an insight for connecting the dressed photon with the external free photon, based on the method obtained up to Section 3. In addition, we will discuss how to control the dressed photon from the external degree of freedom. Finally, Section 5 summarizes this paper.

2. Theoretical Model of a Dressed-Photon System

2.1. Quantum Master Equation

From the experimental situation for a nanophotonics system, one can understand that the system always exists under an environment with the external photoexcitation and the dissipation, and the balance of the input and the output is maintained. This is a non-equilibrium open system. For describing the dressed-photon dynamics, the dressed photon is assumed to be a carrier bounded in a nanomatter system, and a part of energy dissipates to the external field as the free photon, where the optical coherence is disappeared. In other words, it is a problem to analyze the internal states of the dressed photon distributed in a non-equilibrium open system.

A nanomatter with an arbitrary shape is expressed as a collection of nodes that bind the dressed photon, and are freely arranged inside a matter. To avoid misunderstanding, note that the node does not mean the atomic site, but a center of mass for the dressed photon with spatial spreading. Therefore, the nodes are not restricted by a periodic array structure representing the translational symmetry of such an electron wave, and can set freely. This paper is not intended to describe a rigorous structure of a matter, but rather to represent adequately the essence of dressed-photon mediating phenomena. From this point of view, this model is equivalent to a quantum walk on a graph. Several studies have also been reported that suggest that dressed-photon phenomena correspond to some stationary solution in a quantum-walk system [8,9].

The dressed photon as a carrier is assumed to be transferred among the nodes by the hopping conduction, such that the coupling strength is expressed as a function of distance between a target node and all the others. Figure 1 illustrates a dressed-photon system, where a nanoscale two-dimensional taper structure and a nanomatter are expressed as just a collection of nodes without distinguishing the two separated parts. In this system, the dressed photon is injected from the upper part of a taper structure, released to the external field radiatively, and returns to the input side non-radiatively. This model is a non-equilibrium open system. The equation of motion, that is a quantum master equation, in such a system can be described using the quantum density operator $\rho(t)$ as follows [10–12],

$$\frac{\partial \rho^I(t)}{\partial t} = -\frac{i}{\hbar}\left[H_{\text{int}}^I + H_{\text{exc}}^I, \rho^I(t)\right] + \mathcal{L}^{(\text{nr})}\rho^I(t) + \mathcal{L}^{(\text{r})}\rho^I(t), \quad (1)$$

where the superscript I for each operator represents the interaction picture, and the hopping energy transfer and the coherent excitation are expressed as H_{int} and H_{exc}, respectively. The square brackets represent the commutation relation, and $\mathcal{L}^{(\text{r})}$ and $\mathcal{L}^{(\text{nr})}$ mean the Lindblad-type radiative and the non-radiative dissipations. The following devotes explanation of each component in (1), where the superscript I for the interaction picture is omitted to avoid the complexity of the subscript and superscript expressions. In defining the operators that are used in this research, the basis states are assumed to be a one or zero dressed photon. This means an assumption of the weak excitation limit. In the future, the many-body interaction of the dressed photon, i.e., the nonlinear problem, should be considered, and it will be reported somewhere.

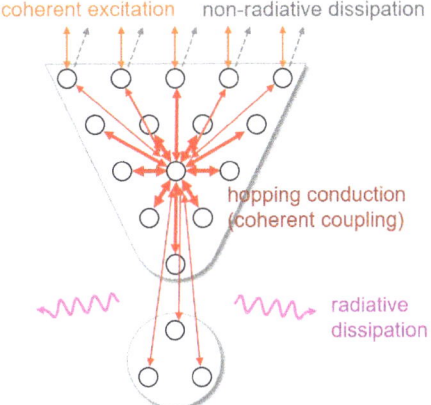

Figure 1. Schematic illustration of a dressed-photon system that consists of plural arbitrarily arranged nodes and models a taper structure of an optical fiber probe and a nanomatter. It is not necessary to distinguish between the taper and the nanomatter, as it is regarded as just a collection of nodes. In this system, the dressed photon is coherently excited from the upper part of the taper structure, and transfers via the hopping conduction among nodes with the coupling strength according to the distance. Some dressed photon dissipates out of the system as the free photon, and some returns to the input side non-radiatively.

2.1.1. Dressed-Photon Excitation by External Field

The external excitation of the dressed photon is assumed to be given coherently from the upper part in a taper structure in Figure 1. When the creation and annihilation operators $a_i^\dagger$ and a_i of the dressed photon at a node i are predetermined, the excitation is expressed as

$$H_{\text{exc}} = \sum_{i \in \text{edge}} \hbar A (a_i + a_i^\dagger), \quad (2)$$

where $\hbar A$ denotes the strength of the excitation that is related to the amplitude of the external input field. The form of (2) is inspired by the theoretical description of the conventional electric dipole excitation.

2.1.2. Inter-Node Energy Transfer

The hopping energy transfer means mathematically an exchange of the dressed photon between two different nodes, which is given by the following equation,

$$H_{\text{int}} = \sum_{i \neq j} \hbar V(|\mathbf{r}_i - \mathbf{r}_j|)(a_i^\dagger a_j + a_i a_j^\dagger), \tag{3}$$

where the coupling strength $\hbar V(r)$ is assumed to have a finite interaction range for expressing the localization nature of the dressed photon. Readers with knowledge of quantum theory may pay attention to a positive sign of the interaction Hamiltonian in comparison with some known models of material systems, such as the Bose–Hubbard model and the tight-binding model [13]. The interaction Hamiltonian is based on the theoretical derivation of the transition probability of the electronic excitation between two nanomatters in our published reports [14–16], where the transition probability was obtained by assuming that the constraint of the energy and momentum conservation lows can be overcome. According to the detailed explanation in [17], the coupling strength $\hbar V(r)$ with a finite interaction distance and a positive sign is derived as the form so-called Yukawa potential,

$$V(r) = \frac{V_0 e^{-m_{\text{eff}} r}}{r}, \tag{4}$$

where V_0 and m_{eff} are an appropriate constant and an effective mass which determines the interaction range, respectively. The Yukawa function often appears to give a screening effect in a many-body interaction system. In the case of the dressed-photon energy transfer, degrees of freedom of an environment leads to the equivalent effect to the many-body interaction.

2.1.3. Radiative Dissipation

The Lindblad-type radiative dissipation in (1), which shows the emission of the free photon into an external space, is given as the following equation,

$$\mathcal{L}^{(\text{r})}\rho(t) = \frac{\gamma^{(\text{r})}}{2} \sum_{i,j} \left(2a_i \rho(t) a_j^\dagger - \left\{ a_i^\dagger a_j, \rho(t) \right\} \right), \tag{5}$$

where $\gamma^{(\text{r})}$ represents the relaxation constant via the free photon in an external space, and the curly brackets are the notation of the anti-commutation relation. It is worth noting the summation of nodes labeled by the indices i and j. The relaxation involves both allowed and forbidden transitions of the free photon depending the symmetry of the spatial distribution of the total dressed photon excitation.

2.1.4. Non-Radiative Dissipation

As shown in Figure 1, the dressed photon is simultaneously excited and dissipated from the input side of a nanomatter system because it is an open system. Since the actual system of interest should be regarded as a microscopic part of an infinite system, it is difficult to accurately model the whole picture of the matter structure that is continuously connected from microscopic to the macroscopic systems. In our formulation, the Lindblad-type non-radiative dissipation is assumed for simply realizing a non-equilibrium open system. This assumption is approximately inadequate, but deep physical consideration in this topic is beyond the scope of this paper. It is expected a theoretical model will be built that accurately incorporates the macroscopic system hidden in the background. There are several studies for connecting a microscopic system with a macroscopic one [18,19].

Here, the non-radiative dissipation, i.e., the third term in (1), is given qualitatively as a similar manner in (5) as

$$\mathcal{L}^{(\text{nr})}\rho(t) = \frac{\gamma^{(\text{nr})}}{2} \sum_{i,j \in \text{edge}} \left(2a_i \rho(t) a_j^\dagger - \left\{ a_i^\dagger a_j, \rho(t) \right\} \right), \tag{6}$$

where $\gamma^{(\mathrm{nr})}$ is the non-radiative relaxation constant of the local dressed photon that is obviously faster than the radiative one. This is almost the same as (5), but the region with the dissipation is limited to a part of a taper structure.

2.2. Spatial Mode Expansion

In this subsection, the basis states for expressing the spatial distribution of the dressed photon are discussed using the quantum master equation formulated in Section 2.1. So far, the basis states of the dressed photon are set as the dressed photon exists or not at local nodes in a nanomatter system as an implicit understanding. In Figure 2, a steady-state solution in the case of a two-dimensional taper structure is calculated and mapped with the color gradation that represents the occupancy probability of the dressed photon. Figure 2a–c denote the snapshots of the temporal evolution at the time steps, $t = 5$, 50, and 5000, respectively. The simulation parameters used in these calculations are written in the caption in Figure 2, and are commonly used in the following calculations. At each time step, the spatial distribution of the dressed photon reflects the weight coefficient c_i of the basis states in a quantum superposition state $|\phi\rangle = c_0|0,\cdots,0\rangle + c_1|1,0,\cdots,0\rangle + c_2|0,1,0,\cdots,0\rangle + \cdots + c_N|0,\cdots,0,1\rangle$, where, for example, $|0,1,0,\cdots,0\rangle$ represents a state in which the dressed photon exists at the node labeled as the position 2. The temporal evolution can be interpreted as follows; in the early stage, the dressed photon runs down as the ballistic conduction at a part of the taper slopes, and then is reflected at a boundary of the taper tip, i.e., a spatial singular point of the system, leading to a steady state. Finally, it is found that the dressed photon makes spatial localization near around the tip, similar to a standing wave. In addition, there are locations inside the taper where the occupancy probability of the dressed photon is highly established quasi-periodically. The spatial distribution is, of course, determined depending on the shape of a matter system, such as the size of the taper structure and the steepness of the taper slopes. It also depends on the coupling strength $\hbar V(r)$.

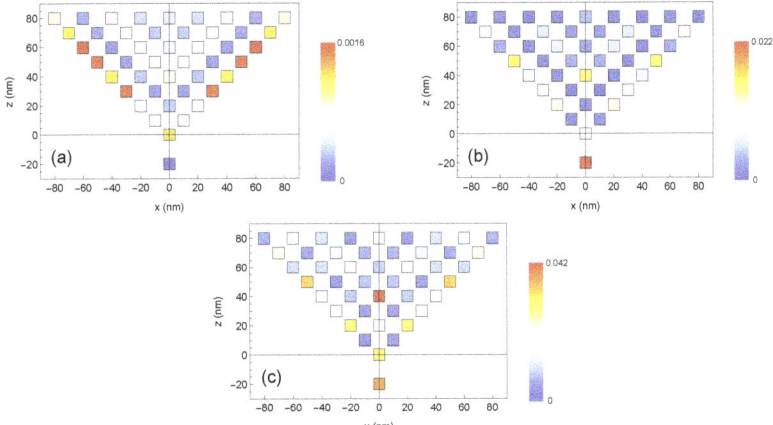

Figure 2. Temporal snapshot of the occupancy probability for the dressed photon at the time steps (**a**) $t = 5$, (**b**) 50, and (**c**) 5000. In this calculation, the parameters are set as $\hbar A = 1$, $\hbar V_0 = 27.2$, $m_{\mathrm{eff}} = 0.1$, $\gamma^{(\mathrm{r})} = 0.01$, and $\gamma^{(\mathrm{nr})} = 10$, and the matter system is assumed as a two-dimensional taper structure which is expressed by the 47 nodes. The dressed photon initially transfers on the taper slopes, and converges into a steady state with the spatial localization similar to a generation of standing wave caused by a system asymmetry.

As mentioned in the Introduction, the dressed photon should be controlled in a nanomatter system, and observed via the free photon radiated from the system. In the following, a way to extract the characteristics of the spatial distribution of the dressed photon is discussed from a viewpoint of the basis transformation. Although the Fourier transformation and/or the Bloch's theorem, which are based on translational symmetry, are used in the cases of the conventional optics and solid-state physics to catch the clear description of a wave nature, they cannot be applied for the description of the dressed photon because of the spatial singularity of the matter boundary and the impurity. Therefore, focusing on the fact that this system converges to a non-equilibrium steady state, the basis transformation which diagonalizes the steady state is proposed. According to the obtained basis states, there is no energy transfer between such basis states at a steady state, and the dressed photon dynamics can be separable depending on the spatial distribution of the basis states which strongly reflects a geometrical nature of a nanomatter.

From the steady-state solution (Figure 2c), the matrix U that diagonalizes the quantum density matrix can be determined numerically and uniquely. As a result of this transformation, (1) is rewritten as

$$\frac{\partial \rho_{st}(t)}{\partial t} = -\frac{i}{\hbar}[H_{int,st} + H_{exc,st}, \rho_{st}(t)] + \mathcal{L}_{st}^{(nr)}\rho_{st}(t) + \mathcal{L}_{st}^{(r)}\rho_{st}(t), \qquad (7)$$

$$O_{st} \equiv U^{-1}OU, \qquad (8)$$

$$\mathcal{L}_{st}^{(nr,r)}\rho_{st} \equiv \frac{\gamma^{(nr,r)}}{2}\left(2a_{st}\rho_{st}(t)a_{st}^\dagger + \left\{a_{st}^\dagger a_{st}, \rho_{st}(t)\right\}\right), \qquad (9)$$

where the subscript "st" means the operators after the basis transformation as the quantum density matrix being diagonalized, and O is an arbitrary operator. To decompose the individual row of the matrix U is intuitive because the elements of a certain row are constructed from the weight coefficients of the linear combination of the basis states in the local-node description, and it is sorted in descending order of the occupancy probability. The basis states can be visualized as shown in Figure 3.

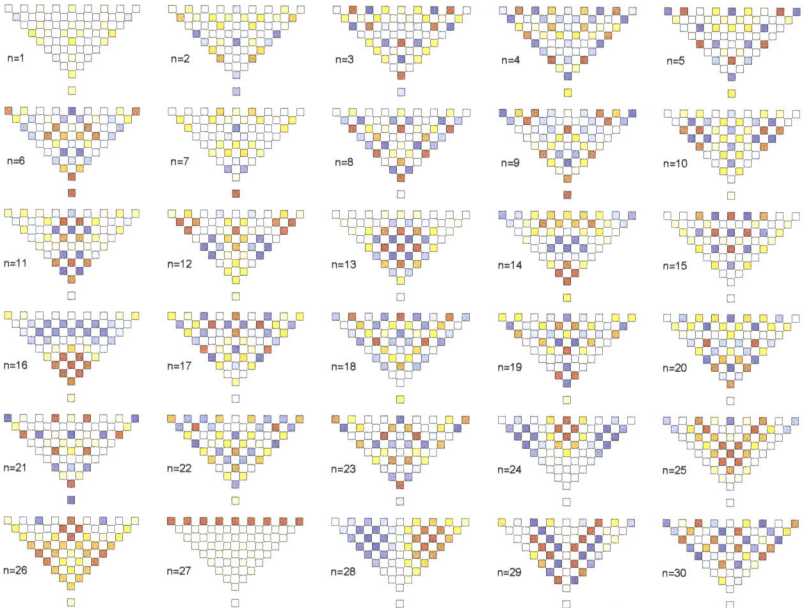

Figure 3. Color map images of the basis states reconstructed from the transformation matrix U in (8). Since the state $n = 27$ corresponds to the coherent excitation, there is no meaning in the state over $n = 27$, and almost of those are excluded from visualization.

From the perspective of the spatial distribution, there are several characteristic basis states. The state of $n = 27$ in Figure 3 apparently corresponds to the excitation due to the external field at an input interface, and thus, the states in the region labeled $n > 27$ are no longer excited in this system, and most of these are excluded from the drawing. The states $n = 14, 16$, and 24 have quasi-periodic spatial structures that resemble standing waves in a waveguide. In the states of $n = 8$ and 12, the dressed photon occupies the taper slopes. Several basis states of $n \leq 9$ show localization of the dressed photon at a taper tip; therefore, it is predicted that these states couple strongly with each other.

The dynamics of the quantum density matrix for the transformed basis states (Figure 3) can be recalculated numerically. In Figure 4, the density matrix elements are depicted as the color map images, where the time steps are similarly set as $t = 5, 50$, and 5000, and the colors represent absolute values of the density matrix elements. In an early stage of a time evolution, the occupancy probability (diagonal elements) concentrates in the basis states with a localization nature ($n \leq 7$), and the off-diagonal elements which represent the transition probability between the different basis states also change actively. After some time, the central area of the color map becomes active, in which there are a few characteristic basis states with high occupancy probability. In the final stage, the system goes to the steady state that consists only of the diagonal matrix elements. The following two points from this basis transformation approach are noticeable. One is that the basis states labeled by $n > 27$ are not excited and negligible, and this contributes to decrease the numerical calculation volume and the calculation time. The other is that there are components growing slowly and unidirectionally without exchange of energies among the other basis states. These are reminiscent of the dissipation process for the free photon.

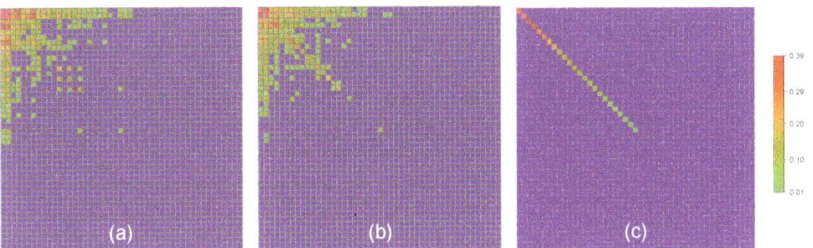

Figure 4. Color map images of the quantum density matrices at the time steps of (**a**) $t = 5$, (**b**) 50, and (**c**) 5000, respectively. The occupancy probability and the transition matrices of the dressed photon are represented as the diagonal and off-diagonal matrix elements, respectively. All simulation parameters are the same in Figure 2. Meanwhile, in the early state, the dressed photon concentrates in the states with a localization nature and goes and returns aggressively among themselves; the basis states with the intermediate spatial size show slightly calm movement, which is reminiscent of the radiative dissipation to the external field of the free photon.

3. Renormalization of Quasi-Static Basis States

In the previous section, novel basis states inspired by a non-equilibrium steady state are proposed to capture the spatial property that distinguishes the dressed-photon dynamics, and the temporal evolution of the dressed photon is visualized numerically in a space of the quantum density matrix. This seems to suggest the distinction between the matter-like and the free photon-like properties of the dressed photon. Based on this insight, this section is devoted to discussing a way to focus the principal modes of the dressed photon with a localization nature.

First, let us pay attention to the coupling strength between the unitary transformed basis states that can be observed in the interaction Hamiltonian, $H_{int,st}$. The interaction Hamiltonian before and after the basis transformation is visualized as the color map images in Figure 5. In the case before the transformation, a quasi-periodic structure appears depending on the lattice structure of the nodes as illustrated in Figure 1. The unitary transformation drastically changes the appearance, which is shown in Figure 5b. The effective transition among the basis states restricts in the several basis states, and many basis states stay in their own modes that are described as the diagonal matrix elements, which represent the energy shift in the system dynamics. In the following, the projection operator method is applied to extract the principal basis states with a localization nature of the dressed photon, and to eliminate the basis states with the weak contribution.

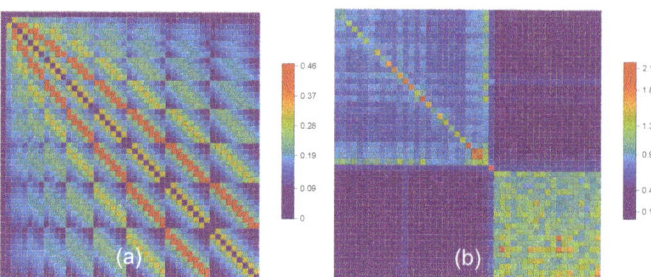

Figure 5. Color map images of matrix elements of the interaction Hamiltonian H_{int}, which is given in (3). (**a**) The matrix before the unitary transformation has a quasi-periodic structure reflected by the range-dependent coupling strength among a certain node and nearly arranged ones, and all matrix elements in the diagonal part are zero. (**b**) The matrix after the unitary transformation shows characteristic structure. There are two distinct areas divided at $n = 27$, which corresponds to the mode of the dressed-photon excitation. In the base $n \leq 27$, the diagonal matrix elements have large values, i.e., staying in their own modes, and it is found that several basis states dominantly contribute to the dressed-photon dynamics via off-diagonal matrix elements.

3.1. Projection Operator Method

The projection operator method is a mathematical technique that divides the entire system into a target space (P) and a complementary space (Q), and inserts the influence of the complementary space into the target space [14,20]. A state vector of the entire system $|\psi_{\text{st}}\rangle$ is divided into the two sub-spaces using the projection operators,

$$|\psi_{\text{st}}^P\rangle = P|\psi_{\text{st}}\rangle, \tag{10a}$$

$$|\psi_{\text{st}}^Q\rangle = Q|\psi_{\text{st}}\rangle, \tag{10b}$$

where the projection operators P and Q satisfy the following relations,

$$P + Q = 1, \tag{11a}$$

$$P^2 = P, \tag{11b}$$

$$Q^2 = Q. \tag{11c}$$

Using the Schrödinger equation,

$$H_{\text{exc,st}}|\psi_{\text{st}}\rangle = \Delta E|\psi_{\text{st}}\rangle, \tag{12}$$

the state vector in the Q-space can be expressed as the sum of the contributions from the state vector in the P-space, i.e.,

$$|\psi_{\text{st}}^Q\rangle = \sum_{n=1}^{\infty} \left(\Delta E^{-1} Q H_{\text{int,st}}\right)^n |\psi_{\text{st}}^P\rangle \approx \Delta E^{-1} Q H_{\text{int,st}}|\psi_{\text{st}}^P\rangle. \tag{13}$$

In (12), ΔE corresponds to the energy shift of the basis states unitary transformed from the basis states expressed by the local nodes. It should be noted that the contribution of the radiative and non-radiative dissipations, and the excitation of the dressed photon are ignored in (12) and (13) because the dissipation and the excitation originate from the interaction with the external field, but it is qualitatively negligible by assuming that only the hopping conduction of the dressed photon contributes to the transition between the P and the Q-spaces. In the last part of (13), the first-order perturbation is applied by assuming that the basis states in the Q-space weakly affect the P-space dynamics.

3.2. Modified Quantum Master Equation

Applying the approximate expression given in Section 3.1, the equation of motion for the quantum density operator can be transformed in the P-space representation, where the influence of the Q-space is renormalized into the original interaction Hamiltonian, and the creation and annihilation operators in the dissipation terms. Omitting the redundant mathematical transformations, the quantum master equation is modified as follows,

$$\frac{\partial \rho_{st}(t)}{\partial t} \approx \frac{\partial \rho_{st}^P(t)}{\partial t} = -\frac{i}{\hbar}[H_{int,st}^{P'} + H_{ext,st}^P, \rho_{st}^P(t)] + \mathcal{L}_{st}^{(nr)'} \rho_{st}^P(t) + \mathcal{L}_{st}^{(r)'} \rho_{st}^P(t), \quad (14)$$

where the quantum density matrix operator in the P-space is $\rho_{st}^P(t) = P\rho_{st}(t)P$, and the modified interaction Hamiltonian reads

$$H_{int,st}^{P'} \equiv PH_{int,st}P + \sum_{m \in Q} \frac{PH_{int,st}|\phi_m^Q\rangle\langle\phi_m^Q|H_{int,st}P}{\langle\phi_m^Q|H_{int,st}|\phi_m^Q\rangle}. \quad (15)$$

In (15), the operator Q is rewritten by the intermediate states $|\phi_m^Q\rangle$ for clear understanding, i.e.,

$$Q = \sum_{m \in Q} |\phi_m^Q\rangle\langle\phi_m^Q|, \quad (16)$$

where the summation is applied to the artificially selected basis states in the Q-space. (15) means that the interaction Hamiltonian with the coherent dynamics is corrected by the transition between the basis states in the Q- and the P-spaces.

The dissipation terms in (5) and (6) are similarly rewritten as the following form,

$$\mathcal{L}_{st}^{(r,nr)'} \rho_{st}^P(t) = \frac{\gamma^{(r,nr)}}{2} \sum_{i,j} \left(2a_i^{P'} \rho_{st}^P a_j^{P'\dagger} - \{a_i^{P'\dagger} a_j^{P'}, \rho_{st}^P(t)\}\right), \quad (17)$$

where

$$a_i^{P'} \equiv Pa_iP + \sum_{m \in Q} \frac{Pa_i|\phi_m^Q\rangle\langle\phi_m^Q|H_{int,st}P}{\langle\phi_m^Q|H_{int,st}|\phi_m^Q\rangle}. \quad (18)$$

Ideally, the contribution of the dissipation should be renormalized into the relaxation constants $\gamma^{(r,nr)}$, and the creation and annihilation operators should be left as the original form of the basis states transformed by a non-equilibrium steady state. However, (17) is only an approximate expression for the operators, since the theoretical formulation has not been completed in this stage. This is a problem to be solved in the future. In (18), the second term means that there are dissipation processes with the energy flow from the P-space to the Q-space.

3.3. Numerical Demonstration of Renormalization

Using the above formulation, the concrete temporal evolution of the quantum density matrix is calculated numerically, and the validity of the approximation is evaluated. Figure 6 shows the steady-state solution for the three steps of the coarse graining, which are the original result without approximation, the result simply removing the basis states over $n = 27$, and the result after renormalization using (14)–(17). Prior to the renormalization, the Q-space components are selected as $n = 17, 19, 20, 22$, and 23, by referring the correction term of $H_{int,st}/\langle\phi_m^Q|H_{int,st}|\phi_m^Q\rangle$, that weakly couple to the basis state for the excitation. Despite reducing the number of the basis states, the obtained steady-state solutions are almost the same in all three cases, and the calculation time has been significantly reduced. In the case of Figure 6, the number of the basis states for obtaining the calculation results has been reduced by less than half against no coarse graining, and thus the number of the differential equations to be solved is 22% less. To confirm the validity of this approach, the spatial distribution of the occupancy probability of the dressed photon is reconstructed from the quantum density matrix by applying renormalization or not, that is shown in Figure 7. Both color map images of the occupancy probability before and after renormalization are in good agreement with each other.

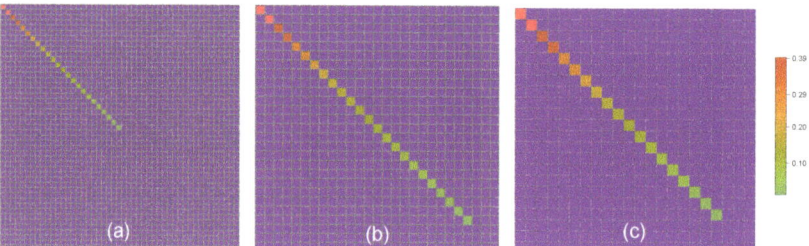

Figure 6. Color map images of steady-state solutions for the quantum density matrix in the cases of (**a**) no eliminating the extra basis states, eliminating the states of $n > 27$, and additional renormalization of the states $n = 17, 19, 20, 22,$ and 23. The number of the matrix elements decreases from (**a**–**c**) as 47^2, 27^2, and 22^2. In all three cases, the steady-state solutions converge to only diagonal elements, and the occupancy probability can be reproduced after coarse graining using renormalization of the quasi-static basis states.

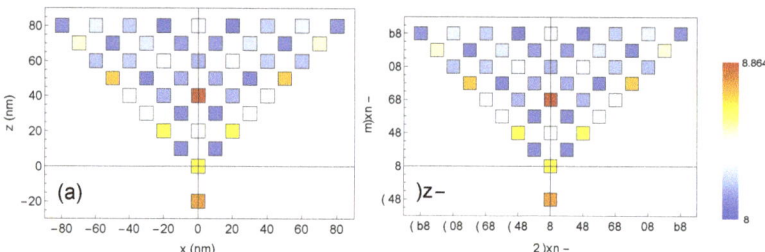

Figure 7. Steady-state solutions of occupancy probability for the dressed photon are mapped in the geometrical structure of taper that are calculated using (**a**) the original basis states defined by nodes, and (**b**) reconstructed from the basis coarse-grained by eliminating extra base and renormalization. The renormalization condition is the same as that in Figure 6.

So far, a method to distinguish the heavy and the light components of the dressed photon has been proposed using the original basis transformation, and the numerical demonstration shows the potential for reducing the amount of computation. As a similar approach, a method where a macroscopic system is expressed with a small number of basis states using the basis states that are predetermined by the steady-state solutions in a small space step by step has been already published [18,19]. These papers report a large reduction in the amount of the quantum calculation. This method is very similar to our approach, in which basis transformation and renormalization are used for reducing the number of the principal basis states. Meanwhile, our main purpose in this research is to observe and control a behavior of the dressed photon localized in a nanometer space. This point will be considered in the next section.

4. Discussion on Control of Dressed Photon Distribution

This section discusses the physical meaning for renormalizing particular basis states. In Section 3.3, from the characteristics of the basis states defined by a steady-state solution, the basis states with the weak contribution can be converted to dissipative component in the system by applying the renormalization method in the first-order perturbation approximation. Such a situation is equivalent to a free photon reservoir. According to the intuitive image, the dressed photon can be regarded as stripping off the mass caused by the interaction with the environment and changes into the massless free photon, where the dressed-photon basis states staying in a nanomatter system are responsible for the stripped mass via renormalization.

On the other hand, it is interesting to consider how to affect the spatial distribution characteristics of the dressed photon that stays inside a nanomatter system. As an example, let us consider extracting a certain principal basis state with the strong localization of the dressed photon into the Q-space. When the localization basis state is selected as $n = 7$ in Figure 3, where the dressed photon energy concentrates at a tip position, is assigned in the Q-space, the quantum density matrix is calculated in the same manner as explained in the previous section, where the approximation of the weak coupling has been already exceeded. Figure 8a is the numerical result of the simulation, and the quantum density matrix cannot converge on the diagonal matrix elements. If the strict quantitativeness is neglected, this corresponds to change of a steady-state solution, i.e., the spatial distribution of the dressed photon can be modified by extracting artificially the principal localization basis state. In Figure 8b, the steady-state solutions are shown as a color map image in the taper geometry reconstructed from Figure 8a. One can observe that the localization of the dressed photon at a tip position disappears after such renormalization. It should be noted that this result represents the characteristic behavior of dressed-photon mediated phenomena. Removing the dressed photon out of a nanomatter system for an experimental observation makes another new internal state of the spatial distribution of the dressed photon in the system. For controlling and optimizing dressed-photon mediated phenomena, the renormalization of the basis states of interest, that is proposed in this paper, will be an extremely important concept.

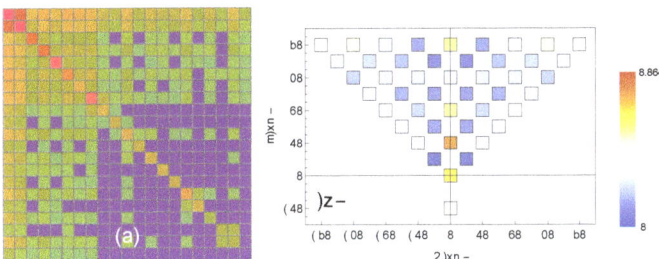

Figure 8. Numerical calculation result of the quantum density matrix when the basis state of $n = 7$ is additionally extracted as the Q-space. (**a**) Color map image of a steady-state solution for the density matrix elements, and (**b**) reconstructed color map image on the geometrical structure of taper. The extraction of the state actively contributing to the localization drastically changes convergence property of the quantum density matrix as well as spatial distribution of the dressed photon in a nanomatter.

5. Conclusions

In this paper, a phenomenological model that regards the dressed photon as a particle localized at a certain node in a collection of nodes representing nanomatter has been proposed, and its spatio-temporal dynamics has been formulated using the quantum density operator. This system includes the radiative and non-radiative dissipation processes that are given by the Lindblad-type dissipation based on the first-order Born–Markov approximation, and the external excitation, and thus, the system dynamics converges to a non-equilibrium steady state. For such a model, a mechanism for extracting a part of the dressed-photon energy to the external field, which corresponds to observation instruments, has been considered to access the localized state of the dressed photon, and to explain interesting experimental facts mediated by the dressed photon. Specifically, the methods to describe the dressed photon by characteristic basis states inspired by a non-equilibrium steady state as well as to separate the basis states into the target and the complementary spaces have been proposed and formulated using the projection operators. Contribution of the complementary space is renormalized in the target space by means of the lowest-order perturbation approximation. These theoretical and numerical approaches are a pioneering study that elucidates the principle of continuously connecting the dressed photon to the free photon. In this research, the process in which the bound or massive dressed photon dissociates its mass and is converted to the free photon has been interpreted by considering the energy transfer among the basis states with different spatial characteristics.

In the last part of this paper, a concept for accessing the principal basis states in a nanomatter system has been discussed using the same manner of renormalization. This is a qualitative proposal, but an important finding that the external manipulation of the dressed photon associated with the concept of renormalization.

The basis transformations using a predetermined steady state are inconsistent for the purpose of simulating the dressed-photon dynamics in an unknown system. However, in the experimental systems in which the dressed photon is mediated, the structural changes of the nanomatter always appears, such as an optimal rearrangement of atoms. Therefore, our approach to focus on changes from the steady states seems to be effective for explaining the experimental facts. In that sense, our proposed method is worth enough aiming at solving a dressed-photon optimization problem.

In the present research stage, the theoretical formulation is somewhat insufficient to explain the experimental facts quantitatively, but this paper has provided a meaningful consideration as a challenge by stepping into the essence of the underlying physical mechanism of the dressed photon and an off-shell science. It is expected to lead to a detailed understanding of dressed-photon physics and industrial applications in the near future.

Author Contributions: Conceptualization, H.S. and S.S.; methodology, S.S.; validation, S.S.; investigation, S.S.; writing—original draft preparation, S.S. Both authors have read and agreed to the published version of the manuscript.

Funding: This research received no external funding.

Institutional Review Board Statement: Not applicable.

Informed Consent Statement: Not applicable.

Data Availability Statement: The data presented in this study are available on request from the corresponding author.

Acknowledgments: The authors thank anonymous reviewers for their comments to improve the quality of this paper.

Conflicts of Interest: The authors declare no conflict of interest.

References

1. Kawazoe, T.; Mueed, M.A.; Ohtsu, M. Highly efficient and broadband Si homojunction structured near-infrared light emitting diodes based on the phonon-assisted optical near-field process. *Appl. Phys. B* **2011**, *104*, 747–754. [CrossRef]
2. Ohtsu, M. *Silicon Light-Emitting Diodes and Lasers*; Springer: Berlin, Germany, 2016.
3. Yatsui, T.; Nobusada, K. Near-field assisted chemical reactions and its applications. In *Progress in Nanophotonics 4. Nano-Optics and Nanophotonics*; Ohtsu, M., Yatsui, T., Eds.; Springer: Cham, Switzerland, 2017; pp. 57–85.
4. Kawazoe, T.; Kobayashi, K.; Ohtsu, M. Near-field optical chemical vapor deposition using $Zn(acac)_2$ with a non-adiabatic photochemical process. *Appl. Phys. B* **2006**, *84*, 247–251. [CrossRef]
5. Tate, N.; Kawazoe, T.; Nomura, W.; Ohtsu, M. Current-induced giant polarization rotation using a ZnO single crystal doped with nitrogen ions. *Sci. Rep.* **2015**, *5*, 12763. [CrossRef] [PubMed]
6. Yatsui, T. (Ed.) *Progress in Nanophotonics 5. Nano-Optics and Nanophotonics*; Springer: Cham, Switzerland, 2018.
7. Ohtsu, M. Route to Off-Shell Science. OffShell: 2006R.001.v1. Available online: http://offshell.rodrep.org/?p=283 (accessed on 25 June 2020).
8. Higuchi, Y.; Segawa, E. A dynamical system induced by quantum walk. *J. Phys. A Math. Theor.* **2019**, *52*, 395202. [CrossRef]

9. Hamano, M.; Saigo, H. Quantum walk and dressed photon. In Proceedings of the 9th International Conference on Quantum Simulation and Quantum Walks, QSQW 2020, Marseille, France, 20–24 January 2020; EPTCS 315; pp. 93–99.
10. Carmichael, H.J. *Statistical Methods in Quantum Optics 1*; Springer: Berlin/Heidelberg, Germany, 1999; pp. 1–74.
11. Breuer, H.-P.; Petruccione, F. *The Theory of Open Quantum Systems*; Oxford University Press: New York, NY, USA, 2002.
12. Manzano, D. A short introduction to the Lindblad master equation. *AIP Adv.* **2020**, *10*, 025106. [CrossRef]
13. Greiner, M.; Mandel, O.; Esslinger, T.; Hänsch, T.W.; Bloch, I. Quantum phase transition from a superfluid to a Mott insulator in a gas of ultracold atoms. *Nature* **2002**, *415*, 39–44. [CrossRef] [PubMed]
14. Kobayashi, K.; Sangu, S.; Ito, H.; Ohtsu, M. Near-field optical potential for a neutral atom. *Phys. Rev. A* **2000**, *63*, 013806. [CrossRef]
15. Sangu, S.; Kobayashi, K.; Shojiguchi, A.; Ohtsu, M. Logic and functional operations using a near-field optically coupled quantum-dot system. *Phys. Rev. B* **2004**, *69*, 115334. [CrossRef]
16. Knoester, J.; Mukamel, S. Nonlinear optics using the multipolar Hamiltonian: The Bloch-Maxwell equation and local fields. *Phys. Rev. A* **1989**, *39*, 1899–1914. [CrossRef] [PubMed]
17. Sangu, S.; Kobayashi, K.; Shojiguchi, A.; Kawazoe, T.; Ohtsu, M. Theory and principles of operation of nanophotonic functional devices. In *Progress in Nano-Electro-Optics Photonics V*; Ohtsu, M., Ed.; Springer: Berlin/Heidelberg, Germany, 2006; pp. 1–62.
18. Finazzi, S.; Boité, A.L.; Storme, F.; Baksic, A.; Ciuti, C. Corner space renormalization method for driven-dissipative 2D correlated systems. *Phys. Rev. Lett.* **2015**, *115*, 080604. [CrossRef] [PubMed]
19. Donatella, K.; Denis, Z.; Boité, A.L.; Ciuti, C. Continuous-time dynamics and error scaling of noisy highly-entangling quantum circuits. *arXiv* **2021**, arXiv:2102.04265.
20. Breuer, H.-P. Non-Markovian quantum dynamics and the method of correlated projection super-operators. In *Theoretical Foundations of Quantum Information Processing and Communication: Selected Topics*; Brüning, E., Petruccione, F., Eds.; Springer: Berlin/Heidelberg, Germany, 2010; pp. 125–139.

Article

Relation between Quantum Walks with Tails and Quantum Walks with Sinks on Finite Graphs

Norio Konno [1], Etsuo Segawa [2,*] and Martin Štefaňák [3]

[1] Department of Applied Mathematics, Yokohama National University, Yokohama 240-8501, Japan; konno-norio-bt@ynu.ac.jp
[2] Graduate School of Environment Information Sciences, Yokohama National University, Yokohama 240-8501, Japan
[3] Department of Physics, Faculty of Nuclear Sciences and Physical Engineering, Czech Technical University in Prague, Břehová 7, 115 19 Praha 1, Czech Republic; martin.stefanak@fjfi.cvut.cz
* Correspondence: segawa-etsuo-tb@ynu.ac.jp

Abstract: We connect the Grover walk with sinks to the Grover walk with tails. The survival probability of the Grover walk with sinks in the long time limit is characterized by the centered generalized eigenspace of the Grover walk with tails. The centered eigenspace of the Grover walk is the attractor eigenspace of the Grover walk with sinks. It is described by the persistent eigenspace of the underlying random walk whose support has no overlap to the boundaries of the graph and combinatorial flow in graph theory.

Keywords: quantum walk; survival probability; attractor eigenspace; dressed photon

Citation: Konno, N.; Segawa, E.; Štefaňák, M. Relation between Quantum Walks with Tails and Quantum Walks with Sinks on Finite Graphs. *Symmetry* **2021**, *13*, 1169. https://doi.org/10.3390/sym13071169

Academic Editor: Motoichi Ohtsu

Received: 7 May 2021
Accepted: 24 June 2021
Published: 29 June 2021

Publisher's Note: MDPI stays neutral with regard to jurisdictional claims in published maps and institutional affiliations.

Copyright: © 2021 by the authors. Licensee MDPI, Basel, Switzerland. This article is an open access article distributed under the terms and conditions of the Creative Commons Attribution (CC BY) license (https://creativecommons.org/licenses/by/4.0/).

1. Introduction

A simple random walker on a finite and connected graph starting from any vertex hits an arbitrary vertex in a finite time. This fact implies that, if we consider a subset of the vertices of this graph as sinks, where the random walker is absorbed, then the survival probability of the random walk in the long time limit converges to zero. However, for quantum walks (QW) [1], the situation is more complicated and the survival probability depends in general on the graph, coin operator, and the initial state of the walk. For a two-state quantum walk on a finite line with sinks on both ends and a non-trivial coin, the survival probability is also zero, as shown by the studies of the corresponding absorption problem [2–5]. However, for a three-state quantum walk with the Grover coin [6], the survival probability on a finite line is non-vanishing [7] due to the existence of trapped states. These are the eigenstates of the unitary evolution operator which do not have a support on the sinks. Trapped states crucially affect the efficiency of quantum transport [8] and lead to counter-intuitive effects, e.g., the transport efficiency can be improved by increasing the distance between the initial vertex and the sink [9,10]. We find a similar phenomena to this quantum walk model in the experiment on the energy transfer of the dressed photon [11] through the nanoparticles distributed in a finite three-dimensional grid [12]. The output signal intensity increases when the depth direction is larger. Although, when the depth is deeper, a lot of "detours" newly appear to reach to the position of the output from the classical point of view, the output signal intensity of the dressed photon becomes stronger. The existence of trapped states also results in infinite hitting times [13,14].

In this paper, we analyze such counter-intuitive phenomena for the Grover walk on a general connected graph using spectral analysis. The Grover walk is an induced quantum walk of the random walk from the viewpoint of the spectral mapping theorem [15].

To this end, first, we connect the Grover walk with sinks to the Grover walk with tails. The tails are the semi-infinite paths attached to a finite and connected graph. We call the set of vertices connecting to the tails the boundary. The Grover walk with tail was introduced by [16,17] in terms of the scattering theory. If we set some appropriate bounded initial state so that the support is included in the tail, the existence of the fixed point of the dynamical system induced by the Grover walk with tails is shown, and the stable generalized eigenspace $\mathcal{H}_s$, in which the dynamical system lives, is orthogonal to the centered generalized eigenspace $\mathcal{H}_c$ [18] at every time step [19]. The centered generalized eigenspace is generated by the generalized eigenvectors of the principal submatrix of the time evolution operator of the Grover walk with respect to the internal graph, and all the corresponding absolute values of the eigenvalues are 1. This eigenstate is equivalent to the attractor space [8] of the Grover walk with sink. Indeed, we show that the stationary state of the Grover walk with sink is attracted to this centered generalized eigenstate. Secondly, we characterize this centered generalized eigenspace using the persistent eigenspace of the underlying random walk whose supports have no overlaps to the boundary, also using the concept of "flow" from graph theory. From this result, we see that the existence of the persistent eigenspace of the underlying random walk significantly influences the asymptotic behavior of the corresponding Grover walk, although it has little effect on the asymptotic behavior of the random walk itself. Moreover, we clarify that the graph structure which constructs the symmetric or anti-symmetric flow satisfying the Kirchhoff's law contributes to the non-zero survival probability of the Grover walk, as suggested in [8,15].

This paper is organized as follows. In Section 2, we prepare the notations of graphs and give the definition of the Grover walk and the boundary operators which are related to the chain. In Section 3, we give the definition of the Grover walk on a graph with sinks. In Section 4, a necessary and sufficient condition for the surviving of the Grover walk is described. In Section 5, we give an example. Section 6 is devoted to the relation between the Grover walk with sink and the Grover walk with tail. In Section 7, we partially characterize the centered generalized eigenspace using the concept of flow from graph theory.

2. Preliminary

2.1. Graph Notation

Let $G = (V, A)$ be a connected and *symmetric digraph* such that an arc $a \in A$ if and only if its inverse arc $\bar{a} \in A$. The *origin and terminal vertices* of $a \in A$ are denoted by $o(a) \in V$ and $t(a) \in V$, respectively. Assume that G has no multiple arcs. If $t(a) = o(a)$, we call such an arc a the *self-loop*. In this paper, we regard $\bar{a} = a$ for any self-loops. We denote A_σ as the set of all self-loops. The *degree* of $v \in V$ is defined by

$$\deg(v) = |\{a \in A \mid t(a) = v\}|.$$

The *support edge* of $a \in A \setminus A_\sigma$ is denoted by $|a|$ with $|a| = |\bar{a}|$. The set of *(non-directed) edges* is

$$E = \{|a| \mid a \in A \setminus A_\sigma\}.$$

A *walk* in G is a sequence of arcs such that $p = (a_0, a_1, \ldots, a_{r-1})$ with $t(a_j) = o(a_{j+1})$ for any $j = 0, \ldots, r-2$, which may have the same arcs in p. The *cycle* in G is a subgraph of G which is isomorphic to a sequence of arcs $(a_0, a_1, \ldots, a_{r-1})$ $(r \geq 3)$ satisfying $t(a_j) = o(a_{j+1})$ with $a_j \neq \bar{a}_{j+1}$ for any $j = 0, \ldots, r-1$, where the subscript is the modulus of r. We identify $(a_k, a_{k+1}, \ldots, a_{k+r-1})$ with $(a_0, a_1, \ldots, a_{r-1})$ for $k \in \mathbb{Z}$. The *spanning tree* of G is a connected subtree of G covering all vertices of G. A *fundamental cycle* induced by the spanning tree is the cycle in G generated by recovering an arc which is outside of the spanning tree to the spanning tree. There are two choices of orientations for each support of the fundamental cycle, but we choose only one of them as the representative. Fixing a spanning tree, we denote the set of fundamental cycles by Γ. Then, the cardinality of Γ is $|E| - |V| + 1 =: b_1$. We call b_1 the *first Betti number*.

2.2. Definition of the Grover Walk

Let Ω be a discrete set. The vector space whose standard basis is labeled by each element of Ω is denoted by $\mathbb{C}^\Omega$. The standard basis is denoted by $\delta_\omega^{(\Omega)}$ ($\omega \in \Omega$), i.e.,

$$\delta_\omega^{(\Omega)}(\omega') = \begin{cases} 1 & : \omega = \omega', \\ 0 & : \text{otherwise}. \end{cases}$$

Throughout this paper, the inner product is standard, i.e.,

$$\langle \psi, \phi \rangle_\Omega = \sum_{\omega \in \Omega} \bar{\psi}(\omega)\phi(\omega),$$

for any $\psi, \phi \in \mathbb{C}^\Omega$, and the norm is defined by

$$||\psi||_\Omega = \sqrt{\langle \psi, \psi \rangle_\Omega}.$$

For any $\psi \in \mathbb{C}^\Omega$, the support of ψ is defined by

$$supp(\psi) := \{\omega \in \Omega \mid \psi(\omega) \neq 0\}.$$

For subspaces $M, N \subset \mathbb{C}^\Omega$, the relation

$$\mathbb{C}^\Omega = M \oplus N,$$

means that M and N are complementary spaces in $\mathbb{C}^\Omega$, i.e., for any $f \in \mathbb{C}^\Omega$, $g \in M$ and $h \in N$ are uniquely determined such that $f = g + h$, which means, if $u' + u'' = 0$ for some $u' \in \Omega'$ and $u'' \in \Omega''$, then u' and u'' must be $u' = u'' = 0$. Note that $\langle g, h \rangle_\Omega \neq 0$ in general, i.e., M and N are not necessarily orthogonal subspaces. Especially in this paper, we treat an operator which is a submatrix of a unitary operator, and we are not ensured that it is a normal operator. The vector space describing the whole system of the Grover walk is $\mathbb{C}^A$. The time evolution operator of the Grover walk on G is defined by

$$(U_G \psi)(a) = -\psi(\bar{a}) + \frac{2}{\deg(o(a))} \sum_{t(b)=o(a)} \psi(b)$$

for any $\psi \in \mathbb{C}^A$ and $a \in A$. Note that, since U_G is a unitary operator on $\mathbb{C}^A$, U_G preserves the ℓ^2 norm, i.e., $||U_G \psi||_A^2 = ||\psi||_A^2$. Let $\psi_n \in \mathbb{C}^A$ be the nth iteration of the Grover walk $\psi_n = U_G \psi_{n-1}$ ($n \geq 1$) with the initial state ψ_0. Then, the probability distribution at time n, $\mu_n : V \to [0,1]$, can be defined by

$$\mu_n(v) = \sum_{t(a)=v} |\psi_n(a)|^2$$

if the norm of the initial state is unity. Our interest is the asymptotic behavior of the sequence of probabilities μ_n and also of amplitudes ψ_n on the graph comparing with the behavior of the corresponding random walk.

2.3. Boundary Operators

Let $G = (V, A)$ be the original graph. The set of sinks is denoted by $V_s \subset V$. The subgraph of G; $G_0 = (V_0, A_0)$, is defined by

$$V_0 = V \setminus V_s, \quad A_0 = \{a \in A \mid t(a), o(a) \notin V_s\}.$$

The set of self-loops in G_0 is denoted by $A_{0,\sigma} \subset A_0$ (see Figure 1). The set of the fundamental cycles in G_0 is denoted by Γ hereafter. The set of boundary vertices of G_0 is defined by
$$\delta G_0 = \{o(a) \mid a \in A, \, o(a) \in V \setminus V_s, \, t(a) \in V_s\}.$$
This means that δG_0 consists of the origins of arcs flowing into the sinks. Under the above settings of graphs, let us now prepare some notations to show our main theorem.

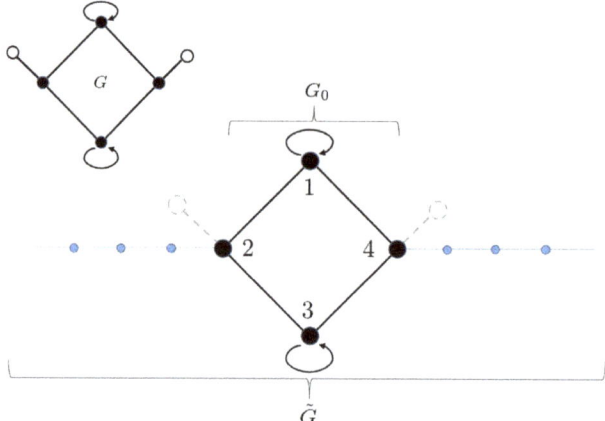

Figure 1. The setting of graphs: The original graph G is depicted in the left corner. The sinks V_s are the white vertices. The subgraph G_0 of G is the black colored graph in the center. The set of boundary vertices δV is $\{2,4\}$. The semi-infinite graph $\tilde{G}$ is constructed by connecting the infinite length path to each boundary vertex of G_0.

Definition 1. *Let $\deg(u)$ be the degree of u in the original graph G. Let $G_0 = (V_0, A_0)$ be the subgraph as above. Then, the boundary operators $d_1 : \mathbb{C}^{A_0} \to \mathbb{C}^{V_0}$ and $\partial_2 : \mathbb{C}^{\Gamma} \to \mathbb{C}^{A_0}$ are denoted by*
$$(d_1\psi)(v) = \frac{1}{\sqrt{\deg(v)}} \sum_{t(a)=v} \psi(a), \quad (\partial_2 \Psi)(a) = \sum_{a \in A(c) \subset A_0} \Psi(c),$$
respectively, for any $\psi \in \mathbb{C}^A$, $\Psi \in \mathbb{C}^{\Gamma}$ and $v \in V_0, a \in A_0$. Here, $A(c)$ is the set of arcs of $c \in \Gamma$.

The boundary operator d_1 has the following matrix representation
$$(d_1)_{u,a} = \begin{cases} 1/\sqrt{\deg(u)} & : t(a) = u, \\ 0 & : \text{otherwise,} \end{cases}$$
while the boundary operator ∂_2 has the following matrix representation
$$(\partial_2)_{a,c} = \begin{cases} 1 & : a \in A(c), \\ 0 & : \text{otherwise.} \end{cases}$$

Note that $\deg(u)$ is the degree of G; thus, if $u \in \delta G_0$, then $\deg(u)$ is greater than the degree in G_0. The adjoint operators of d_1 and ∂_2 are defined by
$$\langle f, d_1\psi \rangle_{V_0} = \langle d_1^* f, \psi \rangle_{A_0}, \quad \langle \psi, \partial_2 \Psi \rangle_{A_0} = \langle \partial_2^* \psi, \Psi \rangle_{\Gamma}$$
which imply
$$(d_1^* f)(a) = f(t(a)), \quad (\partial_2^* \psi)(c) = \sum_{a \in A(c)} \psi(a).$$

Let $S : \mathbb{C}^{A_0} \to \mathbb{C}^{A_0}$ be a unitary operator defined by $(S\psi)(a) = \psi(\bar{a})$. We prove that the composition of $d_1(I - S) \circ \partial_2$ is identically equal to zero as follows.

Lemma 1. *Let d_1 and ∂_2 be the above. Then, we have*

$$d_1(I - S)\partial_2 = 0.$$

Proof. For any $c \in \Gamma$, let $\delta_c^{(\Gamma)} \in \mathbb{C}^\Gamma$ be the delta function, i.e.,

$$\delta_c^{(\Gamma)}(c') = \begin{cases} 1 & : c = c', \\ 0 & : c \neq c'. \end{cases}$$

Then, it is enough to see that $d_1(I - S)\partial_2 \delta_c^{(\Gamma)} = 0$ for any $c \in \Gamma$. Indeed, we find

$$d_1(I - S)\partial_2 \delta_c^{(\Gamma)} = d_1 \left(\sum_{a \in A(c)} \delta_a^{(A)} - \sum_{a \in A(c)} \delta_{\bar{a}}^{(A)} \right)$$

$$= \sum_{a \in A(c)} \frac{1}{\sqrt{\deg(t(a))}} \delta_{t(a)}^{(V)} - \sum_{a \in A(c)} \frac{1}{\sqrt{\deg(t(\bar{a}))}} \delta_{t(\bar{a})}^{(V)}$$

$$= 0,$$

which is the desired conclusion. □

Let us set the function $\xi_c^{(+)}$ induced by $c \in \Gamma$ by

$$\xi_c^{(+)} := (I - S)\partial_2 \delta_c^{(\Gamma)}.$$

In other words, $\mathrm{supp}(\xi_c^{(+)}) = A(c) \cup A(\bar{c})$ and

$$(\xi_c^{(+)})(a) = \begin{cases} 1 & : a \in A(c), \\ -1 & : \bar{a} \in A(c), \\ 0 & : \text{otherwise}. \end{cases}$$

The function $\xi_c^{(+)}$ represents the fundamental cycle c. Let us introduce $\chi_S : \mathbb{C}^A \to \mathbb{C}^{A_0}$ by

$$(\chi_S \phi)(a) = \phi(a)$$

for all $a \in A_0$. The adjoint $\chi_S^* : \mathbb{C}^{A_0} \to \mathbb{C}^A$ is described by

$$(\chi_S^* f)(a) = \begin{cases} f(a) & : a \in A_0, \\ 0 & : \text{otherwise}. \end{cases}$$

A matrix representation of χ_S is expressed as follows:

$$\chi_S \cong [\, I_{A_0} \mid 0 \,],$$

which is a $|A_0| \times |A|$ matrix. The function $\xi_c^{(+)}$ satisfies the following properties:

Proposition 1. *For any fundamental cycle c in $G_0 \subset G$, we have $\chi_S^* \xi_c^{(+)} \in \ker(1 - U_G)$.*

Proof. The following direct computation gives the consequence:

$$(U_G \chi_S^* \xi_c^{(+)})(a) = -(\chi_S^* \xi_c^{(+)})(\bar{a}) + \frac{2}{\deg(o(a))} \sum_{t(b)=o(a)} (\chi_S^* \xi_c^{(+)})(b)$$

$$= (\chi_S^* \xi_c^{(+)})(a) + \frac{2}{\sqrt{\deg(o(a))}} (d_1 \chi_S^* \xi_c^{(+)})(o(a))$$

$$= (\chi_S^* \xi_c^{(+)})(a).$$

Here, the first equality derives from the definition of U_G. In the second equality, since $\mathrm{supp}(\xi_c^{(+)}) \subset A_0 \subset A$ and the summation of RHS in the first equality is essentially the same as the one over A_0, we can apply the definition of d_1 to this. We use Lemma 1 in the last equality. □

We set $\mathcal{K} \subset \mathbb{C}^{A_0}$ by

$$\mathcal{K} = \mathrm{span}\{\chi_S \xi_c^{(+)} \mid c \in \Gamma \subset G_0\}. \tag{1}$$

The self-adjoint operator

$$T := (\chi_S d_1) S (\chi_S d_1)^*$$

on $\mathbb{C}^{A_0}$ is similar to the transition probability operator P' with the Dirichlet boundary condition on δV_0; i.e.,

$$P' = D^{-1/2} T D^{1/2},$$

where $(Df) = \deg(u) f(u)$. Here, the matrix representation of P' is described by

$$(P')_{u,v} := \langle \delta_u^{(V_0)}, P' \delta_v^{(V_0)} \rangle_{V_0} = \begin{cases} 1/\deg(u) & : \text{if } u \text{ and } v \text{ are connected,} \\ 0 & : \text{otherwise,} \end{cases}$$

for any $u, v \in V_0$. If $Tf = xf$ and $Tg = yg$ ($x \neq y$), then we find the orthogonality such that

$$\langle (1 - e^{i \arccos x} S) d_1^* f, (1 - e^{-i \arccos y} S) d_1^* g \rangle = 0,$$

$$\langle (1 - e^{i \arccos x} S) d_1^* f, (1 - e^{i \arccos y} S) d_1^* g \rangle = 0,$$

$$\langle (1 - e^{i \arccos x} S) d_1^* f, (1 - e^{-i \arccos y} S) d_1^* g \rangle = 0.$$

Then, we set $\mathcal{T} \subset \mathbb{C}^{A_0}$ by

$$\mathcal{T} = \bigoplus_{|\lambda|=1} \{(1 - \lambda S) d_1^* f \mid f \in \ker((\lambda + \lambda^{-1})/2 - T), \ \mathrm{supp}(f) \subset V_0 \setminus \delta V_0\}. \tag{2}$$

This is the subspace of $\mathbb{C}^{A_0}$ lifted up from the eigenfunctions in $\mathbb{C}^{V_0}$ of the Dirichlet cut random walk T by $(1 - \lambda S) d_1^* f$. It is shown that $\mathrm{Spec}(E) \subset \mathbb{D}$, where $\mathbb{D}$ is the unit disc $\{z \in \mathbb{C} \mid |z| \leq 1\}$ in Proposition 3, and $\mathcal{T} = \oplus_{|\lambda|=1, \lambda \neq \pm 1} \ker(\lambda - E)$, where $E := \chi_S U_G \chi_S^*$ in Lemma 3.

3. Definition of the Grover Walk on Graphs with Sinks

Let $G = (V, A)$ be a finite and connected graph with sinks $V_s = \{v_1, \ldots, v_q\} \subset V$. We consider the subgraph $G_0 = (V_0, A_0)$ as defined in Section 2.3. Assume that G_0 is connected. For simplicity, in this paper, we consider the initial state of the Grover walk ϕ_0 that satisfies the condition $\mathrm{supp}(\phi_0) \subset A_0$. (If we consider general initial state ϕ_0' such that $\mathrm{supp}(\phi_0') \cap (A \setminus A_0) \neq \emptyset$, replacing ϕ_0' into $\phi_0 = \phi_1'$, we can reproduce the QW with this initial state after $n \geq 1$ by our setting.) The time evolution of the Grover walk with sinks V_s with such an initial state ϕ_0 is defined by

$$\phi_n(a) = \begin{cases} (U_G \phi_{n-1})(a) & : t(a) \in V \setminus V_s, \\ 0 & : t(a) \in V_s, \end{cases} \quad (3)$$

This means that a quantum walker at a sink falls into a pit trap. We are interested in the survival probability of the Grover walk defined by

$$\gamma := \lim_{n \to \infty} \sum_{a \in A} |\phi_n(a)|^2.$$

It is the probability that the quantum walker remains in the graph without falling into the sinks forever. Considering the corresponding isotropic random walk with sinks such that

$$p_n(v) = \begin{cases} (Pp_{n-1})(v) & : v \in V \setminus V_s, \\ 0 & : v \in V_s, \end{cases}$$

we find that its survival probability is zero,

$$\gamma^{RW} := \lim_{n \to \infty} \sum_{v \in V} p_n(v) = 0,$$

because the first hitting time of a random walk to an arbitrary vertex for a finite graph is finite. On the other hand, in the case of the Grover walk, the survival probability becomes positive, up to the initial state. In this paper, we clarify a necessary and sufficient condition for $\gamma > 0$.

4. Main Theorem

We consider the case study on G_0 by

Case A: $A_{0,\sigma} = \emptyset$ and G_0 is a bipartite graph;

Case B: $A_{0,\sigma} = \emptyset$ and G_0 is a non-bipartite graph;

Case C: $A_{0,\sigma} \neq \emptyset$ and $G_0 \setminus A_{0,\sigma}$ is a bipartite graph;

Case D: $A_{0,\sigma} \neq \emptyset$ and $G_0 \setminus A_{0,\sigma}$ is a non-bipartite graph.

For a subspace $\mathcal{H} \subset \mathbb{C}^{A_0}$, the projection operator onto $\mathcal{H}$ is denoted by $\Pi_\mathcal{H}$. Then, we obtain the following theorem.

Theorem 1. *Let ϕ_n be the nth iteration of the Grover walk on $G = (V, A)$ with sinks. Let the survival probability at time n be defined by*

$$\gamma_n = \sum_{a \in A} |(\phi_n)|^2.$$

The subspaces $\mathcal{A}, \mathcal{B}, \mathcal{C}, \mathcal{D}$ of $\mathbb{C}^{A_0}$ are defined in (7),..., (10), respectively. Then, we have

1. $\lim_{n \to \infty} \gamma_n = \gamma$ exists.
2. *The survival probability γ is expressed by*

$$\gamma = ||\Pi_\mathcal{T} \chi_S \phi_0||^2 + ||\Pi_\mathcal{K} \chi_S \phi_0||^2 + \begin{cases} ||\Pi_\mathcal{A} \chi_S \phi_0||^2 & : \text{Case A} \\ ||\Pi_\mathcal{B} \chi_S \phi_0||^2 & : \text{Case B} \\ ||\Pi_\mathcal{C} \chi_S \phi_0||^2 & : \text{Case C} \\ ||\Pi_\mathcal{D} \chi_S \phi_0||^2 & : \text{Case D} \end{cases}$$

Proof. Part 1 of Theorem 1 is obtained by the consequences of Proposition 3 and Part 2 derives from Propositions 5 and 6. □

From this theorem, we obtain useful sufficient conditions for non-zero survival probability as follows.

Corollary 1. *Assume G_0 is a finite and connected graph. If G_0 is not a tree or G_0 has more than two self-loops, then $\gamma > 0$.*

Remark 1. *The eigenspaces $\mathcal{A}, \mathcal{B}, \mathcal{C}, \mathcal{D}$ correspond to the p-attractors defined in [8].*

5. Example

Let us consider a simple example in Figure 1. $G_0 = (V_0, A_0)$ with $V_0 = \{1, 2, 3, 4\}$ and $A_0 = \{a_1, a_2, a_3, a_4, \bar{a}_1, \bar{a}_2, \bar{a}_3, \bar{a}_4, b_1, b_2\}$, where a_1 has the origin 1 and the terminus 2; a_2 has the origin 2 and the terminus 3; a_3 has the origin 1 and the terminus 4; a_4 has the origin 1 and the terminus 1; and b_1 and b_2 are the self loops on 1 and 3, respectively.

This graph fits into Case C. Thus, let q be the closed walk by $q = (a_1, a_2, a_3, a_4)$ and q' be the walk between two selfloops by (b_1, a_1, a_2, b_2). Then, $\xi_q^{(+)}$, and the functions defined by (6) and Definition 2 are given by

$$\xi_q^{(+)} = (\delta_{a_1} + \delta_{a_2} + \delta_{a_3} + \delta_{a_4}) - (\delta_{\bar{a}_1} + \delta_{\bar{a}_2} + \delta_{\bar{a}_3} + \delta_{\bar{a}_4},)$$
$$\xi_q^{(-)} = (\delta_{a_1} + \delta_{\bar{a}_1}) - (\delta_{a_2} + \delta_{\bar{a}_2}) + (\delta_{a_3} + \delta_{\bar{a}_3}) - (\delta_{a_4} + \delta_{\bar{a}_4}),$$
$$\eta_{b_1 - b_2} = \delta_{b_1} - (\delta_{a_1} + \delta_{\bar{a}_1}) + (\delta_{a_2} + \delta_{\bar{a}_2}) - \delta_{b_2}.$$

The matrix representation of the self adjoint operator T is expressed by

$$T = \frac{1}{3}\begin{bmatrix} 1 & 1 & 0 & 1 \\ 1 & 0 & 1 & 0 \\ 0 & 1 & 1 & 1 \\ 1 & 0 & 1 & 0 \end{bmatrix}.$$

The eigenvector of T which has no overlaps to $\delta V_0 = \{2, 4\}$ is easily obtained by

$$f = [1, 0, -1, 0]^\top$$

which satisfies $Tf = (1/3)f$. Here, the symbol "⊤" is the transpose. The eigenfunctions lifted up to $\mathbb{C}^{\mathcal{A}}$ from f is

$$(\varphi_\pm)(a) = f(t(a)) - \lambda_\pm f(o(a))$$

by (2), where

$$\lambda_\pm = \frac{1}{3}(1 \pm i\sqrt{8}) = e^{\pm i\theta}, \quad \theta = \arccos \frac{1}{3}.$$

Then, we have

$$\varphi_\pm(a_1) = -\lambda_\pm, \ \varphi_\pm(a_2) = -1, \ \varphi_\pm(a_3) = \lambda_\pm, \ \varphi_\pm(a_4) = 1,$$
$$\varphi_\pm(\bar{a}_1) = 1, \ \varphi_\pm(\bar{a}_2) = \lambda_\pm, \ \varphi_\pm(\bar{a}_3) = -1, \ \varphi_\pm(\bar{a}_4) = -\lambda_\pm,$$
$$\varphi_\pm(b_1) = 1 - \lambda_\pm, \ \varphi_\pm(b_2) = -1 + \lambda_\pm.$$

It holds that $E\varphi_\pm = \lambda_\pm \varphi_\pm$. We obtain

$$\mathcal{T} = \mathbb{C}\varphi_+ \oplus \mathbb{C}\varphi_-,$$
$$\mathcal{K} = \mathbb{C}\xi_{(a_1,a_2,a_3,a_4)}^{(+)},$$
$$\mathcal{C} = \mathbb{C}\xi_{(a_1,a_2,a_3,a_4)}^{(-)} \oplus \mathbb{C}\eta_{b_1 - b_2}.$$

After the Gram–Schmidt procedure to $\mathcal{C}$, we have

$$\mathcal{C} = \mathbb{C}\xi^{(-)}_{(a_1,a_2,a_3,a_4)} \oplus \mathbb{C}(\eta_{b_1-b_2} + \eta'_{b_1-b_2}).$$

Here, we denote

$$\eta'_{b_1-b_2} = \delta_{b_1} - (\delta_{a_4} + \delta_{\bar{a}_4}) + (\delta_{a_3} + \delta_{\bar{a}_3}) - \delta_{b_2}$$

(see Figure 2). We express the functions $\varphi_\pm$, $\xi^{(+)}_{(a_1,a_2,a_3,a_4)}$, $\eta_{b_1-b_2}$, $\eta'_{b_1-b_2}$, $\eta_{b_1-b_2} + \eta'_{b_1-b_2}$ by weighted sub-digraphs of G_0. Then, the time evolution of the asymptotic dynamics of this quantum walk is described by

$$U^n \sim \frac{1}{8}|\xi^{(+)}_{(a_1,a_2,a_3,a_4)}\rangle\langle\xi^{(+)}_{(a_1,a_2,a_3,a_4)}|$$
$$+ (-1)^n\left(\frac{1}{8}|\xi^{(-)}_{(a_1,a_2,a_3,a_4)}\rangle\langle\xi^{(-)}_{(a_1,a_2,a_3,a_4)}| + \frac{1}{16}|\eta_{b_1-b_2} + \eta'_{b_1-b_2}\rangle\langle\eta_{b_1-b_2} + \eta'_{b_1-b_2}|\right)$$
$$+ e^{in\theta}\frac{3}{32}|\varphi_+\rangle\langle\varphi_+| + e^{-in\theta}\frac{3}{32}|\varphi_-\rangle\langle\varphi_-|. \quad (4)$$

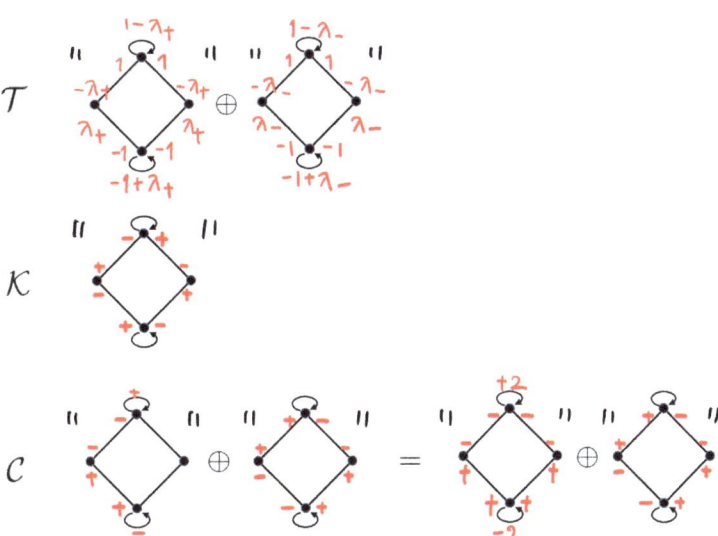

Figure 2. The centered eigenspace of the example: The centered eigenspace to which Grover walk with sinks asymptotically belongs in this example is $\mathcal{T} \oplus \mathcal{K} \oplus \mathcal{C}$. Each weighted sub-digraph represents a function in $\mathbb{C}^{A_0}$; the complex value at each arc is the returned value of the function. Each eigenspace, $\mathcal{T}$, $\mathcal{K}$, and $\mathcal{C}$, is spanned by the functions represented by these weighted sub-digraphs.

Finally, for example, if the initial state is $\varphi_0 = \delta_{b_1}$, then the survival probability can be computed by

$$\gamma = ||\Pi_\mathcal{T}\varphi_0||^2 + ||\Pi_\mathcal{K}\varphi_0||^2 + ||\Pi_\mathcal{C}\varphi_0||^2$$
$$= \frac{1}{16}|\langle\eta_{b_1-b_2} + \eta'_{b_1-b_2}, \varphi_0\rangle|^2 + \frac{3}{32}|\langle\varphi_+, \varphi_0\rangle|^2 + \frac{3}{32}|\langle\varphi_-, \varphi_0\rangle|^2$$
$$= \frac{1}{16}|2|^2 + \frac{3}{32}|1-\lambda_+|^2 + \frac{3}{32}|1-\lambda_-|^2$$
$$= 1/2.$$

The second equality derives from the fact that the orthonormalized eigenvectors in the centered generalized eigenspace which have an overlap with the self-loop b_1 are given by $(1/4)(\eta_{b_1-b_2} + \eta'_{b_1-b_2})$ and $\sqrt{3/32}\, \varphi_\pm$.

6. Relation between Grover Walk with Sinks and Grover Walk with Tails

6.1. Grover Walk on Graphs with Tails

Let $G = (V, A)$ be a finite and connected graph with the set of sinks $V_s \subset V$. We introduce the infinite graph $\tilde{G} = (\tilde{V}, \tilde{A})$ by adding the semi-infinite paths to each vertex of $\delta V = \{v_1, \ldots, v_r\}$, that is,

$$\tilde{V} = (V \setminus V_s) \cup (\cup_{j=1}^r V(\mathbb{P}_j)),$$
$$\tilde{A} = \cup_{j=1}^r A(\mathbb{P}_j) \cup (A \setminus \{a \in A \mid t(a) \in V_s \text{ or } o(a) \in V_s\}).$$

Here, $\mathbb{P}_j$s are the semi-infinite paths named the tail whose origin vertex is identified with v_i ($i = 1, \ldots, r$) (see Figure 1). Recall that $G_0 = (V_0, A_0)$ is the subgraph of G eliminating the sinks V_s. Recall also that $\chi_S : \mathbb{C}^A \to \mathbb{C}^{A_0}$ is

$$(\chi_S \phi)(a) = \phi(a)$$

for all $a \in A_0$. In the same way, we newly introduce $\chi_T : \mathbb{C}^{\tilde{A}} \to \mathbb{C}^{A_0}$ by

$$(\chi_T \phi)(a) = \phi(a)$$

for all $a \in A_0$. The adjoint $\chi_T^* : \mathbb{C}^{A_0} \to \mathbb{C}^{\tilde{A}}$ is

$$(\chi_T^* f)(a) = \begin{cases} f(a) & : a \in A_0, \\ 0 & : \text{otherwise.} \end{cases}$$

The only difference between χ_S and χ_T is the domain. A matrix representation of χ_T is

$$\chi_T \cong [\, I_{A_0} \mid 0 \,]$$

which is a $|A_0| \times \infty$ matrix because $|\tilde{A} \setminus A_0| = \infty$. The following theorem was proven by [19].

Theorem 2 ([19]). *Let $\tilde{G} = (\tilde{V}, \tilde{A})$ be the graph with infinite tails $\{\mathbb{P}_j\}_{j=1}^r$ induced by G_0 and its boundaries δV_0. Assume the initial state ψ_0 is*

$$\psi_0(a) = \begin{cases} \alpha_1 & : a \in A(\mathbb{P}_1),\ \mathrm{dist}(o(a), v_1) > \mathrm{dist}(t(a), v_1), \\ \vdots & \\ \alpha_r & : a \in A(\mathbb{P}_r),\ \mathrm{dist}(o(a), v_r) > \mathrm{dist}(t(a), v_r), \\ 0 & : \text{otherwise.} \end{cases}$$

Then, $\lim_{n \to \infty} \psi_n(a) =: \psi_\infty(a)$ exists and $\psi_\infty(a)$ is expressed by

$$\psi_\infty(a) = \frac{\alpha_1 + \cdots + \alpha_r}{r} + \mathrm{j}(a).$$

Here, $\mathrm{j}(\cdot)$ is the electric current flow on the electric circuit assigned the resistance value 1 at each edge, that is, $\mathrm{j}(\cdot)$ satisfies the following properties:

$$d_1 \mathrm{j} = 0,\ \mathrm{j}(\bar{a}) = -\mathrm{j}(a) \quad \text{(Kirchhoff's current law)}$$
$$\partial_2^* \mathrm{j} = 0 \quad \text{(Kirchhoff's voltage law)}$$

with the boundary conditions
$$j(e_i) = \alpha_i - \frac{\alpha_1 + \cdots + \alpha_r}{r} \tag{5}$$
for any e_i ($i = 1, \ldots, r$) such that $t(e_i) = v_j$ and $o(e_i) \in V(\mathbb{P}_i)$.

Remark 2. *The stationary state ψ_∞ satisfies the equation*
$$\psi_\infty(a) = (U_{\tilde{G}}\psi_\infty)(a)$$
for any $a \in A$ and $\psi_\infty \in \ell^\infty$, however $\|\psi_\infty\|_{\tilde{A}} = \infty$.

Remark 3. *The function $\xi_c^{(+)} = (1-S)\partial_2 \delta_c^{(\Gamma)}$ also satisfies*
$$\chi_T^* \xi_c^{(+)}(a) = (U_{\tilde{G}} \chi_T^* \xi_c^{(+)})(a)$$
and Kirchhoff's current and voltage laws if the internal graph G_0 is not a tree, while it does not satisfy the boundary condition (5) because the support of this function $\chi_T^* \xi_c^{(+)}$ has no overlaps to the tails but is included in the fundamental cycle c in the internal graph G_0.

6.2. Relation between Grover Walk with Sinks and Grover Walk with Tails

Let us consider the Grover walk on G with sinks V_s and with the initial state $\psi_0^{(S)} \in \mathbb{C}^A$. We describe U_G as the time evolution operator of Grover walk on G. The nth iteration of this walk following (3) is denoted by $\psi_n^{(S)}$. Let us also consider the Grover walk on $\tilde{G}$ with the tails and with the "same" initial state
$$\psi_0^{(T)}(a) = \begin{cases} \psi_0^{(S)}(a) & : a \in A_0, \\ 0 & : \text{otherwise.} \end{cases}$$

Note that the initial state $\psi_0^{(S)}$ is different from the one in the setting of Theorem 2. Putting the time evolution operator on $\tilde{G}$ by $U_{\tilde{G}}$, we denote the nth iteration of this walk by $\psi_n^{(T)} = U_{\tilde{G}} \psi_{n-1}^{(T)}$. Then, we obtain a simple but important relation between QW with sinks and QW with tails.

Lemma 2. *Let the setting of the QW with sinks and QW with tails be as the above. Then, for any time step n, we have*
$$\chi_S \psi_n^{(S)} = \chi_T \psi_n^{(T)}.$$

Proof. The initial state of $\chi_S \psi_0^{(S)}$ coincides with $\chi_T \psi_0^{(T)}$ because of the setting. Note that $\chi_J^* \chi_J$ is the projection operator onto $\mathbb{C}^{A_0}$ while $\chi_J \chi_J^*$ is the identity operator on $\mathbb{C}^{A_0}$ ($J \in \{S, T\}$). Since $\psi_n^{(S)}(a) = 0$ for any $a \in V_s$, we have
$$(1 - \chi_S^* \chi_S) \psi_n^{(S)} = 0$$
for any $n \in \mathbb{N}$. Then, putting $\chi_S \psi_n^{(S)} =: \phi_n^{(S)}$ and $\chi_S U_G \chi_S^* =: E$, we have
$$\begin{aligned}
\phi_n^{(S)} &= \chi_S \psi_n^{(S)} = \chi_S U_G \psi_{n-1}^{(S)} \\
&= \chi_S U_G (\chi_S^* \chi_S + (1 - \chi_S^* \chi_S)) \psi_{n-1}^{(S)} \\
&= E \phi_{n-1}^{(S)} + (\chi_S U_G (1 - \chi_S^* \chi_S)) \psi_{n-1}^{(S)} \\
&= E \phi_{n-1}^{(S)}.
\end{aligned}$$

It is easy to see that $E = \chi_S U_G \chi_S^* = \chi_T U_{\tilde{G}} \chi_T^*$. Since the support of the initial state is included in the internal graph, the inflow never comes into the internal graph from the tail for any time n, which implies

$$(\chi_T U_{\tilde{G}}(1 - \chi_T^* \chi_T))\psi_n^{(T)} = 0.$$

It holds that $E = \chi_S \tilde{U} \chi_S^* = \chi_T U_{\tilde{G}} \chi_T^*$. Then, putting $\phi_n^{(T)} := \chi_T \psi_n^{(T)}$, in the same way as $\psi_n^{(S)}$, we have

$$\phi_n^{(T)} = \chi_T U_{\tilde{G}}(\chi_T^* \chi_T + (1 - \chi_T^* \chi_T))\psi_{n-1}^{(T)}$$
$$= E \phi_{n-1}^{(T)}.$$

Therefore, $\chi_S \psi_n^{(S)}$ and $\chi_T \psi_n^{(T)}$ follow the same recurrence and have the same initial state which means $\chi_S \psi_n^{(S)} = \chi_T \psi_n^{(T)}$ for any $n \in \mathbb{N}$. □

Corollary 2. *Let the initial state for the Grover walk with sinks be ϕ_0 with $\mathrm{supp}(\phi_0) \subset A_0$. The survival probability γ can be expressed by*

$$\gamma = ||\phi_0||_A^2 - \sum_{n=0}^{\infty} \tau_n,$$

where τ_n is the outflow of the QW with tails from the internal graph G_0, i.e.,

$$\tau_n = \sum_{o(a) \in \delta V,\ t(a) \notin A_0} |(U_{\tilde{G}} \chi_T^* \phi_{n-1}^{(T)})(a)|^2$$

Remark 4. *The time evolution for $\phi_n^{(T)}$ is given by*

$$\phi_n^{(T)} = E \phi_{n-1}^{(T)} + \rho,$$

where $\rho = \chi_T U_{\tilde{G}} \psi_0^{(T)}$. In this case, the inflow is $\rho = 0$. On the other hand, in the setting of Theorem 2, ρ is given by a nonzero constant vector.

Let us now consider a QW with tails with a general initial state $\Psi_0 \in \mathbb{C}^{\tilde{A}}$ on $\tilde{G}$. We denote $\nu = \chi_T \Psi_0$ and $\rho = \chi_T U_{\tilde{G}}(1 - \chi^* \chi) \Psi_0$. We summarize the relation between a QW with sinks and a QW for the setting of Theorem 2 in Table 1 from the viewpoint of a QW with tails.

Table 1. Relatiion beteween QWs with tails and sinks.

	ρ	ν	State in G_0
QW with tails in the setting of Theorem 2 [19]	$\neq 0$	$= 0$	$\in \mathcal{H}_s$ (for any n)
QW with sinks	$= 0$	$\neq 0$	$\in \mathcal{H}_c$ (asymptotically)

7. Centered Generalized Eigenspace of E for the Grover Walk Case

7.1. The Stationary States from the Viewpoint of the Centered Generalized Eigenspace

From the above discussion, we see the importance of the spectral decomposition

$$E = \chi_S U_G \chi_S^* = \chi_T U_{\tilde{G}} \chi_T^*,$$

to obtain both limit behaviors. The operator E is no longer a unitary operator, and, moreover, it is not ensured that it is diagonalizable. The centered generalized eigenspace of E is defined by

$$\mathcal{H}_c := \{\psi \in \mathbb{C}^{A_0} \mid \exists\, m \geq 1 \text{ and } \exists\, |\lambda| = 1 \text{ such that } (E^m - \lambda)\psi = 0\}$$

Let $\mathcal{H}_s$ be defined by

$$\mathbb{C}^{A_0} = \mathcal{H}_c \oplus \mathcal{H}_s.$$

Here, "$\oplus$" means $\mathcal{H}_c$ and $\mathcal{H}_s$ are complementary spaces, that is, if $u_c + u_v = 0$ for some $u_c \in \mathcal{H}_c$ and $u_v \in \mathcal{H}_s$, then u_c and u_v must be $u_c = u_v = 0$. Note that, since E is not a normal operator on a vector space $\mathcal{H}_c \oplus \mathcal{H}_s$, it seems that in general $\langle u_c, u_v \rangle \neq 0$ for $u \in \mathcal{H}_c$ and $\mathcal{H}_s \in N$. However, we can see some important properties of the spectrum of E in the following proposition.

Proposition 2 ([19]).
1. For any $\lambda \in \mathrm{Spec}(E)$, it holds that $|\lambda| \leq 1$, i.e.,

$$\mathcal{H}_s = \{\psi \mid \exists\, m \in \mathbb{N}, \exists\, |\lambda| < 1, (U - \lambda)^m \psi) = 0\}.$$

2. Let P_c be the projection operator on $\mathcal{H}_c$ along with $\mathcal{H}_s$; that is, $P_c E = E P_c$ and $P_c^2 = P_c$. Then, P_c is the orthogonal projection onto $\mathcal{H}_c$, i.e., $P_c = P_c^*$.
3. The operator E acts as a unitary operator on $\mathcal{H}_c$, that is, $\mathcal{H}_c = \oplus_{|\lambda|=1} \ker(\lambda - E)$ and $U_G \chi_S^* \varphi = \lambda \chi_S^* \varphi$ for any $\varphi \in \ker(\lambda - E)$ with $|\lambda| = 1$.

We call $\mathcal{H}_c$ and $\mathcal{H}_s$ the *centered eingenspace* and the *stable eigenspace* [18], respectively.

Corollary 3. For any $\psi \in \mathcal{H}_s$ and $\phi \in \mathcal{H}_c$, it holds that $\langle \psi, \phi \rangle = 0$.

Now, let us see the stationary states from the viewpoint of the *orthogonal* decomposition of $\mathcal{H}_c \oplus \mathcal{H}_s$.

Proposition 3.
1. The state $\chi_T \psi_n$ in Theorem 2 belongs to $\mathcal{H}_s$ for any time step $n \in \mathbb{N}$.
2. The state of QW with sinks, $\chi_S \phi_n$, asymptotically belongs to $\mathcal{H}_c$ in the long time limit n.

Proof. The inflow $\rho = \chi^* U \psi_0$ is orthogonal to $\mathcal{H}_c$ by a direct consequence of Lemma 3.5 in [19], which implies $E^n \rho \in \mathcal{H}_s$ for any $n \in \mathbb{N}$ by Proposition 2. Since the stationary state of Part 1 is described by the limit of the following recurrence

$$\chi_T \psi_n = E \chi_T \psi_{n-1} + \rho, \quad \chi_T \psi_0 = 0,$$

we obtain the conclusion of Part 1. On the other hand, let us consider the proof of Part 2 in the following. The time evolution in G_0 obeys $\chi_S \phi_n = E \chi_S \phi_{n-1}$. The overlap of $\chi_S \phi_n$ to the space $\mathcal{H}_s$ decreases more quickly than polynomial times because all the absolute values of the generalized eigenvalues of $\mathcal{H}_s$ are strictly less than 1 (see Proposition 4 for more detailed order of the convergence). Then, only the contribution of the centered eigenspace, whose eigenvalues lie on the unit circle in the complex plain, remains in the long time limit. □

Let $W = P_c E = E P_c = P_c E P_c$ be the operator restricted to the centered eigenspace $\mathcal{H}_c$. Then, we have

$$\lim_{n \to \infty} |\chi_S \phi_n(a) - W^n \chi_S \phi_0(a)| = 0$$

for any $a \in A_0$ uniformly by Proposition 3. This means that, in the long time limit, the time evolution is reduced to W, which is a unitary operator on $\mathcal{H}_c$.

Proposition 4. *The survival probability is re-expressed by*

$$\gamma = ||P_c \chi_S \phi_0||^2.$$

The convergence speed ($f(n) = O(g(n))$ *means* $\lim_{n\to\infty} |f(n)/g(n)| < \infty$ *if the limit exists*) *is estimated by* $O(n^\kappa r_{max}^n)$, *where* $\kappa = \dim \mathcal{H}_s$, $r_{max} = \max\{|\lambda|\ ;\ \lambda \in \mathrm{Spec}(E), |\lambda| < 1\}$.

Proof. Putting $E(1 - P_c) = W'$, we have

$$W + W' = E, \quad WW' = 0,$$

by Proposition 2 (2). Note that the operator E^n is similar to

$$\bigoplus_{\lambda \in \mathrm{Spec}(E)} J^n(\lambda; k_\lambda)$$

with some natural numbers k_λs. Here, $J(\lambda; k)$ is the k-dimensional matrix by

$$J(\lambda; k) = \begin{bmatrix} \lambda & 1 & & & \\ & \lambda & 1 & & \\ & & \ddots & \ddots & \\ & & & \ddots & 1 \\ & & & & \lambda \end{bmatrix}.$$

We obtain that the survival probability at each time n is described by

$$\begin{aligned}
\gamma_n &= ||U_G \chi_S^* E^{n-1} \chi_S \phi_0||^2 \\
&= ||U_G \chi_S^* (W^{n-1} + W'^{n-1}) \chi_S \phi_0||^2 \\
&= ||(W^{n-1} + W'^{n-1}) \chi_S \phi_0||^2 \\
&= ||W^{n-1} \chi_S \phi_0||^2 + ||W'^{n-1} \chi_S \phi_0||^2.
\end{aligned}$$

In the third equality, we use the fact that U_G is unitary; the last equality follows from Corollary 3. The second term decreases to zero by Proposition 2 (2) with the convergence speed at least $O(n^\kappa r_{max}^n)$ because the Jordan matrix $J(\lambda; k)$ can be estimated by $J(\lambda; k)^n = O(n^k |\lambda|^n)$. Hence, we find for γ_n

$$\begin{aligned}
\gamma_n &= ||W^{n-1} \chi_S \phi_0||^2 + O(n^\kappa r_{max}^n) \quad (n \gg 1) \\
&= ||W^{n-1} P_c \chi_S \phi_0||^2 + O(n^\kappa r_{max}^n) \\
&= ||P_c \chi_S \phi_0||^2 + O(n^\kappa r_{max}^n),
\end{aligned}$$

where in the second equality we use that $W = W P_c$ and the last equality follows from Proposition 2 (3). □

Therefore, the characterization of $\mathcal{H}_c$ is important to obtain the asymptotic behavior of ϕ_n.

7.2. Characterization of Centered Generalized Eigenspace by Graph Notations

The centered generalized eigenspace of E can be rewritten by using the boundary operator d_1 and the self-adjoint operator $T = d_1 S d_1^*$ as follows.

Lemma 3 ([19]). *Assume* $\lambda \in \mathrm{Spec}(E)$ *with* $|\lambda| = 1$. *Then, we have*
1. $\lambda = \pm 1$ *if and only if* $\ker(\lambda - E) = \ker(-\lambda - S) \cap \ker d_1$.
2. $\lambda \neq \pm 1$ *if and only if* $\mathrm{supp}(g) \subset V_0 \setminus \delta V_0$ *for any* $g \in \ker((\lambda + \lambda^{-1})/2 - T) \neq 0$.

In the following, we consider the characterization of $\ker(\pm 1 - E)$ using some walks on graph G_0 up to the situations of the graph (Cases (A)–(D)). First, we prepare the following notations. For each support edge $e \in E_0$, there are two arcs a and $\bar{a}$ such that $|a| = |\bar{a}|$. Let us choose one of the arcs from each $e \in E_0$ and denote A_+ as the set of selected arcs. Then, $|A_+| = |E_0|$ and $a \in A_+$ if and only if $\bar{a} \notin A_+$ holds. We set $A_{rep} = A_{0,\sigma} \cup A_+$. Let us introduce the map $\iota : \mathbb{C}^{A_0} \to \mathbb{C}^{A_{rep}}$ defined by $(\iota\psi)(a) = \psi(a)$ for any $\psi \in \mathbb{C}^{A_0}$ and $a \in A_{rep}$.

Let us define the boundary operator $\partial_+ : \mathbb{C}^{A_{rep}} \to \mathbb{C}^{V_0}$ by

$$(\partial_+ \varphi)(u) = \sum_{t(a)=u \text{ in } A_+} \varphi(a) - \sum_{o(a)=u \text{ in } A_+} \varphi(a)$$

for any $\varphi \in \mathbb{C}^{A_{rep}}$ and $u \in V_0$. On the other hand, let us also define the boundary operator $\partial_- : \mathbb{C}^{A_{rep}} \to \mathbb{C}^{V_0}$ by

$$(\partial_- \varphi)(u) = \begin{cases} \sum_{t(a)=u} \varphi(a) + \sum_{o(a)=u} \varphi(a) & : u \text{ has no selfloop,} \\ \sum_{t(a)=u} \varphi(a) + \sum_{o(a)=u} \varphi(a) - \varphi(a_s) & : u \text{ has a selfloop } a_s, \end{cases}$$

for any $\varphi \in \mathbb{C}^{A_{rep}}$ and $u \in V_0$. We obtain the following lemma.

Lemma 4. Let $G_0 = (V_0, A_0)$ be a graph with self-loops. We set E_0 as the set of support edges of $A_0 \setminus A_{0,\sigma}$ such that $E_0 = \{|a| \mid a \in A_0 \setminus A_{0,\sigma}\}$. Then, we have

$$\dim[\ker(1-E)] = |E_0| - |V_0| + 1,$$

$$\dim[\ker(1+E)] = \begin{cases} |E_0| - |V_0| + 1 & : \text{Case A,} \\ |E_0| - |V_0| & : \text{Case B,} \\ |E_0| - |V_0| + |A_{0,\sigma}| & : \text{Cases C and D,} \end{cases}$$

Proof. Note that, if $\psi \in \ker(1+S)$, then $\psi(\bar{a}) = -\psi(a)$ for any $a \in A_+$, and, if $\psi \in \ker(d)$, then $\sum_{t(a)=u} \psi(a) = 0$ for any $u \in V_0$. We remark that, since $(S\psi)(a_s) = \psi(a_s)$ for any $a_s \in A_{0,\sigma}$, we have $\psi(a_s) = 0$ if $\psi \in \ker(1+S)$. Therefore, if $\psi \in \ker(1+S) \cap \ker(d)$, then

$$\sum_{t(a)=u \text{ in } A_+} (\iota\psi)(a) - \sum_{o(a)=u \text{ in } A_+} (\iota\psi)(a) = (\partial_+ \iota\psi)(u) = 0$$

holds. Then, $\ker(1+S) \cap \ker d$ is isomorphic to $\{\varphi \in \ker \partial_+ \mid supp(\varphi) \subset A_+\}$. Let us consider $\ker \partial_+$. By the definition of ∂_+, we have $\partial_+ \delta_a^{(A_{rep})} = 0$ for any $a \in A_s$. Hence, we should eliminate the subspace of $\ker \partial_+$ induced by the self-loops. The dimension of this subspace is $|A_{0,\sigma}|$. The adjoint operator $\partial_+^* : \mathbb{C}^{V_0} \to \mathbb{C}^{A_+}$ of ∂_+ is described by

$$(\partial_+^* f)(a) = f(t(a)) - f(o(a)),$$

for any $f \in \mathbb{C}^{V_0}$ and $a \in A_{rep}$. If $\partial_+^* f = 0$ holds, then $f(t(a)) = f(o(a))$ for any $a \in A_+$. This means $f(u) = c$ for any $u \in V_0$ with some non-zero constant c. Thus, $\dim \ker(\partial_+^*) = 1$. Therefore, the fundamental theorem of linear algebra (for a linear map $g : X \to Y$, $\dim \ker g = \dim X - \dim Y + \dim \ker g^*$) implies

$$\dim \ker(1+S) \cap \ker d = \dim \ker(\partial_+) - |A_{0,\sigma}|$$
$$= (|A_{rep}| - |V_0| + 1) - |A_{0,\sigma}|$$
$$= |E_0| - |V_0| + 1.$$

Next, let us consider $\dim(\ker(1-S) \cap \ker d_1)$. Note that, if $\psi \in \ker(1-S)$, then $\psi(\bar{a}) = \psi(a)$. Assume that $\psi \in \ker(1-S) \cap \ker(d_1)$; then,

$$\sum_{t(a)=u} (\iota\psi)(a) = 0 \text{ for any } u \in V_0,$$

which is equivalent to
$$\partial_- \iota\psi = 0.$$

The adjoint of ∂_- is described by

$$(\partial_-^* f)(a) = \begin{cases} f(t(a)) + f(o(a)) & : a \in A_+, \\ f(t(a)) & : a \in A_{0,\sigma}. \end{cases}$$

Let us consider $f \in \ker(\partial_-^*)$ in the cases for both $A_{0,\sigma} = \emptyset$ and $A_{0,\sigma} \neq \emptyset$.
$A_{0,\sigma} = \emptyset$ **case**:
If G_0 is a bipartite graph, then we can decompose the vertex set V into $X \cup Y$, where every edge connects a vertex in X to one in Y. Then, $f(x) = k$ for any $x \in X$ and $f(y) = -k$ for any $y \in Y$ with some nonzero constant k. Hence, $\dim \ker(\partial^*) = 1$ if $A_{0,\sigma} = \emptyset$ and G_0 is bipartite. On the other hand, if G_0 is non-bipartite, then there must exist an odd length fundamental cycle $c = (a_0, a_1, \ldots, a_{2m})$. We have that

$$f(o(a_1)) = -f(o(a_2)) = f(o(a_3)) = \cdots = -f(o(a_{2r})) = f(o(a_0)) = -f(o(a_1)).$$

Then, $f(u) = 0$ for any $u \in V(c)$. Since G_0 is connected, the value 0 is inherited to the other vertices by $f(t(a)) = -f(o(a))$. After all, we have $f = 0$, which implies $\ker(\partial_-^*) = 0$ if $A_{0,\sigma} = \emptyset$ and G_0 is non-bipartite.

$A_{0,\sigma} \neq \emptyset$ **case**: Since $(\partial_-^* f)(a) = f(t(a)) = 0$ if $a \in A_{0,\sigma}$, then f takes the value 0 at the other vertices since $f(t(a)) = -f(o(a))$ for any $a \in A_+$, which implies $\ker(\partial_+^*) = 0$ if $A_{0,\sigma} \neq \emptyset$.

After all, by the fundamental theorem of the linear algebra,

$$\dim \ker \partial_- = |A_{rep}| - |V_0| + \begin{cases} 1 & : A_s = \emptyset, G_0 \text{ is bipartite.} \\ 0 & : \text{otherwise.} \end{cases}$$

Noting that $|A_{rep}| = |E_0| + |A_{0,\sigma}|$, we obtain the desired conclusion. □

In the following, let us find linearly independent eigenfunctions of $\ker(\pm 1 - E)$ using some concepts from graph theory. A walk p in G_0 is a sequence $p = (a_0, a_1, \ldots, a_r)$ of arcs with $t(a_j) = o(a_{j+1})$ $(j = 0, 1, \ldots, r-1)$, which may contain repeated arcs as defined in Section 2.1. We set $\{a_0, a_1, \ldots, a_r\} =: A(p)$, and similarly $\overline{A}(p) = \{\bar{a}_0, \ldots, \bar{a}_r\}$ as *multi* sets. We describe $\tilde{\xi}_p^{(\pm)} : \{a_0, \ldots, a_r\} \cup \{\bar{a}_0, \ldots, \bar{a}_r\} \to \{\pm 1\}$ by

$$\tilde{\xi}_p^{(+)}(a) = \begin{cases} 1 & : a \in A(p), \\ -1 & : \bar{a} \in A(p), \end{cases}$$

$$\tilde{\xi}_p^{(-)}(a) = \begin{cases} 1 & : |a| \in \{|a_j| \mid j \text{ is even}\}, \\ -1 & : |a| \in \{|a_j| \mid j \text{ is odd}\}. \end{cases}$$

Then, we set the functions $\xi_p^{(\pm)} \in \mathbb{C}^A$ by

$$\xi_p^{(\pm)}(a) = \begin{cases} \sum_{b: a=b} \tilde{\xi}_p^{(\pm)}(b) & : a \in A(p) \cup \overline{A}(p), \\ 0 & : \text{otherwise.} \end{cases} \quad (6)$$

Now, we are ready to show the following proposition for $\ker(1-E)$.

Proposition 5. *Let $\xi_c^{(+)}$ be defined as (6). Then, we have*
$$\ker(1 - E) = \operatorname{span}\{\xi_c^{(+)} \mid c \in \Gamma\}.$$

Proof. By the definition of $\xi_c^{(+)}$, we have $\xi_c^{(+)} \in \ker d_1 \cap \ker(1 - S)$, which implies $\xi_c^{(+)} \in \ker(1 - E)$ by Lemma 3. We show the linear independence of $\{\xi_c^{(+)}\}_{c \in \Gamma}$. Let us set $\Gamma = \{c_1, \ldots, c_r\}$ and $\tilde{\xi}_j := \xi_{c_j}^{(+)}$ ($j = 1, \ldots, r$) induced by the spanning tree $\mathbb{T} \subset G$. Assume that
$$\beta_1 \tilde{\xi}_1 + \cdots + \beta_r \tilde{\xi}_r = 0.$$

Put $a_r \in A_0(c_r) \cap (A_0 \setminus A(\mathbb{T}))$. From the definition of the fundamental cycle, we have
$$\beta_1 \tilde{\xi}_1(a_r) + \cdots + \beta_r \tilde{\xi}_r(a_r) = \beta_r = 0.$$

In the same way, let $a_{r-1} \in A(c_{r-1}) \cap (A_0 \setminus A(\mathbb{T}))$; then,
$$\beta_1 \tilde{\xi}_1(a_r) + \cdots + \beta_{r-1} \tilde{\xi}_{r-1}(a_{r-1}) = \beta_{r-1} = 0.$$

Then, using it recursively, we obtain $\beta_1 = \cdots = \beta_r = 0$, which means $\tilde{\xi}_j$s are linearly independent.

Then, $\dim(\mathcal{K}) = |\Gamma| = |E_0| - |V_0| + 1$. By Lemma 4, we reach the conclusion. □

Define $\Gamma_o, \Gamma_e \subset \Gamma$ as the set of odd and even length fundamental cycles. In the following, to obtain a characterization of $\ker(1 + E) = \ker(1 - S) \cap \ker(d_1)$, we construct the function $\eta_{x,y} \in \ker(1 - S) \cap \ker(d_1)$, which is determined by $x, y \in A_{0,\sigma} \cup \Gamma_o$. The main idea to construct such a function is as follows. By the definition of $\xi_q^{(-)}$ for any walk q, $\xi_q^{(-)} \in \ker(1 - S)$. This is equivalent to assigning the symbols "+" and "−" alternatively to each edge along the walk q. If the walk c is an even length cycle, then a symbol on each edge of c is different from the ones on the neighbor's edges; this means
$$\sum_{t(a)=u} \xi_c^{(-)}(a) = 0,$$

for every u. Then, $\xi_c^{(-)} \in \ker(d_1) \cap \ker(1 - S)$ holds. On the other hand, if the walk $c = (b_1, \ldots, b_r)$ is an odd length cycle, then a "frustration" appears at $u := o(b_1)$; i.e.,
$$\sum_{t(a)=u} \xi_c^{(-)}(a) = 2.$$

There are two ways to vanish this frustration: the first is to make a cancellation by another frustration induced by another odd cycle c' and the second is to push the frustration to a self-loop. That is the reason the domains of x and y are $A_{0,\sigma} \cup \Gamma_o$. We give more precise explanations of the constructions as follows. See also Figure 3.

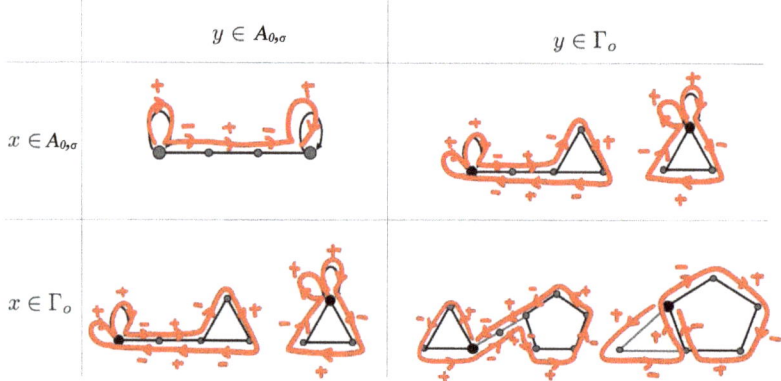

Figure 3. Construction of eigenfunction $\eta_{x,y} \in \mathbb{C}^{A_0}$: Each graph with signs $\pm$ represents the function $\eta_{x,y}$. The support of $\eta_{x,y}$ is included in the arcs of each graphs. The signs are the return values of this function at each arcs. The return values of the inverse arcs are the same as the original arcs. The signs are assigned alternatively along the red colored walks. At each time where the walk runs through an arc, we take the sum of the signs; e.g., in the case for $x \in A_{0,\sigma}, y \in \Gamma_o$, the walk runs through the self-loop twice, and then the return value at the self-loops of the function is $1 + 1 = 2$.

Definition 2. Construction of $\eta_{x,y} \in \mathbb{C}^{A_0}$:

The function $\eta_{x,y}$ is described by $\xi_q^{(-)}$ induced by a walk depending on the indexes of x, y. In this paper, we consider four cases of the domains of x and y: (1) $x \in \Gamma_o, y \in \Gamma_o$; (2) $x \in A_\sigma, y \in A_\sigma$; (3) $x \in A_\sigma, y \in \Gamma_o$; and (4) $x \in \Gamma_o, y \in A_\sigma$.

1. $x \in \Gamma_o, y \in \Gamma_o$ case:

   If G_0 is a bipartite graph, let us fix an odd length fundamental cycle $c_* = (a_0, \ldots, a_{r-1}) \in \Gamma_o$ and pick up another $c \in \Gamma_o = (b_0, \ldots, b_{s-1})$. We set the following walk q and define the function on $\mathbb{C}^{A_0}$; $\xi_q^{(-)} =: \bar{a} a_{c_*-c}$, induced by $c_*, c \in \Gamma_o$:

   (a) $c_0 \cap c \neq \emptyset$ case: We set q as the shortest closed walk starting from a vertex $u_0 \in V(c_0) \cap V(c)$ and visiting all the vertices of $V(c_0)$ and $V(c)$; that is, $q = (a_i, \ldots, a_{i+r}, b_j, \ldots, b_{s+j})$. Here, $o(a_i) = o(b_j) = u_0$ and the suffices are modulus of r and s.

   (b) $c_0 \cap c = \emptyset$ case: Let us fix the shortest path between c_0 and c by $p = (p_1, \ldots, p_t)$. Denoting the vertex in $V(c_*)$ connecting to p by $u_0 \in V(c_*)$, we set q by the shortest closed walk q starting from u_* and visiting all the vertices; that is, $q = (a_i, \ldots, a_{r+i}, p_0 \ldots, p_t, b_j \ldots, b_{s+j}, \bar{p}_t \ldots, \bar{p}_1)$, where $o(a_i) = t(a_{r+i}) = o(p_1) = u_0, t(p_t) = o(b_j) = t(b_{s+j})$.

   Note that, by the definition of the fundamental cycle, the intersection $c_0 \cap c$ is a path in Case (1). Since G_0 is connected, there is a path connecting c_* to c and we fix such a path for every pair of (c_*, c) in Case (2).

2. $x \in A_\sigma$ and $y \in A_\sigma$ case:

   If the number of self-loops $|A_\sigma| \geq 2$, let us fix a self-loop a_* from A_σ and a path between a_* to each $a \in A_\sigma \setminus \{a_*\}$. Let us denote the path between a_* and a by $p = (p_1, \ldots, p_t)$. Then, we set the walk from a_* to a by $q = (a_*, p_1, \ldots, p_t, a)$ and $\xi_q^{(-)} =: \eta_{a_*-a}$.

3. $x \in A_\sigma$ and $y \in \Gamma_o$ case:

   If $|A_\sigma| \geq 1$ and $G \setminus A_\sigma$ is a non-bipartite graph, let us fix a self-loop a_* and pick up an odd cycle $c = (b_1, \ldots, b_t) \in \Gamma_o$; if the self-loop $o(a_*) \in V(c)$, we set the walk starting from a_* visiting all the vertices $V(c)$ and returning back to a_* by $q = (a_*, b_1, \ldots, b_t, a_*)$; and, for $o(a_*) \notin V(c)$, let us fix a path $p = (p_1, \ldots, p_t)$ between $o(a_*)$ and $o(b_1)$ and set the walk starting from a_* visiting all the vertices $V(p) \cup V(c)$ and returning back to a_*; $q = (a_*, p_1, \ldots, p_t, b_0 \ldots, b_t, \bar{p}_t, \ldots, \bar{p}_1, a_*)$. Then, we set $\xi_q^{(-)} =: \eta_{a_*,c}$.

4. $x \in \Gamma_o$ and $y \in A_\sigma$ case:
    Let us fix an odd length fundamental cycle $c_* \in \Gamma_o = (b_1, \ldots, b_{s-1})$ and pick up a self-loop $a \in A_\sigma$. Let us set a short length path p between $o(a)$ and $o(b_1)$. Then, we consider the same walk q as in Case (3) and set $\xi_q^{(-)} =: \eta_{c_*, a}$.

By the construction, we have $\eta_{x,y} \in \ker(1-S) \cap \ker(d_1)$. Using the function $\eta_{x,y}$, we obtain the following characterization of $\ker(-1-E)$.

Proposition 6. *Let $\xi_c^{(-)}$ be defined by (6) and $\eta_{x,y}$ be the above. Let us fix $a_* \in A_\sigma$ and $c_* \in \Gamma_o$. Then, we have*

$$\ker(1+E) = \begin{cases} \mathrm{span}\{\xi_c^{(-)} \mid c \in \Gamma\} & : \text{Case (A)}, \\ \mathrm{span}\{\xi_c^{(-)} \mid c \in \Gamma_e\} \oplus \mathrm{span}\{\eta_{c_*-c} \mid c \in \Gamma_o \setminus \{c_*\}\} & : \text{Case (B)}, \\ \mathrm{span}\{\xi_c^{(-)} \mid c \in \Gamma\} \oplus \mathrm{span}\{\eta_{a_*-a} \mid a \in A_{0,\sigma} \setminus \{a_*\}\} & : \text{Case (C)}, \\ \mathrm{span}\{\xi_c^{(-)} \mid c \in \Gamma_e\} \oplus \mathrm{span}\{\eta_{a_*-y} \mid y \in \Gamma_o \cup (A_{0,\sigma} \setminus \{a_*\})\} & : \text{Case (D)}. \end{cases}$$

Proof. We put

$$\mathcal{A} := \mathrm{span}\{\xi_c^{(-)} \mid c \in \Gamma\}, \tag{7}$$

$$\mathcal{B} := \mathrm{span}\{\xi_c^{(-)} \mid c \in \Gamma_e\} \oplus \mathrm{span}\{\eta_{c_*-c} \mid c \in \Gamma_o \setminus \{c_*\}\}, \tag{8}$$

$$\mathcal{C} := \mathrm{span}\{\xi_c^{(-)} \mid c \in \Gamma\} \oplus \mathrm{span}\{\eta_{a_*-a} \mid a \in A_{0,\sigma} \setminus \{a_*\}\}, \tag{9}$$

$$\mathcal{D} := \mathrm{span}\{\xi_c^{(-)} \mid c \in \Gamma_e\} \oplus \mathrm{span}\{\eta_{a_*-y} \mid y \in \Gamma_o \cup (A_{0,\sigma} \setminus \{a_*\})\} \tag{10}$$

(see also Figure 4). From the construction of $\eta_{x,y}$ and $\xi_c^{(-)}$, the linear independence is immediately obtained. Let us check the dimensions for each case.

In Case (A),
$$\dim(\mathcal{A}) = |\Gamma| = |E_0| - |V_0| + 1.$$

In Case (B),
$$\dim(\mathcal{B}) = |\Gamma_e| + (|\Gamma_o| - 1) = |E_0| - |V_0|.$$

In Case (C),
$$\dim(\mathcal{C}) = |\Gamma| + (|A_{0,\sigma}| - 1) = |E_0| - |V_0| + |A_{0,\sigma}|.$$

In Case (D),
$$\dim(\mathcal{D}) = |\Gamma_e| + (|\Gamma_o| - 1) + (|A_{0,\sigma}| - 1) = |E_0| - |V_0| + |A_{0,\sigma}|.$$

By Lemma 4, we reach the conclusion. □

Remark 5. *"$M \oplus N$" in Proposition 6 means that M and N are just complementary spaces; the orthogonality is not ensured in general.*

Remark 6. *If $|\Gamma_o| = 1$ in Case (B), we have $\mathcal{B} = \mathrm{span}\{\xi_c^{(-)} \mid c \in \Gamma_e\}$. If $|A_{0,\sigma}| = 1$ in Case (C), we have $\mathcal{C} = \mathrm{span}\{\xi_c^{(-)} \mid c \in \Gamma\}$.*

Remark 7. *The subspace $\mathcal{D}$ can be re-expressed by*

$$\mathcal{D} = \mathrm{span}\{\xi_c^{(-)} \mid c \in \Gamma_e\} \oplus \mathrm{span}\{\eta_{c_*-y} \mid y \in (\Gamma_o \setminus \{c_*\}) \cup A_{0,\sigma}\}.$$

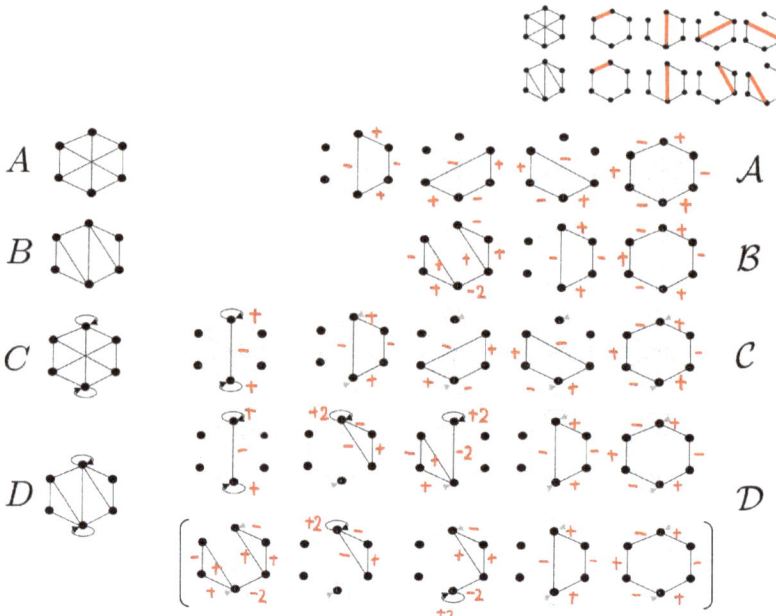

Figure 4. Eigenspaces ($\mathcal{A}$–$\mathcal{D}$): This figure shows examples of four graphs for Cases (**A**)–(**D**) and their induced eigenspaces of the Grover walk ($\mathcal{A}$–$\mathcal{D}$). The figures at the right corner are the fundamental cycles for each case. The weighted graphs represent bases of each eigenspace. The weights are the return values at each arcs of the bases, where every base takes the value 0 at the dashed arcs.

8. Conclusions

We investigated the Grover walk on a finite graph G with sinks using its connection with the walk on the graph G_0 with tails. It was shown that the centered generalized eigenspace of the Grover walk with tails corresponds to the attractor space of the Grover walk with sinks, i.e., it contains all trapped states which do not contribute to the transport of the quantum walker into the sink. Consequently, the attractor space of the Grover walk with sinks can be characterized using the persistent eigenspace of the underlying random walk whose supports have no overlaps to the boundary and the concept of "flow" from graph theory. In particular, we constructed linearly independent basis vectors of the attractor space using the properties of fundamental cycles of G_0. The attractor space can be divided into subspaces $\mathcal{T}$ and $\mathcal{K}$, corresponding to the eigenvalues $\lambda \neq \pm 1$ and $\lambda = 1$, respectively, and an additional subspace which belongs to the eigenvalue $\lambda = -1$. While the basis of $\mathcal{T}$ and $\mathcal{K}$ can be constructed using the same procedure for all finite connected graphs G_0, for the last subspace, we provided a construction based on case separation, depending on if the graph is bipartite or not and if it involves self-loops.

The use of fundamental cycles allowed us to considerably expand the results previously found in the literature, which are often limited to planar graphs. The derived construction of the attractor space enables better understanding of the quantum transport models on graphs. In addition, our results reveal that the attractor space can contain subspaces of eigenvalues different from $\lambda = \pm 1$. In such a case, the evolution of the Grover walk with sink will have more complex asymptotic cycle. In fact, the example presented in Section 5 exhibits an infinite asymptotic cycle, since the phase θ of the eigenvalues $\lambda_\pm \neq \pm 1$ is not a rational multiple of π. This feature is missing, e.g., in the Grover walk on dynamically percolated graphs with sinks, where the evolution converges to a steady state.

Author Contributions: Conceptualization, E.S.; formal analysis, E.S., M.Š., N.K. All authors have read and agreed to the published version of the manuscript.

Funding: E.S. acknowledges financial supports from the Grant-in-Aid of Scientific Research (C) No. JP19K03616, Japan Society for the Promotion of Science and Research Origin for Dressed Photon. M.Š. is grateful for the financial support from MŠMT RVO 14000. This publication was funded by the project "Centre for Advanced Applied Sciences", Registry No. CZ.02.1.01/0.0/0.0/16_019/0000778, supported by the Operational Programme Research, Development and Education, co-financed by the European Structural and Investment Funds and the state budget of the Czech Republic.

Conflicts of Interest: The authors declare no conflict of interest.

References

1. Ambainis, A. Quantum walks and their algorithmic applications. *Int. J. Quantum Inf.* **2003**, *1*, 507–518. [CrossRef]
2. Ambainis, A.; Bach, E.; Nayak, A.; Vishwanath, A.; Watrous, J. One-Dimensional Quantum Walks. In Proceedings of the 33rd Annual ACM Symposium on Theory of Computing 2001, Heraklion, Greece, 6–8 July 2001; p. 37.
3. Konno, N.; Namiki, T.; Soshi, T.; Sudbury, A. Absorption problems for quantum walks in one dimension. *J. Phys. A Math. Gen.* **2003**, *36*, 241. [CrossRef]
4. Bach, E.; Coppersmith, S.; Goldschen, M.P.; Joynt, R.; Watrous, J. One-dimensional quantum walks with absorbing boundaries. *J. Comput. Syst. Sci.* **2004**, *69*, 562. [CrossRef]
5. Yamasaki, T.; Kobayashi, H.; Imai, H. Analysis of absorbing times of quantum walks. *Phys. Rev. A* **2003**, *68*, 012302. [CrossRef]
6. Inui, N.; Konno, N.; Segawa, E. One-dimensional three-state quantum walk. *Phys. Rev. E* **2005**, *72*, 056112. [CrossRef] [PubMed]
7. Štefaňák, M.; Novotný, J.; Jex, I. Percolation assisted excitation transport in discrete-time quantum walks. *New J. Phys.* **2016**, *18*, 023040. [CrossRef]
8. Mareš, J.; Novotný, J.; Jex, I. Percolated quantum walks with a general shift operator: From trapping to transport. *Phys. Rev. A* **2019**, *99*, 042129. [CrossRef]
9. Mareš, J.; Novotný, J.; Štefaňák, M.; Jex, I. A counterintuitive role of geometry in transport by quantum walks. *Phys. Rev. A* **2020**, *101*, 032113. [CrossRef]
10. Mareš, J.; Novotný, J.; Jex, I. Quantum walk transport on carbon nanotube structures. *Phys. Lett. A* **2020**, *384*, 126302. [CrossRef]
11. Ohtsu, M.; Kobayashi, K.; Kawazoe, T.; Yatsui, T.; Naruse, M. *Principles of Nanophotonics*; Taylor and Francis: Boca Raton, FL, USA, 2008.
12. Nomura, W.; Yatsui, T.; Kawazoe, T.; Naruse, M.; Ohtsu, M. Structural dependency of optical excitation transfer via optical near-field interactions between semiconductor quantum dots. *Appl. Phys. B* **2010**, *100*, 181–187. [CrossRef]
13. Krovi, H.; Brun, T.A. Hitting time for quantum walks on the hypercube. *Phys. Rev. A* **2006**, *73*, 032341. [CrossRef]
14. Krovi, H.; Brun, T.A. Quantum walks with infinite hitting times. *Phys. Rev. A* **2006**, *74*, 042334. [CrossRef]
15. Higuchi, Y.; Konno, N.; Sato, I.; Segawa, E. Spectral and asymptotic properties of Grover walks on crystal lattices. *J. Funct. Anal.* **2014**, *267*, 4197–4235. [CrossRef]
16. Feldman, E.; Hillery, M. Quantum walks on graphs and quantum scattering theory. In *Coding Theory and Quantum Computing (Contemporary Mathematics)*; Evans, D., Holt, J., Jones, C., Klintworth, K., Parshall, B., Pfister, O., Ward, H., Eds.; American Mathematical Society: Providence, RI, USA, 2005; Volume 381, pp. 71–96.
17. Feldman, E.; Hillery, M. Modifying quantum walks: A scattering theory approach. *J. Phys. A Math. Theor.* **2007**, *40*, 11343–11359. [CrossRef]
18. Robinson, M. *Dynamical Systems: Stability, Symbolic Dynamics, and Chaos*; CRC Press: Boca Raton, FL, USA, 1995.
19. Higuchi, Y.; Segawa, E. Dynamical system induced by quantum walks. *J. Phys. A Math. Theor.* **2019**, *52*, 39. [CrossRef]

Article

A Discontinuity of the Energy of Quantum Walk in Impurities

Kenta Higuchi [1], Takashi Komatsu [2], Norio Konno [3], Hisashi Morioka [4] and Etsuo Segawa [5,*]

1. Department of Mathematical Sciences, Ritsumeikan University/Noji-Higashi, Kusatsu 525-8577, Japan; ra0039vv@ed.ritsumei.ac.jp
2. Math. Research Institute Calc for Industry/Minami, Hiroshima 732-0816, Japan; t.komatsu.27@cc.it-hiroshima.ac.jp
3. Department of Applied Mathematics, Yokohama National University/Hodogaya, Yokohama 240-8501, Japan; konno-norio-bt@ynu.ac.jp
4. Graduate School of Science and Engineering, Ehime University/Bunkyo-cho 3, Matsuyama, Ehime 790-8577, Japan; morioka@cs.ehime-u.ac.jp
5. Graduate School of Environment Information Sciences, Yokohama National University/Hodogaya, Yokohama 240-8501, Japan
* Correspondence: segawa-etsuo-tb@ynu.ac.jp

Abstract: We consider the discrete-time quantum walk whose local dynamics is denoted by a common unitary matrix C at the perturbed region $\{0, 1, \ldots, M-1\}$ and free at the other positions. We obtain the stationary state with a bounded initial state. The initial state is set so that the perturbed region receives the inflow ω^n at time n ($|\omega|=1$). From this expression, we compute the scattering on the surface of -1 and M and also compute the quantity how quantum walker accumulates in the perturbed region; namely, the energy of the quantum walk, in the long time limit. The frequency of the initial state of the influence to the energy is symmetric on the unit circle in the complex plain. We find a discontinuity of the energy with respect to the frequency of the inflow.

Keywords: quantum walk; scattering theory; energy

Citation: Higuchi, K.; Komatsu, T.; Konno, N.; Morioka, H.; Segawa, E. A Discontinuity of the Energy of Quantum Walk in Impuritie. *Symmetry* **2021**, *13*, 1134. https://doi.org/10.3390/sym13071134

Academic Editor: Motoichi Ohtsu

Received: 29 May 2021
Accepted: 21 June 2021
Published: 24 June 2021

Publisher's Note: MDPI stays neutral with regard to jurisdictional claims in published maps and institutional affiliations.

Copyright: © 2021 by the authors. Licensee MDPI, Basel, Switzerland. This article is an open access article distributed under the terms and conditions of the Creative Commons Attribution (CC BY) license (https://creativecommons.org/licenses/by/4.0/).

1. Introduction

There is no doubt that a study on scattering theory is one of the most interesting topics of the Schrödinger equation. Recently, it has been revealed that the scatterings of some fundamental stationary Schrödinger equations on the real line with not only delta potentials [1–3] but also continuous potential [4] can be recovered by discrete-time quantum walks. These induced quantum walks are given by the following setting: the non-trivial quantum coins are assigned to some vertices in a finite region on the one-dimensional lattice as the impurities and the free-quantum coins are assigned at the other vertices. The initial state is given so that a quantum walker inflows into the perturbed region at every time step. It is shown that the scattering matrix of the quantum walk on the one-dimensional lattice can be explicitly described by using a path counting in [5] and this path counting method can be described by a discrete analogue of the Feynmann path integral [4]. There are some studies for the scattering theory of quantum walks under slightly general settings and related topics [6–12].

Such a setting is the special setting of [13,14] in that the regions where a quantum walker moves freely coincide with tails in [13,14], and the perturbed region can be regarded as a finite and connected graph in [13,14]. The properties of not only the scattering on the surface of the internal graph but also the stationary state in the internal graph for the Szegedy walk are characterized by [15] with a constant inflow from the tails.

By [14], this quantum walk converges to a stationary state. Therefore, let $\vec{\varphi}(\cdot)$: $\mathbb{Z} \to \mathbb{C}^2$ be the stationary state of the quantum walk on $\mathbb{Z}$. The perturbed region is $\Gamma_M := \{0, 1, \ldots, M-1\}$ and we assign the quantum coin

$$C = \begin{bmatrix} a & b \\ c & d \end{bmatrix}$$

to each vertex in Γ_M. The inflow into the perturbed region at time n is expressed by ω^n ($|\omega| = 1$). In this paper, we compute (1) the scattering on the surface of the perturbed region Γ_M in the one-dimensional lattice; (2) the energy of the quantum walk. Here, the energy of quantum walk is defined by

$$\mathcal{E}_M(\omega) = \sum_{x=0}^{M-1} \|\vec{\varphi}(x)\|_{\mathbb{C}^2}^2.$$

This is the quantity that quantum walkers accumulate to the perturbed region Γ_M in the long time limit. We obtain a necessary and sufficient condition for the perfect transmitting, and also obtain the energy. As a consequence of our result on the energy, we observe a discontinuity of the energy with respect to the frequency of the inflow. Moreover, our result implies that the condition for $\theta(\omega) \in \mathbb{N}$ is equivalent to the condition for the perfect transmitting. Then, we obtain that the situation of the perfect transmitting not only releases quantum walker to the opposite outside but also accumulates quantum walkers in the perturbed region. Note that since this quantum walk can be converted to a quantum walk with absorption walls, the problem is reduced to analysis on a finite matrix E_M, which is obtained by picking up from the total unitary time evolution operator with respect to the perturbed region Γ_M. See [16] for a precise spectral results on E_M.

This paper is organized as follows. In Section 2, we explain the setting of this model and give some related works. In Section 3, an explicit expression for the stationary state is computed using the Chebyshev polynomials. From this expression, we obtain the transmitting and reflecting rates and a necessary and sufficient condition for the perfect transmitting. We also give the energy in the perturbed region. In Section 4, we estimate the asymptotics of the energy to see the discontinuity with respect to the incident inflow.

2. The Setting of our Quantum Walk

The total Hilbert space is denoted by $\mathcal{H} := \ell^2(\mathbb{Z}; \mathbb{C}^2) \cong \ell^2(A)$. Here A is the set of arcs of one-dimensional lattice whose elements are labeled by $\{(x; R), (x; L) \mid x \in \mathbb{Z}\}$, where $(x; R)$ and $(x; L)$ represents the arcs "from $x - 1$ to x", and "from $x + 1$ to x", respectively. We assign a 2×2 unitary matrix to each $x \in \mathbb{Z}$ so-called local quantum coin

$$C_x = \begin{bmatrix} a_x & b_x \\ c_x & d_x \end{bmatrix}.$$

Putting $|L\rangle := [1, 0]^\top$, $|R\rangle := [0, 1]^\top$ and $\langle L| = [1, 0]$, $\langle R| = [0, 1]$, we define the following matrix valued weights associated with the motion from x to left and right by

$$P_x = |L\rangle\langle L|C_x, \quad Q_x = |R\rangle\langle R|C_x,$$

respectively. Then, the time evolution operator on $\ell^2(\mathbb{Z}; \mathbb{C}^2)$ is described by

$$(U\psi)(x) = P_{x+1}\psi(x+1) + Q_{x-1}\psi(x-1)$$

for any $\psi \in \ell^2(\mathbb{Z}; \mathbb{C}^2)$. Its equivalent expression on $\ell^2(A)$ is described by

$$\begin{aligned} (U'\phi)(x; L) &= a_{x+1}\phi(x+1; L) + b_{x+1}\phi(x+1; R), \\ (U'\phi)(x; R) &= c_{x-1}\phi(x-1; L) + d_{x-1}\phi(x-1; R) \end{aligned} \tag{1}$$

for any $\psi \in \ell^2(A)$. We call a_x and d_x the transmitting amplitudes, and b_x and c_x the reflection amplitudes at x, respectively. If we put $a_x = d_x = 1$ and $b_x = c_x = \sqrt{-1} = i$, then the primitive form of QW in [17] is reproduced. Remark that U and U' are unitarily equivalent such that letting $\eta : \ell^2(\mathbb{Z};\mathbb{C}^2) \to \ell^2(A)$ be

$$(\eta\psi)(x;R) = \langle R|\psi\rangle, \quad (\eta\psi)(x;L) = \langle L|\psi\rangle,$$

then we have $U = \eta^{-1}U'\eta$. The free quantum walk is the quantum walk where all local quantum coins are described by the identity matrix, i.e.,

$$(U_0\psi)(x) = \begin{bmatrix} 1 & 0 \\ 0 & 0 \end{bmatrix} \psi(x+1) + \begin{bmatrix} 0 & 0 \\ 0 & 1 \end{bmatrix} \psi(x-1).$$

Then, the walker runs through one-dimensional lattices without any reflections in the free case.

In this paper, we set "impurities" on

$$\Gamma_M := \{0, 1, \dots, M-1\}$$

in the free quantum walk on one-dimensional lattice; that is,

$$C_x = \begin{cases} \begin{bmatrix} a & b \\ c & d \end{bmatrix} & : x \in \Gamma_M, \\ I_2 & : x \notin \Gamma_M. \end{cases} \quad (2)$$

We consider the initial state Ψ_0 as follows.

$$\Psi_0(x) = \begin{cases} e^{i\xi x}|R\rangle & : x \leq 0; \\ 0 & : \text{otherwise}, \end{cases}$$

where $\xi \in \mathbb{R}/2\pi\mathbb{Z}$. Note that this initial state belongs to no longer ℓ^2 category. The region Γ_M is obtained a time dependent inflow $e^{-i\xi n}$ from the negative outside. On the other hand, if a quantum walker goes out side of Γ_M, it never come back again to Γ_M. We can regard such a quantum walker as an outflow from Γ_M. Roughly speaking, in the long time limit, the inflow and outflow are balanced and obtain the stationary state with some modification. Indeed, the following statement holds.

Proposition 1 ([14]).

1. *This quantum walk converges to a stationary state in the following meaning:*

$$\exists \lim_{n \to \infty} e^{i(n+1)\xi} \Psi_n(x) =: \Phi_\infty(x).$$

2. *This stationary state is a generalized eigenfunction satisfying*

$$U\Phi_\infty = e^{-i\xi}\Phi_\infty.$$

Relation to an absorption problem

Let the reflection amplitude at time n be $\tilde{\gamma}_n(z) := \langle L|\Phi_n(-1)\rangle$ with $z = e^{i\xi}$. We can see that $\tilde{\gamma}_n(z)$ is rewritten by using U' as follows:

$$z^{-1}\tilde{\gamma}_{n+1}(z) = \langle \delta_{(-1;L)}, U'\delta_{(0;R)}\rangle + \langle \delta_{(-1;L)}, U'^2\delta_{(0;R)}\rangle z$$
$$+ \langle \delta_{(-1;L)}, U'^3\delta_{(0;R)}\rangle z^2 + \dots + \langle \delta_{(-1;L)}, U'^{n+1}\delta_{(0;R)}\rangle z^n$$

The first term is the amplitude that the inflow at time n cannot penetrate into Γ_M; the m-th term is the amplitude that the inflow at time $n-(m-1)$ penetrates into Γ_M and escapes Γ_M from 0 side at time n. Therefore, each term corresponds to the "absorption" amplitude to -1 with the absorption walls -1 and M with the initial state $\delta_{(0;R)}$. Then

Remark 1. *The reflection amplitude $\langle L|\Phi_\infty(-1)\rangle = \lim_{n\to\infty} \tilde{\gamma}_n(z)$ coincides with the generating function of the absorption amplitude to -1 with respect to time n while the transmitting amplitude $\langle R|\Phi_\infty(M)\rangle = \lim_{n\to\infty} \tilde{\tau}_n(z)$ coincides with the generating function of the absorption amplitude to M with respect to time n.*

Put $\gamma_n := |\langle \delta_{(-1;L)}, U'^n \delta_{(0;R)}\rangle|^2$ and $\tau_n := |\langle \delta_{(M;R)}, U'^n \delta_{(0;R)}\rangle|^2$ which are the absorption/first hitting probabilities at positions -1 and M, respectively, starting from $(0:R)$. From the above observation, for example, we can express the m-th moments of the absorption/hitting times to -1 and M as follows:

$$\sum_{n\geq 1} n^m \gamma_n = \int_0^{2\pi} \overline{\langle L|\Phi_\infty(-1)\rangle} \left(-i\frac{\partial}{\partial \xi}\right)^m \langle L|\Phi_\infty(-1)\rangle \frac{d\xi}{2\pi}, \quad (3)$$

$$\sum_{n\geq 1} n^m \tau_n = \int_0^{2\pi} \overline{\langle R|\Phi_\infty(M)\rangle} \left(-i\frac{\partial}{\partial \xi}\right)^m \langle R|\Phi_\infty(M)\rangle \frac{d\xi}{2\pi}. \quad (4)$$

Relation to Scattering of quantum walk

The stationary state Φ_∞ is a generalized eigenfunction of U in $\ell^\infty(\mathbb{Z};\mathbb{C}^2)$. The scattering matrix naturally appears in Φ_∞ (see [5]). In the time independent scattering theory, the inflow can be considered as the incident "plane wave", and the impurity causes the scattered wave by transmissions and reflections. Thus, we can see the transmission coefficient and the reflection coefficient in $\Phi_\infty(x)$ for $x \in \mathbb{Z} \setminus \Gamma_M$. For studies of a general theory of scattering, we also mention the recent work by Tiedra de Aldecoa [12].

3. Computation of Stationary State
3.1. Preliminary

Recall that $|L\rangle$ and $|R\rangle$ represent the standard basis of $\mathbb{C}^2$; that is, $|L\rangle = [1,0]^\top$ and $|R\rangle = [0,1]^\top$. Let $\chi : \ell^2(\mathbb{Z};\mathbb{C}^2) \to \ell^2(\Gamma_M;\mathbb{C}^2)$ be a boundary operator such that $(\chi\psi)(a) = \psi(a)$ for any $a \in \{(x;R),(x;L) \mid x \in \Gamma_M\}$. Here, the adjoint $\chi^* : \ell^2(\Gamma_M;\mathbb{C}^2) \to \ell^2(\mathbb{Z};\mathbb{C}^2)$ is described by

$$(\chi^*\varphi)(a) = \begin{cases} \varphi(a) & : a \in \{(x;R),(x;L) \mid x \in \Gamma_M\}, \\ 0 & : \text{otherwise.} \end{cases}$$

We put the principal submatrix of U with respect to the impurities by $E_M := \chi U \chi^*$. The matrix form of E_M with the computational basis $\chi\delta_0|L\rangle, \chi\delta_0|R\rangle, \ldots, \chi\delta_{M-1}|L\rangle, \chi\delta_{M-1}|R\rangle$ is expressed by the following $2M \times 2M$ matrix:

$$E_M = \begin{bmatrix} 0 & P & & & \\ Q & 0 & P & & \\ & Q & 0 & \ddots & \\ & & \ddots & \ddots & P \\ & & & Q & 0 \end{bmatrix} \quad (5)$$

We express the $((x;J),(x';J'))$ element of E_M by

$$(E_M)_{(x;J),(x';J')} := \left\langle \chi\delta_x|J\rangle, E_M \chi\delta_{x'}|J'\rangle \right\rangle_{\mathbb{C}^{2M}}.$$

Putting $\psi_n := \chi \Psi_n$, we have

$$\psi_{n+1} = \chi U(\chi^*\chi + (1-\chi^*\chi))\Psi_n$$
$$= E_M \psi_n + \chi U(1-\chi^*\chi)\Psi_n$$
$$= E_M \psi_n + e^{-i(n+1)\xi}\chi\delta_0|R\rangle.$$

Then, putting $\phi_n := e^{i(n+1)\xi}\psi_n$, we have

$$e^{-i\xi}\phi_{n+1} = E_M\phi_n + \chi\delta_0|R\rangle. \tag{6}$$

From [14], $\varphi := \exists \lim_{n\to\infty} \phi_n$. Then, the stationary state restricted to Γ_M satisfies

$$(e^{-i\xi} - E_M)\phi_\infty = \chi\delta_0|R\rangle. \tag{7}$$

About the uniqueness of this solution is ensured by the following Lemma since it includes the existence of the inverse of $(e^{-i\xi} - E_M)$.

Lemma 1. *Let E_M be the above with $a \neq 0$.[†] Then $\sigma(E_M) \subset \{\lambda \in \mathbb{C} \mid |\lambda| < 1\}$.*

Proof. Let $\psi \in \ell^2(\Gamma_M, \mathbb{C}^2)$ be an eigenvector of eigenvalue $\lambda \in \sigma(E_M)$. Then

$$|\lambda|^2 ||\psi||^2 = ||E_M\psi||^2 = \langle U\chi^*\psi, \chi^*\chi U\chi^*\psi\rangle \leq \langle U\chi^*\psi, U\chi^*\psi\rangle = ||\chi^*\psi||^2 = ||\psi||^2. \tag{8}$$

Here, for the inequality, we used the fact that $\chi^*\chi$ is the projection operator onto

$$\mathrm{span}\{\delta_x|L\rangle, \delta_x|R\rangle \mid x \in \Gamma_M\} \subset \ell^2(\mathbb{Z}; \mathbb{C}^2)$$

while for the final equality, we used the fact that $\chi\chi^*$ is the identity operator on $\ell^2(\Gamma_M; \mathbb{C}^2)$. If the equality in (8) holds, then $\chi^*\chi U\chi^*\psi = U\chi^*\psi$ holds. Then, we have the eigenequation $U\chi^*\psi = \lambda\chi^*\psi$ by taking χ^* to both sides of the original eigenequation $\chi U\chi^*\psi = \lambda\psi$. However, there are no eigenvectors having finite supports in a position independent quantum walk on $\mathbb{Z}$ with $a \neq 0$ since its spectrum is described by only a continuous spectrum in general. Thus, $|\lambda|^2 < 1$. □

Now, let us solve this Equation (7). The matrix representation of E_M with the permutation of the labeling such that $(x; R) \leftrightarrow (x; L)$ for any $x \in \Gamma_M$ to (5) is

$$E_M \cong \begin{bmatrix} 0 & 0 & 0 & 0 & & & & & \\ 0 & 0 & b & a & & & & & \\ d & c & 0 & 0 & 0 & 0 & & & \\ 0 & 0 & 0 & 0 & b & a & & & \\ & & d & c & \ddots & & \ddots & & \\ & & 0 & 0 & & & & & \\ & & & & \ddots & & \ddots & 0 & 0 \\ & & & & & & & b & a \\ & & & & & & d & c & 0 & 0 \\ & & & & & & 0 & 0 & 0 & 0 \end{bmatrix}$$

Then, the Equation (7) is expressed by

$$\begin{bmatrix} z & 0 & 0 & 0 & & & & & \\ 0 & z & -b & -a & & & & & \\ -d & -c & z & 0 & & & & & \\ & & 0 & z & -b & -a & & & \\ & & -d & -c & z & 0 & & & \\ & & & & \ddots & & \ddots & & \\ & & & & & & 0 & z & -b & -a \\ & & & & & & -d & -c & z & 0 \\ & & & & & & & & 0 & z \end{bmatrix} \begin{bmatrix} \varphi(0;R) \\ \varphi(0;L) \\ \varphi(1;R) \\ \varphi(1;L) \\ \vdots \\ \varphi(M-2;R) \\ \varphi(M-2;L) \\ \varphi(M-1;R) \\ \varphi(M-1;L) \end{bmatrix} = \begin{bmatrix} 1 \\ 0 \\ 0 \\ 0 \\ \vdots \\ 0 \\ 0 \\ 0 \\ 0 \end{bmatrix}.$$

Here, we changed the way of blockwise of E_M and we put $z = e^{-i\xi}$. Putting

$$A_z := \begin{bmatrix} 0 & z \\ -d & -c \end{bmatrix}, \quad B_z := \begin{bmatrix} -b & -a \\ z & 0 \end{bmatrix},$$

we have

$$[z \; 0] \vec{\varphi}(0) = 1, \; A_z \vec{\varphi}(0) + B_z \vec{\varphi}(1) = 0, \; A_z \vec{\varphi}(1) + B_z \vec{\varphi}(2) = 0, \ldots$$
$$\ldots, A_z \vec{\varphi}(M-2) + B_z \vec{\varphi}(M-1) = 0, \; [0 \; z] \vec{\varphi}(M-1) = 0, \tag{9}$$

where $\vec{\varphi}(x) = [\varphi(x;R), \varphi(x;L)]^\top$ for any $x \in \Gamma_M$. The inverse matrix of B_z exists since $z \neq 0$. Then, we have

$$\vec{\varphi}(1) = T\vec{\varphi}(0), \; \vec{\varphi}(2) = T^2 \vec{\varphi}(0), \ldots, \vec{\varphi}(M-1) = T^{M-1} \vec{\varphi}(0), \tag{10}$$

where

$$T = -B_z^{-1} A_z = \frac{1}{az} \begin{bmatrix} \Delta|a|^2 & -\Delta a \bar{b} \\ -\Delta \bar{a} b & z^2 + \Delta|b|^2 \end{bmatrix}.$$

Here $\Delta = \det(P + Q) = \det \begin{bmatrix} a & b \\ c & d \end{bmatrix}$. For the boundaries, there exists κ such that

$$\vec{\varphi}(0) = [z^{-1} \; \kappa], \; [0 \; z] \vec{\varphi}(M-1) = 0. \tag{11}$$

By (10) and (11), κ satisfies

$$\left\langle \begin{bmatrix} 0 \\ 1 \end{bmatrix}, T^{M-1} \begin{bmatrix} z^{-1} \\ \kappa \end{bmatrix} \right\rangle = 0 \tag{12}$$

which is equivalent to

$$\kappa = -\frac{z^{-1}(T^{M-1})_{2,1}}{(T^{M-1})_{2,2}}.$$

Now, the problem is reduced to considering the n-th power of T because the eigenvector is expressed by $\vec{\varphi}(n) = T^n \vec{\varphi}(0)$. Since T is a just 2×2 matrix, we can prepare the following lemma.

Lemma 2. *Let A be a 2-dimensional matrix denoted by*

$$A = \begin{bmatrix} \alpha & \beta \\ \gamma & \delta \end{bmatrix}.$$

1. $(\alpha - \delta)^2 + 4\beta\gamma = 0$ and $A \neq \epsilon I$ for some ϵ case. Let $\lambda = (\alpha + \delta)/2$. Then

$$A^n = \begin{bmatrix} \lambda^n + \frac{\alpha-\delta}{2}n\lambda^{n-1} & \beta n\lambda^{n-1} \\ \gamma n\lambda^{n-1} & \lambda^n - \frac{\alpha-\delta}{2}n\lambda^{n-1} \end{bmatrix}$$

2. Otherwise. Let $\zeta_n := (\det(A)^{1/2})^{n-1}U_{n-1}(\frac{\text{tr}(A)}{2\det(A)^{1/2}})$ for $n \geq 1$. Then

$$A^n = \begin{bmatrix} \zeta_{n+1} - \delta\zeta_n & \beta\zeta_n \\ \gamma\zeta_n & \zeta_{n+1} - \alpha\zeta_n \end{bmatrix},$$

where $U_n(\cdot)$ is the n-th Chebyshev polynomial of the second kind.

Remark 2. *The condition "$(\alpha - \delta)^2 + 4\beta\gamma = 0$ and $A \neq \epsilon I$" is equivalent to the non-diagonalizability of A.*

Remark 3. *For $A = T$ case, the condition of 1. is reduced to*

$$\omega := \Delta^{-1/2}z \in \{\epsilon_1|a| + \epsilon_2 i|b| \mid \epsilon_1, \epsilon_2 \in \{\pm 1\}\} =: \partial B.$$

Remark 4. *For $A = T$ case, the variable of the Chebyshev polynomial in 2. is reduced to*

$$\text{tr}(T)/(2\det(T)^{1/2}) = (\omega + \omega^{-1})/(2|a|).$$

Moreover, if $\omega = e^{ik}$, the Chebyshev polynomial is described by $U_{-1}(\cdot) = 0$,

$$U_n(\cos k/|a|) = \frac{\lambda_+^{n+1} - \lambda_-^{n+1}}{\lambda_+ - \lambda_-} \quad (n \geq 0).$$

Here, $\lambda_\pm$ in RHS are the roots of the quadratic equation

$$\lambda^2 - \frac{2\cos k}{|a|}\lambda + 1 = 0$$

with $|\lambda_-| \leq |\lambda_+|$.

3.2. Transmitting and Reflecting Rates

Let us divide the unit circle in the complex plain as follows:

$$B_{in} = \{e^{ik} \mid |\cos k| < |a|\}, \; \partial B = \{e^{ik} \mid |\cos k| = |a|\}, \; B_{out} = \{e^{ik} \mid |\cos k| > |a|\}. \tag{13}$$

By the unitarity of $\begin{bmatrix} a & b \\ c & d \end{bmatrix}$ and using the Chebyshev recursion; $U_{n+1}(x) = 2xU_n(x) - U_{n-1}(x)$, we insert (1) and (2) in Lemma 2 into (10), and we have an explicit expression for the stationary state as follows.

Theorem 1. *Let the stationary state restricted to $\Gamma_M = \{0, 1, \ldots, M-1\}$ be ϕ_∞ and $\vec{\varphi}(n) := [\phi_\infty(n; R) \; \phi_\infty(n; L)]^\top$. Then we have*

$$\vec{\varphi}(n) = \begin{cases} \frac{z^{-1}(a\Delta^{-1/2})^{-n}}{\omega\zeta'_M - |a|\zeta'_{M-1}} \begin{bmatrix} \omega\zeta'_{M-n} - |a|\zeta'_{M-n-1} \\ ab\zeta'_{M-n-1} \end{bmatrix} & : \omega \notin \partial B \\ \frac{\Delta^{-1/2}\lambda^n}{\epsilon_R|a| + i\epsilon_I M|b|} \begin{bmatrix} \epsilon_R\alpha(\epsilon_R|a| + i\epsilon_I|b|(M-n)) \\ b(M-n-1) \end{bmatrix} & : \omega \in \partial B \end{cases} \tag{14}$$

for $n = 0, 1, \ldots, M-1$, where $\alpha = a/|a|$ and $\zeta'_m = U_{m-1}(\frac{\omega + \omega^{-1}}{2|a|})$ $(m \geq 0)$, $\lambda = \text{sgn}(\epsilon_R)\alpha^{-1}\Delta^{1/2}$. Here $\epsilon_R = \text{sgn}(Re(\omega))$ and $\epsilon_I = \text{sgn}(Im(\omega))$.

Since the transmitting and reflecting rates are computed by

$$T(\omega) = \left|\left\langle \begin{bmatrix} 1 \\ 0 \end{bmatrix}, \vec{\varphi}(M-1) \right\rangle \times d\right|^2,$$

$$R(\omega) = \left|\left\langle \begin{bmatrix} 0 \\ 1 \end{bmatrix}, \vec{\varphi}(0) \right\rangle \times a + \left\langle \begin{bmatrix} 1 \\ 0 \end{bmatrix}, \vec{\varphi}(0) \right\rangle \times b\right|^2,$$

we obtain explicit expressions for them as follows.

Corollary 1. *Assume $abcd \neq 0$. For any $\omega \in \mathbb{R}/(2\pi\mathbb{Z})$, we have*

$$T(\omega) = \frac{|a|^2}{|a|^2 + |b|^2 \zeta'^2_M} \tag{15}$$

$$R(\omega) = \frac{|b|^2 \zeta'^2_M}{|a|^2 + |b|^2 \zeta'^2_M} \tag{16}$$

Note that the unitarity of the time evolution can be confirmed by $T + R = 1$. By Corollary 1, we can find a necessary and sufficient conditions for the perfect transmitting; that is, $T = 1$.

Corollary 2. *Assume $abcd \neq 0$. Let $\omega = e^{ik}$ with some real value k. Then the perfect transmitting happens if and only if*

$$\arccos\left(\frac{\cos k}{|a|}\right) \in \left\{ \frac{\ell}{M}\pi \mid \ell \in \{0, \pm 1, \ldots, \pm(M-1)\} \right\}.$$

On the other hand, the perfect reflection never occurs.

Remark that if $\omega \notin B_{in}$, then the perfect transmitting never happens.

3.3. Energy in the Perturbed Region

Taking the square modulus to $\vec{\varphi}(n)$ in Theorem 1, the relative probability at position $n \in \Gamma_M = \{0, \ldots, M-1\}$ can be computed as follows.

Proposition 2. *Assume $abcd \neq 0$. Then, the relative probability is described by*

$$\|\vec{\varphi}(n)\|^2 = \begin{cases} \frac{1}{|a|^2 + |b|^2 \zeta'^2_M}\left(|a|^2 + |b|^2 \zeta'^2_{M-n-1} + |b|^2 \zeta'^2_{M-n}\right) & : \omega \notin \partial B \\ \frac{1}{|a|^2 + M^2|b|^2}\left\{|a|^2 + |b|^2(M-n)^2 + |b|^2(M-n-1)^2\right\} & : \omega \in \partial B \end{cases} \tag{17}$$

Proof. Let us consider the case for $\omega \notin \partial B$. Using the property of the Chebyshev polynomial, we have $\zeta'_{m+1}\zeta'_{m-1} = \zeta'^2_m - 1$ and $(\omega + \omega^{-1})/|a| \cdot \zeta'_m = \zeta'_{m+1} + \zeta'_{m-1}$. It holds that

$$(\omega + \omega^{-1})\zeta'_m\zeta'_{m-1} = |a|(\zeta'_{m+1} + \zeta'_{m-1})\zeta'_{m-1}$$
$$= |a|(\zeta'^2_m + \zeta'^2_{m-1} - 1).$$

Since $\zeta'_m \in \mathbb{R}$, we have

$$q(m) := |\omega \zeta'_m - |a|\zeta'_{m-1}|^2 = \zeta'^2_m + |a|^2 \zeta'^2_{m-1} - |a|^2(\omega + \omega^{-1})\zeta'_m \zeta'_{m-1}$$
$$= |b|^2 \zeta'^2_m + |a|^2,$$

Then, we have

$$||\vec{\varphi}(n)||^2 = \frac{1}{q(M)}(q(M-n) + |b|^2 \zeta'^2_{M-n-1})$$
$$= \frac{|b|^2 \zeta'^2_{M-n} + |a|^2 + |b|^2 \zeta'^2_{M-n-1}}{|b|^2 \zeta'^2_M + |a|^2}.$$

□

Then, we can see how much quantum walkers accumulate in the perturbed region $\Gamma_M = \{0, \ldots, M-1\}$ by

$$\mathcal{E}_M(\omega) =: \sum_{n=0}^{M-1} ||\vec{\varphi}(n)||^2.$$

We call it the energy of quantum walk. The dependency of the energy on ω is symmetric on the unit circle in the complex plain.

Corollary 3. *Let $\mathcal{E}_M(\omega)$ be the above and assume $abcd \neq 0$. Then we have*

$$\mathcal{E}_M(\omega) = \frac{1}{|a|^2 + |b|^2 \zeta'^2_M} \left\{ M|a|^2 + \frac{|b|^2}{(\lambda_+ - \lambda_-)^2} \left(\zeta'^2_{M+1} - \zeta'^2_{M-1} - 4M \right) \right\} \quad (18)$$

In particular, $\mathcal{E}_M(\cdot)$ is continuous at every $\omega_* \in \partial B$ and

$$\mathcal{E}_M(\omega_*) = \frac{1}{3} \frac{M}{|a|^2 + |b|^2 M^2} \left(3|a|^2 + |b|^2 + 2|b|^2 M^2 \right).$$

Proof. Using the properties of the Chebyshev polynomial for example, $U_n^2 - U_{n+1} U_{n-1} = 1$, $T_n = (U_n - U_{n-2})/2$, we have

$$(\lambda_+^{m-1} + \lambda_-^{m-1})\zeta'_M = 2T_{m-1} U_{m-1} = \zeta'^2_m - \zeta'^2_{m-1} + 1.$$

Then, we have

$$\sum_{n=0}^{m-1} \zeta'^2_n = \sum_{n=0}^{m-1} \left(\frac{\lambda_+^m - \lambda_-^m}{\lambda_+ - \lambda_-} \right)^2$$
$$= \frac{1}{(\lambda_+ - \lambda_-)^2} \left\{ (\lambda_+^{m-1} + \lambda_-^{m-1})\zeta'_m - 2m \right\}$$
$$= \frac{1}{(\lambda_+ - \lambda_-)^2} (\zeta'^2_m - \zeta'^2_{m-1} - 2m + 1) \quad (19)$$

Then, we have

$$\sum_{n=0}^{M-1} ||\vec{\varphi}(n)||^2 = \frac{1}{|a|^2 + |b|^2 \zeta'^2_M} \left(M|a|^2 + |b|^2 \sum_{n=0}^{M-1} \zeta'^2_{M-n-1} + \zeta'^2_{M-n} \right)$$
$$= \frac{1}{|a|^2 + |b|^2 \zeta'^2_M} \left\{ M|a|^2 + \frac{|b|^2}{(\lambda_+ - \lambda_-)^2} \left(\zeta'^2_{M+1} - \zeta'^2_{M-1} - 4M \right) \right\}$$

Here, we used (19) in the last equality.

If $\omega \in \partial B$, then by directly computation taking summation of (17) over $n \in \Gamma_M = \{0, 1, \ldots, M-1\}$, we obtain the conclusion. Let us see $\mathcal{E}_M(\cdot)$ is continuous at ∂B. We put $x := (1/|a|)\cos k$ and $\zeta'_m(x) := \zeta'_m$. Remark that $\omega \to \omega_*$ implies $|x| \to 1$. In the following, we consider $x \to 1$ case. The Taylor expansion of $\zeta'_m(x)$ around $x = 1$ is

$$\zeta'_m(1-\epsilon) = m - \frac{m}{3}(m^2-1)\epsilon + O(\epsilon^2).$$

The reason for obtaining the expansion until ϵ^1 order is

$$\zeta'^2_{M+1} - \zeta'^2_{M-1} - 4M = O(\epsilon^2).$$

around $x = 1$. Note that $(\lambda_+ - \lambda_-)^2 = 4(x^2 - 1)$. Then

$$(\lambda_+ - \lambda_-)^2 = -8\epsilon + O(\epsilon)$$

around $x = 1$. Then inserting all of them into (18), we obtain

$$\lim_{\omega \to \omega_*} \mathcal{E}_M(\omega) = \frac{M}{|a|^2 + |b|^2 M^2}\left(|a|^2 + \frac{|b|^2}{3} + \frac{2|b|^2}{3}M^2\right).$$

□

4. Asymptotics of Energy

If $\omega \in \partial B$, then by Corollary 3, it is immediately obtained that

$$\lim_{M \to \infty} \frac{\mathcal{E}_M(\omega)}{M} = \frac{2}{3}. \tag{20}$$

Let us consider the case of $\omega \in B_{in} \cup B_{out}$ as follows. Note that

$$\lambda_\pm = \begin{cases} \text{sgn}(\cos k) e^{\pm \theta} & : \omega \in B_{out}, \\ e^{\pm i\theta} & : \omega \in B_{in}, \end{cases}$$

where $(1/|a|)\cos k = \cosh\theta$ ($\omega \in B_{out}$), while $(1/|a|)\cos k = \cos\theta$ ($\omega \in B_{in}$) such that $\sin\theta > 0$ and $\sinh\theta > 0$. To observe the asymptotics of $\mathcal{E}_M(\omega)$ for $\omega \notin \partial B$, we rewrite $\mathcal{E}_M(\omega)$ as follows:

$$\mathcal{E}_M(\omega) = \begin{cases} \frac{1}{|a|^2 \sinh^2\theta + |b|^2 \sinh^2 M\theta}\left\{(-|b|^2 + |a|^2 \sinh^2\theta)M + \frac{|b|^2}{4}\frac{\sinh 2M\theta \sinh 2\theta}{\sinh^2\theta}\right\} & : \omega \in B_{out} \\ \frac{1}{|a|^2 \sin^2\theta + |b|^2 \sin^2 M\theta}\left\{(|b|^2 + |a|^2 \sin^2\theta)M - \frac{|b|^2}{4}\frac{\sin 2M\theta \sin 2\theta}{\sin^2\theta}\right\} & : \omega \in B_{in} \end{cases} \tag{21}$$

From now on, let us consider the asymptotics of $\mathcal{E}_M(\omega)$ for large M. We summarize our results on the asymptotics of $\mathcal{E}_M(\omega)$ in Table 1. In the following, we regard $\mathcal{E}_M(\omega)$ as a function of θ, M; that is $\mathcal{E}(M, \theta)$ because θ can be expressed by ω and consider the asymptotics for large M.

4.1. $\omega \in B_{out}$

Let us see that

$$\lim_{M \to \infty} \mathcal{E}_M(\omega) = \frac{\cosh\theta}{\sinh\theta} = \frac{\left|\frac{\cos k}{a}\right|}{\sqrt{\left|\frac{\cos k}{a}\right|^2 - 1}}. \tag{22}$$

Note that $\sinh M\theta \sim e^{M\theta}/2 \gg M$. Then by (21), we have

$$\mathcal{E}_M(\omega) \sim \frac{1}{|b|^2 e^{2M\theta}} \times \frac{|b|^2}{4} \frac{e^{2M\theta} \sinh 2\theta}{\sinh^2 \theta} = \frac{\cosh \theta}{\sinh \theta}.$$

By (22), if $\omega \to \omega_* \in \partial B$, then $\mathcal{E}_M(\omega) \sim 1/\theta \to \infty$. To connect it to the limit for the case of $\omega_* \in \partial B$ described by (20) continuously, we consider $M \to \infty$ and $\theta \to 0$ simultaneously, so that $M\theta \sim \theta_* \in (0, \infty)$. Let us see that

$$\mathcal{E}_M(\omega) \sim \frac{1}{\sinh^2 \theta_*}\left(-1 + \frac{\sinh 2\theta_*}{2\theta_*}\right) M \qquad (23)$$

Noting that $\sinh m\theta = \sinh m\theta_* \neq 0$, for $m = 1, 2$ and $\sinh \theta \sim \theta_*/M$, we have

$$\mathcal{E}_M(\omega) \sim \frac{1}{|b^2| \sinh^2 \theta_*}\left\{-|b|^2 M + \frac{|b|^2}{4}\frac{\sinh 2\theta_* \times (2\theta_*/M)}{(\theta_*/M)^2}\right\}$$

$$= \frac{1}{\sinh^2 \theta_*}\left(-1 + \frac{\sinh 2\theta_*}{2\theta_*}\right) M$$

Therefore, if we design the parameter θ_* so that

$$\frac{2}{3} = \frac{1}{\sinh^2 \theta_*}\left(-1 + \frac{\sinh 2\theta_*}{2\theta_*}\right), \qquad (24)$$

then the energy of B_{out} continuously closes to that of ∂B in the sufficient large system size M.

4.2. $\omega \in B_{in}$

In this paper, since we determine θ satisfying $\sin \theta > 0$, we set $\theta \in (0, \pi)$. Remark that $\mathcal{E}_M(\omega^{-1}) = \mathcal{E}_M(\omega)$ for any $\omega \in B_{in}$ because $e^{i\theta}$ is invariant under this deformation.

By (21), if $\sin \theta \asymp \sin M\theta \asymp 1$, we have

$$\mathcal{E}_M(\omega) \sim \left(\frac{|a|^2 \sin^2 \theta + |b|^2}{|a|^2 \sin^2 \theta + |b|^2 \sin^2 M\theta}\right) M, \qquad (25)$$

for sufficiently large M, which implies that

$$M \lesssim \mathcal{E}_M(\omega) \lesssim \left(1 + \frac{|b|^2}{|a|^2 \sin^2 \theta}\right) M \qquad (26)$$

if $\theta \notin \{0, \pi\}$ is fixed. Then, we conclude that $\mathcal{E}_M(\omega) = O(M)$ if $\theta \notin \mathbb{Z}\pi$ is fixed for $\omega \in B_{in}$. On the other hand, if we design θ so that the condition of the perfect transmitting is satisfied; $\theta = \pi\ell/M$, $|\ell| \in \{1, \ldots, M-1\}$ (see Corollary 1) and choose ℓ which is very close to 0 or M, then $|\sin \theta| \ll 1$. Note that if $|\sin \theta| \to 0$, which means $\omega \to \omega_* \in \partial B$, then the coefficient of the upper bound in (26) diverges.

Then, from now on, let us consider the following three cases having a magnitude relation between θ and M;

(i) $1 \ll M \ll 1/\sin \theta$; (ii) $M \asymp 1/\sin \theta$; (iii) $1/\sin \theta \ll M$.

1. Case (i): $1 \ll M \ll 1/\sin \theta$

   Let us start to evaluate RHS of (21). Since

$$\frac{\sin 2M\theta \sin 2\theta}{4 \sin^2 \theta} \sim M\left\{1 - \frac{1}{3}(1 + 2M^2)\theta\right\},$$

the "{ }" part in RHS of (21) can be evaluated by $2|b|^2 M^3 \theta^2/3$. The denominator of (21) is evaluated by $1/(|b|^2 M^2 \theta^2)$. Combining them, we have

$$\mathcal{E}_M(\omega) \sim \frac{2M}{3} \tag{27}$$

This is consistent with (20).

2. Case (ii): $M \asymp 1/|\sin \theta|$
    Under this condition, the parameter θ lives around 0 or π if M is large. Since we consider $\theta \in (0, \pi)$, we can evaluate $\sin \theta$ by $\sin \theta \sim \theta$, or $\sin \theta \sim (\pi - \theta)$ for large M. We define $\theta' = \theta$ if $0 < \theta < \pi/2$ and $\theta' = \pi - \theta$ if $\pi/2 \le \theta < \pi$. Because $M \sin \theta \asymp 1$ by the assumption, we have $M\theta' \asymp 1$. Therefore, we put $M\theta' = \theta_* + \epsilon$ with $\theta_* \asymp 1$ and $|\epsilon| \ll 1$. Then up to the value θ_*, let us see

$$\mathcal{E}_M(\omega) \sim \begin{cases} \frac{1}{\sin^2 \theta_*}\left(1 - \frac{\sin 2\theta_*}{2\theta_*}\right)M & : \theta_* \notin \mathbb{Z}\pi, \\ \frac{|b|^2}{|a|^2 \theta_*^2} M^3 & : \theta_* \in \mathbb{Z}\pi \text{ and } \epsilon M \ll 1 \\ \frac{M}{\epsilon^2} & : \theta_* \in \mathbb{Z}\pi \text{ and } \epsilon M \gg 1 \end{cases} \tag{28}$$

Note that if $\theta_* \notin \mathbb{Z}\pi$, then $\sin \theta = \sin \theta' \sim \theta_*/M$ and $\sin^2 M\theta = \sin^2 M\theta' \sim \sin^2 \theta_* \ne 0$, $\sin 2M\theta = \sin 2M\theta' \sim \sin 2\theta_*$ and so on. Inserting them into (21), we have

$$\mathcal{E}_M(\omega) \sim \frac{1}{|a|^2 \theta_*^2/M^2 + |b|^2 \sin^2 \theta_*}\left\{(|a|^2\theta_*^2/M^2 + |b|^2)M - \frac{|b|^2}{4}\frac{\sin 2\theta_* \cdot 2\theta_*/M}{\theta_*^2/M^2}\right\}$$
$$\sim \frac{1}{\sin^2 \theta_*}\left(1 - \frac{\sin 2\theta_*}{2\theta_*}\right)M$$

On the other hand, if $\theta_* \in \mathbb{Z}\pi$, since $\sin \theta \sim \theta_*/M$ and $\sin M\theta_* \sim \epsilon$, by (21), we have

$$\mathcal{E}_M(\omega) \sim \frac{1}{|a|^2 \theta^2 + |b|^2 \epsilon^2}\left\{|b|^2 M - \frac{|b|^2}{4}\frac{2\epsilon \cdot 2\theta_*/M}{(\theta_*/M)^2}\right\}$$
$$\sim \frac{|b|^2 M}{|a|^2 \theta'^2 + |b|^2 \epsilon^2}$$
$$\sim \begin{cases} \frac{|b|^2}{|a|^2 \theta_*^2} M^3 & : \epsilon \ll \theta_*/M \\ M/\epsilon^2 & : \epsilon \gg \theta_*/M \end{cases}$$

3. Case (iii): $1/|\sin \theta| \ll M$
    The "{ }" part in (21) is estimated by $(|b|^2 + |a|^2 \sin^2 \theta)M$ because $M\theta \gg 1$. Then, we have

$$\mathcal{E}_M(\omega) \sim \left(\frac{|a|^2 \sin^2 \theta + |b|^2}{|a|^2 \sin^2 \theta + |b^2|\sin^2 M\theta}\right)M, \tag{29}$$

for sufficiently large M which is the same as (25). Let us consider the following case study:

(a) $\max\{|\sin \theta|, |\sin M\theta|\} \asymp 1$; (b) $|\sin \theta|, |\sin M\theta| \ll 1$.

(a) Let us see $\mathcal{E}_M(\omega) = O(M)$ in this case. If $\sin \theta \asymp \sin \theta M \asymp 1$, then the coefficient of M in (29) is a finite value, then we have (26). On the other hand, if each of $\sin \theta$ or $\sin M\theta \ll 1$, then (29) implies

$$\mathcal{E}_M(\omega) \sim \begin{cases} \frac{1}{\sin^2 M\theta} M & : \sin \theta \ll \sin M\theta \asymp 1 \\ (1 + \frac{|b|^2}{|a|^2 \sin^2 \theta})M & : \sin M\theta \ll \sin \theta \asymp 1 \end{cases} \tag{30}$$

(b) Since $|\sin M\theta| \ll 1$, we evaluate $|\sin M\theta|$ by

$$|\sin M\theta| \sim \min\{|M\theta|, |\pi - M\theta|, \ldots, |M\pi - M\theta|\} =: \delta.$$

Then, there exists a natural number m such that $|\theta - m\pi/M| = \delta/M$. Note that $|\sin \theta|$ is also sufficiently small. Then, the natural number m must be $m/M \ll 1$ if $0 < \theta < \pi/2$ and $(M-m)/M \ll 1$ if $\pi/2 \leq \theta < \pi$. Putting $m' := \min\{m, M-m\}$, we have

$$|\sin \theta| \sim \left|\frac{m'}{M}\pi \pm \frac{\delta}{M}\right| \sim \frac{\delta}{M}.$$

Therefore, $|\sin \theta| \ll |\sin M\theta| \ll 1$ holds. Then, (29) implies

$$\mathcal{E}_M(\omega) \sim \frac{M}{\delta^2}.$$

We summarize the above statements in the following theorem by setting $\theta = O(1/M)$, $\epsilon = 1/M^\alpha$ as a special but natural design of the parameters.

Theorem 2. *Let us set $\omega \in B_{in}$ so that*

$$\theta = \theta(M) = \left(x\pi + \frac{1}{M^\alpha}\right)\frac{1}{M}$$

with the parameters $x \in (0, M) \subset \mathbb{R}$ and $\alpha \geq 0$. If $x \to 0$ or $x \to M$ with fixed M, then $\mathcal{E}_M(\omega) = O(M)$. On the other hand, if we take $M \to \infty$ and fix $x' = \min\{x, M-x\} \asymp 1$, then we have

$$\mathcal{E}_M(\omega) = \begin{cases} O(M^3) & : x' \text{ is natural number and } \alpha \geq 1, \\ O(M^{1+2\alpha}) & : x' \text{ is natural number and } 0 \leq \alpha < 1, \\ O(M) & : \text{otherwise.} \end{cases}$$

Table 1. Asymptotics of the energy of $\mathcal{E}_M(\omega)$: $\cos\theta = (\omega + \omega^{-1})/(2|a|)$, $M\theta = \theta_* + \epsilon$.

	$1 \ll M \ll 1/\theta$	$1 \ll M \asymp 1/\theta$	$1/\theta \ll M$
$\omega \in \partial B$	-	-	$O(M)$
$\omega \in B_{out}$	$O(M)$		$\begin{cases} O(\theta^{-1}) & : 1/\theta \gg 1 \\ O(1) & : 1/\theta \asymp 1 \end{cases}$
$\omega \in B_{in}$	$O(M)$		$\begin{cases} O(M^3/\theta_*^2) & : \theta_* \in \mathbb{Z}\pi, \epsilon M \ll 1 \\ O(M\epsilon^{-2}) & : \theta_* \in \mathbb{Z}\pi, \epsilon M \gg 1 \\ O(M) & : \theta_* \notin \mathbb{Z}\pi \end{cases}$

5. Conclusions

We considered the quantum walk on the line with the perturbed region $\{0, 1, \ldots, M\}$; that is, an non-trivial quantum coin is assigned at the perturbed region and the free quantum coin is assigned at the other region. We set an ℓ^∞ initial state so that free quantum walkers are inputted at each time step to the perturbed region. A closed form of the stationary state of this dynamical system was obtained and we computed the energy of the quantum walk in the perturbed region. This energy represents how quantum walker feels "comfortable" in the perturbed region. We showed that the "feeling" of quantum walk depends on the frequency of the initial state. We can divide the region of the frequency into three parts to classify the asymptotics of the energy for large M; B_{in}, B_{out}, δB. The region B_{in} coincides with the continuous spectrum of the quantum walk with $M \to \infty$ [5]. We showed that quantum walkers prefer to the initial state whose frequency corresponds to the continuous spectrum in the infinite system. More precisely, the energy of the quantum walk in the perturbed region is estimated by $O(1)$ if $\theta \in B_{out}$, while one is estimated by $O(M)$ if

$\theta \in \delta B$ and *almost all* pseudo momentum θ gives $O(M)$-energy, but some momentum gives $O(M^3)$ if $\theta \in B_{in}$ (Theorem 2). Such an initial state exactly exists but it is quite rare from the view point of the Lebesgue measure. The most comfortable initial state for quantum walkers has the frequency whose pseudo momentum θ lives in some neighborhood of the boundary ∂B and accomplishes the perfect transmitting. If the momentum of the initial state exceeds the boundary ∂B from the internal region B_{in}, then the energy is immediately reduced to $O(1)$. It suggests that the control of the frequency of the initial state to give the maximal energy in the perturbed region is quite sensitive from the view point of an implementation.

The spectrum of the boundary ∂B for $M \to \infty$ produces the two singular points of the density function of the Konno limit distribution and is characterized by the Airy functions. In [16], details of the spectrum behavior around ∂B is discussed. Indeed, a kind of "speciality" also appears as the non-diagonalizability of T when $\theta \in \partial B$ in our work (Lemma 2). Note that the infinite system does not have any *edges*, which means every node is "impurity", while our quantum walker feels the *edges* of the impurities; nodes 0 and M. Therefore, to see the effect of such a finiteness on the behavior of the quantum walker comparing with the infinite system, computing how a quantum walker is distributed in the perturbed region is interesting which may be possible from the explicit expression of the stationary state in Theorem 1. Moreover, to consider the escaping time from the perturbed region seems to be useful to estimate the finesse as the interferometer motivated by quantum walk and it would be possible to extract some information from (3) and (4). This remains one of the interesting problems for the future.

Author Contributions: Conceptualization, E.S.; Formal analysis, E.S., H.M., T.K., K.H. and N.K. All authors have read and agreed to the published version of the manuscript.

Funding: HM was supported by the grant-in-aid for young scientists No. 16K17630, JSPS. ES acknowledges financial supports from the Grant-in-Aid of Scientific Research (C) No. JP19K03616, Japan Society for the Promotion of Science and Research Origin for Dressed Photon.

Institutional Review Board Statement: Not applicable.

Informed Consent Statement: Not applicable.

Conflicts of Interest: The authors declare no conflict of interest.

References

1. Higuchi, Y.; Konno, N.; Sato, I.; Segawa, E. Quantum graph walk I: mapping to quantum walks. *Yokohama Math. J.* **2013**, *59*, 33–53.
2. Matsue, K.; Matsuoka, L.; Ogurisu, O.; Segawa, E. Resonant-tunneling in discrete-time quantum walk. *Quantum Stud. Math. Found.* **2018**, *6*, 35–44. [CrossRef]
3. Tanner, G. From quantum graphs to quantum random walks, Non-Linear Dynamics and Fundamental Interactions, NATO Science Series II: Mathematics. *Phys. Chem.* **2006**, *213*, 69–87.
4. Higuchi, K. Feynman-type representation of the scattering matrix on the line via a discrete-time quantum walk. *J. Phys. A-Math. Theor.* **2021**, *33*, 23.
5. Konno, N.; Komatsu, T.; Morioka, H.; Segawa, E. Generalized eigenfunctions for quantum walks via path counting approach. *Rev. Math. Phys.* **2021**, *33*, 2150019.
6. Konno, N.; Komatsu, T.; Morioka, H.; Segawa, E. Asymptotic properties of generalized eigenfunctions for multi-dimensional quantum walks. *arXiv*, **2021**, arXiv:2104.00836.
7. Morioka, H. Generalized eigenfunctions and scattering matrices for position-dependent quantum walks. *Rev. Math. Phys.* **2019**, *31*, 1950019. [CrossRef]
8. Morioka, H.; Segawa, E. Detection of edge defects by embedded eigenvalues of quantum walks. *Quantum Inf. Process.* **2019**, *18*, 283. [CrossRef]
9. Richard, S.; Suzuki, A.; de Aldecoa, R.T. Quantum walks with an anisotropic coin I: spectral theory. *Lett. Math. Phys.* **2018**, *108*, 331–357. [CrossRef]
10. Richard, S.; Suzuki, A.; de Aldecoa, R.T. Quantum walks with an anisotropic coin II: scattering theory. *Lett. Math. Phys. First Online* **2018**. [CrossRef]
11. Suzuki, A. Asymptotic velocity of a position-dependent quantum walk. *Quantum Inf. Process* **2016**, *15*, 103–119. [CrossRef]
12. de Aldecoa, R.T. Stationary scattering theory for unitary operators with an application to quantum walks. *J. Funct. Anal.* **2020**, *279*, 108704. [CrossRef]

13. Feldman, E.; Hillery, M. Quantum walks on graphs and quantum scattering theory, Coding Theory and Quantum Computing, edited by D. Evans, J. Holt, C. Jones, K. Klintworth, B. Parshall, O. Pfister, and H. Ward. *Contemp. Math.* **2005**, *381*, 71–96.
14. Higuchi, Y.; Segawa, E. Dynamical system induced by quantum walks. *J. Physiscs A Math. Theor.* **2009**, *52*, 395202. [CrossRef]
15. Mohamed, S.; Higuchi, Y.; Segawa, E. Electric circuit induced by quantum walks. *J. Stat. Phys.* **2020**, *181*, 603–617.
16. Kuklinski, P. Conditional probability distributions of finite absorbing quantum walks. *Phys. Rev. A* **2020**, *101*, 032309. [CrossRef]
17. Feynman, R.P.; Hibbs, A.R. *Quantum Mechanics and Path Integrals*; emended edition; Dover Publications, Inc.: Mineola, NY, USA, 2010.

Article

Maze Solving by a Quantum Walk with Sinks and Self-Loops: Numerical Analysis

Leo Matsuoka [1,*], Kenta Yuki [2], Hynek Lavička [3] and Etsuo Segawa [4]

[1] Faculty of Engineering, Hiroshima Institute of Technology, Hiroshima 731-5193, Japan
[2] Independent Researcher, Tokyo 160-0023, Japan; k-yuki@middenii.com
[3] Blocksize Capital GmbH, 60329 Frankfurt am Main, Germany; hl@blocksize-capital.com
[4] Graduate School of Environment Information Sciences, Yokohama National University, Yokohama 240-8501, Japan; segawa-etsuo-tb@ynu.ac.jp
* Correspondence: r.matsuoka.65@cc.it-hiroshima.ac.jp

Abstract: Maze-solving by natural phenomena is a symbolic result of the autonomous optimization induced by a natural system. We present a method for finding the shortest path on a maze consisting of a bipartite graph using a discrete-time quantum walk, which is a toy model of many kinds of quantum systems. By evolving the amplitude distribution according to the quantum walk on a kind of network with sinks, which is the exit of the amplitude, the amplitude distribution remains eternally on the paths between two self-loops indicating the start and the goal of the maze. We performed a numerical analysis of some simple cases and found that the shortest paths were detected by the chain of the maximum trapped densities in most cases of bipartite graphs. The counterintuitive dependence of the convergence steps on the size of the structure of the network was observed in some cases, implying that the asymmetry of the network accelerates or decelerates the convergence process. The relation between the amplitude remaining and distance of the path is also discussed briefly.

Keywords: discrete-time quantum walk; scattering quantum random walk; Grover walk; pathfinding; network

1. Introduction

Maze-solving methods are important because they have practical applications and provide insight into the invisible intelligence that underlies them. Maze-solving problems can be regarded as a subset of the shortest path problem [1], which is a practical problem in daily life. To solve the maze problem, a maze can be expressed as a network and then solved by an algorithm, such as the depth-first search or the breadth-first search algorithm [2]. There are also maze-solving methods that exploit natural phenomena.

Such methods have been studied experimentally using the Belousov–Zhabotinsky reaction mixtures [3], amoeboid organisms [4], gas discharge [5], and photons in a waveguide array [6]. In these experiments, the result of maze-solving has a symbolic aspect in that it represents the autonomous optimization of the natural system. In this way, the pursuit and modeling of the optimization process in maze solving by a natural phenomenon, can provide a path to a deeper understanding of that phenomenon.

The quantum walk model, which has been studied as a quantum counterpart of random walk, has been applied to describe various transportation phenomena in nature [7]. It was first studied as the time-evolution of probability distribution, mainly on a one-dimensional network. In the discrete-time quantum walk (DTQW) model, each node has a state vector of complex amplitudes whose dimension corresponds to the number of neighboring nodes. Each evolution is composed of a coin operation and a shift operation; after multiplying the unitary matrix (coin operation), the complex amplitude is transferred into an element of the state vector of a neighboring node (shift operation). By considering time-dependent or site-dependent unitary matrices, the quantum walk can express many kinds of transport dynamics.

The study of quantum walks was extended to arbitrarily connected networks from an early stage [8] because the quantum search on graphs by quantum walks was proposed [9–11] as an alternative to Grover's search algorithm [12]. When dealing with discrete-time quantum walks on an arbitrarily connected network, the concept of scattering quantum walks (SQWs) can simplify the model [13].

In an SQW, the state vectors are placed on the edges rather than the nodes. The dimension of each state vector is two: this corresponds to the two directions of an edge between two nodes. Moreover, each node has a scattering matrix that corresponds to the unitary matrix in the coin operation. The time evolution is composed of an intrusion in the node, the multiplication of the scattering matrix, and an escape from the node. The dynamics of an SQW are equivalent to those of a DTQW except for the location of the state vectors.

Recently, the concepts of consecutive injection and corresponding emission into and from the system were incorporated into quantum walks on arbitrarily connected networks [14,15]. For quantum walks on a network with entrances and/or exits, the steady-state [14], trapped-state [15], analogy to an electrical circuit [16], and relationship to the dressed photon phenomenon [17] have been discussed. In particular, the emergence of a trapped state between two self-loops on a network with an exit sink [15] directly motivated the present study, which applies this concept to maze-solving.

Maze-solving using quantum walks has been studied by Hillery, Koch, and Reitzner on an N-tree maze [18] and a chain of stars [19,20]. Their works are the extension of their studies on quantum search and finding structural anomalies in networks [21–27]. They characterized the start and goal nodes in the maze by reflection with phase inversion, which can be regarded as a pair of structural anomalies.

In this paper, we numerically examine a maze-solving method that uses a quantum walk on a network. The presented method is an application of the emergence of a trapped eigenstate on a network with sinks, and it provides an alternative to previously reported methods [18–20]. Although the mathematical foundation of this method was given by Konno, Segawa, and Štefaňák [28], the results presented here are non-trivial because the interaction among multiple trapped eigenstates and the initial condition is generally difficult to characterize as of now.

We show the effectiveness of the method for some examples of the maze with and without cycles and also show the undesirable cases for which this method does not work. The dependence of the number of steps for convergence (convergence steps) on the size of the network structure was also investigated and found to be counterintuitive in certain cases. We also make a tentative discussion about the amount of amplitude remaining on a path and its relative amount among the multiple paths from the numerical results.

2. Model and Method

In this study, the maze is composed of nodes and edges that connect pairs of nodes. The number of nodes is finite, but pairs of nodes can be connected arbitrarily without limit. The distance between two nodes is given by the smallest number of edges connecting them. Therefore, only distances expressed in positive integers are considered. The start and goal can be placed at any node in the network, even at nodes that are not dead ends. To run the quantum walk, scattering matrices and state vectors are placed on nodes and edges, respectively, as in previous studies on SQWs [13].

The state vectors consist of two complex amplitudes, which express the two directions of the quantum walkers on the edges. As in quantum mechanics, the density of the walkers on an edge is given by the square of the complex amplitude. At each evolution of time, the vector of the incoming component is multiplied by the scattering matrix, generating the vector of the outgoing component. The scattering matrix of the d-dimensional unitary matrix is placed at each node, where d is the number of edges connected to that node.

Specifically, we use the scattering matrix of the Grover walk, which, in concrete form, is given by

$$\begin{pmatrix} b_1 \\ b_2 \\ b_3 \\ \vdots \\ b_d \end{pmatrix} = \begin{pmatrix} \frac{2}{d}-1 & \frac{2}{d} & \frac{2}{d} & \cdots & \frac{2}{d} \\ \frac{2}{d} & \frac{2}{d}-1 & \frac{2}{d} & \cdots & \frac{2}{d} \\ \frac{2}{d} & \frac{2}{d} & \frac{2}{d}-1 & \cdots & \frac{2}{d} \\ \vdots & \vdots & \vdots & \ddots & \vdots \\ \frac{2}{d} & \frac{2}{d} & \frac{2}{d} & \cdots & \frac{2}{d}-1 \end{pmatrix} \begin{pmatrix} a_1 \\ a_2 \\ a_3 \\ \vdots \\ a_d \end{pmatrix}, \qquad (1)$$

where a_i is the incoming complex amplitude from the i-th edge, and b_i is the outgoing complex amplitude to the i-th edge. An example with $d = 3$ is given in Figure 1a.

To implement maze-solving, two self-loops and a sink are introduced, and the conceptual diagram is shown in Figure 1b. Self-loops are the same as edges except that they are only attached to a single node. As a result, a self-loop has a one-dimensional state vector, where the outgoing amplitude from the node becomes the next incoming amplitude without being modified. For this method, one self-loop is attached to the start node, and the other is attached to the goal node to which a sink node is also attached. The sink node has only one edge, which is connected to the goal node, and its scattering matrix is a zero matrix. The sink serves as the exit from the network for complex amplitudes.

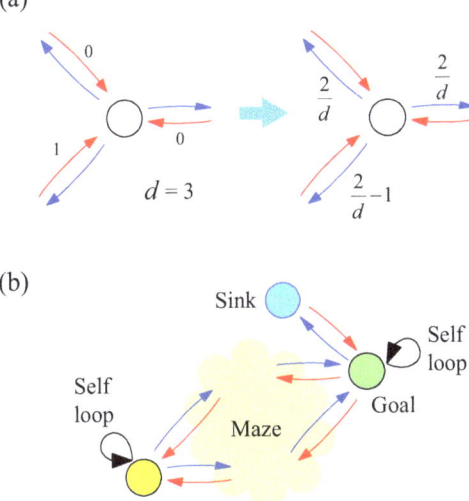

Figure 1. Conceptual schematics of the numerical model. (**a**) Example of the time-evolution for a node with three edges injected with the amplitude 1 from one edge. (**b**) Setup of the start and goal with self-loops and a sink. The colors of the start (yellow), the goal (green), and the sink (blue) are unified in all the examples given later.

The initial amplitude "1" is placed at the self-loop of the start node. To discover the correct path, the initial amplitude should be placed on the path between the start and goal, and it should be kept at a distance from the sink node. In this method, placing the localized amplitude at the self-loop of the start node is the best initial condition for solving the maze correctly without requiring any prior knowledge of the structure of the maze. Finally, note that all the amplitudes in the system are denoted by the real numbers even though the quantum walks are defined using complex amplitudes.

Maze solving was studied for simple structures only because of the large amount of computational time involved by the current code (by the current code on our standard personal computer, the calculation of 10^5 steps took several hours because of unoptimized function–call overhead). For the maze without a cycle, a tree-like structure and a single line with branches were investigated. For the maze with a cycle, independent multiple paths and a ladder-like structure were investigated.

Two undesirable cases, namely, a maze with odd cycles and a maze showing eternal vibration are also investigated. For each kind of structure, the dependence of convergence steps on the size of the structure was investigated. The convergence was judged by the stability of the second decimal place for all the amplitudes in the network, and the convergence steps were expressed with an accuracy of one (or two) significant digits.

For discussion regarding the amount of amplitude remaining, about five digits after the decimal point were considered. The numerical error estimated from the squared sum of the amplitudes was of nearly the same order as the double-precision real number error computed using code written in Python. The source code is available in the repository [29].

3. Results

3.1. Tree-like Structure

We first examine maze-solving for the tree-like structures. This structure has no cycles, and there is only one path from the start to the goal. Figure 2a–c show the results of the amplitude distribution and the number of steps after convergence for the tree-like structures of 2^N leaves for $N = 1, 2$, and 3. From the results, we observed that only the shortest path emerges as a chain of the eternally remaining densities, whereas the densities on the dead ends vanish during the evolution. The number of convergence steps seems to increase by digits according to the increase of N in these cases. The case of $N = 4$ was also examined. However, the distribution did not converge even after 10^6 steps that took three days.

Figure 2d shows the time profiles of the densities on selected edges, where the label 0–3, for example, denotes the edge between nodes 0 and 3. The densities fluctuate strongly at first and then converge to zero or to positive values. The speed of convergence varies according to the position of the edge; the greater the distance to the sink node is, the slower the speed of convergence.

To consider the influence of the extra branching at dead ends on the convergence steps, the cases of decreased and increased extra branching based on Figure 2c were examined. For the case with decreased branching as shown in Figure 2e, the convergence steps decreased, which was an intuitive result. However, the decrease in convergence steps was more for the case with increased extra branching as shown in Figure 2f. This counterintuitive dependence is difficult to explain for the present. However, it can be suggested that the extent of asymmetry in the network accelerated the convergence.

For the cases of Figure 2c,e,f, the absolute values of the converged amplitudes on the correct paths, including self-loops, were all 0.08. That value seems to have been determined by the distance between the start and the goal nodes for the case of the network without cycles. Table 1 lists the relation between the distance between the start and the goal and the absolute value of the amplitude remaining on an edge for each case. Edges indicates the number of edges on a path including self-loops. (Edges = 2 × Distance + 2).

A rational expression approximating the amount of amplitude was attached for each case. For these cases, the amplitudes can be expressed by the inverse of the number of edges included in the path. Namely, the sum of amplitudes along the path is "1.0" for all the cases. However, note that the "1.0" does not indicate all the amplitudes injected into the system because that is not the square sum of the amplitudes.

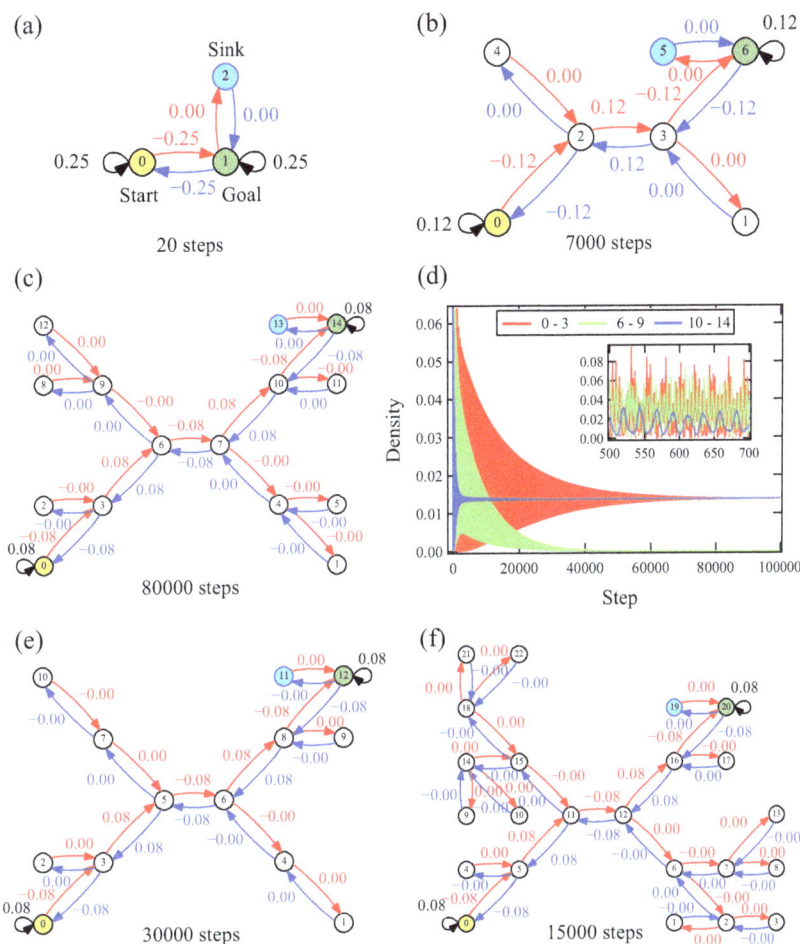

Figure 2. The results of maze-solving for the tree-like structure with 2^N leaves. (**a**) Amplitude distribution and the number of steps after convergence for $N = 1$. (**b**) Amplitude distribution and the number of steps after convergence for $N = 2$. (**c**) Amplitude distribution and the number of steps after convergence for $N = 3$. (**d**) Time profiles of the densities on selected edges for $N = 3$. The inset focuses on the vibrational behavior of each profile. (**e**) Amplitude distribution and the number of steps after convergence for the case where the branches were eliminated from the dead ends in (**c**). (**f**) Amplitude distribution and the number of steps after convergence for the case where the branches were added to the dead ends in (**c**).

Table 1. The relation between the distance and remaining amplitude for Figure 2 (The distance between the start and goal on the correct path, the number of edges in the path, the amplitude remaining on an edge on the path, and an approximate rational expression of the amplitude).

Figure	Distance	Edges	Amplitude	Rational Expression
Figure 2a	1	4	0.25000	1/4
Figure 2b	3	8	0.12500	1/8
Figure 2c	5	12	0.08333	1/12
Figure 2e	5	12	0.08333	1/12
Figure 2f	5	12	0.08333	1/12

3.2. A Line with Branches

To investigate the dependence of the convergence steps on the placement of the branches, the maze-solving for various patterns of a line with shallow dead ends was examined. Figure 3a shows the result for a simple line constructed based on the correct path of Figure 2c. The number of convergence steps decreased by two orders of magnitude from the case shown in Figure 2c. Figure 3b shows the result for a line with four shallow dead-ends. Nearly the same result as Figure 2e was obtained, as the difference between them was only the length of the dead ends.

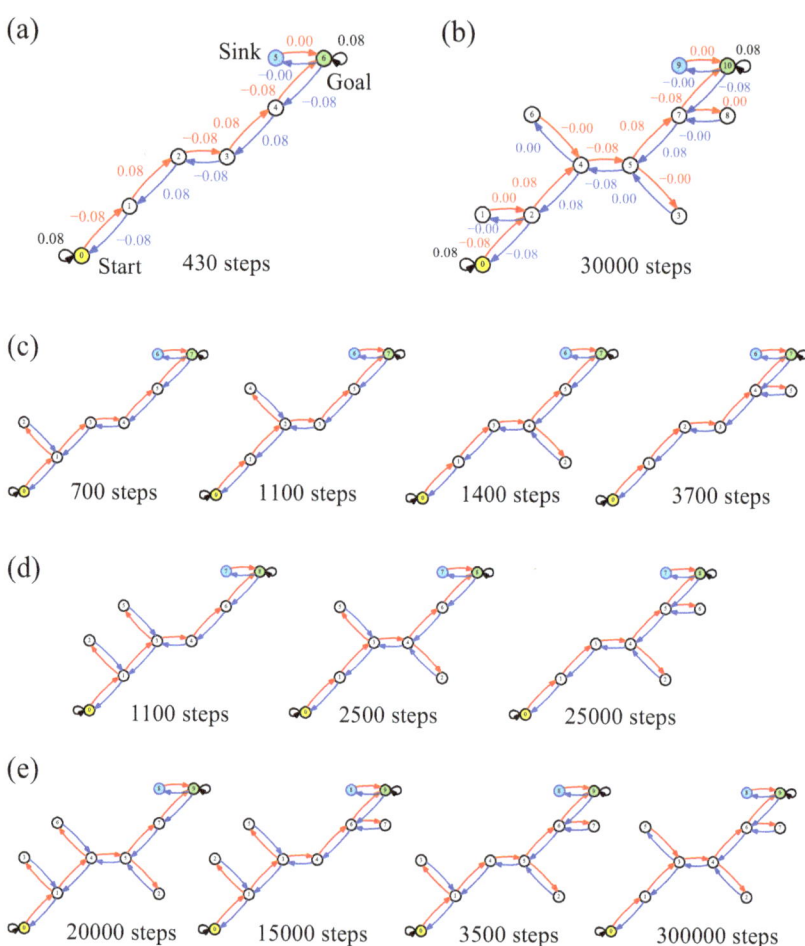

Figure 3. The results of maze-solving for a line with various placements of shallow dead ends. (**a**) Amplitude distribution and the number of steps after convergence for a single line of five edges. (**b**) Amplitude distribution and the number of steps after convergence for a line with four shallow dead ends. (**c**) The structures and the numbers of steps of convergence for a line with a single shallow dead-end at four positions. (**d**) The structures and the numbers of steps of convergence for a line with two shallow dead-ends at three patterns. (**e**) The structures and the numbers of steps of convergence for a line with three shallow dead-ends at four patterns.

Figure 3c–e shows the results for patterns of placement of one to three dead ends, respectively. The distribution of the amplitudes is omitted, but ±0.08, which is the same as Figure 2c,e,f, is on the correct path, and 0.00 is on the dead-end edges in all cases. The convergence steps varied not only by the number of dead ends but also by the positions. As the trend shows, the convergence steps became larger with increasing dead ends; however, exceptions were observed depending on the positions of the dead ends. The convergence steps became larger for the case where dead ends were attached closed to the goal node. This seems counterintuitive considering the quick convergence near the sink, which was observed in Figure 2d.

The number of convergence steps for the case of Figure 3e was much larger than for Figure 3b or Figure 2c. For these cases, the asymmetry significantly decelerated the convergence speed, which is in contrast to the acceleration due to asymmetry observed in Figure 2e,f. A maze without cycles can be solved by this method; however, the dependence of the convergence steps on the network structure is difficult to predict intuitively.

3.3. Independent Multiple Paths

Next, we examined maze-solving on multiple independent paths of different lengths. This structure includes cycles, which makes maze-solving difficult even in classical schemes. Figure 4a–c,e,f shows the numerical results for the networks with M paths, where the length of the Mth path is $2M$. After convergence, in all the examples shown here, the densities remain on all the paths between the start and the goal; however, the maximum densities are only observed on the shortest path, while smaller densities are observed farther from the shortest path. By regarding the path of the maximum densities as the correct path, the maze-solving was successful for these examples.

Figure 4d shows the time profiles of the edges on each path. The speed of convergence was higher than in the case of other structures of a similar scale. The reason for this is unclear, but a lack of branching on the paths may be responsible for the high speed. Among the three paths, the speeds of convergence did not differ significantly, and they did not depend on the distance from the sink unlike in the tree-like structure. In general, the convergence steps increased by the addition of other paths. However, a counter-intuitive decrease of the convergence steps was observed in Figure 4e,f.

The absolute values of amplitudes, after convergence, decrease as the length of the path becomes longer; however, they are not constant for the length of paths because a slight decrease was observed by additional paths. Table 2 lists the relation between the distances of paths and amplitude remaining on an edge. For Figure 4a, the amplitude is the inverse of the number of edges included in the path, which is the same as given in Table 1. However, the rule looks broken in the case of multiple paths.

Table 2. The relation between the distance and remaining amplitude for Figure 4 (The waypoint of a path, the distance between the start and goal on the path, the number of edges in the path, the amplitude remaining on an edge on the path, and an approximate rational expression of the amplitude. Only the relative ratios are shown for Figure 4f because an appropriate rational number was not found).

Figure	Waypoint	Distance	Edges	Amplitude	Rational Expression
Figure 4a	Node 1	2	6	0.16667	1/6
Figure 4b	Node 2	2	6	0.14286	2/14
	Node 3	4	10	0.07143	1/14
Figure 4c	Node 4	2	6	0.13043	3/23
	Node 5	4	10	0.06522	$(3/2) \times (1/23)$
	Node 6	6	14	0.04348	1/23
Figure 4e	Node 7	2	6	0.01245	6/49
	Node 8	4	10	0.06122	$(3/2) \times (2/49)$
	Node 9	6	14	0.04082	2/49
	Node 10	8	18	0.03061	$(3/4) \times (2/49)$
Figure 4f	Node 11	2	6	0.11673	$5 \times (F)$
	Node 12	4	10	0.05837	$(5/2) \times (F)$
	Node 13	6	14	0.03891	$(5/3) \times (F)$
	Node 14	8	18	0.02918	$(5/4) \times (F)$
	Node 15	10	22	0.02335	(F)

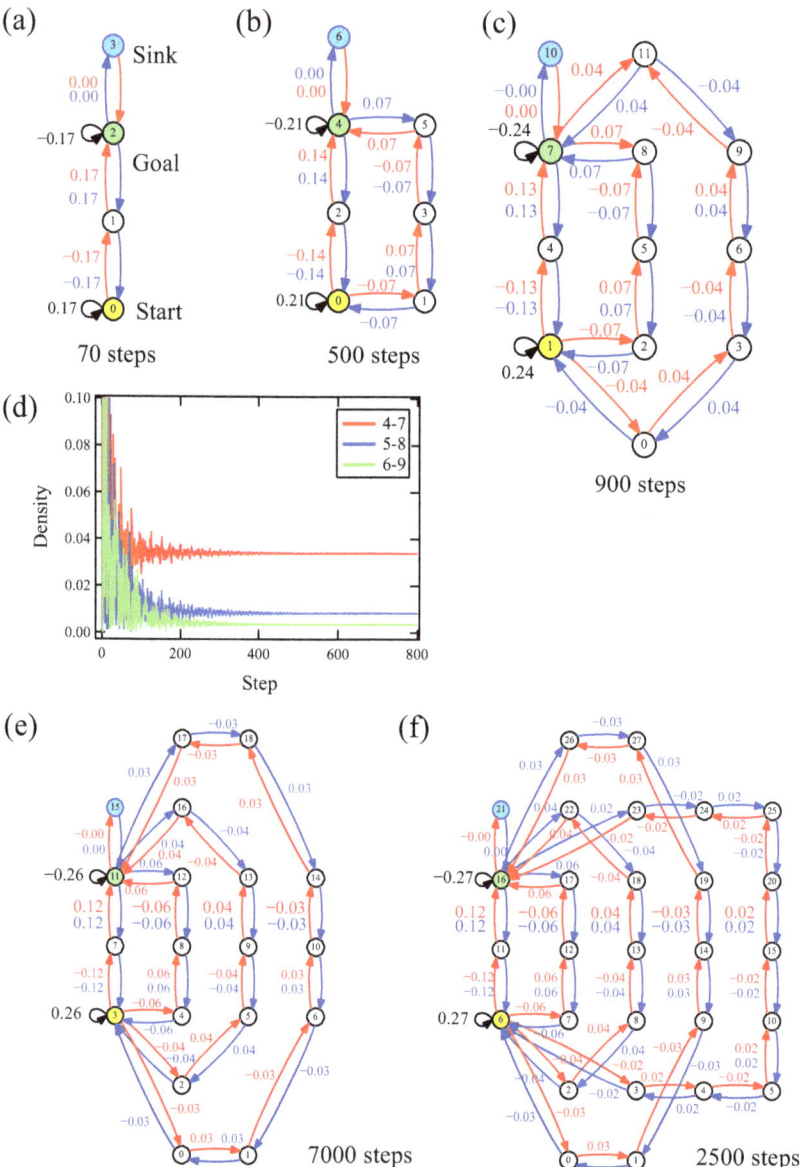

Figure 4. The results of maze-solving for the structures with multiple independent M paths from the start to the goal. The length of Mth path is $2M$. (**a**) Amplitude distribution and the number of steps after convergence for $M = 1$. (**b**) Amplitude distribution and the number of steps after convergence for $M = 2$. (**c**) Amplitude distribution and the number of steps after convergence for $M = 3$. (**d**) Time profiles of the densities on selected edges for $M = 3$. (**e**) Amplitude distribution and the number of steps after convergence for $M = 4$. (**f**) Amplitude distribution and the number of steps after convergence for $M = 5$.

Most of the amplitudes were assigned rational expressions; however, the rule determining the absolute value (or a positive integer of the denominator) is not clear. However, the relative amounts of amplitudes among paths in each case were found to be in inverse proportion to the distance between the start and goal exactly for these cases. The relative amounts of amplitude were determined not by the number of edges but by the distances.

3.4. Ladder-like Structure

As in other small examples of mazes with cycles, the ladder-like structures with L paths were examined. The difference from the previous subsection is that the edges are shared among the different paths. Figure 5a,b,d shows the results of $L = 1$, 3, and 4, respectively. For the cases shown here, the shortest paths are indicated by the chain of maximum densities, while smaller densities are observed farther from the shortest path, meaning that the maze-solving was successful. The absolute values of amplitude after convergence seem to correspond to the distance of each path by considering Figure 5b,d. However, this is not the case in Figure 5a.

For the cases of $L = 2$ and 5, undesirable eternal vibrations were observed and maze-solving could not work, which will be discussed in a later subsection. For the case of $L = 6$, the convergence was difficult to realize owing to the limitation of the computational times. However, it was not an eternal vibration judging from the actual calculations.

Figure 5c shows the time profiles of the edges in each path of Figure 5b. For the three paths, the speeds of convergence did not differ significantly, and they did not depend on the distance from the sink unlike what was observed in the tree-like structure. The convergence is faster than for the tree-like structure but slower than for the independent multiple paths. The number of convergence steps in Figure 5d is smaller than that in Figure 5b, exhibiting the difficulty faced in predicting the convergence speed from the structure of the maze.

Table 3 lists the relation between the distances of paths and amplitude remaining on an edge in Figure 5. The amplitudes can be expressed by rational numbers; however, the meanings of the denominator numbers are not clear as in Figure 4. The absolute values of the amplitudes in Figure 5 are generally smaller than those of the same scale case in Figure 4.

The ratio among the paths seems to have meaning; however, the reason has not been determined except for the relation between the longest and second-longest paths. The relative ratio of the longest path and the second-longest path is thought to be in inverse proportion to the ratio of the length of the non-shared part of each path. This hypothesis is complemented in the next subsection.

Table 3. The relation between the distance and remaining amplitude for Figure 5 (The waypoint of a path, the distance between the start and goal on the path, the number of edges in the path, the amplitude remaining on an edge on the path, and an approximate rational expression of the amplitude).

Figure	Waypoint	Distance	Edges	Amplitude	Rational Expression
Figure 5a	Node 2	4	10	0.10000	1/10
Figure 5b	Node 4	4	10	0.0735	5/68
	Node 5	6 (= 4 + 2)	14	0.0294	2/68
	Node 6	8 (= 4 + 4)	18	0.0147	1/68
Figure 5d	Node 5	4	10	0.07303	13/178
	Node 6	6	14	0.02809	5/178
	Node 7	8 (= 6 + 2)	18	0.01124	2/178
	Node 8	10 (= 6 + 4)	22	0.00562	1/178

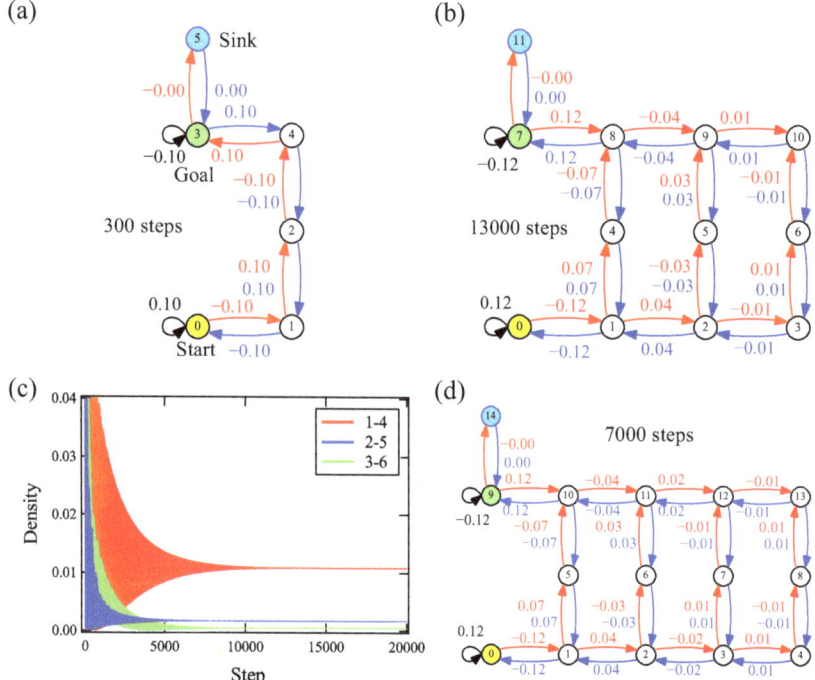

Figure 5. The results of maze-solving for the ladder-like structures with L paths from the start to the goal. (**a**) Amplitude distribution and the number of steps after convergence for $L = 1$. (**b**) Amplitude distribution and the number of steps after convergence for $L = 3$. (**c**) Time profiles of the densities on selected edges for $L = 3$. (**d**) Amplitude distribution and the number of steps after convergence for $L = 4$.

3.5. Small Maze

To demonstrate slightly complicated cases, solutions of small mazes by the method are presented. The maze includes some dead ends and two paths to the goal as shown in Figure 6a. As in the other related cases shown above, the maximum density remains on the shortest path, and the densities of the dead-end paths vanish. The maze-solving worked correctly for a small maze with both dead-ends and cycles.

Figure 6b shows the time profiles of the densities on selected edges. The convergence speeds were not so different from each other, as in the case of ladder-like structures.

The result of another maze that is slightly modified from Figure 6a is shown in Figure 6c. The convergence step was 22,000 for this example; however, a drastic increase of convergence steps was often observed by another slight modification of the structure. It might be in rare cases that the complex maze could be solved in a permissible computational time.

Table 4 lists the relations between the distances of paths and amplitude remaining on an edge in Figure 6. The hypothesis that the relative ratio of the longest path and the second-longest path is in inverse proportion to the ratio of the distances of the non-shared part of each path was also confirmed for these cases.

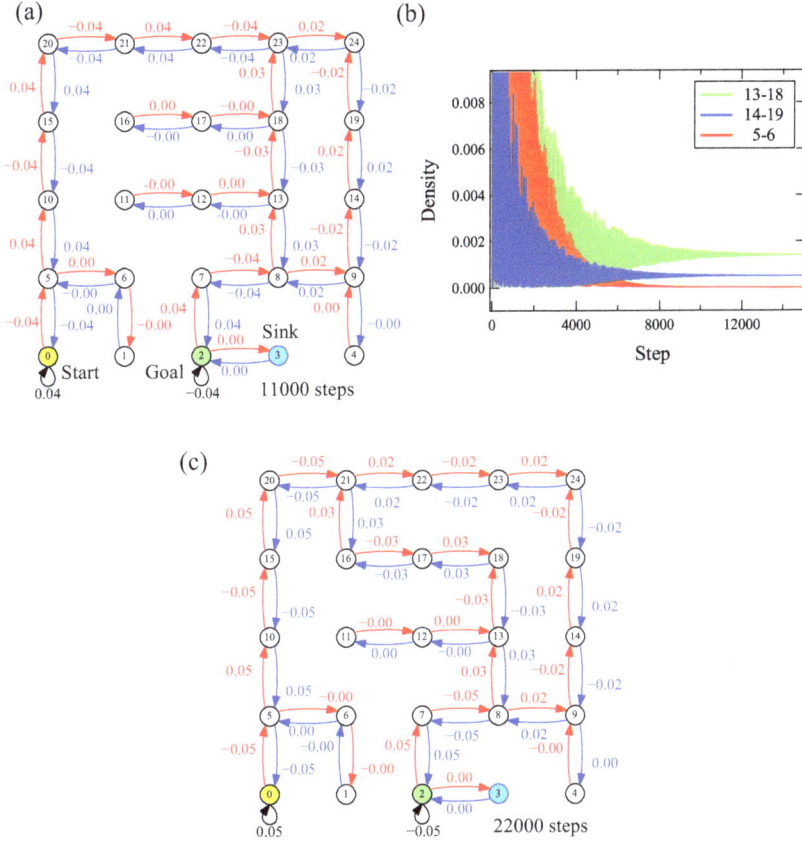

Figure 6. The results of maze-solving for small mazes with dead ends and two paths to the goal. (**a**) Amplitude distribution and the number of steps after convergence for a maze. (**b**) Time profiles of the densities on selected edges for (**a**). (**c**) Amplitude distribution and the number of steps after convergence for a slightly modified maze.

Table 4. The relation between the distance and remaining amplitude for Figure 6 (The waypoint of a path, the distance between the start and goal on the path, the amplitude remaining on an edge on the path, and an approximate rational expression of the amplitude).

Figure	Waypoint	Distance	Amplitude	Rational Expression
Figure 6a	Node 18	9 + 3	0.0263	1/38
	Node 19	9 + 5	0.0158	(3/5) × (1/38)
Figure 6c	Node 13	7 + 5	0.027	1/37
	Node 14	7 + 7	0.019	(5/7) × (1/37)

3.6. Undesirable Cases 1: Odd Cycle

Here, we show some examples of undesirable cases where maze-solving did not work. First, this method cannot be applicable for a maze that includes odd cycles. Figure 7a shows a network with a single odd cycle whose length is 5. The cycle that consists of nodes 1, 2, 5, 6, and 3 is the odd cycle. When the amplitude distribution converged, the absolute value of the amplitude between the exit of the cycle and the goal (edges between nodes 4 and 5) became small. The correct path was not indicated by the maximum densities, meaning that the maze-solving went wrong.

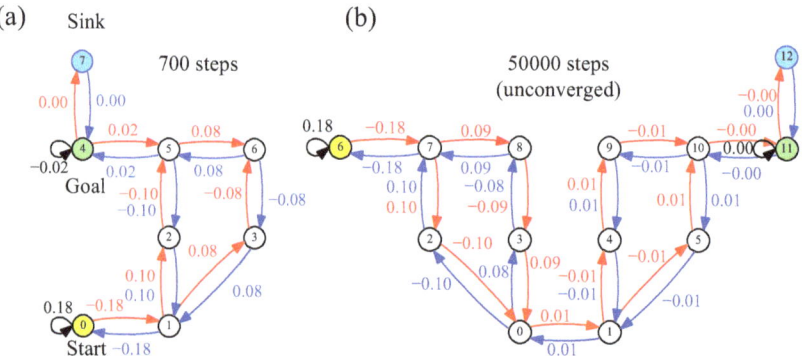

Figure 7. The results of the attempt of maze-solving for a network that includes an odd-cycle. (**a**) Amplitude distribution and the number of steps after convergence for a network with one odd cycle. (**b**) Amplitude distribution and the number of steps after convergence for of a network with two sequential odd cycles. The amplitude distribution that is nearly converged but not completely is shown because of the limitation of the computational time.

Figure 7b shows an attempt of solving for the network with two sequential odd-cycles. The effects of the two odd-cycles were not canceled out, and only a small amplitude reached the goal. The solving method presented cannot apply to the network with odd-cycles.

3.7. Undesirable Cases 2: Eternal Vibration

Even though the odd cycle was not involved in the network, undesirable eternal vibration was observed in some cases. Figure 8a shows the network of the ladder-like structure for $L = 2$, which is exhibiting eternal vibration. In this case, only the edges between nodes 5 and 6, were stabilized. The amplitudes of other edges, from the start to the cycle, exhibit a constant vibration pattern eternally. Figure 8b shows the time profiles of the densities of some edges. The constant amplitude vibrations seem to continue eternally and not converge. The inset shows the details of the vibrational behavior. The same patterns are seen to be repeating. The eternal vibration was observed only for the ladder-like structure of $L = 2$ and 5.

We found that the eternal vibration was suppressed by the addition of an extra dead end. Figure 8c shows the network in which one dead-end is attached to Figure 8a. The amplitude distribution converged, and the shortest path was indicated by the maximum densities. Figure 8d shows the time profile of the density for some selected edges in Figure 8c. The reason for the stabilization is unclear at present; however, a small perturbation of the network may have a significant influence on the behavior of quantum walks.

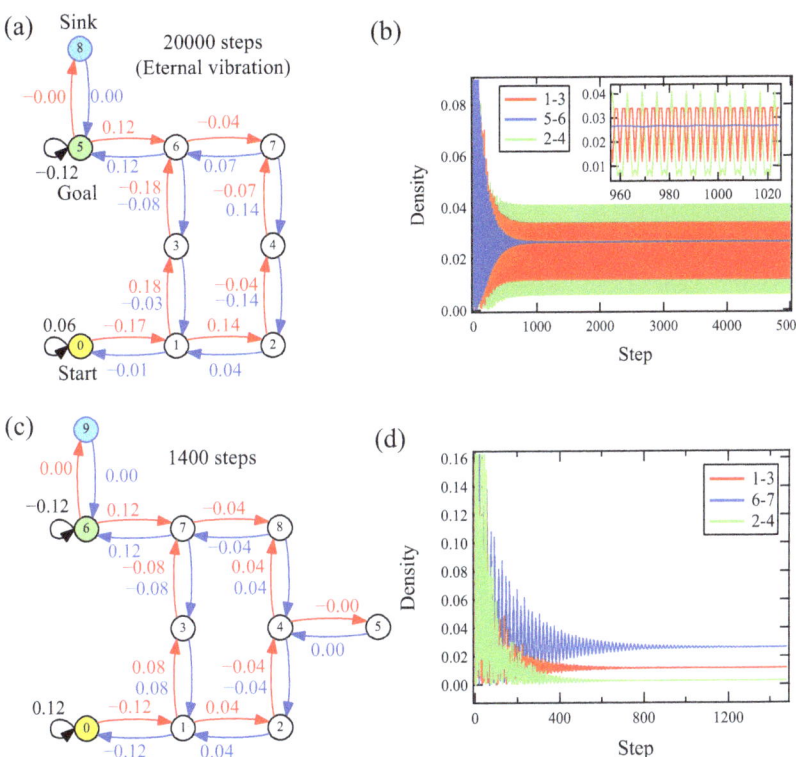

Figure 8. The results of the attempts of maze-solving for a structure where the eternal vibration was observed. (**a**) Amplitude distribution after 20,000 steps for the ladder-like structure of $L = 2$. (**b**) Time profiles of the densities on selected edges in (**a**). The inset shows the vibrational behavior in detail. (**c**) Amplitude distribution and the number of steps after convergence for the network in (**a**) where a dead-end is attached. (**d**) Time profiles of the densities on selected edges in (**c**).

4. Discussion

In applying the proposed method to mazes without odd cycles, we verified that the paths between the start and goal emerge as trapped states of the quantum walk, and the density on the shortest path was maximized autonomously. As the network without odd cycles is regarded as a bipartite graph, we concluded that the method can be applied to the bipartite graph except for the case where the eternal vibration emerges. The condition for the occurrence of the eternal vibration is not clear as of now as only a few examples were considered.

The key features of the proposed method are the self-loops at the start and the goal and the sink node attached to the goal. In previous studies, the start and goal were marked by reflection with phase inversion placed at the dead ends [18–20]. The correct path was then judged by the transient profile of the probabilities. Our method partially improves upon past works by incorporating self-loops, which can be placed anywhere in the maze, and by determining the correct path according to the eternally remaining densities.

We now consider the remaining densities on the correct path in terms of knowledge that has been proven mathematically. The eigenstate of the time evolution operator of the quantum walk with sinks was constructed on the path between two-self loops [28]. This eigenstate is called the trapped state, and it is not absorbed by the sink. In the Grover walk, the eigenstates are constructed between two self-loops and also around the cycles [28].

To generate a trapped state, the initial amplitude should be placed on the edge that is to be included in the trapped state. This was the reason why the initial amplitude was placed on the self-loop of the start node. If the initial amplitude is placed randomly at the edge, the trapped state on the correct path does not always emerge because the initial edge may not be included on the path between the start and the goal. Even if the initial state is on the correct path, a trapped state may also emerge in the cyclic structure that includes the initial edge. In this case, the shortest path may not have the maximum density. When placing the initial amplitude on a self-loop, the initial edge is not included in any cyclic structure in the network, and only the paths between the start and the goal emerge.

The role of the sink should also be considered. The dynamics of this type of Grover walk can be separated into an electric current component that propagates rapidly, and a random-walk component that propagates slowly [16]. The emergence of the trapped state results from the electric current component; hence, to observe the trapped state, the random-walk component must be eliminated by the sink.

Even without the mathematical knowledge above, the amplitude distribution after convergence can be interpreted by the simple rules observed in the numerical results. The key rule for determining amplitude distribution is that the sum of incoming/outgoing amplitudes to/from a node must be zero, separately. This rule is mathematically and numerically exact at all the nodes in the examples that converged. Figure 9a shows an example of amplitude distribution around a node on the correct path in the maze.

As the sum of incoming and outgoing amplitudes should be zero separately, amplitudes of plus and minus emerge alternately on the line. Figure 9b shows an example of an amplitude distribution around a dead-end node. As only one amplitude is incoming to the dead-end node, that should be zero to make the sum of the incoming amplitude zero. This is why the amplitudes vanish on the path to the dead-end.

Figure 9c shows an example of amplitude distribution around a self-loop. In this case, the amplitude on the self-loop acts as both incoming and outgoing amplitudes to keep the sum zero for both. This is the reason why the signs of the amplitudes are the same on the edges connected to the node involving the self-loop. These facts fit all the nodes included in the numerical results after convergence.

The sum rule above can be used to also explain the amplitude distribution around the even cycle and odd cycle. Figure 9d shows an example of the amplitude distribution around an even cycle. When the large positive amplitude enters the cycle, two small negative amplitudes are generated at the first branching node. Both amplitudes move on the cycle by changing the sign alternately and meet again on the join node. If the cycle is an even cycle, two small negative amplitudes make a large positive amplitude to the outside of the cycle to keep the sum rule. For the case of an odd cycle (Figure 9e), two amplitudes meet at the join node with different signs. To maintain the sum rule, only the smaller amplitude, which is nearly zero, generates the output. This is the reason why the maze, including the odd cycle, cannot be solved by this method.

The maze-solving speed of this method is clearly considerably slower than that of other known algorithms. Although the examples were limited, the convergence steps were difficult to predict by intuition in observing the structure of the network. At present, the intuitive unified parameter that connects the network structure and convergence speed has not been determined mathematically. Further analysis, considering some other aspect, such as the symmetry of the graph, may be required.

The general reason that the maximum densities emerge on the shortest path remains unclear at present; however, some tentative rules were observed numerically. In many cases, the absolute values of amplitude that remained could be approximated to a rational number composed of integers. When there is only one path to the goal, the absolute values of amplitudes on an edge become the inverse number of the number of edges included in the path. This is observed in Figures 2, 3, 4a and 5a. The preserved amount is not the square of the amplitude but the absolute value of amplitude. It is the same as the sum rule discussed above.

When there are multiple paths to the goal and they do not share edges mutually, the ratio of the absolute values of amplitudes is in inverse proportion to the ratio of the distance of the paths. This is observed in Figure 4b–f. When there are two paths to the goal and they share some edges, the ratio of the absolute values of amplitudes is in inverse proportion to the ratio of the distance of the non-shared part of the paths. This is observed in Figure 6a,c. When there are more than two paths to the goal and they share some edges, the dependence of the relative amount of amplitudes on the distance is unclear; however, certain rules clearly exist. This was seen in Figure 5b,d.

To apply the method presented for actual problems of the shortest path finding, the lengths of all the paths should be expressed by positive integers. The odd-loops must not be included; however, the odd-loops would be eliminated by a slight modification of the distance in the process of discretization of the network. The eternal vibration is still the obstacle of the path-finding problem. This should be analyzed more both mathematically and numerically. Additionally, this method cannot involve the negative distance that is considered in some classical algorithms.

Studying this maze-solving method may not appear to be of much use from the viewpoint of computational algorithms; however, it may help to understand the mechanisms of autonomous features that can be observed in a natural system because the quantum walk is a toy model that can be applied to the energy transportation in quantum fields, such as dressed photon phenomena [30].

While the emergence of the shortest path or some other optimized structure in a natural phenomenon may seem mysterious at first glance, they may have an analogy in maze-solving using the quantum walks. Moreover, the implicit existence of the sink node may play an important role in such systems.

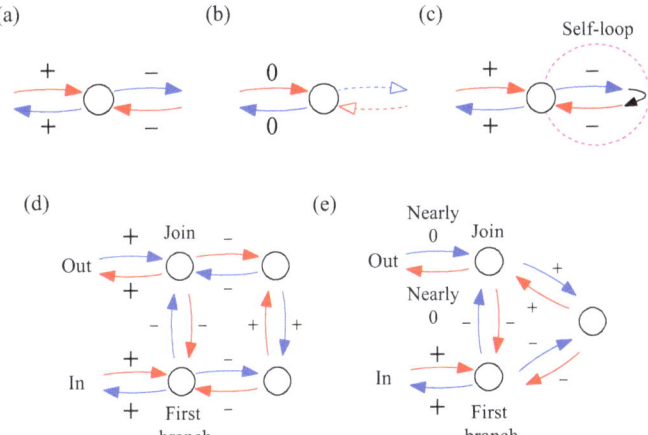

Figure 9. Schematic for the interpretation of the amplitude distribution after convergence based on the sum rule on each node. (**a**) An example of distribution around a node on the correct path in the maze. The sums of incoming amplitudes (red arrows) and outgoing amplitudes (blue arrows) should be zero, respectively. (**b**) An example of distribution around a node at a dead-end. To make the sums of incoming/outgoing amplitudes zero, respectively, no amplitude should enter the dead-end. (**c**) An example of distribution around a node with a self-loop. Amplitude on the self-loop acts as both incoming and outgoing amplitudes. (**d**) An example of distribution around an even-cycle. (**e**) An example of distribution around an odd-cycle.

Author Contributions: Conceptualization, L.M.; methodology, L.M. and E.S.; software, K.Y. and H.L.; validation, L.M., E.S. and H.L.; formal analysis, K.Y. and H.L.; investigation, L.M. and E.S.; resources, all authors; data curation, L.M. and K.Y.; writing—original draft preparation, L.M.; writing—review and editing, L.M.; visualization, K.Y. and H.L.; supervision, L.M.; project administration, L.M.; funding acquisition, L.M. All authors have read and agreed to the published version of the manuscript.

Funding: This research received no external funding.

Data Availability Statement: The data presented in this study are available on request from the corresponding author.

Acknowledgments: We thank Osamu Ogurisu and Hayato Saigo for helpful discussions.

Conflicts of Interest: The authors declare no conflict of interest.

References

1. Dijkstra, E.W. A note on two problems in connexion with graphs. *Numer. Math.* **1959**, *1*, 269–271. [CrossRef]
2. Cormen, T.H.; Leiserson, C.E.; Rivest, R.L.; Stein, C. *Introduction to Algorithms*, 3rd ed.; The MIT Press: London, UK, 2009; pp. 589–612.
3. Steinbock, O.; Tóth, A.; Showalter, K. Navigating Complex Labyrinths: Optimal Paths from Chemical Waves. *Science* **1995**, *267*, 868–871. [CrossRef] [PubMed]
4. Nakagaki, T.; Yamada, H.; Tóth, Á. Maze-solving by an amoeboid organism. *Nature* **2000**, *407*, 470. [CrossRef]
5. Reyes, D.R.; Ghanem, M.M.; Whitesides, G.M.; Manz, A. Glow discharge in microfluidic chips for visible analog computing. *Lab Chip* **2002**, *2*, 113–116. [CrossRef] [PubMed]
6. Caruso, F.; Crespi, A.; Ciriolo, A.G.; Sciarrino, F.; Osellame, R. Fast escape of a quantum walker from an integrated photonic maze. *Nat. Commun.* **2016**, *7*, 11682. [CrossRef]
7. Venegas-Andraca, S.E. Quantum walks: A comprehensive review. *Quantum Inf. Process* **2012**, *11*, 1015–1106. [CrossRef]
8. Kempe, J. Quantum random walks: An introductory overview. *Contemp. Phys.* **2009**, *50*, 339–359. [CrossRef]
9. Aaronson, S.; Ambainis, A. Quantum search of spatial regions. *Theory Comput.* **2005**, *1*, 47–79. [CrossRef]
10. Childs, A.M.; Goldstone, J. Spatial search by quantum walk. *Phys. Rev. A* **2004**, *70*, 022314. [CrossRef]
11. Shenvi, N.; Kempe, J.; Whaley, K. A Quantum Random Walk Search Algorithm. *Phys. Rev. A* **2002**, *67*, 052307. [CrossRef]
12. Grover, L.K. Quantum Mechanics Helps in Searching for a Needle in a Haystack. *Phys. Rev. Lett.* **1997**, *79*, 325–328. [CrossRef]
13. Hillery, M.; Bergou, J.; Feldman, E. Quantum walks based on an interferometric analogy. *Phys. Rev. A* **2003**, *68*, 032314. [CrossRef]
14. Higuchi, Y.; Segawa, E. A dynamical system induced by quantum walk. *J. Phys. A Math. Theor.* **2019**, *52*, 395202. [CrossRef]
15. Mareš, J.; Novotný, J.; Štefaňák, M.; Jex, I. Counterintuitive role of geometry in transport by quantum walks. *Phys. Rev. A* **2020**, *101*, 032113. [CrossRef]
16. Higuchi, Y.; Sabri, M.; Segawa, E. Electric Circuit Induced by Quantum Walk. *J. Stat. Phys.* **2020**, *181*, 603–617. [CrossRef]
17. Hamano, M.; Saigo, H. Quantum Walk and Dressed Photon. *Electron. Proc. Theor. Comput. Sci.* **2020**, *315*, 93–99. [CrossRef]
18. Koch, D.; Hillery, M. Finding paths in tree graphs with a quantum walk. *Phys. Rev. A* **2018**, *97*, 012308. [CrossRef]
19. Reitzner, D.; Hillery, M.; Koch, D. Finding paths with quantum walks or quantum walking through a maze. *Phys. Rev. A* **2017**, *96*, 032323. [CrossRef]
20. Hillery, M. Finding more than one path through a simple maze with a quantum walk. *J. Phys. A Math. Theor.* **2021**, *54*, 095301. [CrossRef]
21. Reitzner, D.; Hillery, M.; Feldman, E.; Bužek, V. Quantum searches on highly symmetric graphs. *Phys. Rev. A* **2009**, *79*, 012323. [CrossRef]
22. Hillery, M.; Reitzner, D.; Bužek, V. Searching via walking: How to find a marked clique of a complete graph using quantum walks. *Phys. Rev. A* **2010**, *81*, 062324. [CrossRef]
23. Feldman, E.; Hillery, M.; Lee, H.; Reitzner, D.; Zheng, H.; Bužek, V. Finding structural anomalies in graphs by means of quantum walks. *Phys. Rev. A* **2010**, *82*, 040301(R). [CrossRef]
24. Hillery, M.; Zheng, H.; Feldman, E.; Reitzner, D.; Bužek, V. Quantum walks as a probe of structural anomalies in graphs. *Phys. Rev. A* **2012**, *85*, 062325. [CrossRef]
25. Cottrell, S.; Hillery, M. Finding Structural Anomalies in Star Graphs Using Quantum Walks. *Phys. Rev. Lett.* **2014**, *112*, 030501. [CrossRef] [PubMed]
26. Cottrell, S.S. Finding structural anomalies in star graphs using quantum walks: A general approach. *J. Phys. A Math. Theor.* **2015**, *48*, 035304. [CrossRef]
27. Koch, D. Scattering quantum random walks on square grids and randomly generated mazes. *Phys. Rev. A* **2019**, *99*, 012330. [CrossRef]
28. Konno, N.; Segawa, E.; Štefaňák, M. Relation between Quantum Walks with Tails and Quantum Walks with Sinks on Finite Graphs. *Symmetry* **2021**, *13*, 1169. [CrossRef]

29. Yuki, K. GitHub Repository. Available online: https://github.com/kyuki-rp/qw-maze-solving (accessed on 18 November 2021).
30. Ohtsu, M. History, current developments, and future directions of near-field optical science. *Opto-Electron. Adv.* **2020**, *3*, 190046. [CrossRef]

Article

Investigation of Eigenmode-Based Coupled Oscillator Solver Applied to Ising Spin Problems

Shintaro Murakami, Okuto Ikeda, Yusuke Hirukawa and Toshiharu Saiki *

Graduate School of Science and Technology, Keio University, Yokohama 223-8522, Japan; murashin1218@keio.jp (S.M.); okuto.ikeda@saiki.elec.keio.ac.jp (O.I.); yusuke.hirukawa@saiki.elec.keio.ac.jp (Y.H.)
* Correspondence: saiki@elec.keio.ac.jp

Abstract: We evaluate a coupled oscillator solver by applying it to square lattice (N × N) Ising spin problems for N values up to 50. The Ising problems are converted to a classical coupled oscillator model that includes both positive (ferromagnetic-like) and negative (antiferromagnetic-like) coupling between neighboring oscillators (i.e., they are reduced to eigenmode problems). A map of the oscillation amplitudes of lower-frequency eigenmodes enables us to visualize oscillator clusters with a low frustration density (unfrustrated clusters). We found that frustration tends to localize at the boundary between unfrustrated clusters due to the symmetric and asymmetric nature of the eigenmodes. This allows us to reduce frustration simply by flipping the sign of the amplitude of oscillators around which frustrated couplings are highly localized. For problems with N = 20 to 50, the best solutions with an accuracy of 96% (with respect to the exact ground state) can be obtained by simply checking the lowest ~N/2 candidate eigenmodes.

Keywords: combinatorial optimization; Ising spin glass; coupled oscillator; eigenmode; clustering

1. Introduction

The spin glass model originates from condensed matter physics, where it was applied to physical systems in which magnetic atoms are randomly distributed in a non-magnetic host and induce ferromagnetic and antiferromagnetic interactions between neighboring magnetic moments. The physical system is mathematically modeled by a weighted graph where each vertex corresponds to a spin and each edge represents the interaction between spins with positive and negative signs [1,2]. In the Ising spin model, the spin is a binary variable that takes the value ± 1 [3,4]. The Ising problem is to find a binary spin configuration that minimizes the total energy function (the number of frustrated edges) for a given set of edges. A variety of combinatorial optimization problems, such as sequencing and ordering problems, resource allocation problems, and clustering problems [5,6], can be mapped to the Ising problem [7].

To solve the Ising problem using a brute force combination approach, we need to check 2^n possibilities, where n is the total number of spins. The branch and bound method, which based on a tree search algorithm, is commonly used to find the exact ground state without an exhaustive search [8]. However, this method still requires a lot of CPU time and memory and is only applicable to instances with a small number of spins. The potential applications of the Ising model to optimization problems have motivated the development of heuristic algorithms for finding high-quality solutions for instances with a large number of spins [9,10]. Although heuristic algorithms generally do not guarantee an optimal solution, they can yield good time-to-solution in practice.

Simulated annealing (SA), one of the most common heuristic algorithms, mimics the physical process of annealing, where a material is slowly cooled to obtain the lowest energy state [11–13]. Its algorithm is based on Monte Carlo simulation. Starting with an initial spin configuration, a new candidate configuration is selected in each iteration

of the simulation. If the total energy decreases for the new candidate, that candidate is accepted and the iterative process continues. Otherwise, it is accepted with a probability given by the Boltzmann factor, which decreases with temperature. This random acceptance allows the algorithm to escape local minima. The system eventually cools into the global minimum in the spin configuration space.

The growth of data size in Ising problems has spurred interest in physical hardware systems that directly minimize the energy function [14–21]. Such systems are called Ising machines. An example of an Ising machine is the quantum annealing machine from D-Wave Systems, which was implemented using superconducting qubits [22,23]. The machine operates at a cryogenic temperature. The connectivity between qubits is limited to rather simple structures. Quantum adiabatic optimization inspired a new heuristic algorithm for the Ising problem, called simulated bifurcation, which simulates adiabatic evolution of classical nonlinear oscillators that exhibit bifurcation [24,25].

We recently developed a heuristic algorithm for the Ising problem in which the Ising spin system is replaced by a coupled oscillator system, which is possible owing to the equivalence of their equations of motion [26]. We obtained exact ground states for problems with a small number of spins by simply calculating the lowest mode of the coupled oscillators (i.e., the lowest eigenvalue and eigenvector of the matrix representing the equations of motion). We also developed an error correction algorithm that modifies the coupling strength depending on the amplitude of individual oscillators. This heuristic algorithm is a kind of annealing process since the energy landscape in the dipole configuration space is optimized in such a way that the correct configuration is equivalent to the lowest eigenmode. Based on this concept, we proposed an Ising machine composed of plasmon particles with dipole–dipole interaction, whose strength can be modified by a phase-change material inserted between neighboring particles [27].

In the present paper, we reconsider the coupled oscillator solver (COS) described above from the following viewpoints: (1) the lowest mode of the coupled oscillators may not always provide a minimally frustrated spin configuration (exact ground state) for large-sized Ising problems; and (2) it is desirable to replace the time-consuming error correction algorithm with a better algorithm inspired by an analysis of good candidate solutions (i.e., the lowest eigenmodes). We apply the COS to two-dimensional N × N oscillators for N values of up to 50. A map of the oscillation amplitudes (eigenvector components) of lower-frequency eigenmodes enables us to visualize unfrustrated clusters. We found that frustration tends to localize at the boundary between clusters due to the symmetric and asymmetric nature of the eigenmodes. This allows us to reduce frustration simply by flipping the sign of the amplitude of highly frustrated oscillators.

2. Coupled Oscillator Solver Applied to Ising Spin Problems

Here, we consider a square lattice (N × N) Ising spin glass problem without an external magnetic field. The spin configuration that minimizes the Ising energy is given by

$$E_{\text{Ising}} = -\sum_{i=1}^{N \times N} \sum_{j=1}^{N \times N} J_{ij} s_i s_j \quad (1)$$

where s_i denotes the ith spin with a value of 1 or -1, and J_{ij} is the coupling coefficient between the ith and jth spins having both positive (+J; ferromagnetic coupling) and negative ($-J$; antiferromagnetic coupling) values. In this study, only four nearest neighbor couplings are taken into account. For a given spin configuration, when $J_{ij} s_i s_j > 0$, the coupling J_{ij} is satisfied, otherwise it is frustrated. Minimizing the Ising energy is equivalent to maximizing the number of satisfied couplings.

We start with an instance of 10 × 10 (N = 10) spins with 200 couplings. Problems were generated by randomly assigning ferromagnetic and antiferromagnetic couplings with a number ratio of 1:1. Figure 1a shows the distribution of frustrated couplings (bold lines) for the exact ground state provided by a public domain [28], where an algorithm in [29] is used. In this algorithm, the original graph underlying the Ising problem is transformed into a dual graph, and minimum weight perfect matching is calculated. For the backward transformation, the matching leads to an Eulerian subgraph, the weight of which is also minimized. Owing to the one-to-one correspondence between the Eulerian subgraphs (cycles) and cuts in the original graph, the optimum Eulerian subgraphs provide the exact ground state for the Ising problem. The red circles and blue diamonds represent up-spin and down-spin states, respectively. The number of satisfied couplings of the exact ground state was found to be $n^E = 166$.

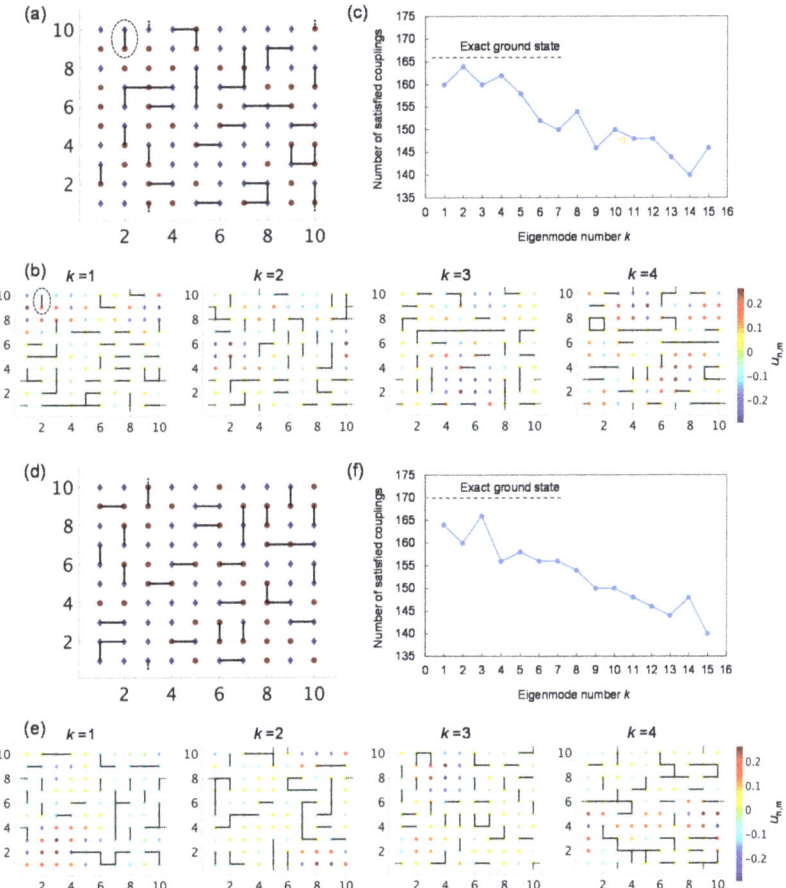

Figure 1. Instance of square lattice (10 × 10) Ising spin problem solved by the COS. (**a**) Spin configuration of the exact ground state. The red circles and blue diamonds represent up-spin and down-spin states, respectively. Frustrated couplings are indicated by bold lines. (**b**) Mapping of oscillation amplitude $u_{n,m}$ for the lowest four eigenmodes $k = 1$ to 4. The circles and diamonds respectively represent positive and negative signs of $u_{n,m}$. Frustrated couplings are indicated by bold lines. (**c**) Plot of the number of satisfied couplings n^{CO} as a function of eigenmode number k. (**d**–**f**) Results for another instance.

To solve the problem, we converted it to a classical coupled oscillator model by replacing the ferromagnetic and antiferromagnetic couplings with positive and negative couplings, respectively, between neighboring oscillators, as illustrated in Figure 2a. A normal attractive spring connecting neighboring masses gives rise to a positive interaction, and the masses tend to move in the same direction at lower frequency. A negative interaction is implemented by a repulsive spring (which does not exist in reality) to allow the masses to move in opposite directions. Due to the mathematical similarity between the inter-spin and inter-oscillator interactions, we anticipate that the sign of the oscillator amplitude for the lowest mode is the same or close to the spin configuration for the exact ground state for the original Ising problem.

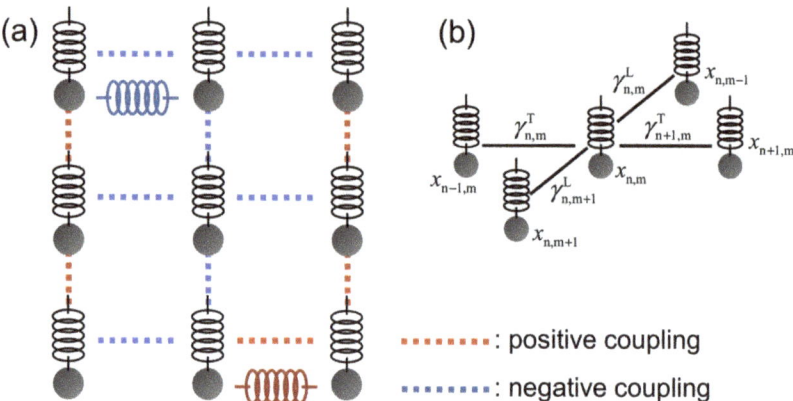

Figure 2. (a) Coupled oscillator model that includes both positive (ferromagnetic-like) and negative (antiferromagnetic-like) coupling. (b) Definition of the superscripts and subscripts associated with γ.

The equation of motion for the masses on the square lattice is given by

$$\ddot{x}_{n,m} = \alpha^2(\gamma^T_{n,m}x_{n-1,m} + \gamma^L_{n,m}x_{n,m-1} + \gamma^T_{n+1,m}x_{n+1,m} + \gamma^L_{n,m+1}x_{n,m+1}) \quad (2)$$

where $x_{n,m}$ is the displacement of a mass at the (n, m) lattice site and α is the square root of the spring constant divided by the mass, which represents the strength of the coupling between neighboring oscillators. Here, $\gamma_{n,m}$ is +1 for positive interaction and −1 for negative interaction, and "T" and "L" indicate the transverse and longitudinal directions, respectively. The definition of the superscripts and subscripts associated with γ is given in Figure 2b. The eigenmodes of the collective motion of oscillators can be calculated by substituting $x_{n,m} = u_{n,m}\exp(-i\omega t)$ into Equation (2) to obtain

$$\omega^2 u_{n,m} = \alpha^2(\gamma^T_{n,m}u_{n-1,m} + \gamma^L_{n,m}u_{n,m-1} + \gamma^T_{n+1,m}u_{n+1,m} + \gamma^L_{n,m+1}u_{n,m+1}) \quad (3)$$

By assuming a periodic boundary condition for $\gamma_{n,m}$, Equation (3) for the N × N system can be reduced to the problem of calculating the eigenvalue (frequency) ω and eigenvector (amplitude) $u_{n,m}$ for N^2 elements. Figure 1b shows a map of the oscillation amplitude $u_{n,m}$ of the lowest four eigenmodes (eigenmode number k = 1 to 4) for the original Ising problem. The circles and diamonds respectively represent positive and negative signs of $u_{n,m}$. The distribution of $u_{n,m}$ is not localized; it covers the entire system. If two neighboring oscillators connected by positive (negative) coupling move in opposite directions (the same direction), they are considered to be frustrated, analogous to the Ising spin model. Frustrated couplings are indicated by bold lines in Figure 1b. For instance, the two oscillators enclosed by the dotted ellipse in Figure 1b move in opposite directions, as indicated by $u_{n,m} < 0$ for the upper oscillator and $u_{n,m} > 0$ for the lower oscillator. Since the coupling is positive, which is evident by the frustrated coupling (connected by the bold line) of the two corresponding spins with opposite signs shown in Figure 1a, the oscillators are also frustrated for the eigenmode with k = 1. A lower frequency (eigenmode number) typically yields a smaller number of frustrated couplings (but not strictly, as demonstrated in Figure 1c).

The number of satisfied couplings n^{CO} as a function of eigenmode number k is plotted in Figure 1c. n^{CO} is maximized at the second lowest mode ($k = 2$) and tends to decrease with k. The maximum n^{CO} (n^{CO}_{max}) is 164, which corresponds to 98.7% of n^E (=166). Figure 1d–f show the results for another instance of the system. Also in this case, the distribution of the amplitude $u_{n,m}$ is delocalized. n^{CO} is a maximum at $k = 3$, for which n^{CO}_{max} is 166 or 97.6% of n^E (=170). Table 1 summarizes the values of k that maximize n^{CO} and n^{CO}_{max}/n^E for nine different instances. For all cases, n^{CO} is a maximum at $k \leq 3$ and n^{CO}_{max}/n^E is larger than 94.1%.

Table 1. Values of k required to maximize n^{CO} and n^{CO}_{max}/n^E for nine instances of problem with N = 10.

Sample#	1	2	3	4	5	6	7	8	9
k	1	2	2	1	1	2	1	1	3
n^{CO}_{max}/n^E (%)	94.2	95.3	98.8	96.4	96.6	96.5	96.4	98.8	97.6

3. Eigenmode Mapping to Visualize Frustration Localization

Next, we increase the problem size to 20 × 20 (N = 20). The distribution of frustrated couplings for the exact ground state is shown in Figure 3a. The problem was converted to the coupled oscillator model and the eigenvalues and eigenvectors were calculated. Figure 3b shows a map of the oscillation amplitude and frustrated couplings for eigenmode numbers of $k = 1$ to 5. Figure 3d,e show the results for another instance. In contrast to the smaller problem with N = 10, the collective oscillation is spatially localized and clusters form depending on k. It is reasonable that the distribution of the signs of $u_{n,m}$ in each cluster is in complete agreement with that of the spin configuration in the exact ground state. The formation of such unfrustrated clusters can specify the region where frustration occurs with high probability since the oscillator system lowers the eigenfrequency by reducing the amplitude of the oscillators around which frustrated couplings are localized. In particular, for lower eigenmodes, the unfrustrated clusters tend to extend as widely as possible, making frustrated couplings as localized as possible at the boundary between unfrustrated clusters. In Figure 3b, there are many oscillators around which three of the four couplings are frustrated. For these oscillators, the number of frustrated couplings can be reduced from three to one by flipping the sign of the amplitude. Figure 3c shows n^{CO} before and after the flipping process as a function of k, demonstrating the effectiveness of flipping in reducing frustration. n^{CO}_{max} is obtained for $k = 4$ after flipping and n^{CO}_{max}/n^E reaches 97.7%. For the other problem (Figure 3f), n^{CO}_{max}/n^E is a maximum (97.6%) at $k = 3$.

Table 2 shows the results for nine instances, including the value of k required to maximize n^{CO} and n^{CO}_{max}/n^E before and after flipping, to evaluate the effectiveness of flipping. For all cases, n^{CO} is a maximum at $k \leq 8$ and n^{CO}_{max}/n^E after flipping is larger than 96.7%. The eigenmode calculation is useful for visualizing unfrustrated clusters to find a fairly good solution, in which frustrated couplings are strongly localized around specific oscillators. The solution is effectively improved by flipping the sign of the amplitude to reduce frustration. It should be mentioned that it is relatively less probable for the lowest eigenmode ($k = 1$) to provide the highest n^{CO}_{max}/n^E. This might be due to the fact that the amplitude distribution has more nodes between unfrustrated clusters for a few higher eigenmodes and the frustration is more localized in the vicinity of the nodes. To summarize, what the COS does before flipping is to find the eigenmode consisting of clusters without nodes (locally symmetric), and simultaneously localizing nodes at the cluster boundaries (globally asymmetric).

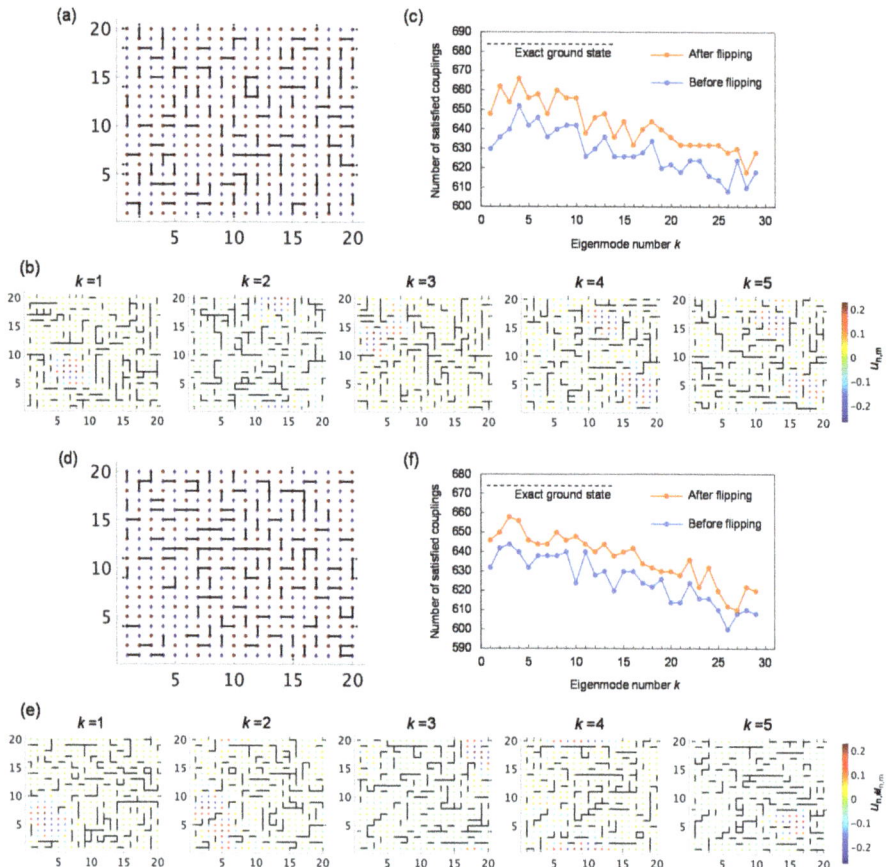

Figure 3. Instance of square lattice (20 × 20) Ising spin problem solved by the COS. (**a**) Spin configuration of the exact ground state. The red circles and blue diamonds represent up-spin and down-spin states, respectively. Frustrated couplings are indicated by bold lines. (**b**) Mapping of oscillation amplitude $u_{n,m}$ for the lowest five eigenmodes $k = 1$ to 5. The circles and diamonds respectively represent positive and negative signs of $u_{n,m}$. Frustrated couplings are indicated by bold lines. (**c**) Plot of the number of satisfied couplings n^{CO} before and after flipping as a function of eigenmode number k. (**d**–**f**) Results for another instance.

Table 2. Values of k required to maximize n^{CO} and n^{CO}_{max}/n^E before and after flipping for nine instances of problem with N = 20.

Sample#	1	2	3	4	5	6	7	8	9
k	2	6	8	5	6	4	2	8	3
n^{CO}_{max}/n^E before flipping (%)	94.7	96.2	96.2	95.0	95.3	95.6	94.7	95.3	95.5
n^{CO}_{max}/n^E after flipping (%)	96.7	97.9	97.4	97.4	97.6	97.7	96.7	97.1	97.6

4. Application to Larger Problems and Benchmark

To demonstrate the performance of the algorithm, we applied it to larger problems. Tables 3 and 4 summarizes the value of k required to maximize n^{CO} and n^{CO}_{max}/n^E before and after flipping for nine instances of problems with N = 30 and 40, respectively. It is confirmed that lower eigenmodes provide good candidates and that the flipping process effectively improves the candidates. For N = 30, n^{CO} is a maximum at $k \leq 9$ and n^{CO}_{max}/n^E after flipping is larger than 96.6%. For N = 40, n^{CO} is a maximum at $k \leq 13$ and n^{CO}_{max}/n^E after flipping is larger than 96.7%. Overall, for N = 10 to 40, the best solution can be found by checking the lowest ~N/2 candidates.

Table 3. Values of k required to maximize n^{CO} and n^{CO}_{max}/n^E before and after flipping for nine instances of problem with N = 30.

Sample#	1	2	3	4	5	6	7	8	9
k	7	2	2	7	9	2	5	2	6
n^{CO}_{max}/n^E before flipping (%)	95.9	94.9	95.3	95.4	95.8	95.1	95.7	95.4	95.2
n^{CO}_{max}/n^E after flipping (%)	97.2	96.6	97.4	97.6	97.1	97.1	97.5	97.3	96.9

Table 4. Values of k required to maximize n^{CO} and n^{CO}_{max}/n^E before and after flipping for nine instances of problem with N = 40.

Sample#	1	2	3	4	5	6	7	8	9
k	7	1	13	6	1	10	10	4	10
n^{CO}_{max}/n^E before flipping (%)	95.0	94.9	95.4	94.8	95.0	95.6	94.8	94.9	94.9
n^{CO}_{max}/n^E after flipping (%)	97.1	97.3	97.3	97.6	97.2	97.5	97.3	96.7	97.1

As a benchmark study, the computation time is compared between the COS and a standard SA algorithm for ten instances of problems with N = 50. All trials were performed on a MacBook Pro with a 2.6-GHz Intel® Core i7 processor (6 cores) and 16 GB of RAM. The COS generated n^{CO}_{max} in 2.74 s, including the time required for the flipping process. Figure 4 shows the evolution of the number of satisfied couplings with iteration number in SA for a given problem. n^{CO}_{max} and n^E are also indicated. After 27 iterations, SA provides a better solution than that provided by the COS. The computation time required to reach n^{CO}_{max} (27 iterations) was 8.63 s. Table 5 compares the computation time required to reach n^{CO}_{max} between the COS and SA for ten instances. Assuming that an n^{CO}_{max}/n^E value of 97% is satisfactory, the COS is three times faster than SA in generating the solution.

Table 5. n^{CO}_{max}/n^E and computation time required to reach n^{CO}_{max} with the COS (T_{CO}) and SA (T_{SA}).

Sample#	1	2	3	4	5	6	7	8	9	10
k	15	12	13	4	25	19	2	5	21	7
n^{CO}_{max}/n^E (%)	97.2	97.5	97.0	97.0	96.8	97.5	96.9	97.0	97.4	97.3
TCO	2.74	2.71	2.74	2.73	2.75	2.74	2.73	2.73	2.76	2.74
TSA	8.89	9.50	7.60	8.20	8.21	8.40	7.37	7.65	8.83	8.60

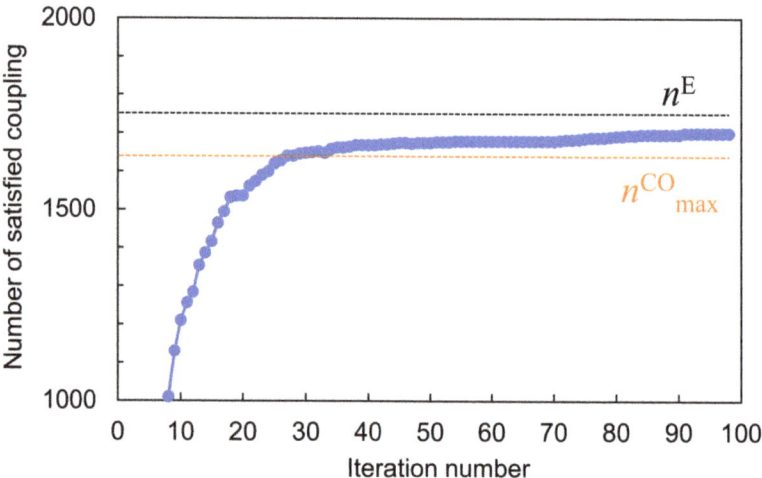

Figure 4. Evolution of the number of satisfied couplings with iteration number in SA for a given problem.

5. Conclusions

We evaluated the COS for Ising spin problems based on eigenmode characterization. After a square lattice (N × N) Ising problem was converted to a coupled oscillator model that includes positive and negative coupling, the equation of motion, which was reduced to an eigenmode problem, was solved. For smaller problems (N = 10), the oscillation amplitude (eigenvector) was delocalized (i.e., it covered the entire oscillator lattice) and a fairly good solution was obtained. For larger problems, the oscillation became localized, forming oscillator clusters with low frustration density (unfrustrated clusters). From a map of unfrustrated clusters for lower eigenmodes, we found that frustration tends to localize at the boundary between clusters. Frustration localization, where three of the four couplings are frustrated, is useful for reducing frustration by flipping the sign of the amplitude. Localization and the flipping method were applied to problems with N = 40. Good solutions with an accuracy of 97.2% in average (with respect to the exact ground state) were obtained simply by checking the lowest 13 ($\leq N/2$) candidate eigenmodes. A benchmark study demonstrated that the computation time required to reach a fairly good solution (n^{CO}_{max}) for the COS is three times shorter than that for SA.

Author Contributions: Conceptualization, T.S.; software, S.M., O.I. and Y.H.; formal analysis, S.M., O.I. and Y.H.; investigation, S.M., O.I. and Y.H.; writing—original draft preparation, S.M.; writing—review and editing, T.S.; funding acquisition, T.S. All authors have read and agreed to the published version of the manuscript.

Funding: This work was partially supported by JSPS KAKENHI (grant number 18H04490 and 20H04645) and partially by MEXT Quantum Leap Flagship Program Grant No. JPMXS0118067246.

Institutional Review Board Statement: Not applicable.

Informed Consent Statement: Not applicable.

Data Availability Statement: The data presented in this study are available on request from the corresponding author.

Conflicts of Interest: The authors declare no conflict of interest.

References

1. Nishimori, H. *Statistical Physics of Spin Glasses and Information Processing: An Introduction*; Clarendon Press: Oxford, UK, 2001.
2. Mezard, M.; Parisi, G.; Virasoro, M. *Spin Glass Theory and Beyond*; World Scientific: Singapore, 1998.

3. Ising, E. Beitrag zur Theorie des Ferromagnetismus. *Z. Physik.* **1925**, *31*, 253–258. [CrossRef]
4. Barahona, F. On the computational complexity of Ising spin glass models. *J. Phys. A Math. Gen.* **1982**, *15*, 3241–3253. [CrossRef]
5. Peres, F.; Castelli, M. Combinatorial Optimization Problems and Metaheuristics: Review, Challenges, Design, and Development. *Appl. Sci.* **2021**, *11*, 6449. [CrossRef]
6. Tanahashi, K.; Takayanagi, S.; Motohashi, T.; Tanaka, S. Application of Ising Machines and a Software Development for Ising Machines. *Jpn. J. Appl. Phys.* **2019**, *88*, 061010. [CrossRef]
7. Andrew, L. Ising formulations of many NP problems. *Front. Phys.* **2014**, *2*, 5.
8. Simone, C.D.; Diehl, M.; Jünger, M.; Mutzel, P.; Reinelt, G.; Rinaldi, G. Exact ground states of Ising spin glasses: New experimental results with a branch-and-cut algorithm. *J. Stat. Phys.* **1995**, *80*, 487–496. [CrossRef]
9. Blum, C.; Roli, A. Metaheuristics in combinatorial optimization: Overview and conceptual comparison. *ACM Comput. Surv.* **2003**, *35*, 268–308. [CrossRef]
10. Gendreau, M.; Potvin, J.Y. Metaheuristics in Combinatorial Optimization. *Ann. Oper. Res.* **2005**, *140*, 189–213. [CrossRef]
11. Kirkpatrick, S.; Gelatt, C.D.; Vecchi, M.P. Optimization by Simulated Annealing. *Science* **1983**, *220*, 671–680. [CrossRef] [PubMed]
12. Marinari, E.; Parisi, G. Simulated Tempering: A New Monte Carlo Scheme. *EPL Europhys. Lett.* **1992**, *19*, 451–458. [CrossRef]
13. Isakov, S.V.; Zintchenko, I.N.; Rønnow, T.F.; Troyer, M. Optimised simulated annealing for Ising spin glasses. *Comput. Phys. Commun.* **2015**, *192*, 265–271. [CrossRef]
14. Marandi, A.; Wang, Z.; Takata, K.; Byer, R.L.; Yamamoto, Y. Network of time-multiplexedoptical parametric oscillators as a coherent Ising machine. *Nat. Photonics* **2014**, *8*, 937–942. [CrossRef]
15. Inagaki, T.; Haribara, Y.; Igarashi, K.; Sonobe, T.; Tamate, S.; Honjo, T.; Marandi, A.; McMahon, P.L.; Umeki, T.; Enbutsu, K.; et al. A coherent Ising machine for 2000-node optimization problems. *Science* **2016**, *354*, 603–606. [CrossRef]
16. McMahon, P.L.; Marandi, A.; Haribara, Y.; Hamerly, R.; Langrock, C.; Tamate, S.; Inagaki, T.; Takesue, H.; Utsunomiya, S.; Aihara, K.; et al. A fully programmable 100-spin coherent Ising machine with all-to-all connections. *Science* **2016**, *354*, 614–617. [CrossRef] [PubMed]
17. Pierangeli, D.; Marcucci, G.; Conti, C. Large-scale photonic Ising machine by spatial light modulation. *Phys. Rev. Lett.* **2019**, *122*, 213902. [CrossRef]
18. Pierangeli, D.; Marcucci, G.; Brunner, D.; Conti, C. Noise-enhanced spatial-photonic Ising machine. *Nanophotonics* **2020**, *9*, 4109–4116. [CrossRef]
19. Yamaoka, M.; Yoshimura, C.; Hayashi, M.; Okuyama, T.; Aoki, H.; Mizuno, H. A 20k-spin Ising chip to solve combinatorial optimization problems with CMOS annealing. *IEEE J. Solid State Circ.* **2015**, *51*, 303–309.
20. Tsukamoto, S.; Takatsu, M.; Matsubara, S.; Tamura, H. An accelerator architecture for combinatorial optimization problems. *Fujitsu Sci. Tech. J.* **2017**, *53*, 8–13.
21. Aramon, M.; Rosenberg, G.; Valiante, E.; Miyazawa, T.; Tamura, H.; Katzgraber, H.G. Physics-inspired optimization for quadratic unconstrained problems using a digital annealer. *Front. Phys.* **2019**, *7*, 48. [CrossRef]
22. Johnson, M.W.; Amin, M.H.S.; Gildert, S.; Lanting, T.; Hamze, F.; Dickson, N.; Harris, R.; Berkley, A.J.; Johansson, J.; Bunyk, P.; et al. Quantum annealing with manufactured spins. *Nature* **2011**, *473*, 194–198. [CrossRef]
23. Boixo, S.; Rønnow, T.F.; Isakov, S.V.; Wang, Z.; Wecker, D.; Lidar, D.A.; Martinis, J.M.; Troyer, M. Evidence for quantum annealing with more than one hundred qubits. *Nat. Phys.* **2014**, *10*, 218–224. [CrossRef]
24. Goto, H. Bifurcation-based adiabatic quantum computation with a nonlinear oscillator network. *Sci. Rep.* **2016**, *6*, 21686. [CrossRef] [PubMed]
25. Goto, H.; Tatsumura, K.; Dixon, A.R. Combinatorial optimization by simulating adiabatic bifurcations in nonlinear Hamiltonian systems. *Sci. Adv.* **2019**, *5*, eaav2372. [CrossRef] [PubMed]
26. Kanazawa, S.; Kuwamura, K.; Kihara, Y.; Hirukawa, Y.; Saiki, T. Computations with near-field coupled plasmon particles interacting with phase-change materials. *Appl. Phys. A* **2015**, *121*, 1323–1327. [CrossRef]
27. Saiki, T. Switching of localized surface plasmon resonance of gold nanoparticles using phase-change materials and implementation of computing functionality. *Appl. Phys. A* **2017**, *123*, 577. [CrossRef]
28. The Program is Available on the Server. Available online: https://software.cs.uni-koeln.de/spinglass/client.html (accessed on 6 September 2021).
29. Pardella, G.; Liers, F. Exact ground states of large two-dimensional planar Ising spin glasses. *Phys. Rev. E* **2008**, *78*, 056705. [CrossRef]

MDPI
St. Alban-Anlage 66
4052 Basel
Switzerland
Tel. +41 61 683 77 34
Fax +41 61 302 89 18
www.mdpi.com

Symmetry Editorial Office
E-mail: symmetry@mdpi.com
www.mdpi.com/journal/symmetry

www.ingramcontent.com/pod-product-compliance
Lightning Source LLC
LaVergne TN
LVHW070152120526
838202LV00013BA/915